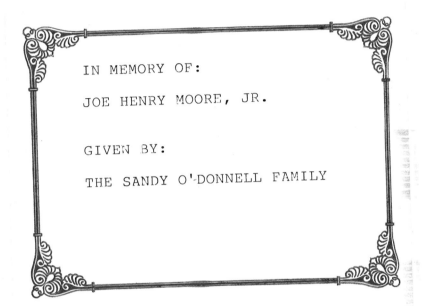

IN MEMORY OF:

JOE HENRY MOORE, JR.

GIVEN BY:

THE SANDY O'DONNELL FAMILY

IN THEIR
OWN WORDS

IN THEIR OWN WORDS

Copy 1

AUTOBIOGRAPHICAL WRITINGS OF
SOCRATES/PLATO • JULIUS CAESAR
AUGUSTUS CAESAR • MARCUS AURELIUS
MARTIN LUTHER • FREDERICK THE GREAT
THOMAS JEFFERSON • ALEXANDER HAMILTON
ROBERT BURNS • NAPOLEON BONAPARTE
SIR WALTER SCOTT • ABRAHAM LINCOLN
CHARLES DARWIN • CHARLES DICKENS
RICHARD WAGNER • QUEEN VICTORIA
OSCAR WILDE

COMPILED BY

RANDALL GIBBONS

GRAMERCY BOOKS
New York • Avenel

This edition is published by Gramercy Books, distributed by Random House
Value Publishing, Inc., 40 Engelhard Avenue, Avenel, New Jersey 07001.

Random House
New York • Toronto • London • Sydney • Auckland

Printed and bound in the United States of America

Library of Congress Cataloging-in-Publication Data
In their own words.
p. cm.
ISBN 0-517-12228-6
1. Autobiographies. I. Gramercy Books (Firm)
CT101.I66 1995
920.02—dc20   95-10996
                                                              CIP

8 7 6 5 4 3 2 1

CONTENTS

FOREWORD

THE LIVES of the great are constant sources of fascination and inspiration. While there have been numerous biographies of the famous historical figures in this book, the words they have written themselves, sometimes fragmentary and sometimes comprehensive, provide a special perspective.

Four of the greatest leaders of the ancient world have left partial accounts of their lives. In the fifth century B.C., the Greek philosopher Socrates was tried by the Athenian state for blasphemy against the gods and for corrupting the city's youth. The *Apology* of Socrates, his defense and estimate of his own life, was chronicled by Plato, the martyred philosopher's student. Among Julius Caesar's famous *Commentaries* are those on the Roman Civil War, in which he discusses his role in the struggle for power with Pompey. Augustus Caesar, the first Roman emperor, left a public statement of all his achievements, which was inscribed upon a monument in Rome and then duplicated in other cities. The *Meditations* of the extraordinary second-century Roman emperor Marcus Aurelius are introspective essays about his family, friends, and personal values and on living a virtuous and exemplary life.

Martin Luther, one of the world's most important religious figures, left memoirs in the form of letters and other writings; these were gathered into a narrative by the French author Michelet, whose *Life of Luther* is reprinted in this book. In the eighteenth century, King Frederick the Great of Prussia furnished an account of his early wars and his theories of statecraft in *The History of My Own Time*. Another military genius, Napoleon, provided an assessment of his career and of the political situation in Europe in a document prepared shortly before his death for his son.

Three great American statesmen, Thomas Jefferson, Alexander Hamilton, and Abraham Lincoln, also left abbreviated stories of their lives. In his old age, Jefferson worked on a detailed record of his public deeds and his role in the birth of the United States; his narrative covers the years up to 1790. Another Founding Father, Alexander Hamilton, wrote little about himself; but he did give a concise account of his life in a letter to a distant relative in Scotland. Lincoln's autobiography is also brief, ending in the year of his election to the presidency; it was written to be used as a biography of the Republican party's presidential candidate in 1860.

Among the literary figures represented in this collection are Robert Burns, Sir Walter Scott, Charles Dickens, and Oscar Wilde. Burns, Scotland's national poet, included a short outline of his life in a letter to a friend. Sir Walter Scott, the author of *Ivanhoe, Kenilworth,* and other historical adventures, provided his biographer and son-in-law, J. G. Lockhart, with a sketch of his early life; six years before his death, he added copious footnotes commenting on later events. Charles Dickens's celebrated novels, such as *David Copperfield* and *Little Dorrit,* are based upon the writer's youthful experiences. For his biography, by his friend John Forster, Dickens supplied a brief description of his own childhood. Oscar Wilde, the author of *The Picture of Dorian Gray* and *The Importance of Being Earnest,* spent two years in prison in the late 1890s on charges of violating British morality statutes. Wilde wrote a defense of his career and description of his mental suffering in jail, *De Profundis,* the autobiographical portion of which is presented in this book. Also included is another fragmentary memoir of an artistic genius, the revolutionary German opera composer Richard Wagner.

Finally, there are self-revealing writings by two of the giants of nineteenth-century England. Charles Darwin's theories on evolution and natural selection changed the course of philosophy, religion, and biological science. Darwin's intimate "Recollection of the Development of My Mind and Character" was incorporated in *The Life and Letters of Charles Darwin,* written by his son Francis. Queen Victoria, whose long rule defined a nation for most of a century, was a conscientious diarist. The selections in *In Their Own Words* deal primarily with her childhood and the first years of her reign, up to and including her marriage to Prince Albert in 1840.

RANDALL GIBBONS

New York, 1995

SOCRATES

SOCRATES

469-399 B. C.

INTRODUCTORY NOTE

Socrates, the Athenian, was the earliest of those remarkable Greek philosophers whom our own age reveres as the originator of man's effort to understand his world. We are thus peculiarly fortunate in having Socrates' own estimate of his life, his doctrines and his own value to the world around him. His favorite command to his disciples, his favorite expression as to the aim of all philosophy, was, "Know thyself," a phrase which has become historic as the master word of his teaching. The Greek religious oracle once declared Socrates to be the wisest of men, but he interpreted the seeming praise most humbly by saying that it was true, for he alone among men realized that he really knew nothing.

Like many a later philosopher, Socrates taught doctrines so far beyond his times that he was persecuted. At first, indeed, his instructions were eagerly sought. The ablest of the younger Athenians became his pupils. But many of these were of the aristocratic class and became involved in an effort to overthrow the Athenian democracy. Socrates was suspected of aiding or at least encouraging these plots, and at the age of seventy he was tried by the people's court as being a corrupter of the Athenian youth. He was adjudged guilty by a bare majority of the five hundred judges of the court, and was condemned to drink hemlock poison. This he did with quiet simplicity, declaring his continued obedience to the State, and refusing the schemes of escapes urged upon him by his friends.

His celebrated "Apology" which we here present was his defense before the court which condemned him. In it he reviewed his whole life to show what had been his real influence upon the Athenian youth. The "Apology" comes to us not from his own pen but from that of his favorite pupil, Plato, his successor as the leader of philosophy. Plato wrote among his own books what he tells us was his master's speech, and from allusions to it by other authors we know that the speech must really have been almost, if not exactly, as Plato has recorded it. The

3

"Apology" has generally been regarded as the most valuable piece of genuine autobiography preserved to us from before the time of Christ.

THE APOLOGY OF SOCRATES

How you have felt, O men of Athens, at hearing the speeches of my accusers, I cannot tell; but I know that their persuasive words almost made me forget who I was, such was the effect of them; and yet they have hardly spoken a word of truth. But many as their falsehoods were, there was one of them which quite amazed me: I mean when they told you to be upon your guard, and not to let yourselves be deceived by the force of my eloquence. They ought to have been ashamed of saying this, because they were sure to be detected as soon as I opened my lips and displayed my deficiency; they certainly did appear to be most shameless in saying this, unless by the force of eloquence they mean the force of truth; for then I do indeed admit that I am eloquent. But in how different a way from theirs! Well, as I was saying, they have hardly uttered a word, or not more than a word, of truth; but you shall hear from me the whole truth: not, however, delivered after their manner, in a set oration duly ornamented with words and phrases. No, indeed! but I shall use the words and arguments which occur to me at the moment; for I am certain that this is right, and that at my time of life I ought not to be appearing before you, O men of Athens, in the character of a juvenile orator: let no one expect this of me. And I must beg of you to grant me one favor, which is this, —If you hear me using the same words in my defense which I have been in the habit of using and which most of you may have heard in the agora [market place], and at the tables of the money-changers, or anywhere else, I would ask you not to be surprised at this, and not to interrupt me. For I am more than seventy years of age, and this is the first time that I have ever appeared in a court of law, and I am quite a stranger to the ways of the place; and therefore I would have you regard me as if I were really a stranger, whom you would excuse if he spoke in his native tongue, and after the fashion of his country: that I think is not an unfair request. Never mind the manner, which may or may not be good;

but think only of the justice of my cause, and give heed to that: let the judge decide justly and the speaker speak truly.

And first, I have to reply to the older charges and to my first accusers, and then I will go on to the later ones. For I have had many accusers, who accused me of old, and their false charges have continued during many years; and I am more afraid of them than of Anytus [1] and his associates, who are dangerous, too, in their own way. But far more dangerous are these, who began when you were children, and took possession of your minds with their falsehoods, telling of one Socrates, a wise man, who speculated about the heaven above, and searched into the earth beneath, and made the worse appear the better cause. These are the accusers whom I dread; for they are the circulators of this rumor, and their hearers are too apt to fancy that speculators of this sort do not believe in the gods. And they are many, and their charges against me are of ancient date, and they made them in days when you were impressible—in childhood, or perhaps in youth—and the cause when heard went by default, for there was none to answer. And hardest of all, their names I do not know and cannot tell; unless in the chance case of a comic poet. [2] But the main body of these slanderers who from envy and malice have wrought upon you—and there are some of them who are convinced themselves, and impart their convictions to others—all these, I say, are most difficult to deal with; for I cannot have them up here, and examine them, and therefore I must simply fight with shadows in my own defense, and examine when there is no one who answers. I will ask you then to assume with me, as I was saying, that my opponents are of two kinds—one recent, the other ancient; and I hope that you will see the propriety of my answering the latter first, for these accusations you heard long before the others, and much oftener.

Well, then, I will make my defense, and I will endeavor

[1] The chief accuser of Socrates. He hated Socrates for having influenced his son to study philosophy. He is said to have gone into exile after the death of Socrates to escape the vengeance of the repentant people.

[2] Aristophanes, twenty-five years before the trial of Socrates, wrote a comedy called The Clouds, in which he ridiculed the philosopher, representing him as a visionary with his head in the clouds, oblivious of mundane affairs, and so misleading his followers.

in the short time which is allowed to do away with this evil opinion of me which you have held for such a long time; and I hope that I may succeed, if this be well for you and me, and that my words may find favor with you. But I know that to accomplish this is not easy—I quite see the nature of the task. Let the event be as God wills: in obedience to the law I make my defense.

I will begin at the beginning, and ask what the accusation is which has given rise to this slander of me, and which has encouraged Meletus [3] to proceed against me. What do the slanderers say? They shall be my prosecutors, and I will sum up their words in an affidavit: "Socrates is an evil-doer, and a curious person, who searches into things under the earth and in heaven, and he makes the worse appear the better cause; and he teaches the aforesaid doctrines to others." That is the nature of the accusation, and that is what you have seen yourselves in the comedy of Aristophanes, who has introduced a man whom he calls Socrates, going about and saying that he can walk in the air, and talking a deal of nonsense concerning matters of which I do not pretend to know either much or little—not that I mean to say anything disparaging of any one who is a student of natural philosophy. I should be very sorry if Meletus could lay that to my charge. But the simple truth is, O Athenians, that I have nothing to do with studies. Very many of those here present are witnesses to the truth of this, and to them I appeal. Speak then, you who have heard me, and tell your neighbors whether any of you have ever known me hold forth in few words or in many upon matters of this sort. . . . You hear their answer. And from what they say of this you will be able to judge of the truth of the rest.

As little foundation is there for the report that I am a teacher, and take money; that is no more true than the other. Although, if a man is able to teach, I honor him for being paid. There is Gorgias of Leontium, and Prodicus of Ceos, and Hippias of Elis,[4] who go the round of the cities, and are able to persuade the young men to leave their own citizens,

[3] An obscure young tragic poet, who made the formal accusation against Socrates. He was the tool of Anytus and was stoned to death by the people in their revulsion of feeling after the death of Socrates.
[4] Popular Sophists of the day.

by whom they might be taught for nothing, and come to them whom they not only pay, but are thankful if they may be allowed to pay them. There is actually a Parian philosopher [5] residing in Athens, of whom I have heard; and I came to hear of him in this way: I met a man who has spent a world of money on the Sophists, Callias the son of Hipponicus, and knowing that he had sons, I asked him: "Callias," I said, "if your two sons were foals or calves, there would be no difficulty in finding some one to put over them; we should hire a trainer of horses, or a farmer probably, who would improve and perfect them in their own proper virtue and excellence; but as they are human beings, whom are you thinking of placing over them? Is there any one who understands human and political virtue? You must have thought about this as you have sons: is there any one?" "There is," he said. "Who is he?" said I, "and of what country? and what does he charge?" "Evenus the Parian," he replied; "he is the man, and his charge is five minæ." [6] Happy is Evenus, I said to myself, if he really has this wisdom, and teaches at such a modest charge. [7] Had I the same, I should have been very proud and conceited; but the truth is that I have no knowledge of the kind, O Athenians.

I dare say that some one will ask the question, "Why is this, Socrates, and what is the origin of these accusations of you: for there must have been something strange which you have been doing? All this great fame and talk about you would never have arisen if you had been like other men: tell us, then, why this is, as we should be sorry to judge hastily of you." Now I regard this as a fair challenge, and I will endeavor to explain to you the origin of this name of "wise," and of this evil fame. Please to attend, then. And although some of you may think that I am joking, I declare that I will tell you the entire truth. Men of Athens, this reputation of mine has come of a certain sort of wisdom which I possess. If you ask me what kind of wisdom, I reply, such wisdom as is attainable by man, for to that extent I am inclined to believe that I am wise; whereas the persons of whom I was speaking

[5] Evenus of Paros, a poet, and rhetorician.

[6] About eighty or ninety dollars.

[7] Gorgias and Portagoras received as much as one hundred minæ ($1600 to $1800).

have a superhuman wisdom, which I may fail to describe, because I have it not myself; and he who says that I have, speaks falsely, and is taking away my character. And here, O men of Athens, I must beg you not to interrupt me, even if I seem to say something extravagant. For the word which I will speak is not mine. I will refer you to a witness who is worthy of credit, and will tell you about my wisdom—whether I have any, and of what sort—and that witness shall be the God of Delphi [Apollo]. You must have known Chærephon; he was early a friend of mine, and also a friend of yours, for he shared in the exile of the people,[8] and returned with you. Well, Chærephon, as you know, was very impetuous in all his doings, and he went to Delphi and boldly asked the oracle to tell him whether—as I was saying, I must beg you not to interrupt—he asked the oracle to tell him whether there was any one wiser than I was, and the Pythian prophetess answered, that there was no man wiser. Chærephon is dead himself, but his brother, who is in court, will confirm the truth of this story.

Why do I mention this? Because I am going to explain to you why I have such an evil name. When I heard the answer, I said to myself, What can the god mean? and what is the interpretation of this riddle? for I know that I have no wisdom, small or great. What can he mean when he says that I am the wisest of men? And yet he is a god and cannot lie; that would be against his nature. After a long consideration, I at last thought of a method of trying the question. I reflected that if I could only find a man wiser than myself, then I might go to the god with a refutation of wisdom in my hand. I should say to him "Here is a man who is wiser than I am; but you said that I was the wisest." Accordingly I went to one who had the reputation of wisdom, and observed him—his name I need not mention; he was a politician whom I selected for examination—and the result was as follows: When I began to talk with him, I could not help thinking that he was not really wise, although he was thought wise by many, and wiser still by himself; and I went and tried

[8] The Peloponnesian War (431-404 B. C.) was a conflict between Athens and Sparta in which Athens was defeated, and her most patriotic citizens sent into exile.

to explain to him that he thought himself wise, but was not really wise; and the consequence was that he hated me, and his enmity was shared by several who were present and heard me. So I left him, saying to myself, as I went away: Well, although I do not suppose that either of us knows anything really beautiful and good, I am better off than he is—for he knows nothing, and thinks that he knows. I neither know nor think that I know. In this latter particular, then, I seem to have slightly the advantage of him. Then I went to another who had still higher philosophical pretensions, and my conclusion was exactly the same. I made another enemy of him, and of many others beside him.

After this I went to one man after another, being not unconscious of the enmity which I provoked, and I lamented and feared this: but necessity was laid upon me,—the word of God, I thought, ought to be considered first. And I said to myself, Go I must to all who appear to know, and find out the meaning of the oracle. And I swear to you, Athenians, by the dog [9] I swear!—for I must tell you the truth—the result of my mission was just this: I found that the men most in repute were all but the most foolish; and that some inferior men were really wiser and better. I will tell you the tale of my wanderings and of the "Herculean" labors, as I may call them, which I endured only to find at last the oracle irrefutable. When I left the politicians, I went to the poets; tragic, dithyrambic, and all sorts. And there, I said to myself, you will be detected: now you will find out that you are more ignorant than they are. Accordingly, I took them some of the most elaborate passages in their own writings, and asked what was the meaning of them—thinking that they would teach me something. Will you believe me? I am almost ashamed to speak of this, but still I must say that there is hardly a person present who would not have talked better about their poetry than they did themselves. That showed me in an instant that not by wisdom do poets write poetry, but by a sort of genius and inspiration; they are like diviners or soothsayers who also say many fine things, but do not understand the meaning of them. And the poets appeared to me to be much in the same case; and I further observed that upon the

* An oath, of possibly Egyptian origin, often used by Socrates.

strength of their poetry they believed themselves to be the wisest of men in other things in which they were not wise. So I departed, conceiving myself to be superior to them for the same reason that I was superior to the politicians.

At last I went to the artisans, for I was conscious that I knew nothing at all, as I may say, and I was sure that they knew many fine things; and in this I was not mistaken, for they did know many things of which I was ignorant, and in this they certainly were wiser than I was. But I observed that even the good artisans fell into the same error as the poets; because they were good workmen they thought that they also knew all sorts of high matters, and this defect in them overshadowed their wisdom—therefore I asked myself on behalf of the oracle, whether I would like to be as I was, neither having their knowledge nor their ignorance, or like them in both; and I made answer to myself and the oracle that I was better off as I was.

This investigation has led to my having many enemies of the worst and most dangerous kind, and has given occasion also to many calumnies. And I am called wise, for my hearers always imagine that I myself possess the wisdom which I find wanting in others: but the truth is, O men of Athens, that God only is wise; and in this oracle he means to say that the wisdom of men is little or nothing: he is not speaking of Socrates, he is only using my name as an illustration, as if he said, He, O men, is the wisest, who, like Socrates, knows that his wisdom is in truth worth nothing. And so I go my way, obedient to the god, and make inquisition into the wisdom of any one, whether citizen or stranger, who appears to be wise; and if he is not wise, then in vindication of the oracle I show him that he is not wise; and this occupation quite absorbs me, and I have no time to give either to any public matter of interest or to any concern of my own, but I am in utter poverty by reason of my devotion to the god.

There is another thing:—young men of the richer classes, who have not much to do, come about me of their own accord; they like to hear the pretenders examined, and they often imitate me, and examine others themselves; there are plenty of persons, as they soon enough discover, who think that they know something, but really know little or nothing: and then those who are examined by them instead of being angry with themselves are angry with me: This confounded Socrates, they say; this villainous misleader of youth!—and then if somebody asks them, Why, what evil does he practice or teach? they do not know, and cannot tell; but in order that they may not appear to be at a loss, they repeat the ready-made charges which are used against all philosophers about teaching things up in the clouds and under the earth, and having no gods, and making the worse appear the better cause; for they do not like to confess that their pretence of knowledge has been detected—which is the truth: and as they are numerous and ambitious and energetic, and are all in battle array and have persuasive tongues, they have filled your ears with their loud and inveterate calumnies. And this is the reason why my three accusers, Meletus and Anytus and Lycon,[10] have set upon me: Meletus, who has a quarrel with me on behalf of the poets; Anytus, on behalf of the craftsmen; Lycon, on behalf of the rhetoricians: and as I said at the beginning, I cannot expect to get rid of this mass of calumny all in a moment. And this, O men of Athens, is the truth and the whole truth; I have concealed nothing, I have dissembled nothing. And yet, I know that this plainness of speech makes them hate me, and what is their hatred but a proof that I am speaking the truth?—this is the occasion and reason of their slander of me, as you will find out either in this or in any future inquiry.

I have said enough in my defense against the first class of my accusers; I turn to the second class who are headed by Meletus, that good and patriotic man, as he calls himself. And now I will try to defend myself against them: these new accusers must also have their affidavit read. What do they say? Something of this sort: That Socrates is a doer of evil, and corrupter of the youth, and he does not believe in the gods of the State, and has other new divinities of his own. That is the sort of charge; and now let us examine the particular counts. He says that I am a doer of evil, who corrupt the youth; but I say, O men of Athens, that Meletus is a doer of evil, and the evil is that he makes a joke of a

[10] A rhetorician and orator, afterward banished for his part in the prosecution of Socrates.

serious matter, and is too ready at bringing other men to trial from a pretended zeal and interest about matters in which he really never had the smallest interest. And the truth of this I will endeavor to prove.

[Socrates questions Meletus and forces him to confess that he himself is careless about the improvement of the youth. Then Socrates shows it is inconceivable that a man should intentionally injure those among whom he has to live. On Meletus charging that Socrates is an atheist, the philosopher shows the absurdity of charging a disbeliever in all gods with attempting to introduce new ones.]

I have said enough in answer to the charge of Meletus: any elaborate defense is unnecessary: but as I was saying before, I certainly have many enemies, and this is what will be my destruction if I am destroyed; of that I am certain; not Meletus, nor yet Anytus, but the envy and detraction of the world, which has been the death of many good men, and will probably be the death of many more; there is no danger of my being the last of them.

Some one will say: And are you not ashamed, Socrates, of a course of life which is likely to bring you to an untimely end? To him I may fairly answer: There you are mistaken: a man who is good for anything ought not to calculate the chance of living or dying; he ought only to consider whether in doing anything he is doing right or wrong—acting the part of a good man or of a bad. Whereas, according to your view, the heroes who fell at Troy were not good for much, and the son of Thetis above all, who altogether despised danger in comparison with disgrace; and when his goddess mother said to him, in his eagerness to slay Hector, that if he avenged his companion Patroclus, and slew Hector, he would die himself,—"Fate," as she said, "waits upon you next after Hector;" he, hearing this, utterly despised danger and death, and instead of fearing them, feared rather to live in dishonor, and not to avenge his friend. "Let me die next," he replies, "and be avenged of my enemy, rather than abide here by the beaked ships, a scorn and a burden of the earth." Had Achilles any thought of death and danger? For wherever a man's place is, whether the place which he has chosen or that in which he has been placed by a commander, there he ought to remain in the hour of danger; he should not think of death or of anything, but of disgrace. And this, O men of Athens, is a true saying.

Strange, indeed, would be my conduct, O men of Athens, if I who, when I was ordered by the generals whom you chose to command me at Potidæa and Amphipolis and Delium, remained where they placed me, like any other man, facing death,—if, I say, now, when, as I conceive and imagine, God orders me to fulfill the philosopher's mission of searching into myself and other men, I were to desert my post through fear of death, or any other fear; that would indeed be strange, and I might justly be arraigned in court for denying the existence of the gods, if I disobeyed the oracle because I was afraid of death: then I should be fancying that I was wise when I was not wise. For this fear of death is indeed the pretense of wisdom, and not real wisdom, being the appearance of knowing the unknown; since no one knows whether death, which they in their fear apprehend to be the greatest evil, may not be the greatest good. Is there not here conceit of knowledge, which is a disgraceful sort of ignorance? And this is the point in which, as I might think, I am superior to men in general, and in which I might perhaps fancy myself wiser than other men,—that whereas I know but little of the world below,[11] I do not suppose that I know: but I do know that injustice and disobedience to a better, whether God or man, are evil and dishonorable, and I will never fear or avoid a possible good rather than a certain evil. And therefore if you let me go now, and reject the counsels of Anytus, who said that if I were not put to death I ought not to have been prosecuted, and that if I escape now, your sons will all be utterly ruined by listening to my words,—if you say to me, Socrates, this time we will not mind Anytus, and will let you off, but upon one condition, that you are not to inquire and speculate in this way any more, and that if you are caught doing this again you shall die,—if this was the condition on which you let me go, I should reply: Men of Athens, I honor and love you; but I shall obey God rather than you, and while I have life and strength I shall never cease from the practice and teaching of philosophy, exhorting any one whom

[11] Tartarus, the place of punishment for evil souls.

I meet after my manner, and convincing him, saying: O my friend, why do you, who are a citizen of the great and mighty and wise city of Athens, care so much about laying up the greatest amount of money and honor and reputation, and so little about wisdom and truth and the greatest improvement of the soul, which you never regard or heed at all? Are you not ashamed of this? And if the person with whom I am arguing, says, Yes, but I do care: I do not depart or let him go at once; I interrogate and examine and cross-examine him, and if I think that he has no virtue, but only says that he has, I reproach him with undervaluing the greater, and overvaluing the less. And this I should say to every one whom I meet, young and old, citizen and alien, but especially to the citizens, inasmuch as they are my brethren. For this is the command to God, as I would have you know; and I believe that to this day no greater good has ever happened in the State than my service to the God. For I do nothing but go about persuading you all, old and young alike, not to take thought for your persons or your properties, but first and chiefly to care about the greatest improvement of the soul. I tell you that virtue is not given by money, but that from virtue come money and every other good of man, public as well as private. This is my teaching, and if this is the doctrine which corrupts the youth, my influence is ruinous indeed. But if any one says that this is not my teaching, he is speaking an untruth. Wherefore, O men of Athens, I say to you, do as Anytus bids or not as Anytus bids, and either acquit me or not; but whatever you do, know that I shall never alter my ways, not even if I have to die many times.

Men of Athens, do not interrupt, but hear me; there was an agreement between us that you should hear me out. And I think that what I am going to say will do you good: for I have something more to say, at which you may be inclined to cry out; but I beg that you will not do this. I would have you know, that if you kill such a one as I am, you will injure yourselves more than you will injure me. Meletus and Anytus will not injure me: they cannot; for it is not in the nature of things that a bad man should injure a better than himself. I do not deny that he may, perhaps, kill him, or drive him into exile, or deprive him of civil rights; and he may imagine, and others may imagine, that he is doing him a great injury: but in that I do not agree with him; for the evil of doing as Anytus is doing—of unjustly taking away another man's life—is greater far. And now, Athenians, I am not going to argue for my own sake, as you may think, but for yours, that you may not sin against the God, or lightly reject his boon by condemning me. For if you kill me you will not easily find another like me, who, if I may use such a ludicrous figure of speech, am a sort of gadfly, given to the State by the God; and the State is like a great and noble steed who is tardy in his motions owing to his very size, and requires to be stirred into life. I am that gladly which God has given the State, and all day long and in all places am always fastening upon you, arousing and persuading and reproaching you. And as you will not easily find another like me, I would advise you to spare me. I dare say that you may feel irritated at being suddenly awakened when you are caught napping; and you may think that if you were to strike me dead as Anytus advises, which you easily might, then you would sleep on for the remainder of your lives, unless God in his care of you gives you another gadfly. And that I am given to you by God is proved by this: that if I had been like other men, I should not have neglected all my own concerns, or patiently seen the neglect of them during all these years, and have been doing yours, coming to you individually, like a father or elder brother, exhorting you to regard virtue; this, I say, would not be like human nature. And had I gained anything, or if my exhortations had been paid, there would have been some sense in that: but now, as you will perceive, not even the impudence of my accusers dares to say that I have ever exacted or sought pay of any one: they have no witness of that. And I have a witness of the truth of what I say; my poverty is a sufficient witness.

Some one may wonder why I go about in private, giving advice and busying myself with the concerns of others, but do not venture to come forward in public and advise the State. I will tell you the reason of this. You have often heard me speak of an oracle or sign which comes to me, and is the divinity which Meletus ridicules in the indictment.[12] This

[12] Socrates spoke frequently of this voice, calling it his *daemon*, but

sign I have had ever since I was a child. The sign is a voice which comes to me and always forbids me to do something which I am going to do, but never commands me to do anything, and this is what stands in the way of my being a politician. And rightly, as I think. For I am certain, O men of Athens, that if I had engaged in politics, I should have perished long ago, and done no good either to you or to myself. And don't be offended at my telling you the truth: for the truth is, that no man who goes to war with you or any other multitude, honestly struggling against the commission of unrighteousness and wrong in the State, will save his life; he who will really fight for the right, if he would live even for a little while, must have a private station and not a public one.

I can give you as proofs of this, not words only, but deeds, which you value more than words. Let me tell you a passage of my own life, which will prove to you that I should never have yielded to injustice from any fear of death, and that if I had not yielded I should have died at once. I will tell you a story—tasteless, perhaps, and commonplace, but nevertheless true. The only office of state which I ever held, O men of Athens, was that of senator; the tribe Antiochis, which is my tribe, had the presidency at the trial of the generals who had not taken up the bodies of the slain after the battle of Arginusæ; and you proposed to try them all together, which was illegal, as you all thought afterwards; but at the time I was the only one of the prytanes who was opposed to the illegality, and I gave my vote against you; and when the orators threatened to impeach and arrest me, and have me taken away, and you called and shouted, I made up my mind that I would run the risk, having law and justice with me, rather than take part in your injustice because I feared imprisonment and death. This happened in the days of the democracy. But when the oligarchy of the Thirty [13] was in power, they sent for me and four others into the rotunda, and bade us bring Leon the Salaminian from Salamis, as they wanted to execute

the wording is usually too vague to be even so clearly understood as here. The most common modern interpretation is that he meant the voice of conscience, though some scholars think that he believed himself to have a special individual spirit guiding him.

[13] The oligarchical commission, dictated by Sparta, that ruled Athens after its subjugation in the Peloponnesian War.

him. This was a specimen of the sort of commands which they were always giving with the view of implicating as many as possible in their crimes; and then I showed, not in word only but in deed, that, if I may be allowed to use such an expression, I cared not a straw for death, and that my only fear was the fear of doing an unrighteous or unholy thing. For the strong arm of that oppressive power did not frighten me into doing wrong; and when we came out of the rotunda the other four went to Salamis and fetched Leon, but I went quietly home. For which I might have lost my life, had not the power of the Thirty shortly afterwards come to an end. And to this many will witness.

Now do you really imagine that I could have survived all these years, if I had led a public life, supposing that like a good man I had always supported the right and had made justice, as I ought, the first thing? No indeed, men of Athens, neither I nor any other. But I have been always the same in all my actions, public as well as private, and never have I yielded any base compliance to those who are slanderously termed my disciples,[14] or to any other. For the truth is that, I have no regular disciples: but if any one likes to come and hear me while I am pursuing my mission, whether he be young or old, he may freely come. Nor do I converse with those who pay only, and not with those who do not pay; but any one, whether he be rich or poor, may ask and answer me and listen to my words; and whether he turns out to be a bad man or a good one, that cannot be justly laid to my charge, as I never taught him anything. And if any one says that he has ever learned or heard anything from me in private which all the world has not heard, I should like you to know that he is speaking an untruth.

But I shall be asked, Why do people delight in continually conversing with you? I have told you already, Athenians, the whole truth about this: they like to hear the cross-examination of the pretenders to wisdom; there is amusement in this. And this is a duty which the God has imposed upon me, as I am assured by oracles, visions, and in every sort of way in which the will of divine power was ever signified to any one.

[14] Chities, one of the Thirty Tyrants, and Alcibiades, who had in youth mingled with Socrates and his disciples.

This is true, O Athenians; or, if not true, would be soon refuted. For if I am really corrupting the youth, and have corrupted some of them already, those of them who have grown up and have become sensible that I gave them bad advice in the days of their youth should come forward as accusers and take their revenge; and if they do not like to come themselves, some of their relatives, fathers, brothers, or other kinsmen, should say what evil their families suffered at my hands. Now is their time. Many of them I see in the court. There is Crito, who is of the same age and of the same deme [township] with myself; and there is Critobulus his son, whom I also see. Then again there is Lysanias of Sphettus, who is the father of Æschines,—he is present; and also there is Antiphon of Cephisus, who is the father of Epigenes; and there are the brothers of several who have associated with me. There is Nicostratus the son of Theosdotides, and the brother of Theodotus (now Theodotus himself is dead, and therefore he, at any rate, will not seek to stop him); and there is Paralus the son of Demodocus, who had a brother Theages, and Adeimantus the son of Ariston, whose brother Plato is present; and Æantodorus, who is the brother of Apollodorus, whom I also see. I might mention a great many others, any of whom Meletus should have produced as witnesses in the course of his speech; and let him still produce them, if he has forgotten; I will make way for him. And let him say, if he has any testimony of the sort which he can produce. Nay, Athenians, the very opposite is the truth. For all these are ready to witness on behalf of the corrupter, of the destroyer of their kindred, as Meletus and Anytus call me; not the corrupted youth only,—there might have been a motive for that, —but their uncorrupted elder relatives. Why should they too support me with their testimony? Why, indeed, except for the sake of truth and justice, and because they know that I am speaking the truth, and that Meletus is lying.

Well, Athenians, this and the like of this is nearly all the defense which I have to offer. Yet a word more. Perhaps there may be some one who is offended at me, when he calls to mind how he himself on a similar, or even a less serious occasion, had recourse to prayers and supplications with many tears, and how he produced his children in court, which was a moving spectacle, together with a posse of his relations and friends: whereas I, who am probably in danger of my life, will do none of these things. Perhaps this may come into his mind, and he may be set against me, and vote in anger because he is displeased at this. Now if there be such a person among you, which I am far from affirming, I may fairly reply to him: My friend, I am a man, and like other men, a creature of flesh and blood, and not of wood or stone, as Homer says; and I have a family, yes, and sons, O Athenians, three in number, one·of whom is growing up, and the two others are still young; and yet I will not bring any of them hither in order to petition you for an acquittal. And why not? Not from any self-will or disregard of you. Whether I am or am not afraid of death is another question, of which I will not now speak. But my reason simply is, that I feel such conduct to be discreditable to myself, and you, and the whole State. One who has reached my years, and who has a name for wisdom, whether deserved or not, ought not to demean himself. At any rate, the world has decided that Socrates is in some way superior to other men.

And if those among you who are said to be superior in wisdom and courage, and any other virtue, demean themselves in this way, how shameful is their conduct! I have seen men of reputation, when they have been condemned, behaving in the strangest manner: they seemed to fancy that they were going to suffer something dreadful if they died, and that they could be immortal if you only allowed them to live; and I think that they were a dishonor to the State, and that any stranger coming in would say of them that the most eminent men of Athens, to whom the Athenians themselves give honor and command, are no better than women. And I say that these things ought not to be done by those of us who are of reputation; and if they are done, you ought not to permit them; you ought rather to show that you are more inclined to condemn, not the man who is quiet, but the man who gets up a doleful scene, and makes the city ridiculous.

But, setting aside the question of dishonor, there seems to be something wrong in petitioning a judge, and thus procuring an acquittal instead of informing and convincing him. For his duty is, not to make a present of justice, but to give judgment; and he has sworn that he will judge according to the laws, and not according to his own good pleasure; and neither he nor we should get into the habit of perjuring ourselves—there can be no piety in that. Do not then require me to do what I consider dishonorable and impious and wrong, especially now, when I am being tried for impiety on the indictment of Meletus. For if, O men of Athens, by force of persuasion and entreaty, I could overpower your oaths, then I should be teaching you to believe that there are no gods, and convict myself, in my own defense, of not believing in them. But that is not the case; for I do believe that there are gods, and in a far higher sense than that in which any of my accusers believe in them. And to you and to God I commit my cause, to be determined by you as is best for you and me.

[Socrates is convicted. He then arises and speaks:]

There are many reasons why I am not grieved, O men of Athens, at the vote of condemnation. I expected this, and am only surprised that the votes are so nearly equal; for I had thought that the majority against me would have been far larger; but now, had thirty votes gone over to the other side, I should have been acquitted. And I may say that I have escaped Meletus. And I may say more; for without the assistance of Anytus and Lycon, he would not have had a fifth part of the votes, as the law requires, in which case he would have incurred a fine of a thousand drachmæ [$160 to $180], as is evident.

And so he proposes death as the penalty. And what shall I propose on my part,[15] O men of Athens? Clearly that which is my due. And what is that which I ought to pay or to receive? What shall be done to the man who has never had the wit to be idle during his whole life; but has been careless

[15] "In Athenian procedure, the penalty inflicted was determined by a separate vote of the Dikasts" (officers somewhat like our jurymen) "taken after the verdict of guilty. The accuser having named the penalty which he thought suitable, the accused party on his side named some lighter penalty upon himself; and between those two the Dikasts were called on to make their option—no third proposition being admissible. The prudence of an accused party always induced him to propose, even against himself, some measure of punishment which the Dikasts might be satisfied to accept, in preference to the heavier sentence invoked by his antagonist."—Grote's History of Greece.

of what the many care about—wealth, and family interests, and military offices, and speaking in the assembly, and magistracies, and plots, and parties. Reflecting that I was really too honest a man to follow in this way and live, I did not go where I could do no good to you or to myself; but where I could do the greatest good privately to every one of you, thither I went, and sought to persuade every man among you, that he must look to himself, and seek virtue and wisdom before he looks to his private interests, and look to the State before he looks to the interests of the State; and that this should be the order which he observes in all his actions and words. What shall be done to such a one? Doubtless some good thing, O men of Athens, if he has his reward; and the good should be of a kind suitable to him. What would be a reward suitable to a poor man who is your benefactor, who desires leisure that he may instruct you? There can be no more fitting reward than maintenance in the prytaneum,[16] O men of Athens, a reward which he deserves far more than the citizen who has won the prize at Olympia in the horse or chariot race, whether the chariots were drawn by two horses or by many. For I am in want, and he has enough; and he only gives you the appearance of happiness, and I give you the reality. And if I am to estimate the penalty justly, I say that maintenance in the prytaneum is the just return.

Perhaps you may think that I am braving you in saying this, as in what I said before about the tears and prayer. But that is not the case. I speak rather because I am convinced that I never intentionally wronged any one, although I cannot convince you of that—for we have had a short conversation only; but if there were a law at Athens, such as there is in other cities, that a capital cause should not be decided in one day, then I believe I should have convinced you; but now the time is too short. I cannot in a moment refute great slanders; and, as I am convinced that I never wronged another, I will assuredly not wrong myself. I will not say of myself that I deserve any evil, or propose any penalty. Why

[16] A public hotel wherein entertainment was furnished by the government to foreign ambassadors and to citizens whom the State wished to honor.

should I? Because I am afraid of the penalty of death which Meletus proposes? When I do not know whether death is a good or an evil, why should I propose a penalty which would certainly be an evil? Shall I say imprisonment? And why should I live in prison, and be the slave of the magistrates of the year—of the eleven [police commissioners]? Or shall the penalty be a fine, and imprisonment until the fine is paid? There is the same objection. I should have to lie in prison, for money I have none, and cannot pay. And if I say exile (and this may possibly be the penalty which you will affix), I must indeed be blinded by the love of life, if I were to consider that when you, who are my own citizens, cannot endure my discourses and words, and have found them so grievous and odious that you would fain have done with them, others are likely to endure me. No, indeed, men of Athens, that is not very likely. And what a life should I lead, at my age, wandering from city to city, living in ever-changing exile, and always being driven out! For I am quite sure that into whatever place I go, as here so also there, the young men will come to me; and if I drive them away, their elders will drive me out at their desire: and if I let them come, their fathers and friends will drive me out for their sakes.

Some one will say: Yes, Socrates, but cannot you hold your tongue, and then you may go into a foreign city, and no one will interfere with you? Now I have great difficulty in making you understand my answer to this. For if I tell you that this would be a disobedience to a divine command, and therefore that I cannot hold my tongue, you will not believe that I am serious; and if I say again that the greatest good of man is daily to converse about virtue, and all that concerning which you hear me examining myself and others, and that the life which is unexamined is not worth living— that you are still less likely to believe. And yet what I say is true, although a thing of which it is hard for me to persuade you. Moreover, I am not accustomed to think that I deserve any punishment. Had I money I might have proposed to give you what I had, and have been none the worse. But you see that I have none, and can only ask you to proportion the fine to my means. However, I think that I could afford a mina, and therefore I propose that penalty: Plato, Crito,

Critobulus, and Apollodorus, my friends here, bid me say thirty minæ, and they will be the sureties. Well, then, say thirty minæ, let that be the penalty; for that they will be ample security to you.

Not much time will be gained, O Athenians, in return for the evil name which you will get from the detractors of the city, who will say that you killed Socrates, a wise man; for they will call me wise even although I am not wise when they want to reproach you. If you had waited a little while, your desire would have been fulfilled in the course of nature. For I am far advanced in years, as you may perceive, and not far from death. I am speaking now only to those of you who have condemned me to death. And I have another thing to say to them: You think that I was convicted through deficiency of words—I mean, that if I had thought fit to leave nothing undone, nothing unsaid, I might have gained an acquittal. Not so; the deficiency which led to my conviction was not of words—certainly not. But I had not the boldness or impudence or inclination to address you as you would have liked me to address you, weeping and wailing and lamenting, and saying and doing many things which you have been accustomed to hear from others and which, as I say, are unworthy of me. But I thought that I ought not to do anything common or mean in the hour of danger: nor do I now repent of the manner of my defense, and I would rather die having spoken after my manner, than speak in your manner and live. For neither in war nor yet at law ought any man to use every way of escaping death. For often in battle there is no doubt that if a man will throw away his arms, and fall on his knees before his pursuers, he may escape death; and in other dangers there are other ways of escaping death, if a man is willing to say and do anything. The difficulty, my friends, is not in avoiding death, but in avoiding unrighteousness; for that runs faster than death. I am old and move slowly, and the slower runner has overtaken me, and my accusers are keen and quick, and the faster runner, who is unrighteousness, has overtaken them. And now I depart hence condemned by you to suffer the penalty of death, and they too go their ways condemned by the truth to suffer the penalty of villainy and wrong; and I must abide by my award—let them abide by theirs. I suppose that these things may be regarded as fated, —and I think that they are well.

And now, O men who have condemned me, I would fain prophesy to you; for I am about to die, and that is the hour in which men are gifted with prophetic power. And I prophesy to you who are my murderers, that immediately after my death punishment far heavier than you have inflicted on me will surely await you. Me you have killed because you wanted to escape the accuser, and not to give an account of your lives. But that will not be as you suppose: far otherwise. For I say that there will be more accusers of you than there are now; accusers whom hitherto I have restrained: and as they are younger they will be more severe with you, and you will be more offended at them. For if you think that by killing men you can avoid the accuser censuring your lives, you are mistaken; that is not a way of escape which is either possible or honorable; the easiest and the noblest way is not to be crushing others, but to be improving yourselves. This is the prophecy which I utter before my departure to the judges who have condemned me.

Friends, who would have acquitted me, I would like also to talk with you about this thing which has happened, while the magistrates are busy, and before I go to the place at which I must die. Stay then a while, for we may as well talk with one another while there is time. You are my friends, and I should like to show you the meaning of this event which has happened to me. O my judges—for you I may truly call judges—I should like to tell you of a wonderful circumstance. Hitherto the familiar oracle within me has constantly been in the habit of opposing me even about trifles, if I was going to make a slip or error about anything; and now as you see there has come upon me that which may be thought, and is generally believed to be, the last and worst evil. But the oracle made no sign of opposition, either as I was leaving my house and going out in the morning, or when I was going up into this court, or while I was speaking, at anything which I was going to say; and yet I have often been stopped in the middle of a speech, but now in nothing I either said or did touching this matter has the oracle opposed me. What do I take to be the explanation of this? I will tell you. I regard this as a proof that what has happened to me is a good, and that those of us who think that death is an evil are in error. This is a great proof to me of what I am saying, for the customary sign would surely have opposed me had I been going to evil and not to good.

Let us reflect in another way, and we shall see that there is great reason to hope that death is a good, for one of two things: either death is a state of nothingness and utter unconsciousness, or, as men say, there is a change and migration of the soul from this world to another. Now if you suppose that there is no consciousness, but a sleep like the sleep of him who is undisturbed even by the sight of dreams, death will be an unspeakable gain. For if a person were to select the night in which his sleep was undisturbed even by dreams, and were to compare with this the other days and nights of his life, and then were to tell us how many days and nights he had passed in the course of his life better and more pleasantly than this one, I think that any man, I will not say a private man, but even the great king [of Persia] will not find many such days or nights, when compared with the others. Now if death is like this, I say that to die is gain; for eternity is then only a single night. But if death is the journey to another place, and there, as men say, all the dead are, what good, O my friends and judges, can be greater than this? If indeed when the pilgrim arrives in the world below, he is delivered from the professors of justice in this world, and finds the true judges who are said to give judgment there, Minos and Rhadamanthus and Æacus and Triptolemus, and other sons of God who were righteous in their own life, that pilgrimage will be worth making. What would not a man give if he might converse with Orpheus and Musæus and Hesiod and Homer? Nay, if this be true, let me die again and again. I, too, shall have a wonderful interest in a place where I can converse with Palamedes, and Ajax the son of Telamon, and other heroes of old, who have suffered death through an unjust judgment; and there will be no small pleasures, as I think, in comparing my own sufferings with theirs. Above all, I shall be able to continue my search into true and false knowledge; as in this world, so also in that; I shall find out who is wise, and who pretends to be wise, and is not. What

would not a man give, O judges, to be able to examine the
leader of the great Trojan expedition; or Odysseus or Sisy-
phus, or numberless others, men and women too! What infinite delight would there be in conversing with them and asking them questions! For in that world they do not put a
man to death for this; certainly not. For besides being happier in that world than in this, they will be immortal, if what
is said is true.

Wherefore, O judges, be of good cheer about death, and
know this of a truth—that no evil can happen to a good man,
either in life or after death. He and his are not neglected by
the gods; nor has my own approaching end happened by mere
chance. But I see clearly that to die and be released was better for me; and therefore the oracle gave no sign. For which
reason, also, I am not angry with my accusers or my con-
demners; they have done me no harm, although neither of
them meant to do me any good; and for this I may gently
blame them.

Still I have a favor to ask of them. When my sons are
grown up, I would ask you, O my friends, to punish them;
and I would have you trouble them, as I have troubled you,
if they seem to care about riches, or anything, more than
about virtue; or if they pretend to be something when they
are really nothing,—then reprove them, as I have reproved
you, for not caring about that for which they ought to care,
and thinking that they are something when they are really
nothing. And if you do this, I and my sons will have received
justice at your hands.

The hour of departure has arrived, and we go our ways—I
to die, and you to live. Which is better God only knows.

JULIUS CAESAR

JULIUS CÆSAR

100-44 B. C.

INTRODUCTORY NOTE

The writings of Julius Cæsar have been so much referred to by later writers of autobiography, that they may almost be said to stand as the basis and foundation of literary self-study. This rank has been assigned to them by many critics; and so many autobiographical writers, especially military ones, have named Cæsar's works as having inspired them to similar effort that a series like the present can scarcely pass Cæsar by. Yet there is little that is genuinely autobiographical in his writings. He describes campaigns and countries in such a coldly impersonal light, referring always to himself as "Cæsar," that one gets hardly a single glimpse at the man behind the mask.

This is particularly true in his "Commentaries on the Gallic Wars." In his other book of commentaries, the "Civil War," he speaks with more warmth of personal feeling and more directness. The "Civil War" has therefore been selected for presentation here. It is rather fragmentary, the surviving portion breaking abruptly into the midst of Cæsar's struggle with Pompey. Pompey had been master of the Roman world before Cæsar; and as the latter's military strength and political fame grew with the conquest of Gaul, Pompey became jealous and suspicious. He endeavored to break Cæsar's power, and finally compelled the Roman Senate to command Cæsar to surrender his devoted Gallic army. This would have left Cæsar helpless in face of Pompey's army. Cæsar urged that both armies should be dismissed, or else that he and his rival should meet personally and come to some agreement of amity. The Tribunes or people's representatives in Rome upheld Cæsar in this; but Pompey persisted in using his influence within the Roman Senate so as to crush his rival. Cæsar was declared by senatorial decree to be an enemy of the republic. What Cæsar, the strongest, keenest man in all the Roman world, then resolved upon and did, here follows in his own words.

CÆSAR'S COMMENTARIES ON THE CIVIL WAR

WHEN Cæsar heard of the actions of his enemies, he harangued his soldiers; he reminded them "of the wrongs done at all times by his enemies, and complained that Pompey had been alienated from him and led astray by them through envy and a malicious opposition to his glory, though he had always favored and promoted Pompey's honor and dignity. He complained that an innovation had been introduced into the republic, that the intercession of the tribunes, which had been restored a few years before by Sylla, was branded as a crime, and suppressed by force of arms; that Sylla, who had stripped the tribunes of every other power, had, nevertheless, left the privilege of intercession unrestrained; that Pompey, who pretended to restore what they had lost, had taken away the privileges which they formerly had; that whenever the senate decreed, 'that the magistrates should take care that the republic sustained no injury' (by which words and decree the Roman people were obliged to repair to arms), it was only when pernicious laws were proposed; when the tribunes attempted violent measures; when the people seceded, and possessed themselves of the temples and eminences of the city; (and these instances of former times, he showed them were expiated by the fate of Saturninus and the Gracchi): that nothing of this kind was attempted now, nor even thought of: that no law was promulgated, no intrigue with the people going forward, no secession made; he exhorted them to defend from the malice of his enemies the reputation and honor of that general under whose command they had for nine years most successfully supported the state; fought many successful battles, and subdued all Gaul and Germany." The soldiers of the thirteenth legion, which was present (for in the beginning of the disturbances he had called it out, his other legions not having yet arrived), all cry out that they are ready to defend their general, and the tribunes of the commons, from all injuries.

Having made himself acquainted with the disposition of his soldiers, Cæsar set off with that legion to Ariminum, and there met the tribunes, who had fled to him for protection; he called his other legions from winter quarters, and ordered them to follow him. Thither came Lucius Cæsar, a young man, whose father was a lieutenant-general under Cæsar. He, after concluding the rest of his speech, and stating for what purpose he had come, told Cæsar that he had commands of a private nature for him from Pompey, that Pompey wished to clear himself to Cæsar, lest he should impute those actions which he did for the republic, to a design of affronting him; that he had ever preferred the interest of the state to his own private connections; that Cæsar, too, for his own honor, ought to sacrifice his desires and resentment to the public good, and not vent his anger so violently against his enemies, lest in his hope of injuring them, he should injure the republic. He spoke a few words to the same purport from himself, in addition to Pompey's apology. Roscius, the prætor, conferred with Cæsar almost in the same words, and on the same subject, and declared that Pompey had empowered him to do so.

Though these things seemed to have no tendency toward redressing his injuries, yet having got proper persons by whom he could communicate his wishes to Pompey; he required of them both, that, as they had conveyed Pompey's demands to him, they should not refuse to convey his demands to Pompey; if by so little trouble they could terminate a great dispute, and liberate all Italy from her fears. "That the honor of the republic had ever been his first object, and dearer to him than life; that he was chagrined, that the favor of the Roman people was wrested from him by the injurious reports of his enemies; that he was deprived of a half-year's command, and dragged back to the city, though the people had ordered that regard should be paid to his suit for the consulate at the next election, though he was not present; that, however, he had patiently submitted to this loss of honor, for the sake of the republic; that when he wrote letters to the senate, requiring that all persons should resign the command of their armies, he did not obtain even that request; that levies were made throughout Italy; that the two legions which had been taken from him, under the pretense of the Parthian war, were kept at home, and that the state was in arms. To what did all these things tend, unless to his ruin? But, nevertheless, he was ready to condescend to any terms, and to endure everything for the sake of the republic. Let Pompey [1] go to his own province; let them both disband their armies; let all persons in Italy lay down their arms; let all fears be removed from the city; let free elections, and the whole republic be resigned to the direction of the senate and Roman people. That these things might be the more easily performed, and conditions secured and confirmed by oath, either let Pompey come to Cæsar, or allow Cæsar to go to him; it might be that all their disputes would be settled by an interview.''

Roscius and Lucius Cæsar, having received this message, went to Capua, where they met the consuls and Pompey, and declared to them Cæsar's terms. Having deliberated on the matter, they replied, and sent written proposals to him by the same persons, the purport of which was, that Cæsar should return into Gaul, leave Ariminum, and disband his army: if he complied with this, that Pompey would go to Spain. In the meantime, until security was given that Cæsar would perform his promises, that the consuls and Pompey would not give over their levies.

It was not an equitable proposal, to require that Cæsar should quit Ariminum and return to his province; but that Pompey should himself retain his province and the legions that belonged to another, and desire that Cæsar's army should be disbanded, while he himself was making new levies: and that he should merely promise to go to his province, without naming the day on which he would set out; so that if he should not set out till after Cæsar's consulate expired, yet he would not appear bound by any religious scruples about asserting a falsehood. But his not granting time for a conference, nor promising to set out to meet him, made the expectation of peace appear very hopeless. Cæsar, therefore, sent Marcus Antonius, with five cohorts from Ariminum to Arretium; he himself stayed at Ariminum with two legions,

---

[1] When Cæsar and Pompey were reconciled, they and Crassus divided the provinces between them. Cæsar got Hither and Further Gaul; Crassus, Parthia; and Pompey, Spain and Africa. The others set out for their respective provinces. Pompey dispatched his lieutenants to manage his provinces, and remained himself in Italy with an army, which Cæsar thought a great stretch of power, that he should command both his own provinces and Italy at the same time.

with the intention of raising levies there. He secured Pisaurus, Fanum, and Ancona, with a cohort each.

In the meantime, being informed that Thermus the prætor was in possession of Iguvium, with five cohorts, and was fortifying the town, but that the affections of all the inhabitants were very well inclined toward himself, he detached Curio with three cohorts, which he had at Ariminum and Pisaurus. Upon notice of his approach, Thermus, distrusting the affections of the townsmen, drew his cohorts out of it, and made his escape; his soldiers deserted him on the road, and returned home. Curio recovered Iguvium, with the cheerful concurrence of all the inhabitants. Cæsar, having received an account of this, and relying on the affections of the municipal towns, drafted all the cohorts of the thirteenth legion from the garrison, and set out for Auximum, a town into which Attius had brought his cohorts, and of which he had taken possession, and from which he had sent senators round about the country of Picenum, to raise new levies.

Upon news of Cæsar's approach, the senate of Auximum went in a body to Attius Varus; and told him that it was not a subject for them to determine upon: yet neither they, nor the rest of the freemen would suffer Caius Cæsar, a general, who had merited so well of the republic, after performing such great achievements, to be excluded from their town and walls; wherefore he ought to pay some regard to the opinion of posterity, and his own danger. Alarmed at this declaration, Attius Varus drew out of the town the garrison which he had introduced, and fled. A few of Cæsar's front rank having pursued him, obliged him to halt, and when the battle began, Varus is deserted by his troops: some of them disperse to their homes, the rest come over to Cæsar; and along with them, Lucius Pupius, the chief centurion, is taken prisoner and brought to Cæsar. He had held the same rank before in Cneius Pompey's army. But Cæsar applauded the soldiers of Attius, set Pupius at liberty, returned thanks to the people of Auximum, and promised to be grateful for their conduct.

Intelligence of this being brought to Rome, so great a panic spread on a sudden that when Lentulus, the consul, came to open the treasury, to deliver money to Pompey by the senate's decree, immediately on opening the hallowed door he fled from the city. For it was falsely rumored that Cæsar was approaching, and that his cavalry were already at the gates. Marcellus, his colleague, followed him, and so did most of the magistrates. Cneius Pompey had left the city the day before, and was on his march to those legions which he had received from Cæsar, and had disposed in winter quarters in Apulia. The levies were stopped within the city. No place on this side of Capua was thought secure. At Capua they first began to take courage and to rally, and determined to raise levies in the colonies, which had been sent thither by the Julian law: and Lentulus brought into the public market place the gladiators which Cæsar maintained there for the entertainment of the people, and confirmed them in their liberty, and gave them horses and ordered them to attend him; but afterward, being warned by his friends that this action was censured by the judgment of all, he distributed them among the slaves of the district of Campania, to keep guard there.

Cæsar, having moved forward from Auximum, traversed the whole country of Picenum. All the governors in these countries most cheerfully received him, and aided his army with every necessary. Ambassadors came to him even from Cingulum, a town which Labienus had laid out and built at his own expense, and offered most earnestly to comply with his orders. He demanded soldiers: they sent them. In the meantime, the twelfth legion came to join Cæsar; with these two he marched to Asculum, the chief town of Picenum. Lentulus Spinther occupied that town with ten cohorts; but, on being informed of Cæsar's approach, he fled from the town, and, in attempting to bring off his cohorts with him, was deserted by a great part of his men. Being left on the road with a small number, he fell in with Vibullius Rufus, who was sent by Pompey into Picenum to confirm the people in their allegiance. Vibullius, being informed by him of the transactions of Picenum, takes his soldiers from him and dismisses him. He collects, likewise, from the neighboring countries, as many cohorts as he can from Pompey's new levies. Among them he meets with Ulcilles Hirrus fleeing from Camerinum, with six cohorts, which he had in the garrison there; by a junction with which he made up thirteen cohorts. With them he marched by hasty journeys to Corfinium, to Domitius Ænobarbus, and informed him that Cæsar was advancing with two legions. Domitius had collected about twenty cohorts from Alba, and the Marsians, Pelignians, and neighboring states.

Cæsar, having recovered Asculum and driven out Lentulus, ordered the soldiers that had deserted from him to be sought out and a muster to be made; and, having delayed for one day there to provide corn, he marched to Corfinium. On his approach, five cohorts, sent by Domitius from the town, were breaking down a bridge which was over the river, at three miles' distance from it. An engagement taking place there with Cæsar's advanced-guard, Domitius's men were quickly beaten off from the bridge and retreated precipitately into the town. Cæsar, having marched his legions over, halted before the town and encamped close by the walls.

Domitius, upon observing this, sent messengers well acquainted with the country, encouraged by a promise of being amply rewarded, with dispatches to Pompey to Apulia, to beg and entreat him to come to his assistance. That Cæsar could be easily inclosed by the two armies, through the narrowness of the country, and prevented from obtaining supplies: unless he did so, that he and upward of thirty cohorts, and a great number of senators and Roman knights, would be in extreme danger. In the meantime he encouraged his troops, disposed engines on the walls, and assigned to each man a particular part of the city to defend. In a speech to the soldiers he promised them lands out of his own estate; to every private soldier four acres, and a corresponding share to the centurions and veterans.

In the meantime, word was brought to Cæsar that the people of Sulmo, a town about seven miles distant from Corfinium, were ready to obey his orders, but were prevented by Quintus Lucretius, a senator, and Attius, a Pelignian, who were in possession of the town with a garrison of seven cohorts. He sent Marcus Antonius thither, with five cohorts of the eighth legion. The inhabitants, as soon as they saw our standards, threw open their gates, and all the people, both citizens and soldiers, went out to meet and welcome Antonius.

Lucretius and Attius leaped off the walls. Attius, being brought before Antonius, begged that he might be sent to Cæsar. Antonius returned the same day on which he had set out with the cohorts and Attius. Cæsar added these cohorts to his own army, and sent Attius away in safety. The three first days Cæsar employed in fortifying his camp with strong works, in bringing in corn from the neighboring free towns, and waiting for the rest of his forces. Within the three days the eighth legion came to him, and twenty-two cohorts of the new levies in Gaul, and about three hundred horse from the king of Noricum. On their arrival he made a second camp on another part of the town, and gave the command of it to Curio. He determined to surround the town with a rampart and turrets during the remainder of the time. Nearly at the time when the greatest part of the work was completed, all the messengers sent to Pompey returned.

Having read Pompey's letter, Domitius, concealing the truth, gave out in council that Pompey would speedily come to their assistance; and encouraged them not to despond, but to provide everything necessary for the defense of the town. He held private conferences with a few of his most intimate friends, and determined on the design of fleeing. As Domitius's countenance did not agree with his words, and he did everything with more confusion and fear than he had shown on the preceding days, and as he had several private meetings with his friends, contrary to his usual practice, in order to take their advice, and as he avoided all public councils and assemblies of the people, the truth could be no longer hid nor dissembled; for Pompey had written back in answer, "that he would not put matters to the last hazard; that Domitius had retreated into the town of Corfinium without either his advice or consent. Therefore, if any opportunity should offer, Domitius should come to him with the whole force." But the blockade and works round the town prevented his escape.

Domitius's design being noised abroad, the soldiers in Corfinium early in the evening began to mutiny, and held a conference with each other by their tribunes and centurions, and the most respectable among themselves: "that they were besieged by Cæsar; that his works and fortifications were almost finished; that their general, Domitius, on whose hopes and expectations they had confided, had thrown them off, and was meditating his own escape; that they ought to provide for their own safety." At first the Marsians differed in opinion, and possessed themselves of that part of the town which they thought the strongest. And so violent a dispute arose between them, that they attempted to fight and decide it by arms. However, in a little time, by messengers sent from one side to the other, they were informed of Domitius's meditated flight, of which they were previously ignorant. Therefore they all with one consent brought Domitius into public view, gathered round him, and guarded him; and sent deputies out of their number to Cæsar, to say that they were ready to throw open their gates, to do whatever he should order, and deliver up Domitius alive into his hands.

Upon intelligence of these matters, though Cæsar thought it of great consequence to become master of the town as soon as possible, and to transfer the cohorts to his own camp, lest any change should be wrought on their inclinations by bribes, encouragement, or fictitious messages, because in war great events are often brought about by trifling circumstances; yet, dreading lest the town should be plundered by the soldiers entering into it, and taking advantage of the darkness of the night, he commended the persons who came to him, and sent them back to the town, and ordered the gates and walls to be secured. He disposed his soldiers on the works which he had begun, not at certain intervals, as was his practice before, but in one continued range of sentinels and stations, so that they touched each other, and formed a circle round the whole fortification; he ordered the tribunes and general officers to ride round; and exhorted them not only to be on their guard against sallies from the town, but also to watch that no single person should get out privately. Nor was any man so negligent or drowsy as to sleep that night. To so great height was their expectation raised, that they were carried away, heart and soul, each to different objects, what would become of the Corfinians, what of Domitius, what of Lentulus, what of the rest; what event would be the consequence of another.

About the fourth watch, Lentulus Spinther said to our sentinels and guards from the walls, that he desired to have an interview with Cæsar, if permission were given him. Having obtained it, he was escorted out of town; nor did the soldiers of Domitius leave him till they brought him into Cæsar's presence. He pleaded with Cæsar for his life, and entreated him to spare him, and reminded him of their former friendship; and acknowledged that Cæsar's favors to him were very great; in that through his interest he had been admitted into the college of priests; in that after his prætorship he had been appointed to the government of Spain; in that he had been assisted by him in his suit for the consulate. Cæsar interrupted him in his speech, and told him, "that he had not left his province to do mischief to any man, but to protect himself from the injuries of his enemies; to restore to their dignity the tribunes of the people who had been driven out of the city on his account, and to assert his own liberty, and that of the Roman people, who were oppressed by a few factious men." Encouraged by this address, Lentulus begged leave to return to the town, that the security which he had obtained for himself might be an encouragement to the rest to hope for theirs; saying that some were so terrified that they were induced to make desperate attempts on their own lives. Leave being granted him, he departed.

When day appeared, Cæsar ordered all the senators and their children, the tribunes of the soldiers, and the Roman knights to be brought before him. Among the persons of senatorial rank were Lucius Domitius, Publius Lentulus Spinther, Lucius Vibullius Rufus, Sextus Quintilius Varus, the quæstor, and Lucius Rubrius, besides the son of Domitius, and several other young men, and a great number of Roman knights and burgesses, whom Domitius had summoned from the municipal towns. When they were brought before him he protected them from the insolence and taunts of the soldiers; told them in few words that they had not made him a grateful return, on their part, for his very extraordinary kindness to them, and dismissed them all in safety. Sixty sestertia, which Domitius had brought with him and lodged in the public treasury, being brought to Cæsar by the magistrates

of Corfinium, he gave them back to Domitius, that he might
not appear more moderate with respect to the life of men
than in money matters, though he knew that it was public
money, and had been given by Pompey to pay his army.
He ordered Domitius's soldiers to take the oath to himself,
and that day decamped and performed the regular march.[2]
He stayed only seven days before Corfinium, and marched
into Apulia through the country of the Marrucinians,
Frentanians and Larinates.

Pompey, being informed of what had passed at Corfinium, marches from Luceria to Canusium, and thence to
Brundusium.[3] He orders all the forces raised everywhere
by the new levies to repair to him. He gives arms to
the slaves that attended the flocks, and appoints horses for
them. Of these he made up about three hundred horse.
Lucius, the prætor, fled from Alba, with six cohorts: Rutilus
Lupus, the prætor, from Tarracina, with three. These having described Cæsar's cavalry at a distance, which were commanded by Bivius Curius, and having deserted the prætor,
carried their colors to Curius and went over to him. In
like manner, during the rest of his march, several cohorts
fell in with the main body of Cæsar's army, others with
his horse. Cneius Magius, from Cremona, engineer-general
to Pompey, was taken prisoner on the road and brought to
Cæsar, but sent back by him to Pompey with this message:
"As hitherto he had not been allowed an interview, and was
now on his march to him at Brundusium, that it deeply concerned the commonwealth and general safety that he should
have an interview with Pompey; and that the same advantage
could not be gained at a great distance when the proposals
were conveyed to them by others, as if terms were argued
by them both in person."

Having delivered this message he marched to Brundusium
with six legions, four of them veterans: the rest those which
he had raised in the late levy and completed on his march,
for he had sent all Domitius's cohorts immediately from
Corfinium to Sicily. He discovered that the consuls were
gone to Dyrrachium with a considerable part of the army,

[2] The regular march was about twenty Roman miles.
[3] Brundusium, modern Brindisi, a city of Calabria, in the south of Italy.

and that Pompey remained at Brundusium with twenty cohorts; but could not find out, for a certainty, whether Pompey stayed behind to keep possession of Brundusium, that he might the more easily command the whole Adriatic sea, with the extremities of Italy and the coast of Greece, and be able to conduct the war on either side of it, or whether he remained there for want of shipping; and, being afraid that Pompey would come to the conclusion that he ought not to relinquish Italy, he determined to deprive him of the means of communication afforded by the harbor of Brundusium. The plan of his work was as follows:—Where the mouth of the port was narrowest he threw up a mole of earth on either side, because in these places the sea was shallow. Having gone out so far that the mole could not be continued in the deep water, he fixed double floats, thirty feet on either side, before the mole. These he fastened with four anchors at the four corners, that they might not be carried away by the waves. Having completed and secured them, he then joined to them other floats of equal size. These he covered over with earth and mold, that he might not be prevented from access to them to defend them, and in the front and on both sides he protected them with a parapet of wicker work; and on every fourth one raised a turret, two stories high, to secure them the better from being attacked by the shipping and set on fire.

To counteract this, Pompey fitted out large merchant ships, which he found in the harbor of Brundusium: on them he erected turrets three stories high, and, having furnished them with several engines and all sorts of weapons, drove them among Cæsar's works, to break through the floats and interrupt the works; thus there happened skirmishes every day at a distance with slings, arrows, and other weapons. Cæsar conducted matters as if he thought that the hopes of peace were not yet to be given up. And though he was very much surprised that Magius, whom he had sent to Pompey with a message, was not sent back to him; and though his attempting a reconciliation often retarded the vigorous prosecution of his plans, yet he thought that he ought by all means to persevere in the same line of conduct. He therefore sent Caninius Rebilus to have an interview with Scribonius Libo, his intimate friend and relation. He charges him to exhort Libo to effect a peace, but, above all things, requires that he should be admitted to an interview with Pompey. He declared that he had great hopes, if that were allowed him, that the consequence would be that both parties would lay down their arms on equal terms; that a great share of the glory and reputation of that event would redound to Libo, if, through his advice and agency, hostilities should be ended. Libo, having parted from the conference with Caninius, went to Pompey, and, shortly after, returned with answer that, as the consuls were absent, no treaty of composition could be engaged in without them. Cæsar therefore thought it time at length to give over the attempt which he had often made in vain, and act with energy in the war.

When Cæsar's works were nearly half finished, and after nine days were spent in them, the ships which had conveyed the first division of the army to Dyrrachium being sent back by the consuls, returned to Brundusium. Pompey, either frightened at Cæsar's works or determined from the beginning to quit Italy, began to prepare for his departure on the arrival of the ships; and the more effectually to retard Cæsar's attack, lest his soldiers should force their way into the town at the moment of his departure, he stopped up the gates, built walls across the streets and avenues, sunk trenches across the ways, and in them fixed palisadoes and sharp stakes, which he made level with the ground by means of hurdles and clay. But he barricaded with large beams fastened in the ground and sharpened at the ends two passages and roads without the walls, which led to the port. After making these arrangements, he ordered his soldiers to go on board without noise, and disposed here and there, on the wall and turrets, some light-armed veterans, archers and slingers. These he designed to call off by a certain signal, when all the soldiers were embarked, and left row-galleys for them in a secure place.

The people of Brundusium, irritated by the insolence of Pompey's soldiers, and the insults received from Pompey himself, were in favor of Cæsar's party. Therefore, as soon as they were aware of Pompey's departure, while his men were running up and down, and busied about their voyage, they made signs from the tops of the houses: Cæsar, being apprised of the design by them, ordered scaling-ladders to be got ready, and his men to take arms, that he might not lose any opportunity of coming to an action. Pompey weighed anchor at nightfall. The soldiers who had been posted on the wall to guard it, were called off by the signal which had been agreed on, and knowing the roads, ran down to the ships. Cæsar's soldiers fixed their ladders and scaled the walls: but being cautioned by the people to beware of the hidden stakes and covered trenches, they halted, and being conducted by the inhabitants by a long circuit, they reached the port, and captured with their long boats and small craft two of Pompey's ships, full of soldiers, which had struck against Cæsar's moles.

Though Cæsar highly approved of collecting a fleet, and crossing the sea, and pursuing Pompey before he could strengthen himself with his transmarine auxiliaries, with the hope of bringing the war to a conclusion, yet he dreaded the delay and length of time necessary to effect it: because Pompey, by collecting all his ships, had deprived him of the means of pursuing him at present. The only resource left to Cæsar, was to wait for a fleet from the distant regions of Gaul, Picenum, and the straits of Gibraltar. But this, on account of the season of the year, appeared tedious and troublesome. He was unwilling that, in the meantime, the veteran army, and the two Spains, one of which was bound to Pompey by the strongest obligations, should be confirmed in his interest; that auxiliaries and cavalry should be provided, and Gaul and Italy reduced in his absence.

Therefore, for the present, he relinquished all intention of pursuing Pompey, and resolved to march to Spain, and commanded the magistrates of the free towns to procure him ships, and to have them conveyed to Brundusium. He detached Valerius, his lieutenant, with one legion to Sardinia; Curio, the propraetor, to Sicily with three legions; and ordered him, when he had recovered Sicily, to immediately transport his army to Africa. Marcus Cotta was at this time governor of Sardinia: Marcus Cato,[4] of Sicily: and Tubero, by the lots,

---

[4] Marcus Cato, better known by the name of Cato of Utica, was one of the most determined enemies of Cæsar. He continued the struggle until

should have had the government of Africa. The Caralitani,[5] as soon as they heard that Valerius was sent against them, even before he left Italy, of their own accord drove Cotta out of the town; who, terrified because he understood that the whole province was combined [against him], fled from Sardinia to Africa. Cato was in Sicily, repairing the old ships of war, and demanding new ones from the states, and these things he performed with great zeal. He was raising levies of Roman citizens, among the Lucani and Brutii, by his lieutenants, and exacting a certain quota of horse and foot from the states of Sicily. When these things were nearly completed, being informed of Curio's approach, he made a complaint that he was abandoned and betrayed by Pompey, who had undertaken an unnecessary war, without making any preparation, and when questioned by him and other members in the senate, had assured them that everything was ready and provided for the war. After having made these complaints in a public assembly, he fled from his province.

When these affairs were dispatched, Cæsar, that there might be an intermission from labor for the rest of the season, drew off his soldiers to the nearest municipal towns, and set off in person for Rome. Having assembled the senate, he reminded them of the injustice of his enemies; and told them, "that he aimed at no extraordinary honor, but had waited for the time appointed by law,[6] for standing candidate for the consulate, being contented with what was allowed to every citizen. That a bill had been carried by the ten tribunes of the people (notwithstanding the resistance of his enemies, and a very violent opposition from Cato, who in his usual manner, consumed the day by a tedious harangue) that he should be allowed to stand candidate, though absent, even in the consulship of Pompey; and if the latter disapproved of the bill, why did he

---

affairs became desperate, and then committed suicide in Utica, a town of Africa. Cato the elder, surnamed the Censor, was the first distinguished man of the name. Livy remarked of him, that his talents were so great and so versatile, that he could have raised himself to the highest honors of any state in which he might have been born. He was a most deadly foe to Carthage, and concluded every debate in the senate with the well-known words, "delenda est Carthago."

[5] The inhabitants of Carales, now Cagliari, the modern capital of Sardinia, in the south of the island. It was built by the Carthaginians.

[6] Ten years had elapsed since his former consulate.

allow it to pass? if he approved of it, why should he debar him [Cæsar] from the people's favor? He made mention of his own patience, in that he had freely proposed that all armies should be disbanded, by which he himself would suffer the loss both of dignity and honor. He urged the virulence of his enemies, who refused to comply with what they required from others, and had rather that all things should be thrown into confusion, than that they should lose their power and their armies. He expatiated on their injustice, in taking away his legions: their cruelty and insolence in abridging the privileges of the tribunes; the proposals he had made, and his entreaties of an interview which had been refused him. For which reasons, he begged and desired that they would undertake the management of the republic, and unite with him in the administration of it. But if through fear they declined it, he would not be a burden to them, but take the management of it on himself. That deputies ought to be sent to Pompey, to propose a reconciliation; as he did not regard what Pompey had lately asserted in the senate, that authority was acknowledged to be vested in those persons to whom ambassadors were sent, and fear implied in those that sent them. That these were the sentiments of low, weak minds: that for his part, as he had made it his study to surpass others in glory, so he was desirous of excelling them in justice and equity.''

The senate approved of sending deputies, but none could be found fit to execute the commission: for every person, from his own private fears, declined the office. For Pompey, on leaving the city, had declared in the open senate, that he would hold in the same degree of estimation those who stayed in Rome and those in Cæsar's camp. Thus three days were wasted in disputes and excuses. Besides, Lucius Metellus, one of the tribunes, was suborned by Cæsar's enemies, to prevent this, and to embarrass [7] everything else which Cæsar should

[7] Before Cæsar left the city, he took out of the treasury a large sum of money, deposited there as a fund to defray the expenses of any war that might arise from the Gauls, of whom the Romans had a peculiar horror, alleging that, as he conquered the Gauls, there was no use for it. Metellus attempted to prevent him, but he drew his sword in an attitude of menace, saying, ''Young man, it is as easy to do this as to say it.'' The money was soon expended, as Cæsar, not long after, was obliged to borrow money from his officers to pay his soldiers.

propose. Cæsar having discovered his intention, after spending several days to no purpose, left the city, in order that he might not lose any more time, and went to Transalpine Gaul, without effecting what he had intended.

[The narrative moves along in a leisurely fashion till it comes to the final battle and overthrow of Pompey, which took place at Pharsalia in western Asia.]

When Cæsar thought he had sufficiently sounded the disposition of his troops, he thought that he ought to try whether Pompey had any intention or inclination to come to a battle. Accordingly he led his troops out of the camp, and ranged them in order of battle, at first on their own ground, and at a small distance from Pompey's camp: but afterward for several days in succession, he advanced from his own camp, and led them up to the hills on which Pompey's troops were posted, which conduct inspired his army every day with fresh courage. However he adhered to his former purpose respecting his cavalry, for as he was by many degrees inferior in number, he selected the youngest and most active of the advanced guard, and desired them to fight intermixed with the horse, and they by constant practice acquired experience in this kind of battle. By these means it was brought to pass that a thousand of his horse would dare even on open ground, to stand against seven thousand of Pompey's, if occasion required, and would not be much terrified by their number. For even on one of those days he was successful in a cavalry action, and killed one of the two Allobrogians, who had deserted to Pompey, as we before observed, and several others.

Pompey, because he was encamped on a hill, drew up his army at the very foot of it, ever in expectation, as may be conjectured, that Cæsar would expose himself to this disadvantageous situation. Cæsar, seeing no likelihood of being able to bring Pompey to an action, judged it the most expedient method of conducting the war, to decamp from that post and to be always in motion: with this hope, that by shifting his camp and removing from place to place, he might be more conveniently supplied with corn, and also, that by being in motion he might get some opportunity of forcing them to battle, and might by constant marches harass Pompey's army, which was not accustomed to fatigue. These matters being settled, when the signal for marching was given, and the tents struck, it was observed that shortly before, contrary to his daily practice, Pompey's army had advanced further than usual from his intrenchments, so that it appeared possible to come to an action on equal ground. Then Cæsar addressed himself to his soldiers, when they were at the gates of the camp, ready to march out. "We must defer," says he, "our march at present, and set our thoughts on battle, which has been our constant wish; let us then meet the foe with resolute souls. We shall not hereafter easily find such an opportunity." He immediately marched out at the head of his troops.

Pompey also, as was afterward known, at the unanimous solicitation of his friends, had determined to try the fate of a battle. For he had even declared in council a few days before that, before the battalions came to battle, Cæsar's army would be put to the rout. When most people expressed their surprise at it, "I know," says he, "that I promise a thing almost incredible; but hear the plan on which I proceed, that you may march to battle with more confidence and resolution. I have persuaded our cavalry, and they have engaged to execute it, as soon as the two armies have met, to attack Cæsar's right wing on the flank, and inclosing their army on the rear, throw them into disorder, and put them to the rout, before we shall throw a weapon against the enemy. By this means we shall put an end to the war, without endangering the legions, and almost without a blow. Nor is this a difficult matter, as we far outnumber them in cavalry." At the same time he gave them notice to be ready for battle on the day following, and since the opportunity which they had so often wished for was now arrived, not to disappoint the opinion generally entertained of their experience and valor.

After him Labienus spoke, as well to express his contempt of Cæsar's forces, as to extol Pompey's scheme with the highest encomiums. "Think not, Pompey," says he, "that this is the army which conquered Gaul and Germany; I was present at all those battles, and do not speak at random on a subject to which I am a stranger: a very small part of that army now remains, great numbers lost their lives, as must necessarily happen in so many battles, many fell victims to the autumnal

pestilence in Italy, many returned home, and many were left
behind on the continent. Have you not heard that the cohorts
at Brundusium are composed of invalids? The forces which
you now behold, have been recruited by levies lately made in
Hither Spain, and the greater part from the colonies beyond
the Po; moreover, the flower of the forces perished in the two
engagements at Dyrrachium.'' Having so said, he took an
oath, never to return to his camp unless victorious; and he
encouraged the rest to do the like. Pompey applauded his
proposal, and took the same oath; nor did any person present
hesitate to take it. After this had passed in the council they
broke up full of hopes and joy, and in imagination anticipated
victory; because they thought that in a matter of such importance, no groundless assertion could be made by a general of
such experience.

When Cæsar had approached near Pompey's camp, he observed that his army was drawn up in the following manner:
—On the left wing were the two legions, delivered over by
Cæsar at the beginning of the disputes in compliance with the
senate's decree, one of which was called the first, the other
the third. Here Pompey commanded in person. Scipio with
the Syrian legions commanded the center. The Cilician legion
in conjunction with the Spanish cohorts, which we said were
brought over by Afranius, were disposed on the right wing.
These Pompey considered his steadiest troops. The rest he
had interspersed between the center and the wing, and he had
a hundred and ten complete cohorts; these amounted to forty-
five thousand men. He had besides two cohorts of volunteers,
who having received favors from him in former wars, flocked
to his standard: these were dispersed through his whole army.
The seven remaining cohorts he had disposed to protect his
camp, and the neighboring forts. His right wing was secured
by a river with steep banks; for which reason he placed all
his cavalry, archers, and slingers, on his left wing.

Cæsar, observing his former custom, had placed the tenth
legion on the right, the ninth on the left, although it was
very much weakened by the battles at Dyrrachium. He placed
the eighth legion so close to the ninth, as to almost make one
of the two, and ordered them to support one another. He
drew up on the field eighty cohorts, making a total of twenty-

two thousand men. He left two cohorts to guard the camp. He gave the command of the left wing to Antonius, of the right to P. Sulla, and of the center to Cn. Domitius: he himself took his post opposite Pompey. At the same time, fearing, from the disposition of the enemy which we have previously mentioned, lest his right wing might be surrounded by their numerous cavalry, he rapidly drafted a single cohort from each of the legions composing the third line, formed of them a fourth line, and opposed them to Pompey's cavalry, and, acquainting them with his wishes, admonished them that the success of that day depended on their courage. At the same time he ordered the third line, and the entire army not to charge without his command: that he would give the signal whenever he wished them to do so.

When he was exhorting his army to battle, according to the military custom, and spoke to them of the favors that they had constantly received from him, he took especial care to remind them "that he could call his soldiers to witness the earnestness with which he had sought peace, the efforts that he had made by Vatinius to gain a conference [with Labienus], and likewise by Claudius to treat with Scipio, in what manner he had exerted himself at Oricum, to gain permission from Libo to send ambassadors; that he had been always reluctant to shed the blood of his soldiers, and did not wish to deprive the republic of one or other of her armies." After delivering this speech, he gave by a trumpet the signal to his soldiers, who were eagerly demanding it, and were very impatient for the onset.

There was in Cæsar's army, a volunteer of the name of Crastinus, who the year before had been first centurion of the tenth legion, a man of preëminent bravery. He, when the signal was given, says, "Follow me, my old comrades, and display such exertions in behalf of your general as you have determined to do: this is our last battle, and when it shall be won, he will recover his dignity, and we our liberty." At the same time he looked back to Cæsar, and said, "General, I will act in such a manner to-day, that you will feel grateful to me living or dead." After uttering these words he charged first on the right wing, and about one hundred and twenty chosen volunteers of the same century followed.

There was so much space left between the two lines, as sufficed for the onset of the hostile armies: but Pompey had ordered his soldiers to await Cæsar's attack, and not to advance from their position, or suffer their line to be put into disorder. And he is said to have done this by the advice of Caius Triarius, that the impetuosity of the charge of Cæsar's soldiers might be checked, and their line broken, and that Pompey's troops remaining in their ranks, might attack them while in disorder; and he thought that the javelins would fall with less force if the soldiers were kept in their ground, than if they met them in their course; at the same time he trusted that Cæsar's soldiers, after running over double the usual ground, would become weary and exhausted by the fatigue. But to me Pompey seems to have acted without sufficient reason: for there is a certain impetuosity of spirit and an alacrity implanted by nature in the hearts of all men, which is inflamed by a desire to meet the foe. This a general should endeavor not to repress, but to increase; nor was it a vain institution of our ancestors, that the trumpets should sound on all sides, and a general shout be raised; by which they imagined that the enemy were struck with terror, and their own army inspired with courage.

But our men, when the signal was given, rushed forward with their javelins ready to be launched, but perceiving that Pompey's men did not run to meet their charge, having acquired experience by custom, and being practiced in former battles, they of their own accord repressed their speed, and halted almost midway, that they might not come up with the enemy when their strength was exhausted, and after a short respite they again renewed their course, and threw their javelins, and instantly drew their swords, as Cæsar had ordered them. Nor did Pompey's men fail in this crisis, for they received our javelins, stood our charge, and maintained their ranks; and having launched their javelins, had recourse to their swords. At the same time Pompey's horse, according to their orders, rushed out at once from his left wing, and his whole host of archers poured after them. Our cavalry did not withstand their charge: but gave ground a little, upon which Pompey's horse pressed them more vigorously, and began to file off in troops, and flank our army. When Cæsar perceived this, he gave the signal to his fourth line, which he had formed of the six cohorts. They instantly rushed forward and charged Pompey's horse with such fury, that not a man of them stood; but all wheeling about, not only quitted their post, but galloped forward to seek a refuge in the highest mountains. By their retreat the archers and slingers, being left destitute and defenseless, were all cut to pieces. The cohorts, pursuing their success, wheeled about upon Pompey's left wing, while his infantry still continued to make battle, and attacked them in the rear.

At the same time Cæsar ordered his third line to advance, which till then had not been engaged, but had kept their post. Thus, new and fresh troops having come to the assistance of the fatigued, and others having made an attack on their rear, Pompey's men were not able to maintain their ground, but all fled,[8] nor was Cæsar deceived in his opinion, that the victory, as he had declared in his speech to his soldiers, must have its beginning from those six cohorts, which he had placed as a fourth line to oppose the horse. For by them the cavalry were routed; by them the archers and slingers were cut to pieces; by them the left wing of Pompey's army was surrounded, and obliged to be the first to flee. But when Pompey saw his cavalry routed, and that part of his army on which he reposed his greatest hopes thrown into confusion, despairing of the rest, he quitted the field, and retreated straightway on horseback to his camp, and calling to the centurions, whom he had placed to guard the prætorian gate, with a loud voice, that the soldiers might hear: "Secure the camp," says he, "defend it with diligence, if any danger should threaten it; I will visit the other gates, and encourage the guards of the camp." Having thus said, he retired into his tent in utter despair, yet anxiously waiting the issue.

Cæsar having forced the Pompeians to flee into their intrenchment, and thinking that he ought not to allow them any respite to recover from their fright, exhorted his soldiers to take advantage of fortune's kindness, and to attack the camp. Though they were fatigued by the intense heat, for

[8] Historians state that Cæsar on this occasion advised his soldiers to aim at the faces of Pompey's cavalry, who, being composed principally of the young noblemen of Rome, dreaded a scar in the face more than death itself.

the battle had continued till mid-day, yet, being prepared to undergo any labor, they cheerfully obeyed his command. The camp was bravely defended by the cohorts which had been left to guard it, but with much more spirit by the Thracians and foreign auxiliaries. For the soldiers who had fled for refuge to it from the field of battle, affrighted and exhausted by fatigue, having thrown away their arms and military standards, had their thoughts more engaged on their further escape than on the defense of the camp. Nor could the troops who were posted on the battlements, long withstand the immense number of our darts, but fainting under their wounds, quitted the place, and under the conduct of their centurions and tribunes, fled, without stopping, to the high mountains which joined the camp.

In Pompey's camp you might see arbors in which tables were laid, a large quantity of plate set out, the floors of the tents covered with fresh sods, the tents of Lucius Lentulus and others shaded with ivy, and many other things which were proofs of excessive luxury, and a confidence of victory, so that it might readily be inferred that they had no apprehensions of the issue of the day, as they indulged themselves in unnecessary pleasures, and yet upbraided with luxury Cæsar's army, distressed and suffering troops, who had always been in want of common necessaries. Pompey, as soon as our men had forced the trenches, mounting his horse, and stripping off his general's habit, went hastily out of the back gate of the camp, and galloped with all speed to Larissa. Nor did he stop there, but with the same dispatch, collecting a few of his flying troops, and halting neither day nor night, he arrived at the seaside, attended by only thirty horse, and went on board a victualing bark, often complaining, as we have been told, that he had been so deceived in his expectation, that he was almost persuaded that he had been betrayed by those from whom he had expected victory, as they began the fight.

Cæsar having possessed himself of Pompey's camp, urged his soldiers not to be too intent on plunder, and lose the opportunity of completing their conquest. Having obtained their consent, he began to draw lines round the mountain. The Pompeians distrusting the position, as there was no water on the mountain, abandoned it, and all began to retreat toward Larissa; which Cæsar perceiving, divided his troops, and ordering part of his legions to remain in Pompey's camp, sent back a part of his own camp, and taking four legions with him, went by a shorter road to intercept the enemy: and having marched six miles, drew up his army. But the Pompeians observing this, took post on a mountain, whose foot was washed by a river. Cæsar having encouraged his troops, though they were greatly exhausted by incessant labor the whole day, and night was now approaching, by throwing up works cut off the communication between the river and the mountain, that the enemy might not get water in the night. As soon as the work was finished, they sent ambassadors to treat about a capitulation. A few senators who had espoused that party, made their escape by night.

At break of day, Cæsar ordered all those who had taken post on the mountain, to come down from the higher grounds into the plain, and pile their arms. When they did this without refusal, and with outstretched arms, prostrating themselves on the ground, with tears, implored his mercy: he comforted them and bade them rise, and having spoken a few words of his own clemency to alleviate their fears, he pardoned them all, and gave orders to his soldiers, that no injury should be done to them, and nothing taken from them. Having used this diligence, he ordered the legions in his camp to come and meet him, and those which were with him to take their turn of rest, and go back to the camp: and the same day went to Larissa.

In that battle, no more than two hundred privates were missing, but Cæsar lost about thirty centurions, valiant officers. Crastinus, also, of whom mention was made before, fighting most courageously, lost his life by the wound of a sword in the mouth; nor was that false which he declared when marching to battle: for Cæsar entertained the highest opinion of his behavior in that battle, and thought him highly deserving of his approbation. Of Pompey's army, there fell about fifteen thousand; but upwards of twenty-four thousand were made prisoners: for even the cohorts which were stationed in the forts, surrendered to Sylla. Several others took shelter in the neighboring states. One hundred and eighty stands of colors, and nine eagles, were brought to Cæsar.

THE OVERTHROW OF THE GALLIC NATION OF THE NERVII,[1] FROM CÆSAR'S COMMENTARIES ON THE GALLIC WARS

THE Nervii, from early times, because they were weak in cavalry, (for not even at this time do they attend to it, but accomplish by their infantry whatever they can,) in order that they might the more easily obstruct the cavalry of their neighbors if they came upon them for the purpose of plundering, cut young trees, and bent them by means of their numerous branches extending on to the sides, and the quick-briars and thorns springing up between them, they made these hedges present a fortification like a wall, through which it was not only impossible to enter, but even to penetrate with the eye. Since [therefore] the march of our army would be obstructed by these things, the Nervii thought that the chance ought not to be neglected by them.

The nature of the ground which our men had chosen for their camp was this: A hill, declining evenly from the top, extending to the river Sambre: from this river there arose a second hill of like ascent, on the other side and opposite to the former, and open for about 200 paces at the lower part, but in the upper part, woody, so much so that it was not easy to see through it into the interior. Within these woods the enemy kept themselves in concealment; a few troops of horse-soldiers appeared on the open ground, along the river. The depth of the river was about three feet.

Cæsar, having sent his cavalry on before, followed close after them with all his forces; but the plan and order of the march was different from that which had been reported to the Nervii. For as he was approaching the enemy, Cæsar, according to his custom, led on as the van six legions unencumbered by baggage; behind them he had placed the baggage-trains of the whole army; then the two legions which had been last raised closed the rear, and were a guard for the baggage train. Our horse, with the slingers and archers, having passed the river, commenced action with the cavalry of the enemy. While they from time to time betook themselves

---

[1] This description has been here added as being perhaps Cæsar's most desperate battle and one in which he describes himself as taking a vigorous personal part.

into the woods to their companions, and again made an assault out of the wood upon our men, who did not dare to follow them in their retreat further than the limit to which the plain and open parts extended, in the meantime the six legions which had arrived first, having measured out the work, began to fortify the camp. When the first part of the baggage train of our army was seen by those who lay hid in the woods, which had been agreed on among them as the time for commencing action, as soon as they had arranged their line of battle and formed their ranks within the woods, and had encouraged one another, they rushed out suddenly with all their forces and made an attack upon our horse. The latter being easily routed and thrown into confusion, the Nervii ran down to the river with such incredible speed that they seemed to be in the woods, the river, and close upon us almost at the same time. And with the same speed they hastened up the hill to our camp, and to those who were employed in the works.

Cæsar had everything to do at one time: the standard to be displayed, which was the sign when it was necessary to run to arms; the signal to be given by the trumpet; the soldiers to be called off from the works; those who had proceeded some distance for the purpose of seeking materials for the rampart, to be summoned; the order of battle to be formed; the soldiers to be encouraged; the watchword to be given. A great part of these arrangements was prevented by the shortness of time and the sudden approach and charge of the enemy. Under these difficulties two things proved of advantage; first the skill and experience of the soldiers, because, having been trained by former engagements, they could suggest to themselves what ought to be done, as conveniently as receive information from others; and secondly that Cæsar had forbidden his several lieutenants to depart from the works and their respective legions, before the camp was fortified. These, on account of the near approach and the speed of the enemy, did not then wait for any command from Cæsar, but of themselves executed whatever appeared proper.

Cæsar, having given the necessary orders, hastened to and fro into whatever quarter fortune carried him, to animate the troops, and came to the tenth legion. Having encouraged the soldiers with no further speech than that "they should keep up the remembrance of their wonted valor, and not be confused in mind, but valiantly sustain the assault of the enemy;" as the latter were not further from them than the distance to which a dart could be cast, he gave the signal for commencing battle. And having gone to another quarter for the purpose of encouraging [the soldiers], he finds them fighting. Such was the shortness of the time, and so determined was the mind of the enemy on fighting, that time was wanting not only for affixing the military insignia,[2] but even for putting on the helmets [3] and drawing off the covers from the shields.[4] To whatever part any one by chance came from the works (in which he had been employed), and whatever standards he saw first, at these he stood, lest in seeking his own company he should lose the time for fighting.

The army having been marshaled, rather as the nature of the ground and the declivity of the hill and the exigency of the time, than as the method and order of military matters required; while the legions in the different places were withstanding the enemy, some in one quarter, some in another, and the view was obstructed by the very thick hedges intervening, as we have before remarked, neither could proper reserves be posted, nor could the necessary measures be taken in each part, nor could all the commands be issued by one person. Therefore, in such an unfavorable state of affairs, various events of fortune followed.

The soldiers of the ninth and tenth legions, as they had been stationed on the left part of the army, casting their weapons, speedily drove the Atrĕbătes (for that division had been opposed to them,) who were breathless with running and fatigue, and worn out with wounds, from the higher ground into the river; and following them as they were endeavoring to pass it, slew with their swords a great part of

[2] *"Insignia"* here means those ornaments and badges of distinction worn by the Roman soldiers: probably it here refers especially to the devices upon the helmets.

[3] It was the practice of the Roman soldiers when on the march not to wear their helmets, but to carry them slung over their backs, or chests.

[4] As the shields of the soldiers, even at that period, were embellished with curious and expensive ornaments, they kept them, when either in camp or on the march, covered with leather, as a defense against the dust or rain.

them while impeded therein. They themselves did not hesitate to pass the river; and having advanced to a disadvantageous place, when the battle was renewed, they nevertheless
again put to flight the enemy, who had returned and were
opposing them. In like manner, in another quarter two different legions, the eleventh and the eighth, having routed the
Veromandui, with whom they had engaged, were fighting
from the higher ground upon the very banks of the river.
But, almost the whole camp on the front and on the left side
being then exposed, since the twelfth legion was posted in the
right wing, and the seventh at no great distance from it, all
the Nervii, in a very close body, with Boduognatus, who held
the chief command, as their leader, hastened toward that
place; and part of them began to surround the legions on
their unprotected flank, part to make for the highest point of
the encampment.

At the same time our horsemen, and light-armed infantry,
who had been with those, who, as I have related, were routed
by the first assault of the enemy, as they were betaking themselves into the camp, met the enemy face to face, and again
sought flight into another quarter; and the camp-followers [5]
who from the Decuman Gate,[6] and from the highest ridge of
the hill had seen our men pass the river as victors, when,
after going out for the purposes of plundering, they looked
back and saw the enemy parading in our camp, committed
themselves precipitately to flight; at the same time there arose
the cry and shout of those who came with the baggage-train:
and they (affrighted), were carried some one way, some another. By all these circumstances the cavalry of the Treviri
were much alarmed, (whose reputation for courage is extraordinary among the Gauls, and who had come to Cæsar,
being sent by their state as auxiliaries), and, when they saw
our camp filled with a large number of the enemy, the legions
hard pressed and almost held surrounded, the camp-retainers,
horsemen, slingers, and Numidians fleeing on all sides divided

---

[5] These *calones*, it is generally supposed, were slaves. From continual
attendance upon the army they arrived at a considerable degree of skill
in military matters.

[6] The Roman camp had four gates: "*porta prætoria*," nearest to the
enemy; "*porta Decumana*," opposite to that, and thus furthest from
them; "*porta principalis dextra*," and "*porta principalis sinistra*."

and scattered, they, despairing of our affairs, hastened home, and related to their state that the Romans were routed and conquered, [and] that the enemy were in possession of their camp and baggage-train.

Cæsar proceeded, after encouraging the tenth legion, to the right wing; where he perceived that his men were hard pressed, and that in consequence of the standards of the twelfth legion being collected together in one place, the crowded soldiers were a hindrance to themselves in the fight; that all the centurions of the fourth cohort were slain, and the standard-bearer killed, the standard [7] itself lost, almost all the centurions of the other cohorts either wounded or slain and among them the chief centurion of the legion P. Sextius Baculus, a very valiant man, who was so exhausted by many and severe wounds, that he was already unable to support himself; he likewise perceived that the rest were slackening their efforts, and that some, deserted by those in the rear, were retiring from the battle and avoiding the weapons; that the enemy on the other hand though advancing from the lower ground, were not relaxing in front, and were at the same time pressing hard on both flanks; he also perceived that the affair was at a crisis, and that there was not any reserve which could be brought up; having therefore snatched a shield from one of the soldiers in the rear (for he himself had come without a shield), he advanced to the front of the line, and addressing the centurions by name, and encouraging the rest of the soldiers, he ordered them to carry forward the standards, and extend the companies, that they might the more easily use their swords. On his arrival, as hope was brought to the soldiers and their courage restored, while every one for his own part, in the sight of his general, desired to exert his utmost energy, the impetuosity of the enemy was a little checked.

Cæsar, when he perceived that the seventh legion, which stood close by him, was also hard pressed by the enemy, directed the tribunes of the soldiers to effect a junction of the legions gradually, and make their charge upon the enemy with a double front; which having been done, since they

[7] Besides the *aquila* or standard of the legion, there were the subordinate standards of the *cohorts* and the *manipuli*.

brought assistance the one to the other, nor feared lest their rear should be surrounded by the enemy, they began to stand their ground more boldly, and to fight more courageously. In the meantime, the soldiers of the two legions which had been in the rear of the army, as a guard for the baggage-train, upon the battle being reported to them, quickened their pace, and were seen by the enemy on the top of the hill; and Titus Labienus, having gained possession of the camp of the enemy, and observed from the higher ground what was going on in our camp, sent the tenth legion as a relief to our men, who, when they had learned from the flight of the horse and the sutlers in what position the affair was, and in how great danger the camp and the legion and the commander were involved, left undone nothing which tended to dispatch.

By their arrival, so great a change of matters was made, that our men, even those who had fallen down exhausted with wounds, leaned on their shields, and renewed the fight: then the camp-retainers, though unarmed, seeing the enemy completely dismayed, attacked them though armed; the horsemen too, that they might by their valor blot the disgrace of their flight, thrust themselves before the legionary soldiers in all parts of the battle. But the enemy, even in the last hope of safety, displayed such great courage, that when the foremost of them had fallen, the next stood upon them prostrate, and fought from their bodies; when these were overthrown, and their corpses heaped up together, those who survived cast their weapons against our men thence, as from a mound, and returned our darts which had fallen short between the armies; so that it ought not to be concluded, that men of such great courage had injudiciously dared to pass a very broad river, ascend very high banks, and come up to a very disadvantageous place; since their greatness of spirit had rendered these actions easy, although in themselves very difficult.

This battle being ended, and the nation and name of the Nervii being almost reduced to annihilation, their old men, who together with all the boys and women were found to have been collected together in the fenny places and marshes, on this battle having been reported to them, since they were convinced that nothing was an obstacle to the conquerors, and nothing safe to the conquered, sent ambassadors to Cæsar by the consent of all who remained, and surrendered themselves to him; and in recounting the calamity of their state, said that their senators were reduced from 600 to three; that from 60,000 men they were reduced to scarcely 500 who could bear arms; whom Cæsar, that he might appear to use compassion toward the wretched and the suppliant, most carefully spared; and ordered them to enjoy their own territories and towns, and commanded their neighbors that they should restrain themselves and their dependents from offering injury or outrage to them.

Much about the same time, Cassius arrived in Sicily with a fleet of Syrians, Phœnicians, and Cicilians: and as Cæsar's fleet was divided into two parts, Publius Sulpicius the prætor commanding one division at Vibo near the straits, Pomponius the other at Messana, Cassius got into Messana with his fleet, before Pomponius had notice of his arrival, and having found him in disorder, without guards or discipline, and the wind being high and favorable, he filled several transports with fir, pitch, and tow, and other combustibles, sent them against Pomponius's fleet, and set fire to all his ships, thirty-five in number, twenty of which were armed with beaks: and this action struck such terror that though there was a legion in garrison at Messana, the town with difficulty held out, and had not the news of Cæsar's victory been brought at that instant by the horse stationed along the coast, it was generally imagined that it would have been lost, but the town was maintained till the news arrived very opportunely: and Cassius set sail from thence to attack Sulpicius's fleet at Vibo, and our ships being moored to the land, to strike the same terror, he acted in the same manner as before. The wind being favorable, he sent into the port about forty ships provided with combustibles, and the flame catching on both sides, five ships were burned to ashes. And when the fire began to spread wider by the violence of the wind, the soldiers of the veteran legions, who had been left to guard the fleet, being considered as invalids, could not endure the disgrace, but of themselves went on board the ships and weighed anchor, and having attacked Cassius's fleet, captured two five-banked galleys, in one of which was Cassius himself; but he made his escape by taking to a boat. Two three-banked galleys were taken besides. Intelligence was shortly after received of the action in Thessaly, so well authenticated, that the Pompeians themselves gave credit to it; for they had hitherto believed it a fiction of Cæsar's lieutenants and friends. Upon which intelligence Cassius departed with his fleet from that coast.

Cæsar thought he ought to postpone all business and pursue Pompey, whithersoever he should retreat; that he might not be able to provide fresh forces, and renew the war; he therefore marched on every day, as far as his cavalry were able to advance, and ordered one legion to follow him by shorter journeys. A proclamation was issued by Pompey at Amphipolis, that all the young men of that province, Grecians and Roman citizens, should take the military oath; but whether he issued it with an intention of preventing suspicion, and to conceal as long as possible his design of fleeing further, or to endeavor to keep possession of Macedonia by new levies, if nobody pursued him, it is impossible to judge. He lay at anchor one night, and calling together his friends in Amphipolis, and collecting a sum of money for his necessary expenses, upon advice of Cæsar's approach, set sail from that place, and arrived in a few days at Mitylene. Here he was detained two days, and having added a few galleys to his fleet he went to Cilicia, and thence to Cyprus. There he is informed that, by the consent of all the inhabitants of Antioch [8] and Roman citizens who traded there, the castle had been seized to shut him out of the town; and that messengers had been dispatched to all those who were reported to have taken refuge in the neighboring states, that they should not come to Antioch; that if they did, that it would be attended with imminent danger to their lives. The same thing happened to Lucius Lentulus, who had been consul the year before, and to Publius Lentulus a consular senator, and to sev-

---

[8] Antiochia, or Antioch, now called *Antakia*, was founded by Seleucus Nicanor, who named it after his father. It was not only the capital of Syria, but of all Asia, and was once the third city in the world for beauty, size, and population; it was the royal seat of the Syrian kings, and after the Roman conquest became the ordinary residence of the prefect, or governor of the eastern provinces. It was here that the disciples of Christ first received the name of Christians, A.D. 39, having been before commonly called Nazarenes and Galilæans; it was the birthplace of St. Luke, the evangelist.

eral others at Rhodes, who having followed Pompey in his flight, and arrived at the island, were not admitted into the town or port; and having received a message to leave that neighborhood, set sail much against their will; for the rumor of Cæsar's approach had now reached those states.

Pompey, being informed of these proceedings, laid aside his design of going to Syria, and having taken the public money from the farmers of the revenue, and borrowed more from some private friends, and having put on board his ships a large quantity of brass for military purposes, and two thousand armed men, whom he partly selected from the slaves of the tax farmers, and party collected from the merchants, and such persons as each of his friends thought fit on this occasion, he sailed for Pelusium. It happened that king Ptolemy, a minor, was there with a considerable army, engaged in war with his sister Cleopatra, whom a few months before, by the assistance of his relations and friends, he had expelled from the kingdom; and her camp lay at a small distance from his. To him Pompey applied to be permitted to take refuge in Alexandria, and to be protected in his calamity by his powerful assistance, in consideration of the friendship and amity which had subsisted between his father and him. But Pompey's deputies having executed their commission, began to converse with less restraint with the king's troops, and to advise them to act with friendship to Pompey, and not to think meanly of his bad fortune. In Ptolemy's army were several of Pompey's soldiers, of whom Gabinius had received the command in Syria, and had brought them over to Alexandria, and at the conclusion of the war had left with Ptolemy the father of the young king.

The king's friends, who were regents of the kingdom during the minority, being informed of these things, either induced by fear, as they afterward declared, lest Pompey should corrupt the king's army, and seize on Alexandria and Egypt; or despising his bad fortune, as in adversity friends commonly change to enemies, in public gave a favorable answer to his deputies, and desired him to come to the king; but secretly laid a plot against him, and dispatched Achillas, captain of the king's guards, a man of singular boldness, and Lucius Septimius a military tribune to assassinate him. Being kindly addressed by them, and deluded by an acquaintance with Septimius, because in the war with the pirates the latter had commanded a company under him, he embarked in a small boat with a few attendants, and was there murdered by Achillas and Septimius. In like manner, Lucius Lentulus was seized by the king's order, and put to death in prison.

When Cæsar arrived in Asia, he found that Titus Ampius had attempted to remove the money from the temple of Diana at Ephesus; and for this purpose had convened all the senators in the province that he might have them to attest the sum, but was interrupted by Cæsar's arrival, and had made his escape. Thus, on two occasions, Cæsar saved the money of Ephesus. It was also remarked at Elis, in the temple of Minerva, upon calculating and enumerating the days, that on the very day on which Cæsar had gained his battle, the image of Victory which was placed before Minerva, and faced her statue, turned about toward the portal and entrance of the temple; and the same day, at Antioch in Syria, such a shout of an army and sound of trumpets was twice heard that the citizens ran in arms to the walls. The same thing happened at Ptolemais; a sound of drums too was heard at Pergamus, in the private and retired parts of the temple, into which none but the priests are allowed admission, and which the Greeks call Adyta (the inaccessible), and likewise at Tralles, in the temple of Victory, in which there stood a statue consecrated to Cæsar; a palm-tree at that time was shown that had sprouted up from the pavement, through the joints of the stones, and shot up above the roof.

After a few days' delay in Asia, Cæsar, having heard that Pompey had been seen in Cyprus, and conjecturing that he had directed his course into Egypt, on account of his connection with that kingdom,[9] set out for Alexandria with two legions (one of which he ordered to follow him from Thessaly, the other he called in from Achaia, from Fufius, the lieutenant general), and with eight hundred horse, ten ships of war from Rhodes, and a few from Asia. These legions amounted but to three thousand two hundred men; the rest, disabled by wounds received in various battles, by fatigue and the

[9] He had been appointed by the senate, guardian to the young king.

length of their march, could not follow him. But Cæsar, relying on the fame of his exploits, did not hesitate to set forward with a feeble force, and thought that he would be secure in any place. At Alexandria he was informed of the death of Pompey: and at his landing there, heard a cry among the soldiers whom the king had left to garrison the town, and saw a crowd gathering toward him, because the fasces were carried before him; for this the whole multitude thought an infringement of the king's dignity. Though this tumult was appeased, frequent disturbances were raised for several days successively, by crowds of the populace, and a great many of his soldiers were killed in all parts of the city.

Having observed this, he ordered other legions to be brought to him from Asia, which he had made up out of Pompey's soldiers; for he was himself detained against his will, by the etesian winds, which are totally unfavorable to persons on a voyage from Alexandria. In the meantime, considering that the disputes of the princes belonged to the jurisdiction of the Roman people, and of him as consul, and that it was a duty more incumbent on him, as in his former consulate a league had been made with Ptolemy the late king, under sanction both of a law and a decree of the senate, he signified that it was his pleasure that king Ptolemy, and his sister Cleopatra, should disband their armies, and decide their disputes in his presence by justice, rather than by the sword.

A eunuch named Pothinus, the boy's tutor, was regent of the kingdom on account of his youthfulness.[10] He at first began to complain among his friends, and to express his indignation, that the king should be summoned to plead his cause: but afterward, having prevailed on some of those whom he had made acquainted with his views to join him, he secretly called the army away from Pelusium to Alexandria, and appointed Achillas, already spoken of, commander-in-chief of the forces. Him he encouraged and animated by promises both in his own and the king's name, and instructed him both by letters and messages how he should act. By the will of Ptolemy the father, the elder of his two sons and the more advanced in years of his two daughters were declared his

[10] We learn from Appian that the young king was thirteen years old at this time.

heirs, and for the more effectual performance of his intention, in the same will he conjured the Roman people by all the gods, and by the league which he had entered into at Rome, to see his will executed. One of the copies of his will was conveyed to Rome by his embassadors to be deposited in the treasury, but the public troubles preventing it, it was lodged with Pompey: another was left sealed up, and kept at Alexandria.

While these things were debated before Cæsar, and he was very anxious to settle royal disputes as a common friend and arbitrator; news was brought on a sudden that the king's army and all his cavalry, were on their march to Alexandria. Cæsar's forces were by no means so strong that he could trust to them, if he had occasion to hazard a battle without the town. His only resource was to keep within the town in the most convenient places, and get information of Achillas's designs. However he ordered his soldiers to repair to their arms; and advised the king to send some of his friends, who had the greatest influence, as deputies to Achillas, and to signify his royal pleasure. Dioscorides and Serapion, the persons sent by him, who had both been embassadors at Rome, and had been in great esteem with Ptolemy the father, went to Achillas. But as soon as they appeared in his presence, without hearing them, or learning the occasion of their coming, he ordered them to be seized and put to death. One of them, after receiving a wound, was taken up and carried off by his attendants as dead: the other was killed on the spot. Upon this, Cæsar took care to secure the king's person, both supposing that the king's name would have a great influence with his subjects, and to give the war the appearance of the scheme of a few desperate men, rather than of having been begun by the king's consent.

The forces under Achillas did not seem despicable, either for number, spirit or military experience; for he had twenty thousand men under arms. They consisted partly of Gabinius's soldiers, who were now become habituated to the licentious mode of living at Alexandria, and had forgotten the name and discipline of the Roman people, and had married wives there, by whom the greatest part of them had children. To these was added a collection of highwaymen, and freebooters, from Syria, and the province of Cilicia, and the adjacent countries. Besides several convicts and transports had been collected: for at Alexandria all our runaway slaves were sure of finding protection for their persons on the condition that they should give in their names, and enlist as soldiers: and if any of them was apprehended by his master, he was rescued by a crowd of his fellow soldiers, who being involved in the same guilt, repelled, at the hazard of their lives, every violence offered to any of their body. These by a prescriptive privilege of the Alexandrian army, used to demand the king's favorites to be put to death, pillage the properties of the rich to increase their pay, invest the king's palace, banish some from the kingdom, and recall others from exile. Besides these, there were two thousand horse, who had acquired the skill of veterans by being in several wars in Alexandria. These had restored Ptolemy the father to his kingdom, had killed Bibulus's two sons; and had been engaged in war with the Egyptians; such was their experience in military affairs.

Full of confidence in his troops, and despising the small number of Cæsar's soldiers, Achillas seized Alexandria, except that part of the town which Cæsar occupied with his troops. At first he attempted to force the palace; but Cæsar had disposed his cohorts through the streets, and repelled his attack. At the same time there was an action at the port: where the contest was maintained with the greatest obstinacy.[11] For the forces were divided, and the fight maintained in several streets at once, and the enemy endeavored to seize with a strong party the ships of war; of which fifty had been sent to Pompey's assistance, but after the battle in Thessaly, had returned home. They were all of either three or five banks of oars, well equipped and appointed with every necessary for a voyage. Besides these, there were twenty-two vessels with decks, which were usually kept at Alexandria, to guard the port. If they made themselves masters of these, Cæsar being deprived of his fleet, they would have the command of the port and whole sea, and could prevent him from procuring provisions and auxiliaries. Accord-

[11] Otherwise thus, "and that action was productive of by far the greatest danger."

ingly that spirit was displayed, which ought to be displayed when the one party saw that a speedy victory depended on the issue, and the other their safety. But Cæsar gained the day, and set fire to all those ships, and to others which were in the docks, because he could not guard so many places with so small a force; and immediately he conveyed some troops to the Pharos by his ships.

The Pharos is a tower on an island, of prodigious height, built with amazing works, and takes its name from the island. This island lying over against Alexandria, forms a harbor; but on the upper side it is connected with the town by a narrow way eight hundred paces in length, made by piles sunk in the sea, and by a bridge. In this island some of the Egyptians have houses, and a village as large as a town; and whatever ships from any quarter, either through mistaking the channel, or by the storm, have been driven from their course upon the coast, they constantly plunder like pirates. And without the consent of those who are masters of the Pharos, no vessels can enter the harbor, on account of its narrowness. Cæsar being greatly alarmed on this account, while the enemy were engaged in battle, landed his soldiers, seized the Pharos, and placed a garrison in it. By this means he gained this point, that he could be supplied without danger with corn, and auxiliaries; for he sent to all the neighboring countries, to demand supplies. In other parts of the town, they fought so obstinately, that they quitted the field with equal advantage, and neither were beaten (in consequence of the narrowness of the passes); and a few being killed on both sides, Cæsar secured the most necessary posts, and fortified them in the night. In this quarter of the town was a wing of the king's palace, in which Cæsar was lodged on his first arrival, and a theater adjoining the house which served as a citadel, and commanded an avenue to the ports and other docks. These fortifications he increased during the succeeding days, that he might have them before him as a rampart, and not be obliged to fight against his will. In the meantime Ptolemy's younger daughter, hoping the throne would become vacant, made her escape from the palace to Achillas, and assisted him in prosecuting the war. But they soon quarreled about the command, which circumstance enlarged the presents to the soldiers, for each endeavored by great sacrifices to secure their affection. While the enemy was thus employed, Pothinus, tutor to the young king, and regent of the kingdom, who was in Cæsar's part of the town, sent messengers to Achillas, and encouraged him not to desist from his enterprise, nor to despair of success; but his messengers being discovered and apprehended, he was put to death by Cæsar. Such was the commencement of the Alexandrian war.

AUGUSTUS CAESAR

AUGUSTUS CÆSAR

63 B. C.-14 A. D.

INTRODUCTORY NOTE

Gaius Julius Cæsar Octavianus is more commonly known by his title of Augustus, which means the ''august'' or ''consecrated'' Cæsar. He was the grandnephew of Julius Cæsar and as such became his adopted son and heir. The young heir, at first publicly known as Octavian, was only nineteen years old when the mighty Julius was slain; but by much shrewdness and cautious wisdom Octavian gradually got the upper hand of all the foes of his uncle and all his own rivals. Brutus, Cassius, Cicero and Mark Antony, each in turn perished in opposing him. The Roman populace which had been devoted to Julius Cæsar finally became even more devoted to Octavian, and bestowed on him for life the authority of one office after another, until he united in his own person all the powers of chief priest, chief general, chief legislator and chief ''tribune'' or guardian of the people's rights. This complete and universal mastership over all the world of his day, Augustus exercised wisely and with splendid self-control. As he himself records, the Roman temple of the wargod was first closed by him, that is, he held the whole known world in a submissive peace.

Shortly before his death Augustus, somewhat in the spirit of the old Babylonian and Assyrian kings, prepared a public statement of all his achievements. The contrast of his record to that of the Assyrians is, however, very striking. Augustus proclaims his gentleness and justice and generosity; they had proclaimed only their ferocity and supreme power.

This official statement by Augustus was inscribed upon a monument in Rome, and copies of it were set up in other cities. This "Monumentum Ancyranum," the official autobiography of this mightiest of Roman rulers, his own estimate of his great career, is given here. Its wording is stiff and dry and somewhat pompous, representing Augustus to have been all right and his opponents all wrong in every controversy. Yet its very narrowness, its simple striving for approval, is in a way pathetically typical of the emperor himself,

71

of the man of whom the story is told that when approaching death, he had himself carefully dressed and rose upright, saying to his attendants, " Have I played my part well in life? If so applaud me now. "

THE MONUMENTUM ANCYRANUM
OF AUGUSTUS CAESAR [1]

BELOW is a copy of the deeds of the divine Augustus, by which he subjected the whole world to the dominion of the Roman people, and of the amounts which he expended upon the commonwealth and the Roman people, as engraved upon two brazen columns which are set up at Rome.

I

IN my twentieth year, acting upon my own judgment and at my own expense, I raised an army by means of which I restored to liberty the commonwealth which had been oppressed by the tyranny of a faction.[2] On account of this the senate by laudatory decrees admitted me to its order,[3] in the consulship of Gaius Pansa and Aulus Hirtius, and at the same time gave me consular rank in the expression of opinion ; and gave me the *imperium.* It also voted that I as propraetor, together with the consuls, should see to it that the commonwealth suffered no harm.[4] In the same year, moreover, when both consuls had perished in war, the people made me consul, and triumvir for organizing the commonwealth.

---

[1] From a copy of the statement inscribed on the wall of a temple in the Asiatic city of Ancyra.

[2] Such a statement is part of Augustus' scheme to pose as a restorer of the old order. He makes Brutus, Cassius, Pompey and Antony public enemies.

[3] Cicero says "the senate voted that Gaius Caesar, son of Gaius, pontiff, should be a senator, and hold praetorian rank in speaking."

[4] The formula by which in emergencies, extraordinary powers were given to the ordinary magistrates.

II

THOSE who killed my father I drove into exile by lawful judgments, avenging their crime, and afterwards, when they waged war against the commonwealth, I twice defeated them in battle.

III

I UNDERTOOK civil and foreign wars by land and sea throughout the whole world, and as victor I showed mercy to all surviving citizens. Foreign peoples, who could be pardoned with safety, I preferred to preserve rather than to destroy. About five hundred thousand Roman citizens took the military oath of allegiance to me. Of these I have settled in colonies or sent back to their *municipia*, upon the expiration of their terms of service, somewhat over three hundred thousand, and to all these I have given lands purchased by me, or money for farms, out of my own means. I have captured six hundred ships, besides those which were smaller than triremes.

IV

TWICE I have triumphed in the ovation,[5] and three times in the curule triumph,[6] and I have been twenty-one times saluted as imperator.[7] After that, when the senate decreed me many triumphs, I declined them. Likewise I often deposited the laurels in the Capitol in fulfillment of vows which I had also made in battle. On account of enterprises brought to a successful issue on land and sea by me, or by my lieutenants under my auspices, the senate fifty-five times decreed that there should be a thanksgiving to the immortal gods. The number of days, moreover, on which thanksgiving was rendered in accordance with the decree of the senate was eight hundred and ninety. In my triumphs there have been led

[5] The ovation was the lesser triumph. The general entered the city clad as an ordinary magistrate, and on foot, or as here on horseback, decked with myrtle.

[6] In the curule triumph, for important victories, the general was vested in purple, and rode in a four-horse chariot, preceded by the fasces.

[7] The acclamation as *imperator*, on account of success in war, must be carefully distinguished from the title used as a prefix to the name and as a mark of perpetual authority. The title imperator was regularly and permanently assumed at the beginning of each reign, after that of Augustus. To him it was formally assigned by the senate.

before my chariot nine kings, or children of kings. When I wrote these words I had been thirteen times consul, and was in the thirty-seventh year of the tribunitial power.

V

THE dictatorship which was offered to me by the people and the senate, both when I was absent and when I was present, in the consulship of Marcus Marcellus and Lucius Arruntius, I did not accept. At a time of the greatest dearth of grain I did not refuse the charge of the food supply, which I so administered that in a few days, at my own expense, I freed the whole people from the anxiety and danger in which they then were. The annual and perpetual consulship offered to me at that time I did not accept.

VI

DURING the consulship of Marcus Vinucius and Quintus Lucretius, and afterwards in that of Publius and Cnæus Lentulus, and a third time in that of Paullus Fabius Maximus and Quintus Tubero, by the consent of the senate and the Roman people I was voted the sole charge of the laws and of morals, with the fullest power; but I accepted the proffer of no office which was contrary to the customs of the country. The measures of which the senate at that time wished me to take charge, I accomplished in virtue of my possession of the tribunitial power. In this office I five times associated with myself a colleague, with the consent of the senate.

VII

FOR ten years in succession I was one of the triumvirs for organizing the commonwealth. Up to that day on which I write these words I have been *princeps* of the senate through forty years. I have been *pontifex maximus,* augur, a member of the quindecemviral college of the sacred rites, of the septemviral college of the banquets, an Arval Brother, a member of the Titian sodality, and a fetial.

VIII

IN my fifth consulship, by order of the people and the senate, I increased the number of the patricians. Three times I have

revised the list of the senate.[8] In my sixth consulship, with
Marcus Agrippa as colleague, I made a census of the people.
I performed the lustration after forty-one years. In this
lustration the number of Roman citizens was four million and
sixty-three thousand. Again assuming the consular power
in the consulship of Gaius Censorinus and Gaius Asinius, I
alone performed the lustration. At this census the number of
Roman citizens was four million, two hundred and thirty
thousand. A third time, assuming the consular power in the
consulship of Sextus Pompeius and Sextus Appuleius, with
Tiberius Cæsar as colleague, I performed the lustration. At
this lustration the number of Roman citizens was four million,
nine hundred and thirty-seven thousand. By new legislation
I have restored many customs of our ancestors which had
now begun to fall into disuse, and I have myself also committed to posterity many examples worthy of imitation.

IX

THE senate decreed that every fifth year vows for my good
health should be performed by the consuls and the priests.
In accordance with these vows games have been often celebrated during my lifetime, sometimes by the four chief col-
leges, sometimes by the consuls. In private, also, and as
municipalities, the whole body of citizens have constantly
sacrificed at every shrine for my good health.

X

BY a decree of the senate my name has been included in the
Salian hymn, and it has been enacted by law that I should be
sacrosanct, and that as long as I live I should be invested with
the tribunitial power. I refused to be made *pontifex maximus*
in the place of a colleague still living, when the people ten-

[8] During most of the republican history the senate numbered, ideally,
three hundred. In Cicero's time it had over four hundred members.
Julius Cæsar raised it to about nine hundred. Suet. *Aug.*, 35, says: ''By
two separate scrutinies he (Augustus) reduced to their former number
and splendor the senate, which had been swamped by a disorderly crowd;
for they were now more than a thousand, and some of them very mean
persons, who, after Cæsar's death, had been chosen by dint of interest
and bribery, so that they had the name of Orcini among the people.''
They were also called Charonites, because they owed their elevation to
the last will of Cæsar, who had gone into Orcus to Charon.

dered me that priesthood which my father held. I accepted that office after several years, when he was dead who had seized it during a time of civil disturbance; and at the comitia for my election, during the consulship of Publius Sulpicius and Gaius Valgius, so great a multitude assembled as, it is said, had never before been in Rome.

XI

CLOSE to the temples of Honor and Virtue, near the Capena gate, the senate consecrated in honor of my return an altar to Fortune the Restorer, and upon this altar it ordered that the *pontifices* and the Vestal virgins should offer sacrifice yearly on the anniversary of the day on which I returned into the city from Syria, in the consulship of Quintus Lucretius and Marcus Vinucius, and it called the day the Augustalia, from our cognomen.

XII

BY a decree of the senate at the same time a part of the prætors and tribunes of the people with the consul Quintus Lucretius and leading citizens were sent into Campania to meet me, an honor which up to this time has been decreed to no one but me. When I returned from Spain and Gaul after successfully arranging the affairs of those provinces, in the consulship of Tiberius Nero and Publius Quintilius, the senate voted that in honor of my return an altar of the Augustan Peace should be consecrated in the Campus Martius, and upon this altar it ordered the magistrates and priests and vestal virgins to offer sacrifices on each anniversary.

XIII

JANUS QUIRINUS, which it was the purpose of our fathers to close when there was peace won by victory [9] throughout the whole empire of the Roman people on land and sea, and which, before I was born, from the foundation of the city, was reported to have been closed twice in all, the senate three times ordered to be closed while I was *princeps*.

[9] The exact conditions necessary for the closing of the temple, viz., "peace won by victories," were first made known in 1882 by this perfected text of *Res Gestæ*.

XIV

My sons, the Cæsars Gaius and Lucius, whom fortune snatched from me in their youth, the senate and Roman people, in order to do me honor, designated as consuls in the fifteenth year of each, with the intention that they should enter upon that magistracy after five years. And the senate decreed that from the day in which they were introduced into the forum they should share in the public counsels. Moreover the whole body of the Roman knights gave them the title, *principes* of the youth, and gave to each a silver buckler and spear.

XV

To each man of the Roman *plebs* I paid three hundred sesterces in accordance with the last will of my father; [10] and in my own name, when consul for the fifth time, I gave four hundred sesterces from the spoils of the wars; again, moreover, in my tenth consulship I gave from my own estate four hundred sesterces to each man by way of *congiarium;* and in my eleventh consulship I twelve times made distributions of food, buying grain at my own expense; and in the twelfth year of my tribunitial power I three times gave four hundred sesterces to each man. These my donations have never been made to less than two hundred and fifty thousand men. In my twelfth consulship and the eighteenth year of my tribunitial power I gave to three hundred and twenty thousand of the city *plebs* sixty *denarii* apiece. In the colonies of my soldiers, when consul for the fifth time, I gave to each man a thousand sesterces from the spoils; about a hundred and twenty thousand men in the colonies received that triumphal donation. When consul for the thirteenth time I gave sixty *denarii* to the *plebs* who were at that time receiving public grain; these men were a little more than two hundred thousand in number.

XVI

For the lands which in my fourth consulship, and afterwards in the consulship of Marcus Crassus and Cnæus Lentulus, the augur, I assigned to soldiers, I paid money to the *municipia.*

[10] "He (Cæsar) bequeathed to the Roman people his gardens near the Tiber, and three hundred sesterces to each man."

The sum which I paid for Italian farms was about six hundred million sesterces, and that for lands in the provinces was about two hundred and sixty millions. Of all those who have established colonies of soldiers in Italy or in the provinces I am the first and only one within the memory of my age, to do this. And afterward in the consulship of Tiberius Nero and Cnæus Piso, and also in that of Gaius Antistius and Decimus Lælius, and in that of Gaius Calvisius and Lucius Pasienus, and in that of Lucius Lentulus and Marcus Messala, and in that of Lucius Caninius and Quintus Fabricius, I gave gratuities in money to the soldiers whom I sent back to their *municipia* at the expiration of their terms of service, and for this purpose I freely spent four hundred million sesterces.

XVII

FOUR times I have aided the public treasury from my own means, to such extent that I have furnished to those in charge of the treasury one hundred and fifty million sesterces. And in the consulship of Marcus Lepidus and Lucius Arruntius I paid into the military treasury which was established by my advice that from it gratuities might be given to soldiers who had served a term of twenty or more years, one hundred and seventy million sesterces from my own estate.

XVIII

BEGINNING with that year in which Cnæus and Publius Lentulus were consuls, when the imposts failed, I furnished aid sometimes to a hundred thousand men, and sometimes to more, by supplying grain or money for the tribute from my own land and property.

XIX

I CONSTRUCTED the Curia, and the Chalcidicum adjacent thereto, the temple of Apollo on the Palatine, with its porticoes, the temple of the divine Julius, the Lupercal, the portico to the Circus of Flaminius, which I allowed to bear the name, Portico Octavia, from his name who constructed the earlier one in the same place; the Pulvinar at the Circus Maximus, the temples of Jupiter the Vanquisher and Jupiter the Thunderer, on the Capitol, the temple of Quirinus, the temples of

Minerva and Juno Regina and of Jupiter Libertas, on the Aventine, the temple of the Lares on the highest point of the Via Sacra, the temple of the divine Penates on the Velian hill, the temple of Youth, and the temple of the Great Mother on the Palatine.

XX

THE Capitol and the Pompeian theater have been restored by me at enormous expense for each work, without any inscription of my name. Aqueducts which were crumbling in many places by reason of age I have restored, and I have doubled the water which bears the name Marcian by turning a new spring into its course. The Forum Julium and the basilica which was between the temple of Castor and the temple of Saturn, works begun and almost completed by my father, I have finished; and when that same basilica was consumed by fire, I began its reconstruction on an enlarged site, inscribing it with the names of my sons; and if I do not live to complete it, I have given orders that it be completed by my heirs. In accordance with a decree of the senate, while consul for the sixth time, I have restored eighty-two temples of the gods, passing over none which was at that time in need of repair. In my seventh consulship I reconstructed the Flaminian way from the city to Ariminum, and all the bridges except the Mulvian and Minucian.

XXI

UPON private ground I have built with the spoils of war the temple of Mars the Avenger, and the Augustan Forum. Beside the temple of Apollo, I built upon ground, bought for the most part at my own expense, a theater, to bear the name of Marcellus, my son-in-law. From the spoils of war I have consecrated gifts in the Capitol, and in the temple of the divine Julius, and in the temple of Apollo, and in the temple of Vesta, and in the temple of Mars the Avenger; these gifts have cost me about a hundred million sesterces. In my fifth consulship I remitted to the *municipia* and Italian colonies the thirty-five thousand pounds given me as coronary gold on the occasion of my triumphs, and thereafter, as often as I was proclaimed imperator, I did not accept the coronary gold which the *municipia* and colonies kindly voted to me.

XXII

THREE times in my own name, and five times in that of my sons or grandsons, I have given gladiatorial exhibitions; in these exhibitions about ten thousand men have fought. Twice in my own name, and three times in that of my grandson, I have offered the people the spectacle of athletes gathered from all quarters. I have celebrated games four times in my own name, and twenty-three times in the turns of other magistrates. In behalf of the college of quindecemvirs, I, as master of the college, with my colleague Agrippa, celebrated the Secular Games in the consulship of Gaius Furnius and Gaius Silanus. When consul for the thirteenth time, I first celebrated the Martial games, which since that time the consuls have given in successive years. Twenty-six times in my own name, or in that of my sons and grandsons, I have given hunts of African wild beasts in the circus, the forum, the amphitheaters, and about thirty-five hundred beasts have been killed.

XXIII

I GAVE the people the spectacle of a naval battle beyond the Tiber, where now is the grove of the Cæsars.[11] For this purpose an excavation was made eighteen hundred feet long and twelve hundred wide. In this contest thirty beaked ships, triremes or biremes, were engaged, besides more of smaller size. About three thousand men fought in these vessels in addition to the rowers.

XXIV

IN the temples of all the cities of the province of Asia, I, as victor, replaced the ornaments of which he with whom I was at war had taken private possession when he despoiled the temples. Silver statues of me, on foot, on horseback and in quadrigas, which stood in the city to the number of about eighty, I removed, and out of their money value, I placed

[11] Velleius writes: "The divine Augustus in the year when he was consul with Gallus Caninius sated the minds and the eyes of the Roman people at the dedication of the temple of Mars with the most magnificent gladiatorial shows and naval battles." Dio says that traces of the excavation could be seen in his time (c. 200 A. D.), and that the fight represented a battle of Athenians and Persians, in which the former were victorious.

golden gifts in the temple of Apollo in my own name, and in the names of those who had offered me the honor of the statues.

XXV

I HAVE freed the sea from pirates. In that war with the slaves I delivered to their masters for punishment about thirty thousand slaves who had fled from their masters and taken up arms against the state.[12] The whole of Italy voluntarily took the oath of allegiance to me, and demanded me as leader in that war in which I conquered at Actium. The provinces of Gaul, Spain, Africa, Sicily and Sardinia swore the same allegiance to me. There were more than seven hundred senators who at that time fought under my standards, and among these, up to the day on which these words are written, eighty-three have either before or since been made consuls, and about one hundred and seventy have been made priests.

XXVI

I HAVE extended the boundaries of all the provinces of the Roman people which were bordered by nations not yet subjected to our sway. I have reduced to a state of peace the Gallic and Spanish provinces, and Germany, the lands inclosed by the ocean from Gades to the mouth of the Elbe. The Alps from the region nearest the Adriatic as far as the Tuscan Sea I have brought into a state of peace, without waging an unjust war upon any people. My fleet has navigated the ocean from the mouth of the Rhine as far as the boundaries of the Cimbri, where before that time no Roman had ever penetrated by land or sea; and the Cimbri and Charydes and Semnones and other German peoples of that section, by means of legates, sought my friendship and that of the Roman people. By my command and under my auspices two armies at almost the same time have been led into Ethiopia and into Arabia, which is called "the Happy," and very many of the enemy of both peoples have fallen in battle, and many towns have been captured. Into Ethiopia the advance was as far as Nabata, which is next to Meroe. In Arabia the army penetrated as far as the confines of the Sabaei, to the town Mariba.

[12] The allusion is to Sextus Pompeius, whose fleets, manned largely by slaves, cut off the grain ships on their way to Rome.

XXVII

I HAVE added Egypt to the empire of the Roman people. Of greater Armenia, when its king Artaxes was killed I could have made a province, but I preferred, after the example of our fathers, to deliver that kingdom to Tigranes, the son of king Artavasdes, and grandson of king Tigranes; and this I did through Tiberius Nero, who was then my son-in-law. And afterwards, when the same people became turbulent and rebellious, they were subdued by Gaius, my son, and I gave the sovereignty over them to king Ariobarzanes, the son of Artabazes, king of the Medes, and after his death to his son Artavasdes. When he was killed I sent into that kingdom Tigranes, who was sprung from the royal house of the Armenians. I recovered all the provinces across the Adriatic Sea, which extend toward the east, and Cyrenaica, at that time for the most part in the possession of kings, together with Sicily and Sardinia, which had been engaged in a servile war.

XXVIII

I HAVE established colonies of soldiers in Africa, Sicily, Macedonia, the two Spains, Achaia, Asia, Syria, Gallia Narbonensis and Pisidia. Italy also has twenty-eight colonies established under my auspices, which within my lifetime have become very famous and populous.

XXIX

I HAVE recovered from Spain and Gaul, and from the Dalmatians, after conquering the enemy, many military standards which had been lost by other leaders. I have compelled the Parthians to give up to me the spoils and standards of three Roman armies, and as suppliants to seek the friendship of the Roman people. Those standards, moreover, I have deposited in the sanctuary which is in the temple of Mars the Avenger.

XXX

THE Pannonian peoples, whom before I became *princeps*, no army of the Roman people had ever attacked, were defeated by Tiberius Nero, at that time my son-in-law and legate; and I brought them under subjection to the empire of the Roman people, and extended the boundaries of Illyricum to the bank of the river Danube. When an army of the Dacians crossed this river, it was defeated and destroyed, and afterwards my army, led across the Danube, compelled the Dacian people to submit to the sway of the Roman people.

XXXI

EMBASSIES have been many times sent to me from the kings of India, a thing never before seen in the case of any ruler of the Romans. Our friendship has been sought by means of ambassadors by the Bastarnae and the Scythians, and by the kings of the Sarmatae, who are on either side of the Tanais, and by the kings of the Albani, the Hiberi, and the Medes.

XXXII

To me have betaken themselves as suppliants the kings of the Parthians, Tiridates, and later, Phraates, the son of king Phraates; of the Medes, Artavasdes; of the Adiabeni, Artaxares; of the Britons, Dumnobellaunus and Tim——; of the Sicambri, Maelo; and of the Marcomanian Suevi, ——rus. Phraates, king of the Parthians, son of Orodes, sent all his children and grandchildren into Italy to me, not because he had been conquered in war, but rather seeking our friendship by means of his children as pledges. Since I have been *princeps* very many other races have made proof of the good faith of the Roman people, who never before had had any interchange of embassies and friendship with the Roman people.

XXXIII

FROM me the peoples of the Parthians and of the Medes have received the kings they asked for through ambassadors, the chief men of those peoples: the Parthians, Vonones, the son of king Phraates, and grandson of king Orodes; the Medes, Ariobarzanes, the son of king Artavasdes, and grandson of king Ariobarzanes.

XXXIV

IN my sixth and seventh consulships, when I had put an end to the civil wars, after having obtained complete control of affairs by universal consent, I transferred the commonwealth from my own dominion to the authority of the senate and Roman people. In return for this favor on my part I received by decree of the senate the title Augustus, the door-posts of my house were publicly decked with laurels, a civic crown was fixed above my door, and in the Julian Curia was placed a golden shield, which, by its inscription, bore witness that it was given to me by the senate and Roman people on account of my valor, clemency, justice and piety. After that time I excelled all others in dignity, but of power I held no more than those also held who were my colleagues in any magistracy.

XXXV

WHILE I was consul for the thirteenth time the senate and the equestrian order and the entire Roman people gave me the title of father of the fatherland, and decreed that it should be inscribed upon the vestibule of my house and in the Curia, and in the Augustan Forum beneath the quadriga which had been, by decree of the senate, set up in my honor. When I wrote these words I was in my seventy-sixth year.

MARCUS AURELIUS

MARCUS AURELIUS

121-180 A. D.

INTRODUCTORY NOTE

Marcus Aurelius Antoninus is accepted by common consent as the noblest figure in Roman, perhaps in all pagan, history. He was of a patrician Roman family and so notable even in his earliest youth for ability and honesty that he was highly honored by both Hadrian and Antoninus Pius, the two emperors who preceded him. Antoninus adopted him as a son and made him heir to the imperial throne. Aurelius ruled the Roman world from the year 161 until his death. Most of this world's affections disappointed him; both his wife and his adopted brother and co-emperor were notorious for their vicious lives. His friends died; the Barbarians attacked the empire; his whole reign was spent in battle against foreign foes or Roman rebels. Yet he never wittingly did any man injustice, and was ever ready to forgive a foe or befriend a sufferer. He is the most noteworthy of the Stoic philosophers.

The "Meditations" of this high-souled pagan were unknown until about the year 1550 when a manuscript of the work was discovered and published. Since then it has stood as one of the world's most celebrated and most valued books. No other pagan work so nearly approaches the Christian spirit of faith and obedience toward God and love and toleration toward all men.

The "Meditations" were first written in Greek and for the emperor's own study and perusal. They tell little of his outer history, but reveal so much of his inner life, so much of his soul's sorrow and its strength, that they are usually classed as autobiographical. They certainly take the first great step toward our modern conception of autobiography in that, unlike all earlier biographical works, they tell of the effect of the world upon the man rather than of his effect upon the world. They describe not the writer's deeds but his spiritual and mental development.

THE MEDITATIONS OF MARCUS AURELIUS

BOOK I

THE example of my grandfather Verus gave me a good disposition, not prone to anger.

By the recollection of my father's [1] character, I learned to be both modest and manly.

As for my mother, she taught me to have regard for religion, to be generous and open-handed, and not only to forbear from doing anybody an ill turn, but not so much as to endure the thought of it. By her likewise I was bred to a plain, inexpensive way of living, very different from the common luxury of the rich.

I have to thank my great-grandfather that I did not go to a public school, but had good masters at home, and learned to know that one ought to spend liberally on such things.

From my governor I learned not to join either the green or the blue faction on the race-ground, nor to support the Parmularius or Scutarius at the gladiators' shows. He taught me also to put my own hand to business upon occasion, to endure hardship and fatigues, and to throw the necessities of nature into a little compass; that I ought not to meddle with other people's business, nor be easy in giving credit to informers.

From Diognetus, to shun vain pursuits, not to be led away with the impostures of wizards and soothsayers, who pretend they can discharge evil spirits, and do strange feats by the strength of a charm; not to keep quails for the pit, nor to be eager after any such thing. This Diognetus taught me to bear freedom and plain-dealing in others, and apply myself to philosophy. He also procured me the instruction of Bacchius, Tandasis, and Marcianus. He likewise put me upon improving myself by writing dialogues when I was a boy; prevailed with me to prefer a couch covered with hides to a bed of state; and reconciled me to other like rigors of the Grecian discipline.

---

[1] Annius Verus was the name of both his grandfather and father; his mother's name was Domitia Calvilla. The emperor T. Antoninus Pius married the paternal aunt of Marcus Aurelius, and adopted him.

It was Rusticus [2] that first made me desire to live rightly,
and come to a better state; who prevented me from running
into the vanity of sophists, either by writing speculative
treatises, haranguing upon moral subjects, or making a fan-
tastical appearance or display of generosity or discipline.
This philosophy kept me from yielding to the charms of
rhetoric and poetry, from affecting the character of a man of
pleasantry, from wearing my senator's robe in the house, or
anything of this kind which looks like conceit and affectation.
He taught me to write letters in a plain, unornamental style,
like that dated by him from Sinuessa to my mother. By his
instructions I was persuaded to be easily reconciled to those
who had misbehaved themselves and disobliged me, as soon as
they desired reconciliation. And of the same master I learned
to read an author carefully. Not to take up with a superficial
view, or assent quickly to idle talkers. And, to conclude with
him, he gave me his own copy of Epictetus's memoirs.

Apollonius [3] taught me to give my mind its due freedom,
and disengage it from dependence upon chance, and not to
regard, though ever so little, anything uncountenanced by
reason. To maintain an equality of temper, even in acute
pains, and loss of children, or tedious sickness. His practice
was an excellent instance, that a man may be forcible and yet
unbend his humor as occasion requires. The heaviness and
impertinence of his scholars could seldom rouse his ill-temper.
As for his learning, and the peculiar happiness of his manner
in teaching, he was so far from being proud of himself upon
this score, that one might easily perceive, he thought it one of
the least things which belonged to him. This great man let
me into the true secret of receiving an obligation, without
either lessening myself, or seeming ungrateful to my friend.

The philosopher Sextus recommended good-humor to me,
and showed me the pattern of a household governed in a
fatherly manner. He also bade me make nature and reason
my rule to live by. By his precedent I was instructed to appear with an unaffected gravity, to study the temper and circumstances of my friends in order to oblige them. I saw

[2] L. Junius Rusticus was a Stoic philosopher who was put to death by
Domitian.
[3] Apollonius of Chalcis was a Stoic philosopher.

him bearing with the ignorant and undiscerning, complaisant and obliging to all people, so that his conversation was more charming than flattery; and yet at the same time he was held in the highest reverence by others. Conversing with this philosopher helped me to draw up a true, intelligible, and methodical scheme for life and manners, and never so much as to show the least sign of anger, or any other disturbing thought, but to be perfectly calm and indifferent, yet tenderhearted. However, he let me see in himself that a man might show his good-will significantly enough, without noise and display, and likewise possess great knowledge without vanity and ostentation.

Alexander the Grammarian taught me not to be ruggedly critical about words, nor find fault with people for improprieties of phrase or pronunciation, but to set them right by speaking the thing properly myself, and that either by way of answer, assent, or inquiry, or by some such other indirect and suitable correction.

Fronto [4] taught me that envy, tricking, and dissimulation are the character and consequences of tyranny; and that those we call patricians have commonly not much fatherly feeling in them.

Alexander the Platonist advised me, that without necessity I should never say to any one, nor write in a letter, that I am not at leisure, nor make business an excuse to decline frequently the offices of humanity to those we dwell with.

I learned of Catulus [5] not to slight a friend for making a remonstrance, though it should happen to be unreasonable, but rather to endeavor to restore him to his natural humor. That, like Domitius and Athenodotus, I should always speak well of those who had the care of my education, and that I should always preserve an hearty affection for my children.

I am indebted to Severus [6] for the love I bear to my relations, and towards justice and truth. He likewise made me acquainted with the character and sentiments of Cato, Brutus, Thrasea, Helvidius, and Dio; and gave me the idea of an equal commonwealth, with equal rights and equal speech, and

[4] M. Cornelius Fronto was a rhetorician who was the emperor's tutor. Part of Marcus Aurelius' correspondence with him is extant.
[5] Cinna Catulus was a Stoic philosopher.
[6] Claudius Severus was a Stoic philosopher.

also of a monarchy, where the liberty of the subject was principally regarded. To mention some more of my obligations to him:—It was of him I learned not to grow wise by starts and sudden fancies, but to be a constant admirer of philosophy and improvement; that a man ought to be generous and obliging, hope the best of matters, and never question the affection of his friends; to be free in showing a reasonable dislike of another, and no less clear in his own expectations and desires; and not to put his friends to the trouble of divining what he would be at.

I learned from Maximus [7] to command myself, and not to be too much drawn towards anything; to be full of spirits under sickness and misfortune; to appear with modesty, obligingness, and dignity of behavior; to turn off business smoothly as it arises, without drudging and complaint. Whatever he did, all men believed him, that as he spoke, so he thought, and whatever he did, that he did with a good intent. He attained that greatness of mind, not to wonder or start at anything; neither to hurry an enterprise, nor sleep over it; never to be puzzled or dejected, nor to put on an appearance of friendliness; not to be angry or suspicious, but ever ready to do good, and to forgive and speak truth; and all this as one who seemed rather of himself to be straight and right, than ever to have been rectified. Nobody ever could fancy they were slighted by him, or dared to think themselves his betters. Besides all this, he had an agreeable wit.

In my adoptive father I observed a smooth and inoffensive temper, with great steadiness in keeping close to measures judiciously taken; a greatness proof against vanity and the impressions of pomp and power. From him a prince might learn to love business and action, and be constantly at it; to be willing to hear out any proposal relating to public advantage, and undeviatingly give every man his due; to understand the critical seasons and circumstances for rigor or remissness. To have no boy-favorites. Not to stand upon points of state and prerogative, but to leave his nobility at perfect liberty in their visits and attendance; and when he was upon his progress, no man lost his favor for not being at leisure to follow the court. To debate matters nicely and thoroughly

[7] Claudius Maximus was a Stoic philosopher.

at the council-board, and then to stand by what was resolved on, yet not hastily to give up the inquiry, as one easily satisfied with sudden notions and apprehensions. To be constant to a friend, without tiring or fondness. To be always satisfied and cheerful. To reach forward into the future, and manage accordingly. Not to neglect the least concerns, but all without hurry, or being embarrassed. Farther, by observing his methods and administrations, I had the opportunity of learning how much it was the part of a prince to check the excesses of panegyric and flattery. To have his magazines and exchequer well furnished. To be frugal in his expenses, without minding being lampooned for his pains. Not to worship the gods to superstition; not to court the populace, either by prodigality or compliment; but rather to be sober and firm upon all occasions, keeping things in a steady decorum, without chopping and changing of measures. To enjoy the plenty and magnificence of a sovereign fortune without bragging, and yet without making excuse; so as freely to enjoy them when present, but when wanting, not to be mortified at the loss of them. And to behave himself so that no man could charge him with sophistry, or buffooning, or being a pedant. No; he was a person mature and perfect, scorning flattery, and thoroughly qualified to govern himself and others. As for those that were philosophers in earnest, he had a great regard for them, but without reproaching those who were otherwise, nor yet being led away by these. He was condescending and familiar in conversation, and pleasant too, but not to tiresomeness and excess. As for his health, he was not anxious about it, like one fond of living, or over-studious of bodily appearance, and yet managed his constitution with that care as seldom to stand in need of the assistance of physic or outward applications. Farther, he never envied and browbeat those that were eminent in any faculty or science, as eloquence, or knowledge of the laws or morals; but, on the contrary, encouraged them in their ways, and promoted their reputation. He observed fitness and custom in all his actions, and yet did not seem to regard them. He was not fickle and fluttering in his humor, but constant both to place and undertaking; and I have seen him, after violent fits of the headache, return fresh and vigorous to his usual business. He kept but few things to himself, and those were secrets of government. He was very moderate and frugal in shows, public buildings, liberalities, and such like, being one that did not so much regard the popularity as the rightness of an action. It was none of his custom to bathe at unusual hours, or to be overcome with the fancy of building, to study eating and luxury, to value the curiosity of his clothes, or the shape and person of his servants. His cloak came from Lorium, his villa on the coast; at Lanuvium, he wore for the most part only a tunic; and at Tusculum he would scarcely so much as put on a cloak without making an excuse for it. To take him altogether, there was nothing of ruggedness, immodesty, or eagerness in his temper. Neither did he ever seem to drudge and sweat at the helm. Things were dispatched at leisure, and without being felt; and yet the administration was carried on without confusion, with great order, force, and uniformity. Upon the whole, what was told of Socrates is applicable to him; for he was so much master of himself, that he could either take or leave those conveniences of life with respect to which most people are either uneasy without them, or intemperate with them. Now, to hold on with fortitude in one condition and sobriety in the other is a proof of a great soul and an impregnable virtue, such as he showed in the sickness of Maximus.

I have to thank the gods that my grandfathers, parents, sister, preceptors, relations, friends, and domestics were almost all of them persons of probity, and that I never happened to disoblige or misbehave myself towards any of them, notwithstanding that my disposition was such, that, had occasion offered, I might have acted thus; but by the goodness of the gods, I met with no provocations to reveal my infirmities. It is likewise by their providence that my childhood was no longer managed by my grandfather's mistress; that I preserved the flower of my youth; that I was subject to the emperor my father, and bred under him, who was the most proper person living to put me out of conceit with pride, and to convince me that it is possible to live in a palace without the ceremony of guards, without richness and distinction of habit, without torches, statues, or such other marks of royalty and state; and that a prince may shrink himself almost into the figure of a private gentleman, and yet act, nevertheless, with all the force and majesty of his character when the common weal requires it. It is the favor of the gods that I happened to meet with a brother, whose behavior and affection is such as to contribute both to my pleasure and improvement.[8] It is also their blessing that my children were neither stupid nor misshapen; that I made no farther advances in rhetoric, poetry, and such other amusements, which possibly might have engaged my fancy too far, had I found myself a considerable proficient; that, without asking, I gave my governors that share of honor which they seemed to desire, and did not put them off from time to time with promises and excuses, because they were yet but young; that I had the happiness of being acquainted with Apollonius, Rusticus, and Maximus; that I have a clear idea of the life in accordance with nature, and the impression frequently refreshed: so that, considering the extraordinary assistance and directions of the gods, it is impossible for me to miss the road of nature unless by refusing to be guided by the dictates and almost sensible inspirations of heaven. It is by their favor that my constitution has held out so well, under a life of fatigue and business; that I never had to do with Benedicta or Theodotus; and, when I fell into some fits of love, I was soon cured; that when I fell out with Rusticus, as it frequently happened, I was not transported into any act of violence; that I had the satisfaction of my mother's life and company a considerable while, though she was destined to die young; that when I was willing to relieve the necessities of others, I was never told that the exchequer was empty; and, again, it is they that kept me from standing in need of any man's fortune. Farther, it is from them that my wife is so very obedient and affectionate and so remote from luxury; that I had choice of good governors for my children; that remedies were prescribed me in a dream against giddiness and spitting of blood, as at Cajeta, by an ointment; that when I had a mind to look into philosophy, I did not meet with a sophist to instruct me; that I did not spend too much time in reading history, chopping

---

[8] As Marcus Aurelius had no blood brother, this must refer to his adopted brother, Lucius Verus, who certainly did not deserve the praise here bestowed.

logic, or considering the heavens. Now all these points could never have been compassed without a protection from above and the gods presiding over fate.

This was written in the country of the Quadi, at the Granua.

BOOK II

REMEMBER to put yourself in mind every morning, that before night it will be your luck to meet with some busy-body, with some ungrateful, abusive fellow, with some knavish, envious, or unsociable churl or other. Now all this perverseness in them proceeds from their ignorance of good and evil; and since it has fallen to my share to understand the natural beauty of a good action, and the deformity of an ill one— since I am satisfied the person disobliging is of kin to me, and though we are not just of the same flesh and blood, yet our minds are nearly related, being both extracted from the Deity —I am likewise convinced that no man can do me a real injury, because no man can force me to misbehave myself, nor can I find it in my heart to hate or to be angry with one of my own nature and family. For we are all made for mutual assistance, as the feet, the hands, and the eyelids, as the rows of the upper and under teeth, from whence it follows that clashing and opposition is perfectly unnatural. Now such unfriendly disposition exists in resentment and aversion.

This being of mine, all there is of it, consists of flesh, breath, and the ruling part. Away with your books then. Suffer not your mind any more to be distracted. It is not permitted. As for your body, value it no more than if you were just expiring. For what is it? Nothing but a little blood and bones; a piece of network, wrought out of nerves, veins, and arteries twisted together. In the next place, consider what sort of thing your breath is; why, only a little air, and that not constant, but every moment let out of your lungs, and sucked in again. The third part of your composition is the ruling part. Now consider thus: you are an old man: do not suffer this noble part of you under servitude any longer. Let it not be moved by the springs of selfish passions; let it not quarrel with fate, be uneasy at the present, or afraid of the future.

Providence shines clearly through the works of the gods; even the works of chance are not without dependence on Nature, being only an effect of that chain of causes which are under a providential regulation. Indeed, all things flow from this fountain; besides, there is necessity, and the interest of the whole universe, of which you are a part. Now, that which is both the product and support of universal Nature, must by consequence be serviceable to every part of it; but the world subsists upon change, and is preserved by the mutation of the simple elements, and also of things mixed and compounded, and what it loses one way it gets another. Let these reflections satisfy you, and make them your rule to live by. As for books, cast away your thirst after them, that you may not die complaining, but go off in good-humor, and heartily thank the gods for what you have had.

Remember how often you have postponed minding your interest, and let slip those opportunities the gods have given you. It is now high time to consider what sort of world you are part of, and from what kind of governor of it you are descended; that you have a set period assigned you to act in, and unless you improve it to brighten and compose your thoughts, it will quickly run off with you, and be lost beyond recovery.

Take care always to remember that you are a man and a Roman; and let every action be done with perfect and unaffected gravity, humanity, freedom, and justice. And be sure you entertain no fancies, which may give check to these qualities. This is possible, if you will but perform every action as though it were your last; if your appetites and passions do not cross upon your reason; if you keep clear of rashness, and have nothing of insincerity and self-love to infect you, and do not complain of your destiny. You see what a few points a man has to gain in order to attain to a godlike way of living; for he that comes thus far, performs all which the immortal powers will require of him.

Continue to dishonor yourself, my soul! Neither will you have much time left to do yourself honor. For the life of each man is almost up already; and yet, instead of paying a due regard to yourself, you place your happiness in the souls of other men.

Do not let accidents disturb, or outward objects engross your thoughts, but keep your mind quiet and disengaged, that you may be at leisure to learn something good, and cease rambling from one thing to another. There is likewise another sort of roving to be avoided; for some people are busy and yet do nothing; they fatigue and wear themselves out, and yet aim at no goal, nor purpose any general end of action or design.

A man can rarely be unhappy by being ignorant of another's thoughts; but he that does not attend to the motions of his own is certainly unhappy.

These reflections ought always to be at hand:—To consider well the nature of the universe and my own nature, together with the relation betwixt them, and what kind of part it is, of what kind of whole; and that no mortal can hinder me from acting and speaking conformably to the being of which I am a part.

Theophrastus, in comparing the degrees of faults (as men would commonly distinguish them), talks like a philosopher when he affirms that those instances of misbehavior which proceed from desire are greater than those of which anger is the occasion. For a man that is angry seems to quit his hold of reason unwillingly and with pain, and start out of rule before he is aware. But he that runs riot out of desire, being overcome by pleasure, loses all hold on himself, and all manly restraint. Well, then, and like a philosopher, he said that he of the two is the more to be condemned that sins with pleasure than he that sins with grief. For the first looks like an injured person, and is vexed, and, as it were, forced into a passion; whereas the other begins with inclination, and commits the fault through desire.

Manage all your actions, words, and thoughts accordingly, since you may at any moment quit life. And what great matter is the business of dying? If the gods are in being, you can suffer nothing, for they will do you no harm. And if they are not, or take no care of us mortals—why, then, a world without either gods or Providence is not worth a man's while to live in. But, in truth, the being of the gods, and their concern in human affairs, is beyond dispute. And they have put it entirely in a man's power not to fall into any calamity properly so-called. And if other misfortunes had been really evils, they would have provided against them too, and furnished man with capacity to avoid them. But how can that which cannot make the man worse make his life so? I can never be persuaded that the universal Nature neglected these matters through want of knowledge, or, having that, yet lacked the power to prevent or correct the error; or that Nature should commit such a fault, through want of power or skill, as to suffer things, really good and evil, to happen promiscuously to good and bad men. Now, living and dying, honor and infamy, pleasure and pain, riches and poverty— all these things are the common allotment of the virtuous and vicious, because they have nothing intrinsically noble or base in their nature; and, therefore, to speak properly, are neither good nor bad.

Consider how quickly all things are dissolved and re-solved; the bodies and substances themselves into the matter and substance of the world, and their memories into its general age and time. Consider, too, the objects of sense, particularly those which charm us with pleasure, frighten us with pain, or are most admired for empty reputation. The power of thought will show a man how insignificant, despi-cable, and paltry these things are, and how soon they wither and die. It will show him what those people are upon whose fancy and good word the being of fame depends: also the nature of death, which, if once abstracted from the pomp and terror of the idea, will be found nothing more than a pure natural action. Now he that dreads the course of nature is a very child; but this is not only a work of nature, but is also profitable to her. Lastly, we should consider how we are related to the Deity, and in what part of our being, and in what condition of that part.

Nothing can be more unhappy than the curiosity of that man that ranges everywhere, and digs into the earth, as the poet says, for discovery; that is wonderfully busy to force by conjecture a passage into other people's thoughts, but does not consider that it is sufficient to reverence and serve the divinity within himself. And this service consists in this, that a man keep himself pure from all violent passion, and evil affection, from all rashness and vanity, and from all manner of discontent towards gods or men. For as for the gods, their administration ought to be revered upon the score of excellency; and as for men, their actions should be well taken for the sake of common kindred. Besides, they are often to be pitied for their ignorance of good and evil; which incapacity of discerning between moral qualities is no less a defect than that of a blind man, who cannot distinguish between white and black.

Though you were to live three thousand, or, if you please, thirty thousand of years, yet remember that no man can lose any other life than that which he now lives, neither is he possessed of any other than that which he loses. Whence it follows that the longest life, as we commonly speak, and the shortest, come all to the same reckoning. For the present is of the same duration everywhere. Everybody's loss, therefore, is of the same bigness and reaches no further than to a point of time, for no man is capable of losing either the past or the future; for how can one be deprived of what he has not? So that under this consideration there are two notions worth remembering. One is, that Nature treads in a circle, and has much the same face through the whole course of eternity. And therefore it signifies not at all whether a man stands gazing here an hundred, or two hundred, or an infinity of years; for all that he gets by it is only to see the same sights so much the oftener. The other hint is, that when the longest and shortest-lived persons come to die, their loss is equal; they can but lose the present as being the only thing they have; for that which he has not, no man can be truly said to lose.

Monimus, the Cynic philosopher, used to say that all things were but opinion. Now this saying may undoubtedly prove serviceable, provided one accepts it only as far as it is true.

There are several different ways by which a man's soul may do violence to itself; first of all, when it becomes an abscess, and, as it were, an excrescence on the universe, as far as in it lies. For to be vexed at anything that happens is a separation of ourselves from nature, in some part of which the natures of all other things are contained. Secondly, it falls under the same misfortune when it hates any person, or goes against him, with an intention of mischief, which is the case of the angry and revengeful. Thirdly, it wrongs itself when it is overcome by pleasure or pain. Fourthly, when it makes use of art, tricking, and falsehood, in word or action. Fifthly, when it does not know what it would be at in a business, but runs on without thought or design, whereas even the least undertaking ought to be aimed at some end. Now the end of rational beings is to be governed by the law and reason of the most venerable city and constitution.

The extent of human life is but a point; its substance is in perpetual flux, its perceptions dim, and the whole composition of the body tending to corruption. The soul is but a whirl, fortune not to be guessed at, and fame undiscerning—in a word, that which belongs to the body is a flowing river, and what the soul has is but dream and bubble. Life is but a campaign, or course of travels, and after-fame is oblivion. What is it, then, that will stick by a man? Why, nothing but philosophy. Now, this consists in keeping the divinity within us from injury and disgrace, superior to pleasure and pain, doing nothing at random, without any dissembling and pretense, and independent of the motions of another. Farther, philosophy brings the mind to take things as they fall, and acquiesce in their distribution, inasmuch as all events proceed from the same cause with itself; and, above all, to have an easy prospect of death, as being nothing more than a dissolving of the elements of which each thing is composed. Now, if the elements themselves are never the worse for running off one into another, what if they should all change and be dissolved? Why should any man be concerned at the consequence? All this is but Nature's method; now, Nature never does any mischief.

Written at Carnuntum.

BOOK III

We ought not only to remember that life is wearing off, and a smaller part of it is left daily, but also to consider that if a man's life should happen to be longer than ordinary, yet it is uncertain whether his mind will keep pace with his years, and afford him sense enough for business, and power to contemplate things human and divine. For if the man begins to dote, it is true the mere animal life goes on; he may breathe, and be nourished, and be furnished with imagination and appetite; but to make any proper use of himself, to fill up the measure of his duty, to distinguish appearances, and to know whether it is time for him to walk out of the world or not—as to all such noble functions of reason and judgment, the man is perfectly dead already. It concerns us, therefore, to push forward, and make the most of our matters, for death is continually advancing; and besides that, our understanding sometimes dies before us.

It is worth while to observe that the least thing that happens naturally to things natural has something in itself that is pleasing and delightful. Thus, for example, there are cracks and little breaks on the surface of a loaf, which, though never intended by the baker, have a sort of agreeableness in them, which invites the appetite. Thus figs, when they are most ripe, open and gape; and olives, when they fall of themselves and are near decaying, are particularly pretty to look at. The bending of an ear of corn, the brow of a lion, the foam of a boar, and many other things, if you take them singly, are far enough from being beautiful; but when they are looked on as effects of the products of Nature, help to adorn and attract. Thus, if a man has but inclination and thought enough to examine the product of the universe, he will find the most unpromising appearances in the results of Nature not without charm, and that the more remote appendages have somewhat to recommend them. One thus prepared will be no less pleased to see the gaping jaws of living beasts than the imitations of painters and sculptors, and with chastened eyes he will find beauty in the ripeness of age as well as in the blossom of youth. I grant many of these things will not charm every one, but only those who are truly in harmony with Nature and her works.

Hippocrates, who cured so many diseases, himself fell ill and died. The Chaldeans, who foretold other people's death, at last met with their own fate. Alexander, Pompey, and Julius Cæsar, who had destroyed so many towns, and cut off so many thousands of horse and foot in the field, were forced at last to march off themselves. Heraclitus, who argued so much about the universal conflagration, died through water by a dropsy. Democritus was eaten up with vermin; another sort of vermin destroyed Socrates. What are these instances for? Look you: you have embarked, you have made your voyage and your port; debark then without more ado. If you happen to land upon another world, there will be gods enough to take care of you; but if it be your fortune to drop into nothing, why, then you will be no more solicited with pleasure and pain. Then you will have done drudging for your outer covering, which is the more unworthy in proportion as that which serves it is worthy; for the one is all soul, intelligence, and divinity, whereas the other is but dirt and corruption.

For the future, do not spend your thoughts upon other people, unless you are led to it by common interest. For the prying into foreign business—that is, musing upon the talk, fancies, and contrivances of another, and guessing at the what and why of his actions—does but make a man forget himself, and ramble from his own guiding principle. He ought, therefore, not to work his mind to no purpose, nor throw a superfluous link into the chain of thought; and more especially, to avoid curiosity and malice in his inquiry. Accustom yourself, therefore, to think upon nothing but what you could freely reveal, if the question were put to you; so that if your soul were thus laid open, there would nothing appear but what was sincere, good-natured, and public-spirited—not so much as one voluptuous or luxurious fancy, nothing of hatred, envy, or unreasonable suspicion, nor aught else which you could not bring to the light without blushing. A man thus qualified, who does not delay to assume the first rank among mortals, is a sort of priest and minister of the gods, and makes a right use of the Deity within him. By the assistance thereof, he is preserved, uninfected with pleasure, invulnerable against pain—out of the reach of injury, and above the malice of evil people. Thus he wrestles in the noblest fight, to hold his own against all his passions; and penetrated with the spirit of justice, welcomes with his whole heart all that happens and is allotted to him. He never minds other people's speech, thoughts, or actions, unless public necessity and general good require it. No; he keeps himself to his own business, and contemplates that portion of the whole allotted him by the fates, and endeavors to do the first as it should be, and believes that his lot is good. For every man's fate is suitable, since it is suited to him. He considers that the rational principle is akin in all men, and that general kindness and concern for the whole world is no more than a piece of human nature—that not every one's good opinion is not worth the gaining, but only that of those who seek to live in accordance with Nature. As for others, he knows their way of living, both at home and abroad, by day and by night, and their companions in their evil way of life, and he bears it in mind. And, why, indeed, should he value the commendation of such people, who are not able even to please themselves?

Be not unwilling, selfish, unadvised, or passionate in anything you do. Do not affect quaintness and points of wit: neither talk nor meddle more than is necessary. Take care that the divinity within you has a creditable charge to preside over; that you appear in the character of your sex and age. Act like a Roman Emperor that loves his country, and be always in a readiness to quit the field at the first summons; and ere you claim your discharge, manage your credit so, that you need neither swear yourself nor want a voucher. Let your air be cheerful; depend not upon external supports, nor beg your tranquillity of another. And, in a word, never throw away your legs, to stand upon crutches.

If, in the whole compass of human life, you find anything preferable to justice and truth; to temperance and fortitude; to a mind self-satisfied with its own rational conduct, and entirely resigned to fate—if, I say, you know anything better than this, turn to it with your whole soul, and enjoy it, accounting it the best. But if there is nothing more valuable than the divinity implanted within you, and this is master of its appetites, examines all impressions, and has detached itself from the senses, as Socrates used to say, and shows itself submissive to the government of the gods, and helpful and benevolent to mankind—if all things are trifles compared with this, give way to nothing else. For if you are once inclined to any such thing, it will no longer be in your power to give your undivided preference to what is your own peculiar good, for it is not lawful that anything of another kind or nature, as either popular applause, or power, or riches, or pleasures, should be suffered to contest with what is rationally and politically good. All these things, if but for a while they begin to please, presently prevail, and pervert a man's mind. Let your choice therefore run all one way, and be bold and resolute for that which is best. Now what is profitable is best. If that means profitable to man as he is a rational being, stand to it; but if it means profitable to him as a mere animal, reject it, and keep your judgment without arrogance. Only take care to make inquiry secure.

Think nothing for your interest which makes you break your word, quit your modesty, hate, suspect, or curse any person, or inclines you to any practice which will not bear the light and look the world in the face. For he that values his mind and the worship of his divinity before all other things, need act no tragic part, laments under no misfortune, and wants neither solitude nor company; and, which is still more, he will neither fly from life nor pursue it, but is perfectly indifferent about the length or shortness of the time in which his soul shall be encompassed by his body. And if he were to expire this moment, he is as ready for it as for any other action that may be performed with modesty and decency. For all his life long this is his only care—that his mind may always be occupied as befits a rational and social creature.

If you examine a man that has been well-disciplined and purified by philosophy, you will find nothing that is unsound, foul, or false in him. Death can never surprise his life as imperfect, so that nobody can say he goes off the stage before his part is quite played. Besides, there is in him nothing servile or affected; he neither attaches himself too closely to others, nor keeps aloof from them; he is neither responsible to them, nor does he avoid them.

Hold in honor your opinionative faculty, for this alone is able to prevent any opinion from originating in your guiding principle that is contrary to Nature or the proper constitution of a rational creature. Now, a rational constitution enjoins us to do nothing rashly, and to be kindly disposed towards men, and to submit willingly to the gods.

As for other speculations, throw them all out of your head, excepting those few precepts above mentioned—remembering withal, that every man's life lies all within the present,

which is but a point of time; for the past is spent, and the
future is uncertain. Life moves in a very narrow compass;
yes, and men live in a small corner of the world too. And
the most lasting fame will stretch but to a sorry extent; for,
alas! poor transitory mortals who hand it down know little
even of themselves, much less of those who died long before
their time.

To the foregoing hints you may add this which follows:—
make for yourself a particular description and definition of
every object that presents itself to your mind, that you may
thoroughly contemplate it in its own nature, bare and naked,
wholly and separately. And in your own mind call itself and
the parts of which it is composed, and into which it will be
resolved, by its own and proper name; for nothing is so likely
to raise the mind to a pitch of greatness as the power truly
and methodically to examine and consider all things that happen in this life, and so to penetrate into their natures as to
apprehend at once what sort of purpose each thing serves, and
what sort of universe makes use of it—what value it bears
to the whole, and what to man, who is a citizen of that great
capital, in respect of which all other towns are no more than
single families—what is this object which makes an impression on me; how long can it last; what virtue does it require
of me; is it good-nature, fortitude, truth, simplicity, self-
sufficiency, or any of the rest? On each occasion a man
should be ready to pronounce, "This was sent me by heaven,
this by destiny, or the combinations of fate, or by one of the
same clan, or family, or company as myself, who knows not
what is natural for him. But I do know; therefore I am just
and friendly to him, and treat him according to the natural
laws of our communion. However, in things indifferent I
take care to rate them according to their respective value."

If you will be governed by reason, and manage what lies
before you with industry, vigor, and temper; if you will not
run out after new distraction, but keep your divinity pure,
even as though you must at once render it up again, your
mind staunch and well disciplined, as if this trial of behavior
were your last; and, if you will but cleave to this, and be true
to the best of yourself, fearing and desiring nothing, but
living up to your nature, standing boldly by the truth of your

word, and satisfied therewith, then you will be a happy man. But the whole world cannot hinder you from so doing.

As surgeons always have their instruments and knives ready for sudden occasions, so be you always furnished with rules and principles to let you into the knowledge of things human and divine, remembering even in your slightest action the connection these two have with each other. For without a regard for things divine, you will fail in your behavior towards men; and again, the reasoning holds for the other side of the argument.

Wander at random no longer. Alas! you have no time left to peruse your diary, to read over the Greek and Roman history, or so much as your own commonplace book, which you collected to serve you when you were old. Hasten then towards the goal. Do not flatter and deceive yourself. Come to your own aid while yet you may, if you have a kindness for yourself.

Men do not know in how many senses they can take the words to steal, to buy, to sow, to be quiet, to see what should be done; for this is not effected by eyes, but by another kind of vision.

There are three things which belong to a man—body, soul, and mind. Sensation belongs to the body, impulse to the soul, and reason to the mind. To have the senses stamped with the impression of an object is common to brutes and cattle; to be hurried and convulsed with passion is the quality of beasts of prey and men of pleasure—such as Phalaris and Nero—of atheists and traitors, too, and of those who do not care what they do when no man sees them. Now, since these qualities are common, let us find out the mark of a man of probity. His distinction, then, lies in letting reason guide his practice, in contentment with all that is allotted him, keeping pure the divinity within him, untroubled by a crowd of appearances, preserving it tranquil, and obeying it as a god. He is all truth in his words and justice in his actions; and if the whole world should disbelieve his integrity, dispute his character, and question his happiness, he would neither take it ill in the least, nor turn aside from that path that leads to the aim of life, towards which he must move pure, calm, well-prepared, and with perfect resignation in his fate.

BOOK IV

WHEN the mind acts up to Nature, she is rightly disposed, and takes things as they come, and tacks about with her circumstances; as for fixing the condition of her activity, she is not at all solicitous about that. It is true, she is not perfectly indifferent; she moves forward with a preference in her choice; but if anything comes cross, she falls to work upon it, and like fire converts it into fuel; for like this element, when it is weak, it is easily put out, but when once well kindled it seizes upon what is heaped upon it, subdues it into its own nature, and increases by resistance.

Let every action tend to some point, and be perfect in its kind.

It is the custom of people to go to unfrequented places and country places and the seashore and the mountains for retirement; and this you often earnestly desired. But, after all, this is but a vulgar fancy, for it is in your power to withdraw into yourself whenever you desire. Now one's own mind is a place the most free from crowd and noise in the world, if a man's thoughts are such as to insure him perfect tranquillity within, and this tranquillity consists in the good ordering of the mind. Your way is, therefore, to make frequent use of this retirement, and refresh your virtue in it. And to this end, be always provided with a few short, uncontested notions, to keep your understanding true, and send you back content with the business to which you return. For instance: What is it that troubles you? It is the wickedness of the world. If this be your case, out with your antidote, and consider that rational beings were made for mutual advantage, that forbearance is one part of justice, and that people misbehave themselves against their will. Consider, likewise, how many men have embroiled themselves, and spent their days in disputes, suspicion, and animosities; and now they are dead, and burned to ashes. Be quiet, then, and disturb yourself no more. But, it may be, the distribution of the world does not please you. Recall the alternative, and argue thus: either Providence or atoms rule the universe. Besides, you may recall the proofs that the world is, as it were, one great city and corporation. But possibly the ill state of your health afflicts you. Pray reflect, your intellect is not affected by the roughness or smoothness of the currents of sensation, if she will retire and take a view of her own privilege and power. And when she has done this, recollect the philosophy about pleasure and pain, to which you have even now listened and assented. Well! it may be the concern of fame sits hard upon you. If you are pinched here, consider how quickly all things vanish, and are forgotten—what an immense chaos there stands on either side of eternity. Applause! consider the emptiness of the sound, the precarious tenure, the little judgment of those that give it us, and the narrow compass it is confined to; for the whole globe is but a point; and of this little, how small is your habitation, and how insignificant the number and quality of your admirers. Upon the whole, do not forget to retire into the little realm of your own. And, above all things, let there be no straining nor struggling in the case, but move freely, and contemplate matters like a human being, a citizen, and a mortal. And among the rest of your stock, let these two maxims be always ready: first, that things cannot disturb the soul, but remain motionless without, while disturbance springs from the opinion within the soul. The second is, to consider that the scene is just shifting and sliding off into nothing; and that you yourself have seen abundance of great alterations. In a word, the world is all transformation, and life is opinion.

If the faculty of understanding lies in common amongst us all, then reason, the cause of it, must be common too; and that other reason too which governs practice by commands and prohibitions. From whence we may conclude, that mankind are under one common law; and if so, they must be fellow-citizens, and belong to some body politic. From whence it will follow, that the whole world is but one commonwealth; for certainly there is no other society in which mankind can be incorporated. Now this common fund of understanding, reason, and law is a commodity of this same country, or which way do mortals light on it? For as the four distinctions in my body belong to some general head and species of matter; for instance, the earthy part in me comes from the division of earth; the watery belongs to another element; the airy particles flow from a third spring, and those of fire from one distinct from all the former (for nothing can no more produce something, than something can sink into nothing); thus it is evident that our understanding must proceed from some source or other.

Death and generation are both mysteries of nature, and somewhat resemble each other; for the first does but dissolve those elements the latter had combined. Now there is nothing that a man need be ashamed of in all this; nothing that is opposed to his nature as a rational being, and to the design of his constitution.

Practices and dispositions are generally of a piece; such usage from such sort of men is in a manner necessary. To be surprised at it, is in effect to wonder that the fig-tree yields juice. Pray consider that both you and your enemy are dropping off, and that ere long your very memories will be extinguished.

Do not suppose you are hurt, and your complaint ceases. Cease your complaint, and you are not hurt.

That which does not make a man worse, does not make his life worse; and by consequence he has no harm either within or without.

The nature of the general good was obliged to act in this manner.

Take notice that all events turn out justly, and that if you observe nicely, you will not only perceive a connection between causes and effects, but a sovereign distribution of justice, which presides in the administration, and gives everything its due. Observe, then, as you have begun, and let all your actions answer the character of a good man—I mean a good man in the strictness and notion of philosophy.

If a man affronts you, do not accept his opinion or think just as he would have you do. No, look upon things as reality presents them.

Be always provided with principles for these two purposes: —*First,* To engage in nothing but what reason dictates, what the sovereign and legislative part of you shall suggest, for the interest of mankind. *Secondly,* To be disposed to quit your opinion, and alter your measures, when a friend shall give you good grounds for so doing. But then the reasons of changing your mind ought to be drawn from some consideration regarding justice and public good, or some such generous motive, and not because it pleases your fancy, or promotes your reputation.

Have you any sense in your head? Yes. Why do you not make use of it then? For if this faculty does but do its part, I cannot see what more you need wish for.

At present your nature is distinct; but ere long you will vanish into the world. Or, rather, you will be returned into that universal reason which gave you your being.

When frankincense is thrown upon the altar, one grain usually falls before another; but it makes no difference.

Do but turn to the principles of wisdom, and those who take you now for a monkey or a wild beast, will make a god of you in a week's time.

Do not act as if you had ten thousand years to throw away. Death stands at your elbow. Be good for something, while you live and it is in your power.

What a great deal of time and ease that man gains who lets his neighbor's words, thoughts, and behavior alone, confines his inspections to himself, and takes care that his own actions are honest and righteous. "Truly," as Agathon observes, "we should not wander thus, but run straight to the goal without rambling and impertinence."

He that is so very solicitous about being talked of when he is dead, and makes his memory his inclination, does not consider that all who knew him will quickly be gone. That his fame will grow less in the next generation, and flag upon the course; and handed from one to another by men who eagerly desire it themselves, and are quenched themselves, it will be quenched at last; but granting your memory and your men immortal, what is their panegyric to you? I do not say, when you are dead, but if you were living, what would commendation signify, unless for some reason of utility? To conclude; if you depend thus servilely upon the good word of other people, you will be unworthy of your nature.

Whatever is good has that quality from itself; it is finished by its own nature, and commendation is no part of it. Why, then, a thing is neither better nor worse for being praised. This holds concerning things which are called good in the common way of speaking, as the products of nature and art; what do you think, then, of that which deserves this character in the strictest propriety? It wants nothing foreign to complete the idea any more than law, truth, good nature, and sobriety. Do any of these virtues stand in need of a good word, or are they the worse for a bad one? I hope an emerald will shine nevertheless for a man's being silent about the worth of it. Neither is there any necessity of praising gold, ivory, purple, a lyre, a dagger, a little flower, or a shrub.

If human souls have a being after death, which way has the air made room for them from all eternity? Pray, how has the earth been capacious enough to receive all the bodies buried in it? The solution of this latter question will satisfy the former. For as a corpse after some continuance by change and dissolution makes way for another, so when a man dies, and the spirit is let loose into the air, it holds out for some time, after which it is changed, diffused, and kindled in flame, or else absorbed into the generative principle of the universe. And thus they make room for succession. And this may serve for an answer upon the supposition of the soul's surviving the body. Besides, we are only to consider the vast number of bodies disposed of in the manner above mentioned; but what an infinite number are every day devoured by mankind, and other living creatures, and as it were buried in their bodies. And yet by the transmutation of the food into the blood, or into fire and air, there is space enough. And now which way can a man investigate the truth? Why, in order to do this, he must divide the thing in question into the causal and material elements.

Do not run riot; keep your intention honest, and your convictions sure.

Whatever is agreeable to you, O Universe, is so to me too. Nothing is early or late for me that is seasonable for you. Everything is fruit for me which your seasons bring, oh Nature. From you all things proceed, subsist in you, and return to you. And if the poet said, "Dear City of Cecrops," may we not also say, "Dear City of God"?

"If you would live at your ease," says Democritus, "manage but a few things." I think it had been better if he had said, "Do nothing but what is necessary; and what becomes the reason of a social being, and in the order too it prescribes it." For by this rule a man has the double pleasure of making his actions good and few into the bargain. For the greater part of what we say and do, being unnecessary, if this were but once retrenched, we should have both more leisure and less disturbance. And therefore before a man sets forward he should ask himself this question, "Am I not upon the verge of something unnecessary?" Farther, we should apply this hint to what we think, as well as to what we do. For impertinence of thought draws unnecessary action after it.

Make an experiment upon yourself, and examine your proficiency in a life of virtue. Try how you can acquiesce in your fate, and whether your own honesty and good nature will content you.

Have you seen this side? Pray view the other too. Never be disturbed, but let your purpose be single. Is any man guilty of a fault? It is to himself then. Has any advantage happened to you? It is the bounty of fate. It was all of it preordained you by the universal cause, and woven in your destiny from the beginning. On the whole, life is but short, therefore be just and prudent, and make the most of it. And when you divert yourself, be always upon your guard.

The world is either the effect of contrivance or chance; if the latter, it is a world for all that, that is to say, it is a regular and beautiful structure. Now can any man discover symmetry in his own shape, and yet take the universe for a heap of disorder? I say the universe, in which the very discord and confusion of the elements settle into harmony and order.[1]

A black character, an effeminate character, an obstinate character, brutish, savage, childish, silly, false, scurrilous, mercenary, tyrannical.

Not to know what is in the world, and not to know what is done in the world, comes much to the same thing, and a man is one way no less a stranger than the other. He is no better than a deserter that flies from public law. He is a blind man that shuts the eyes of his understanding; and

[1] The Greek word for Universe and Order is the same—*kosmos.*

he is a beggar that is not furnished at home, but wants the assistance of another. He that frets himself because things do not happen just as he would have them, and secedes and separates himself from the law of universal nature, is but a sort of an ulcer of the world, never considering that the same cause which produced the displeasing accident made him too. And lastly, he that is selfish, and cuts off his own soul from the universal soul of all rational beings, is a kind of voluntary outlaw.

This philosopher has never a tunic to his coat, the other never a book to read, and a third is half naked, and yet they are none of them discouraged. One learned man says, "I have no bread, yet I abide by reason." Another, "I have no profit of my learning, yet I too abide by reason."

Be satisfied with your business, and learn to love what you were bred to; and as to the remainder of your life, be entirely resigned, and let the gods do their pleasure with your body and your soul. And when this is done, be neither slave nor tyrant to anybody.

To begin somewhere, consider how the world went in Vespasian's time; consider this, I say, and you will find mankind just at the same pass they are now: some marrying and some concerned in education, some sick and some dying, some fighting and some feasting, some drudging at the plow and some upon the exchange; some too affable and some overgrown with conceit; one full of jealousy and the other of knavery. Here you might find a group wishing for the death of their friends, and there a seditious club complaining of the times. Some were lovers and some misers, some grasped at the consulship and some at the scepter. Well! all is over with that generation long since. Come forward then to the reign of Trajan. Now here you will find the same thing, but they are all gone too. Go on with the contemplation, and carry it to other times and countries, and here you will see abundance of people very busy with their projects, who are quickly resolved into their elements. More particularly recollect those within your own memory, who have been hurried on in these vain pursuits; how they have overlooked the dignity of their nature, and neglected to hold fast to that, and be satisfied with it. And here you must remember to proportion your concern to the weight and importance of each action. Thus, if you refrain from trifling, you may part with amusements without regret.

Those words which were formerly current are now become obsolete. Alas! this is not all; fame tarnishes in time too, and men grow out of fashion as well as language. Those celebrated names of Camillus, Cæso, Volesus, and Leonnatus are antiquated. Those of Scipio, Cato, and Augustus will soon have the same fortune, and those of Hadrian and Antoninus must follow. All these things are transitory, and quickly become as a tale that is told, and are swallowed up in oblivion. I speak this of those who have been the wonder of their age and who shone with unusual luster. But as for the rest, they are no sooner dead than forgotten. And after all, what does fame everlasting mean? Mere vanity. What then is it that is worth one's while to be concerned for? Why nothing but this: to bear an honest mind, to act for the good of society, to deceive nobody, to welcome everything that happens as necessary and familiar, and flowing from a like source.

Put yourself frankly into the hands of fate, and let her spin you out what fortune she pleases.

He that does a memorable action, and those that report it, are all but short-lived things.

Accustom yourself to consider that whatever is produced, is produced by alteration; that nature loves nothing so much as changing existing things, and producing new ones like them. For that which exists at present is, as it were, the seed of what shall spring from it. But if you take seed in the common notion, and confine it to the field or the womb, you have a dull fancy.

You are just taking leave of the world, and yet you have not done with unnecessary desires. Are you not yet above disturbance and suspicion, and fully convinced that nothing without can hurt you? You have not yet learned to be friends with everybody, and that to be an honest man is the only way to be a wise one.

To understand the true quality of people, you must look into their minds, and examine their pursuits and aversions.

Your pain cannot originate in another man's mind, nor

in any change or transformation of your corporeal covering. Where then does it lie? Why, in that part of you that forms judgments about things evil. Do not imagine you are hurt, and you are impregnable. Suppose then your flesh was hacked, burnt, putrefied, or mortified, yet let that part that judges keep quiet; that is, do not conclude that what is common to good or ill men can be good or evil in itself. For that which may be everybody's lot, must in its own nature be indifferent.

You ought frequently to consider that the world is an animal, consisting of one soul and body, that an universal sense runs through the whole mass of matter. You should likewise reflect how nature acts by a joint effort, and how everything contributes to the being of everything: and lastly, what connection and subordination there is between causes and effects.

Epictetus will tell you that you are a living soul, that drags a corpse about with her.

Things that subsist upon change, and owe their being to instability, can neither be considerably good nor bad.

Time is like a rapid river, and a rushing torrent of all that comes and passes. A thing is no sooner well come, but it is past; and then another is borne after it, and this too will be carried away.

Whatever happens is as common and well known as a rose in the spring, or an apple in autumn. Of this kind are diseases and death, calumny and trickery, and every other thing which raises and depresses the spirits of unthinking people.

Antecedents and consequents are dexterously tied together in the world. Things are not carelessly thrown on a heap, and joined more by number than nature, but, as it were, rationally connected with each other. And as the things that exist are harmoniously connected, so those that become exhibit no mere succession, but an harmonious relationship.

Do not forget the saying of Heraclitus, "That the earth dies into water, water into air, air into fire, and so backward." Remember likewise the story of the man that traveled on without knowing to what place the way would bring him; and that many people quarrel with that reason that governs the world, and with which they are daily conversant, and seem perfectly unacquainted with those things which occur daily. Farther, we must not nod over business—for even in sleep we seem to act,—neither are we to be wholly governed by tradition; for that is like children, who believe anything their parents tell them.

Put the case, some god should acquaint you you were to die to-morrow, or next day at farthest. Under this warning, you would be a very poor wretch if you should strongly solicit for the longest time. For, alas! how inconsiderable is the difference? In like manner, if you would reason right, you would not be much concerned whether your life were to end to-morrow or a thousand years hence.

Consider how many physicians are dead that used to knit their brows over their patients; how many astrologers who thought themselves great men by foretelling the death of others; how many philosophers have gone the way of all flesh, after all their learned disputes about dying and immortality; how many warriors, who had knocked so many men's brains out; how many tyrants, who managed the power of life and death with as much insolence as if they had been immortal; how many cities, if I may say so, have given up the ghost: for instance, Helice in Greece, Pompeii and Herculaneum in Italy; not to mention many besides. Do but recollect your acquaintance, and here you will find one man closing another's eyes, then he himself is laid out, and this one by another. And all within a small compass of time. In short, mankind are poor transitory things! They are one day in the rudiments of life and almost the next turned to mummy or ashes. Your way is therefore to manage this minute in harmony with nature, and part with it cheerfully; and like a ripe olive when you drop, be sure to speak well of the mother that bore you, and make your acknowledgments to the tree that produced you.

Stand firm like a rock, against which though the waves batter, yet it stands unmoved, and they fall to rest at last. How unfortunate has this accident made me, cries such an one! Not at all! He should rather say, What a happy mortal am I for being unconcerned upon this occasion! for being neither crushed by the present, nor afraid of what is to come. The thing might have happened to any other man as well as myself; but for all that, everybody would not have been so easy under it. Why then is not the good fortune of the bearing more considerable than the ill fortune of the happening? Or, to speak properly, how can that be a misfortune to a man which does not frustrate his nature? And how can that cross upon a man's nature which is not opposed to the intention and design of it? Now what that intention is, you know. To apply this reasoning: does the present accident hinder your being just, magnanimous, temperate and modest, judicious, truthful, reverent, and unservile? Now, when a man is furnished with these good qualities, his nature has what she would have. Farther, when everything grows troublesome, recollect this maxim: This accident is not a misfortune, but bearing it well turns it to an advantage.

To consider those old people that resigned life so unwillingly, is a common yet not unserviceable aid in facing death. For what are these long-lived mortals more than those that went off in their infancy? What has become of Cadicianus, Fabius, Julianus, and Lepidus, and others like them? They buried a great many, but came at last to it themselves. Upon the whole, the difference between long and short life is insignificant, especially if you consider the accidents, the company, and the body you must go through with. Therefore do not let a thought of this kind affect you. Do but look upon the astonishing notion of time and eternity; what an immense deal has run out already, and how infinite it is still in the future. Do but consider this, and you will find three days and three ages of life come much to the same thing.

Always go the shortest way to work. Now, the nearest road to your business is the road of nature. Let it be your constant method, then, to be sound in word and in deed, and by this means you need not grow fatigued, you need not quarrel, flourish and dissemble like other people.

BOOK V

WHEN you find an unwillingness to rise early in the morning, make this short speech to yourself: I am getting up now to do the business of a man; and am I out of humor for

going about that I was made for, and for the sake of which
I was sent into the world? Was I then designed for nothing
but to doze and keep warm beneath the counterpane? Well!
but this is a comfortable way of living. Granting that: were
you born only for pleasure? were you never to do anything?
Is not action the end of your being? Pray look upon the
plants and birds, the ants, spiders, and bees, and you will
see them all exerting their nature, and busy in their station.
Pray, shall not a man act like a man? Why do you not rouse
your faculties, and hasten to act according to your nature?
For all that, there is no living without rest. True; but nature
has fixed a limit to eating and drinking, and here, too, you
generally exceed bounds, and go beyond what is sufficient.
Whereas in business you are apt to do less than lies in your
power. In earnest, you have no true love for yourself. If
you had, you would love your nature and honor her wishes.
Now, when a man loves his trade, how he will sweat and
drudge to perform to perfection. But you honor your nature
less than a turner does the art of turning, a dancing-master
the art of dancing. And as for wealth and popularity, how
eagerly are they pursued by the vain and the covetous! All
these people when they greatly desire anything, seek to attain
it, might and main, and will scarcely allow themselves necessary refreshment. And now, can you think the exercise of
social duties less valuable than these petty amusements, and
worth less exertion?

What an easy matter it is to stem the current of your
imagination, to discharge a troublesome or improper thought,
and at once return to a state of calm.

Do not think any word or action beneath you which is in
accordance with nature; and never be misled by the apprehension of censure or reproach. Where honesty prompts you
to say or do anything never hold it beneath you. Other
people have their own guiding principles and impulses; mind
them not. Go on in the straight road, pursue your own and
the common interest. For to speak strictly, these two are
approached by one and the same road.

I will march on in the path of nature till my legs sink
under me, and then I shall be at rest, and expire into that
air which has given me my daily breath; fall upon that earth

which has maintained my parents, helped my nurse to her milk, and supplied me with meat and drink for so many years; and though its favors have been often abused, still suffers me to tread upon it.

Wit and smartness are not your talent. What then? There are a great many other good qualities in which you cannot pretend nature has failed you; improve them as far as you can, and let us have that which is perfectly in your power. You may if you please behave yourself like a man of gravity and good faith, endure hardship, and despise pleasure; want but a few things, and complain of nothing; you may be gentle and magnanimous if you please, and have nothing of luxury or trifling in your disposition. Do not you see how much you may do if you have a mind to it, where the plea of incapacity is out of place? And yet you do not push forward as you should do. What then! Does any natural defect force you to grumble, to lay faults upon your constitution, to be stingy or a flatterer, to seek after popularity, boast, and be disturbed in mind? Can you say you are so weakly made as to be driven to these practices? The immortal gods know the contrary. No, you might have stood clear of all this long since; and after all, if your parts were somewhat slow, and your understanding heavy, your way had been to have taken the more pains with yourself, and not to have lain fallow and remained content with your own dullness.

Some men, when they do you a kindness, at once demand the payment of gratitude from you; others are more modest than this. However, they remember the favor, and look upon you in a manner as their debtor. A third sort shall scarce know what they have done. These are much like a vine, which is satisfied by being fruitful in its kind, and bears a bunch of grapes without expecting any thanks for it. A fleet horse or greyhound does not make a noise when they have done well, nor a bee neither when she has made a little honey. And thus a man that has done a kindness never proclaims it, but does another as soon as he can, just like a vine that bears again the next season. Now we should imitate those who are so obliging, as hardly to reflect on their beneficence. But you will say, a man ought not to act without reflection. It is surely natural for one that is generous to be conscious of his generosity; yes, truly, and to desire the person obliged should be sensible of it too. What you say is in a great measure true. But if you mistake my meaning, you will become one of those untoward benefactors I first mentioned; indeed, they too are misled by the plausibility of their reasoning. But if you will view the matter in its true colors, never fear that you will neglect any social act.

A prayer of the Athenians, "Send down, oh! send down rain, dear Zeus, on the plowed fields and plains of the Athenians." Of a truth, we should not pray at all, or else in this simple and noble fashion.

Æsculapius, as we commonly say, has prescribed such an one riding out, walking in his slippers, or a cold bath. Now, with much the same meaning we may affirm that the nature of the universe has ordered this or that person a disease, loss of limbs or estate, or some such other calamity. For as in the first case, the word "prescribed" signifies a direction for the health of the patient, so in the latter it means an application fit for his constitution and fate. And thus these harsher events may be counted fit for us, as stone properly joined together in a wall or pyramid is said by the workmen to fit in. Indeed, the whole of nature consists of harmony. For as the world has its form and entireness from that universal matter of which it consists, so the character of fate results from the quality and concurrence of all other causes contained in it. The common people understand this notion very well. Their way of speaking is: "This happened to this man, therefore it was sent him and appointed for him." Let us then comply with our doom, as we do with the prescriptions of Æsculapius. These doses are often unpalatable and rugged, and yet the desire of health makes them go merrily down. Now that which nature esteems profit and convenience, should seem to you like your own health. And, therefore, when anything adverse happens, take it quietly to you; it is for the health of the universe, and the prosperity of Zeus himself. Depend upon it, this had never been sent you, if the universe had not found its advantage in it. Neither does nature act at random, or order anything which is not suitable to those beings under her government. You have two reasons, therefore, to be contented with your condition.

First, because it has befallen you, and was appointed you from the beginning by the highest and most ancient causes. *Secondly,* The lot even of individuals is in a manner destined for the interest of him that governs the world. It perfects his nature in some measure, and causes and continues his happiness; for it holds in causes, no less than in parts of a whole that if you lop off any part of the continuity and connection, you maim the whole. Now, if you are displeased with your circumstances, you dismember nature, and pull the world in pieces, as much as lies in your power.

Be not uneasy, discouraged, or out of humor, because practice falls short of precept in some particulars. If you happen to be beaten, come on again, and be glad if most of your acts are worthy of human nature. Love that to which you return, and do not go like a schoolboy to his master, with an ill will. No, you must apply to philosophy with inclination, as those who have sore eyes make use of a good receipt. And when you are thus disposed, you will easily acquiesce in reason, and make your abode with her. And here you are to remember that philosophy will put you upon nothing but what your nature wishes and calls for. But you are crossing the inclinations of your nature. Is not this the most agreeable? And does not pleasure often deceive us under this pretense? Now think a little, and tell me what is there more delightful than greatness of mind, and generosity, simplicity, equanimity, and piety? And once more, what can be more delightful than prudence? than to be furnished with that faculty of knowledge and understanding which keeps a man from making a false step, and helps him to good fortune in all his business?

Things are so much perplexed and in the dark that several great philosophers looked upon them as altogether unintelligible, and that there was no certain test for the discovery of truth. Even the Stoics agree that certainty is very hard to come at; that our assent is worth little, for where is infallibility to be found? However, our ignorance is not so great but that we may discover how transitory and insignificant all things are, and that they may fall into the worst hands. Farther, consider the temper of those you converse with, and you will find the best will hardly do; not to men-

tion that a man has work enough to make himself tolerable
to himself. And since we have nothing but darkness and
dirt to grasp at, since time and matter, motion and mortals
are in perpetual flux; for these reasons, I say, I cannot imagine what there is here worth the minding or being eager
about. On the other hand, a man ought to keep up his spirits,
for it will not be long before his discharge comes. In the
meantime, he must not fret at the delay, but satisfy himself
with these two considerations: the one is, that nothing will
befall me but what is in accordance with the nature of the
universe; the other, that I need do nothing contrary to my
mind and divinity, since no one can force me to act thus, or
force me to act against my own judgment.

What use do I put my soul to? It is a serviceable question this, and should frequently be put to oneself. How does
my ruling part stand affected? And whose soul have I now?
That of a child, or a young man, or a feeble woman, or of a
tyrant, of cattle or wild beasts.

What sort of good things those are, which are commonly
so reckoned on, you may learn from hence. For the purpose,
if you reflect upon those qualities which are intrinsically valuable, such as prudence, temperance, justice, and fortitude,
you will not find it possible afterwards to give ear to those,
for this is not suitable to a good man. But if you have once
conceived as good what appears so to the many, you will
hear and gladly accept as suitable the saying of the comic
writer. Thus we see the generality are struck with the distinction, otherwise they would not dislike the liberty in one
case, and allow it in the other, holding it a suitable and witty
jest when it is directed against wealth, and the means that
further luxury and ambition. Now, what significancy and
excellence can there be in these things, to which may be
applied the poet's jest, that excess of luxury leaves no room
for comfort?

My being consists of matter and form, that is, of soul
and body; annihilation will reach neither of them, for they
were never produced out of nothing. The consequence is,
that every part of me will serve to make something in the
world; and this again will change into another part through
an infinite succession of change. This constant method of

alteration gave me my being, and my father before me, and so on to eternity backward: for I think I may speak thus, even though the world be confined within certain determinate periods.

Reason and the reasoning faculty need no foreign assistance, but are sufficient for their own purposes. They move within themselves, and make directly for the point in view. Wherefore, acts in accordance with them are called right acts, for they lead along the right road.

Those things do not belong to a man which do not belong to him as a man. For they are not included in the idea; they are not required of us men; human nature does not promise them; neither is it perfected by them. From whence it follows that they can neither constitute the chief end of man, nor strictly contribute towards it. Farther, if these things were any real additions, how comes the contempt of them, and the being easy without them, to be so great a commendation? To balk an advantage would be folly if these things were truly good. But the case stands otherwise; for we know that self-denial and indifference about these things, and patience when they are taken away, is the character of a good man.

Your manners will depend very much upon the quality of what you really think on; for the soul is as it were tinged with the color and complexion of thought. Be sure therefore to work in such maxims as these. Wherever a man lives, he may live well; by consequence, a life of virtue and that of a courtier are not inconsistent. Again, that which a thing is made for, is that towards which it is carried, and in that which it is naturally carried to, lies the end of the act. Now where the end of a thing is, there the advantage and improvement of it is certainly lodged. Now the happiness of mankind lies in society, since that we were made for this purpose, I have proved already. For is it not plain that the lower order of beings are made for the higher, and the higher for the service of each other? Now as those with souls are superior to the soulless, so amongst all creatures with souls the rational are the best.

To expect an impossibility is madness. Now it is impossible for ill men not to do ill.

There is nothing happens to any person but what was in his power to go through with. Some people have had very severe trials, and yet either by having less understanding, or more pride than ordinary, have charged bravely through the misfortune, and come off without a scratch. Now it is a disgrace to let ignorance and vanity do more with us than prudence and principle.

Outward objects cannot take hold of the soul, nor force their passage into her, nor set any of her wheels going. No, the impression comes from herself, and it is her own motions which affect her. As for the contingencies of fortune, they are either great or little, according to the opinion she has of her own strength.

When we consider we are bound to be serviceable to mankind, and bear with their faults, we shall perceive there is a common tie of nature and relation between us. But when we see people grow troublesome and disturb us in our business, here we are to look upon men as indifferent sort of things, no less than sun or wind, or a wild beast. It is true they may hinder me in the executing part, but all this is of no moment while my inclinations and good intent stand firm, for these can act according to the condition and change. For the mind converts and changes every hindrance into help. And thus it is probable I may gain by the opposition, and let the obstacle help me on my road.

Among all things in the universe, direct your worship to the greatest. And which is that? It is that being which manages and governs all the rest. And as you worship the best thing in nature, so you are to pay a proportionate regard to the best thing in yourself, and this is akin to the Deity. The quality of its functions will discover it. It is the reigning power within you, which disposes of your actions and your fortune.

That which does not hurt the city or body politic cannot hurt the citizen. Therefore when you think you are ill-used, let this reflection be your remedy: If the community is not the worse for it, neither am I. But if the community is injured, your business is to show the person concerned his fault, but not to grow passionate about it.

Reflect frequently upon the instability of things, and how

very fast the scenes of nature are shifted. Matter is in a perpetual flux. Change is always and everywhere at work; it strikes through causes and effects, and leaves nothing fixed and permanent. And then how very near us stand the two vast gulfs of time, the past and the future, in which all things disappear. Now is not that man a blockhead that lets these momentary things make him proud, or uneasy, or sorrowful, as though they could trouble him for long?

Remember what an atom your person is in respect of the universe, what a minute of immeasurable time falls to your share, and what a small concern you are in the empire of fate!

A man misbehaves himself towards me; what is that to me? The action is his, and the disposition that led him to it is his, and therefore let him look to it. As for me, I am in the condition the universal nature assigns me, and am doing what my own nature assigns me.

Whether the motions of your body are rugged or agreeable, do not let your ruling and governing principle be concerned with them; confine the impressions to their respective quarters, and let your mind keep her distance, and not mingle with them. It is true, that which results from the laws of the union through the force of sympathy or constitution, must be felt, for nature will have its course. But though the sensation cannot be stopped, it must not be overrated, nor strained to the quality of good or evil.

We ought to live with the gods. This is done by him who always exhibits a soul contented with the appointments of Providence, and obeys the orders of that divinity which is his deputy and ruler, and the offspring of God. Now this divine authority is neither more nor less than that soul and reason which every man possesses.

Are you angry at a rank smell or an ill-scented breath? What good will this anger do you? But you will say the man has reason, and can, if he takes pains, discover wherein he offends. I wish you joy of your discovery. Well, if you think mankind so full of reason, pray make use of your own. Argue the case with the faulty person, and show him his error. If your advice prevails, he is what you would have him; and then there is no need of being angry.

You may live now if you please, as you would choose to

do if you were near dying. But suppose people will not let you, why then, give life the slip, but by no means make a misfortune of it. If the room smokes I leave it, and there is an end, for why should one be concerned at the matter? However, as long as nothing of this kind drives me out, I stay, behave as a free man, and do what I have a mind to; but then I have a mind to nothing but what I am led to by reason and public interest.

The soul of the universe is of a social disposition. For this reason it has made the lower part of the creation for the sake of the higher. And as for those beings of the higher rank, it has bound them to each other. You see how admirably things are ranged and subordinated according to the dignity of their kind, and cemented together in mutual harmony.

Recollect how you have behaved yourself all along towards the gods, your parents, brothers, wife, and children; towards your instructors, governors, friends, acquaintance, and servants. Whether men can say of you, "He never wronged a man in word or deed." Recollect how much business you have been engaged in, and what you have had strength to endure; that now your task is done, and the history of your life finished. Remember likewise how many fair sights you have seen, how much of pleasure and pain you have despised, how much glory disregarded, and how often you have done good against evil.

Why should skill and knowledge be disturbed at the censures of ignorance? But who are these knowing and skillful people? Why, those who are acquainted with the original cause and end of all things, with that reason which pervades the mass of matter, which renews the world at certain periods, and which governs it through all the lengths of time.

You will quickly be reduced to ashes and skeleton. And it may be you will have a name left you, and it may be not. And what is a name? Nothing but sound and echo. And then for those things which are so much valued in the world, they are miserably empty and rotten, and insignificant. It is like puppies snarling for a bone; and the contests of little children sometimes transported, and then again all in tears about a plaything. And as for modesty and good faith, truth and justice, they have fled "up to Olympus from the wide-spread earth." And now, what is it that can keep you here? For if the objects of sense are floating and changeable, and the organs misty, and apt to be imposed on; if the soul is but a vapor drawn off the blood, and the applause of little mortals insignificant; if the case stands thus, why not have patience till you are either extinguished or removed? And till that time comes, what is to be done? The answer is easy: to worship the gods, and speak honorably of them; to be beneficial to mankind; to bear with them or avoid them; and lastly, to remember that whatever lies without the compass of your own flesh and breath is nothing of yours, nor in your power.

You may be always successful if you do but set out well, and let your thoughts and practice proceed upon right method. There are two properties and privileges common to the soul of God and man and all rational beings. The one is, not to be hindered by anything external; the other, to make virtuous intention and action their supreme satisfaction, and not so much as to desire anything farther.

If this accident is no fault of mine, nor a consequence of it; and besides, if the community is never the worse for it, why am I concerned? Now, how is the community injured?

Do not suffer a sudden impression to overbear your judgment. Let those that want your assistance have it as far as the case requires. But if they are injured in matters indifferent, do not consider it any real damage, for that is a bad habit. But as the old man, when he went away, asked back his foster-child's top, remembering that it was a top, so do in this case also. When you are haranguing in the rostra, a little of this to yourself would not be amiss:—Hark you, friend, have you forgotten what this glitter of honor really is? I grant it is but tinsel, but for all that it is extremely valued. And because other people are fools, must you be so too? I can at once become happy anywhere, for he is happy who has found for himself a happy lot. In a word, happiness lies all in the functions of reason, in warrantable desires and virtuous practice.

BOOK VI

As the substance of the universe is pliable and obedient, so that sovereign reason which gives laws to it has neither motive nor inclination to bring an evil upon anything. It has no evil in its nature, nor does evil, but forms and governs all things, and hurts nothing.

Do but your duty, and do not trouble yourself, whether it is in the cold, or by a good fire, whether you are over-watched, or satisfied with sleep, whether you have a good word or a bad one, whether you are dying, or doing anything else, for this last must be done at one time or other. It is part of the business of life to leave it, and here too it suffices to manage the present well.

Look thoroughly into matters, and let not the peculiar quality or intrinsic value of anything escape you.

The present appearance of things will quickly undergo a change, and be either exhaled into common matter or dispersed.

That intelligent Being that governs the universe has perfect views of His own nature and acts, and of the matter on which He acts.

The best way of revenge is not to imitate the injury.

Be always doing something serviceable to mankind, and let this constant generosity be your only pleasure, not forgetting in the meantime a due regard to the Deity.

The governing part of the mind arouses and alters itself; gives what air it pleases to its own likeness, and to all the accidents and circumstances without.

The particular effects in the world are all wrought by one intelligent nature. This universal cause has no foreign assistant, no interloping principle, either without or within it.

The world is either a medley of atoms that now intermingle and now are scattered apart, or else it is a unity under the laws of order and providence. If the first, what should I stay for, where nature is in such a chaos, and things are so blindly jumbled together? Why do I care for anything else than to return to the element of earth as soon as may be? Why should I give myself any trouble? Let me do what I will, my elements will be scattered. But if there is a Providence, then I adore the great Governor of the world, and am easy and of good cheer in the prospect of protection.

[The "Meditations" contain twelve books in all; but the later books, seven to twelve, contain no material of an autobiographical or even of a personal character, except perhaps in the passages that follow.]

To keep you modest and free from vain glory, remember that it is no longer in your power to spend your life wholly, from youth upwards, in the pursuit of wisdom. Your friends and yourself, too, are sufficiently acquainted how much you fall short of philosophy; you have been liable to disturbance, so that the bare report of being a philosopher is no longer an easy matter for you to compass; you are unqualified by your station. However, since you know how to come at the thing, never be concerned about missing the credit. Be satisfied, therefore, and for the rest of your life let your own rational nature direct you. Mind, then, what she desires, and let nothing foreign disturb you. You are very sensible how much you have rambled after happiness, and failed. Neither learning, nor wealth, nor fame, nor pleasure could ever help you to it. Which way is it to be had then? By acting up to the height of human nature. And how shall a man do this? Why, by getting a right set of principles for impulses and actions. And what principles are those? Such as state and distinguish good and evil. Such as give us to understand that there is nothing properly good for a man but what promotes the virtues of justice, temperance, fortitude, and independence, nor anything bad for him, but that which carries him off to the contrary vices.

At every action ask yourself this question, What will the consequence of this be to me? Am I not likely to repent of it? I shall be dead in a little time, and then all is over with me. If the present undertaking is but suitable to an intelligent and sociable being, and one that has the honor to live by the same rule and reason with God himself; if the case stands thus, all is well, and to what purpose should you look any farther?

Alexander, Julius Cæsar, and Pompey, what were they in comparison of Diogenes, Heraclitus, and Socrates? These philosophers looked through things and their causes, and their ruling principles were in accordance. But as for those great princes, what a load of cares were they pestered with, and to how many things were they slaves!

People will play the same pranks over and over again, though you should burst.

In the first place, keep yourself easy, for all things are governed by the universal nature. Besides, you will quickly go the way of all flesh, as Augustus and Hadrian have done before you. Farther, examine the matter to the bottom, and remember that your business is to be a good man. Therefore, whatever the dignity of human nature requires of you, set about it at once, without "ifs" or "ands"; and speak always according to your conscience, but let it be done in the terms of good nature and modesty and sincerity. . . .

You have no leisure to read books, what then? You have leisure to check your insolence. It is in your power to be superior to pleasure and pain, to be deaf to the charms of ambition. It is in your power not only to forbear being angry with people for their folly and ingratitude, but over and above, to cherish their interest, and take care of them.

Never again let any man hear you censure a court life, nor seem dissatisfied with your own.

Repentance is a reproof of a man's conscience for the neglect of some advantages. Now, whatever is morally good is profitable, and ought to be the concern of a man of probity. But no good man would ever be inwardly troubled for the omission of any pleasure, whence it follows that pleasure is neither profitable nor good.

What is this thing considered in itself? Of what sort of substance, of what material and causal parts does it consist? What share of action has it in the world? and how long is it likely to stay there?

When you find yourself sleepy in a morning, remember that business and doing service to the world is to act up to nature and live like a man. Whereas sleep you have in common with the beasts. Now those actions which fall in with a man's nature are more suitable and serviceable, yes, and more pleasant than others. . . .

O my soul, are you ever to be rightly good, simple, and uniform, unmasked, and made more visible to yourself than the body that hangs about you? Are you ever likely to relish good nature and general kindness as you ought? Will you ever be fully satisfied, get above want and wishing, and never desire to seek your pleasure in anything foreign, either living or inanimate? Not desiring, I say, either time for longer enjoyment nor place for elbow-room, nor climate for good air, nor the music of good company? Can you be contented with your present condition, and be pleased with all that is about you, and be persuaded that you are fully furnished, that all things are well with you; for the gods are at the head of the administration, and they will approve of nothing but what is for the best, and tends to the security and advantage of that good, righteous, beautiful, and perfect being which generates and supports and surrounds all things, and embraces those things which decay, that other resembling beings may be made out of them? In a word, are you ever likely to be so happily qualified as to converse with the gods and men in such a manner as neither to complain of them nor be condemned by them?

Examine what your nature requires, so far as you have no other law to govern you. And when you have looked into her inclinations never balk them, unless your animal nature is likely to be worse for it. Then you are to examine what your animal nature demands; and here you may indulge your appetite as far as you please, provided your rational nature does not suffer by the liberty. Now, your rational nature admits of nothing but what is serviceable to the rest of mankind. Keep firmly to these rules, and you will have regard for nothing else.

Whatever happens, either you have strength to bear it, or you have not. If you have, exert your nature, and never murmur at the matter. But if the weight is too heavy for you, do not complain; it will crush you, and then destroy itself. And here you are to remember that to think a thing tolerable and endurable is the way to make it so if you do but press it strongly on the grounds of interest or duty.

Is any one mistaken? Undeceive him civilly, and show him his oversight. But if you cannot convince him, blame yourself, or not even yourself.

Whatever happens to you was preordained your lot from

the first; and that chain of causes which constitutes fate, tied your person and the event together from all eternity.

Whether atoms or nature rule the world I lay it down in the first place, that I am part of that whole which is all under nature's government. Secondly, I am in some measure related to those beings which are of my own order and species. These points being agreed, I shall apply them. Insomuch then as I am a part of the universe, I shall never be displeased with the general appointment; for that can never be prejudicial to the part which is serviceable to the whole, since the universe contains nothing but what is serviceable to it. For the nature of no being is an enemy to itself. But the world has this advantage above other particular beings, that there is no foreign power to force it to produce anything hurtful to itself. Since, therefore, I am a member of so magnificent a body, I shall freely acquiesce in whatever happens to me. Farther, inasmuch as I have a particular relation to my own species, I will never do anything against the common interest. On the other hand, I shall make it my business to oblige mankind, direct my whole life for the advantage of the public, and avoid the contrary. And by holding to this conduct, I must be happy, as that citizen must needs be who is always working for the benefit of his fellow-citizens, and perfectly satisfied with that interest and station the government assigns him.

The properties of a rational soul are these. She has the privilege to look into her own nature, to cut her qualities and form herself to what character she pleases. She enjoys her product (whereas trees and cattle bring plenty for other folks). Whether life proves long or short, she gains the ends of living. Her business is never spoilt by interruption, as it happens in a dance or a play. In every part and in spite of every interruption, her acts are always finished and entire; so that she may say: I carry off all that belongs to me. Farther, she ranges through the whole world, views its figure, looks into the vacuum on the outside of it, and strains her sight on to an immeasurable length of time.

What a brave soul is that that is always prepared to leave the body and unconcerned about her being either extinguished, scattered, or removed—prepared, I say, upon judgment, and not out of mere obstinacy like the Christians—but with a solemn air of gravity and consideration, and in a way to persuade another and without tragic show.

God sees through the soul of every man as clearly as if it was not wrapped up in matter, nor had anything of the shroud and coarseness of body about it. And God, with his intellectual part alone, touches those beings only that have flowed and proceeded from him. Now, if you would learn to do thus, a great deal of trouble would be saved; for he that can overlook his body will hardly disturb himself about the clothes he wears, the house he dwells in, about his reputation, or any part of this pomp and magnificence. . . .

To those that ask me the reason of my being so earnest in religious worship, and whether I ever saw any of the gods, or which way I am convinced of the certainty of their existence; in the first place, I answer, that the gods are not invisible. But granting they were, the objection would signify nothing, for I never had a sight of my own soul, and yet I have a great value for it. And thus by my constant experience of the power of the gods I have a proof of their being, and a reason for my veneration.

The best provision for a happy life is to dissect everything, view its own nature, and divide it into matter and form. To practice honesty in good earnest, and speak truth from the very soul of you. What remains but to live easy and cheerful, and crowd one good action so close to another that there may not be the least empty space between them.

The light of the sun is but one and the same, though it is divided by the interposition of walls and mountains, and abundance of other opaque bodies. There is but one common matter, though it is parceled out among bodies of different qualities. There is but one sensitive soul too, notwithstanding it is divided among innumerable natures and individual limitations. And lastly, the rational soul, though it seems to be split into distinction, is but one and the same. Now, excepting this last, the other parts above-mentioned, such as breath and matter, though without apprehension, or any common affection to tie them to each other, are yet upheld by an intelligent being, and by that faculty which pushes things of the same nature to the same place; but human understandings have a peculiar disposition to union; they stick together by inclination, and nothing can extinguish such sociable thoughts in them.

What is it you hanker after? Is it bare existence? or sensation? or motion? or strength, that you may lose it again in decay? What? Is it the privilege of speech, or the power of thinking in general? Is any of this worth desiring? If all these things are trifles, proceed to something that is worth your while, and that is to be governed by reason and the Deity. And yet you cannot be said to value these last-mentioned privileges rightly, if you are disturbed because death must take them from you.

What a small part of immeasurable and infinite time falls to the share of a single mortal, and how soon is every one swallowed up in eternity! What a handful of the universal matter goes to the making of a human body, and what a very little of the universal soul too! And on what a narrow clod with respect to the whole earth do you crawl upon! Consider all this, and reckon nothing great, unless it be to act in conformity to your own reason, and to suffer as the universal nature shall appoint you. The great business of a man is to improve his mind, therefore consider how he does this. As for all other things, whether in our power to compass or not, they are no better than lifeless ashes and smoke.

We cannot have a more promising notion to set us above the fear of death, than to consider that it has been despised even by that sect [the Epicureans] who made pleasure and pain the standard of good and evil. He that likes no time so well as the fitting season, he that is indifferent whether he has room for a long progress in reason or not, or whether he has a few or a great many years to view the world in, a person thus qualified will never be afraid of dying.

Hark ye, friend: you have been a burgher of this great city, what matter though you have lived in it five years or three; if you have observed the laws of the corporation, the length or shortness of the time makes no difference. Where is the hardship then if nature, that planted you here, orders your removal? You cannot say you are sent off by a tyrant or unjust judge. No; you quit the stage as fairly as a player does that has his discharge from the master of the revels.

But I have only gone through three acts, and not held out to the end of the fifth. You say well; but in life three acts make the play entire. He that ordered the opening of the first scene now gives the sign for shutting up the last; you are neither accountable for one nor the other; therefore retire well satisfied, for He by whom you are dismissed is satisfied too.

MARTIN LUTHER

MARTIN LUTHER

1483-1546

INTRODUCTORY NOTE

Some explanation is necessary before presenting the work commonly known as Luther's autobiography. Luther never wrote any complete and consecutive account of his career. He did, however, speak very fully about himself in his letters and other writings; and the task of piecing these scattered utterances together so as to make them tell the continuous story of the great reformer's life was undertaken by the celebrated French author Michelet. This work Michelet published under the title of "The Life of Luther, Told by Himself"; and it is this painstaking and accurate book which has since been known, and is here presented, as Luther's autobiography. To prevent any possible confusion, the following pages enclose in quotation marks each passage of Luther's own writing, and so separate his words clearly from the connecting paragraphs by which Michelet unites them into a single narrative.

These memoirs help us much to understand the character and intent of Martin Luther. He has been sometimes pictured as a compound of violence and rugged obstinacy, a coarse and brutal peasant defying popes and princes of the earth, fanatically faithful to the dictates of his conscience, and caring for naught else in his self-appointed path of righteousness. But after reading these memorabilia of the Saxon reformer, we not only see him in his fearless duel with Rome, roaring and fuming at what he held to be ecclesiastical machinations and wrongs; we also see him as a poor, humble, afflicted man, not a particle puffed up with arrogant pride at the tremendous movement he had brought about, but rather abased by the knowledge of his faults and the sense of his own unworthiness. Ideal man has often been described symbolically as the lion coming out of the lamb, and the lamb coming out of the lion. Luther was in his character a singular combination of ferocity and gentleness. At times, no one could have been more terrible in wrath and denunciation, his the rousing voice to awaken Europe from the lethargy of ages; and, again, if we examine his written opinions and views, he proves to be the most moderate of all the reformers. Honest comparison compels this concession. Even in his struggle with the Roman hierarchy you will discover Luther frequently willing to meet his adversaries more than half way. As an instance, we may cite that this very Luther, the Lion of the North, who made so energetic, so immense a use of liberty, was he who revived the Augustinian theory as to the annihilation of liberty, the sacrificing of free-will to grace, man to God, morality to a kind of providential fatality. It is one of the queer twists in history that the theoretically fatalistic Luther should have in practice established freedom of will.

In this autobiography, then, are exhibited his spiritual fights, his assailing doubts, his temptations, his consolations; his love of music, painting, singing and harmless conviviality; his profound piety, so simple and earnest that it needed no cloak of sanctified air. In him we realize not the equal balance of grace and nature, but their fierce and painful struggle. Luther has concealed nothing, kept nothing to himself; he fought the battle out openly, and he has enabled us to see and sound in him this deep and awful wound of our common nature. He, indeed, is one of the few men in whom we can fully study our terrible anatomy.

THE LIFE OF LUTHER, WRITTEN BY HIMSELF

I

"I HAVE often conversed with Melancthon, and related to him my whole life, from point to point. I am the son of a peasant; my father, my grandfather, my great-grandfather were all mere peasants. My father went to Mansfeldt, and became a miner there. It was there I was born. That I was afterwards to become bachelor of arts, doctor of divinity, and what not, was assuredly not written in the stars, at least, not to ordinary readers. How I astonished everybody when I turned monk! and again, when I exchanged the brown cap for another. These things greatly vexed my father—nay, made him quite ill for a time. After that, I got pulling the pope about by the hair of his head; I married a runaway nun; I had children by her. Who saw these things in the stars? Who would have told any one beforehand they were to happen?"

Hans (John) Luther, or Lutter, father of the Luther who became so celebrated, was of Mœrha or Moer, a village in Upper Saxony, near Eisenach. His mother (Gretha, or Margaret Lindemann) was the daughter of a tradesman of the same place, or rather, according to a preferable tradition,

of Nieustadt, in Franconia. The father, who was only a poor
miner, found it a very difficult matter to maintain his family;
and it will be seen further on, that his children were fain at
times to beg alms for their sustenance. Yet, despite his
extreme poverty, instead of making them labor with him at
his own occupation, he sent them to school. He appears to
have been a man of fine unsophisticated honesty and firm
faith.

" 'Tis with me a pious duty," he says, in a letter to Melancthon, announcing John Luther's death, "to weep for him
whom the Father of Mercy destined to give me birth—for
him, by whose labor and sweat God nourished me, and made
me what I am, such as that is. Oh, how I rejoice that he
lived long enough to see the light of truth! Blessed be
God forever, in all his counsels and decrees! Amen."

Martin Luther, or Ludher, or Lutter, or Lother—for he
signed his name all these ways—was born at Eisleben, on the
10th November, 1483, at eleven o'clock in the evening. Sent
at an early age to the free school of Eisenach (1849), he
used to sing before people's houses to gain his daily bread, as
was the wont, at that time and later, with many poor students
in Germany. It is from himself that we learn this circumstance: "Let no one in my presence speak contemptuously
of the poor fellows who go from door to door, singing and
begging bread *propter Deum!* You know the psalm says—
Princes and kings have sung. I myself was once a poor mendi-
cant, seeking my bread at people's houses, particularly at
Eisenach, my own dear Eisenach!"

After a while he obtained a more regular subsistence, and
an asylum in the house of dame Ursula Cotta, widow of
Hans Schweikard, who took compassion on the poor wandering boy. By the assistance of this charitable woman, he was
enabled to study four years at Eisenach. In 1501, he was
entered at the university of Erfurt, in Thuringia, where his
father, now in better circumstances, managed to support him.
Luther, in one of his works, records the goodness of his bene-
factress, in words glowing with emotion; and he was throughout life grateful, in a more especial manner, to the whole sex
for her sake.

After having tried theology, he was induced, by the advice

of his friends, to embrace the study of the law, which, at that period, was a stepping-stone to the most lucrative positions not only in state, but in church. He seems, however, never to have had any liking for this pursuit. He infinitely preferred the *belles lettres* and music. Music, indeed, was his favorite art. He cultivated it assiduously all his life, and taught it to his children. He does not hesitate to say that music appeared to him the first of the arts after theology: "Music is the art of the prophets; it is the only other art, which like theology, can calm the agitations of the soul, and put the devil to flight." He played both the guitar and the flute.

This inclination to music and literature, the assiduous cultivation of the poets, which he alternated with the study of logic and of law, presented no indication that he was at an early period to play so important a part in the history of religion.

In 1505, an accident gave to the career of the youthful Martin an entirely new direction. He saw one of his friends killed at his side by a stroke of lightning. He sent forth a cry at the terrible spectacle: that cry was a vow to St. Anne that he would become a monk, if he were himself spared. The danger passed over, but he did not seek to elude an engagement wrung from him by terror. He solicited no dispensation from his vow. He regarded the blow with which he had seen himself so nearly threatened, as a menace, as an injunction from Heaven. He only delayed the accomplishment of his vow for a fortnight.

On the 17th July, 1505, after having passed a pleasant convivial evening with some musical friends, he entered the Augustine monastery at Erfurt, taking with him nothing but his Plautus and his Virgil.

Next day, he wrote a brief farewell to various persons, sent word to his father of the resolution he had carried into effect, and returned the ring and gown he had received from the university on being admitted to his mastership of arts; and for a month would not allow any one to see him. He felt the hold which the world still had upon him; he feared the possible effect upon him of his father's venerated features, filled with tears. Nor was it until two years had expired, that John Luther gave way, and consented to be present at his son's ordination. A day was selected for the ceremony on which the miner could quit his avocation, and he then came to Erfurt with several friends, and ere he returned, gave to the son he was thus losing, the savings he had managed to put by: twenty florins.

We are not to suppose that in undertaking these formidable engagements, the new priest was impelled by any peculiar degree of religious fervor. We have seen with how mundane an equipment he had furnished himself on entering the cloister; let us now hear his own statement as to what were the feelings he carried with him thither. "When I said my first mass at Erfurt, I was well nigh dead; for I had no faith. My only notion about myself was that I was a very worthy person indeed. I did not regard myself as a sinner at all. The first mass was a striking thing, and produced a good deal of money. They brought in the *horas canonicas*, surrounded by large flambeaux. The *dear young lord*, as the peasants used to call their new pastor, had then to dance with his mother, if she were still alive, the spectators all weeping tears of joy; if she were dead, he put her, as the phrase ran, under the chalice, and saved her from purgatory."

Luther having obtained what he had sought, having become priest, monk, all being accomplished and the door of the world closed upon him, became a prey, we will not say to regret, but to sadness, to perplexities, to temptations of the flesh, to the mischievous shafts and subtleties of the mind.

"When I was a monk," says Luther, "I frequently corresponded with Dr. Staupitz. Once, I wrote to him: *Oh, my sins! my sins! my sins!* Whereto he replied, *You would fain be without sin; you have no right sin, such as murdering of parents, blaspheming, adultery, and the like. Thou hadst better keep a register of right and true sins, that so thou mayst not afflict thyself about small matters. Remember that Christ came hither for the pardon of our sins.*

"I often confessed to Dr. Staupitz, and put to him, not trivial matters, but questions going to the very knot of the question. He answered me as all the other confessors have answered me: *I do not understand.* At last, he came to me one day, when I was at dinner, and said: 'How is it you are so sad, brother Martin?' 'Ah,' I replied, 'I am sad, indeed.' 'You know not,' said he, 'that such trials are good and necessary for you, but would not be so for any one else.' All he meant to imply was, that as I had some learning, I might, but for these trials, have become haughty and super- cilious; but I have felt since that what he said was, as it were, a voice and an inspiration of the Holy Spirit.''

Luther elsewhere relates, that these temptations had re- duced him to such a state, that once for a whole fortnight, he neither ate, drank, nor slept.

''Ah, if St. Paul were alive now, how glad I should be to learn from himself what sort of temptation it was he under- went. It was not the thorn in the flesh; it was not the worthy Tecla, as the papists dream. Oh, no, it was not a sin that tore his conscience. It was something higher than despair result- ing from the sense of sin; it was rather the temptation of which the Psalmist speaks: *My God! my God! why hast thou forsaken me;* as though the Psalmist would have said: *Thou art my enemy without cause;* and, with Job: *Yet I am inno- cent, nor is iniquity in me.* I am sure that the book of Job is a true history, of which a poem was afterwards made. Jerome and other fathers never experienced such trials. They under- went none but trivial temptations, those of the flesh, which indeed, have quite enough pains of their own accompanying them.

''Augustin and Ambrose, too, had their trials, and trembled before the sword: but this is as nothing compared with the Angel of Satan, *who strikes with the fists.* If I live, I will write a book on temptations, for without a knowledge of that subject, no man can thoroughly understand the Holy Scrip- tures, or feel the due love and fear of the Lord.

'' . . . I was lying sick at the infirmary. The most cruel temptations tortured and wore out my frame, so that I could scarcely breathe. No man comforted me: all those to whom I represented my piteous condition, replied, *I know not.* Then, I said to myself: Am I then the only one amongst you who is to be thus sad in spirit? Oh, what specters, what terrible figures did I see constantly before me! But, ten years ago, God sent me a consolation by his dear angels, enabling me to fight and write for Him.''

A long time after this, only the year which preceded that of his death, he himself explains to us the nature of these so terrible temptations. "Even when I was at school, in studying the Epistles of St. Paul, I was seized with the most ardent desire to understand what the apostle meant in his epistle to the Romans. One single phrase stopped me: *Justitia Dei revelatur in illo.* I hated this expression, *Justitia Dei*, because, according to the custom of doctors, I had learned to understand by it that active justice, whereby God is just, and punishes the unjust and sinners. Now, I, who led the life of a harmless monk, and who yet felt painfully within me the uneasy conscience of a sinner, without being able to attain an idea as to the satisfaction I might offer up to God, I did not love, nay, to say the truth, I hated this just God, punisher of sin. I was indignant against Him, and gave silent utterance to murmuring, if not altogether to blasphemy. I said to myself: 'Is it not, then, enough that wretched sinners, already eternally damned for original sin, should be overwhelmed with so many calamities by the decrees of the decalogue, but God must further add misery to misery by his gospel, menacing us even there with his justice and his fierce anger?'

"Thus the trouble of my conscience carried me away, and I always came back to the same passage. At last I perceived that the *justice* of God is that whereby, with the blessing of God, the just man lives, that is to say, *Faith;* and I then saw that the meaning of the passage was thus: *The gospel reveals the justice of God, a passive justice, whereby the merciful God justifies us by faith.* Thereupon, I felt as if born again, and it seemed to me as though heaven's gates stood full open before me, and that I was joyfully entering therein. At a later period, I read St. Augustin's book, *On the Spirit and the Letter,* and I found, contrary to my expectation, that he also understands by the justice of God, that wherewith God clothes us in justifying us. I was greatly rejoiced to find this, though the thing is put somewhat incompletely in the book, and though the father explains himself vaguely and imperfectly, on the doctrine of imputation."

To confirm Luther in the doctrine of grace it only needed for him to visit the people from among whom grace had departed. We refer to Italy. We shall be dispensed from painting in detail that Italy of the Borgias. It certainly presented at this period something which has seldom, nay, which has at no other time, been exhibited in history: a systematic and scientific perversity; a magnificent ostentation of wickedness; in a word, the atheist priest proclaiming himself monarch of the universe.

In one of his conversations, he gives us naïvely an idea of how terrible Italy was to the imaginations of the simple-hearted Germans: ''The Italians only require you to look in a mirror to be able to kill you. They can deprive you of all your senses by secret poisons. In Italy, the air itself is pestilential; at night, they close hermetically every window, and stop up every chink and cranny.'' Luther assures us that both himself and the Brother who accompanied him, were taken ill, solely in consequence of having slept with the casement open, but they ate two pomegranates, by which means it pleased God to save their lives.

He went on his journey, merely passing through Florence without stopping, and at length entered Rome. He proceeded to the convent of his order, near the *Porto del Popolo*. ''On arriving, I fell on my knees, raised my hands to Heaven, and exclaimed: 'Hail, holy Rome! made holy by the holy martyrs, and by the blood which has been spilt here.' '' In his fervor, he adds, he hastened to view the sacred places, saw all, believed all. He soon perceived, however, that he was the only person who did believe; Christianity seemed totally forgotten in this capital of the Christian world. The pope was no longer the scandalous Alexander VI., but the warlike and choleric Julius II. This father of the faithful breathed nothing but blood and ruin.

If our poor German took refuge in the churches, he had not even the consolation of a good mass. The Roman priest dispatched the divine sacrifice with such celerity, that before Luther had got through the gospel, the minister said to him, *Ite, missa est.* ''These Italian priests often say mass in such a manner that I detest them. I have heard them make a boast of their fearful temerity in free-thinking. Repeatedly, in consecrating the host, they would say, 'Bread thou art, and bread thou wilt remain! wine thou art, and wine thou wilt remain!'" The only thing to be done was to flee, veiling the head, and shaking off the dust from the feet: Luther quitted Rome at the end of a fortnight.

He carried back with him into Germany the condemnation of Italy, and of the Roman church. In the rapid and mournful journey he had made, the Saxon had seen sufficient to condemn, but not sufficient to comprehend. And, in truth, for a mind intent upon the moral point of view of Christianity, there needed a rare effort of philosophy, an historical enthusiasm, hardly to be expected in those days, to discover religion in that world of art, of jurisprudence, of politics, which constituted Italy.

"I would not," he says somewhere, "I would not for a hundred thousand florins have missed seeing Rome, (and he repeats these words thrice). I should have always felt an uneasy doubt whether I was not, after all, doing injustice to the pope. As it is, I am quite satisfied on the point."

II

1517-1521

THE papacy was far from suspecting its danger. Ever since the thirteenth century, men had been disputing with it, had been railing against it, but apparently with no effect.

Julius II. conquered for the church; Leo X. for his family. This youthful pope, a thorough man of the world, a man of pleasure, a man of letters, a man of business, in common with all the other Medici, had the passions of his age, as well as those of the former popes, and those of his own particular period. His aim was to make the Medici family monarchs. He himself played the part of the first king of Christendom. Independently of the costly diplomatic relations which he maintained with all the states of Europe, he kept up a scientific correspondence with the most distant regions. He opened communications even with the extreme north, and employed persons to collect the monuments of Scandinavian history. At Rome he was proceeding with St. Peter's, the construction of which had been bequeathed to him by Julius II.; the latter pontiff, in resolving on the work, had not calculated his resources; and indeed, when Michel-Angelo brought such or such a plan, who would have thought for an instant of haggling about the cost?

Leo X. had commenced his pontificate with selling to Francis I. what did not belong to him, the rights of the church of France. At a later period, as a means of raising money, he created thirty-one cardinals at once; but these were small matters. His mines were the old faith of the nations, their easy credulity. He had entrusted the working of this mine in Germany to the Dominicans, who had accordingly succeeded the Augustines in the sale of indulgences. The Dominican, Tetzel, a shameless mountebank, went about from town to town, with great display, pomp, and expense, hawking the commodity in the churches, the public streets, in taverns and ale-houses. He paid over to his employers as little as possible, pocketing the balance, as the pope's legate subsequently proved against him. The faith of the buyers diminishing, it became necessary to exaggerate to the fullest extent the merit of the specific; the article had been so long in the market, and in such great supply, that the demand was falling off. The intrepid Tetzel stretched his rhetoric to the very uttermost bounds of amplification. Daringly piling one lie upon another, he set forth, in reckless display, the long list of evils which this panacea could cure. He did not content himself with enumerating known sins; he set his foul imagination to work, and invented crimes, infamous atrocities, strange, unheard of, unthought of; and when he saw his auditors standing aghast at each horrible suggestion, he would calmly repeat the burden of his song: "Well, all this is expiated the moment your money chinks in the pope's chest."

Luther assures us that up to this time he had no very definite notion what indulgences were. But when he saw the prospectus of them proudly set forth with the name, arms, and authorization of the archbishop of Mayence, whom the pope had charged with the superintendence of their sale in Germany, he was seized with indignation. A problem of mere speculation would never have placed him in antagonism with his ecclesiastical superiors. But this was a question of good sense, of common morality. A doctor of divinity, an influential professor in the university of Wittemberg, which the elector had just founded, provincial vicar of the Augustins, and entrusted by the vicar-general with the pastoral visitation of Misnia and Thuringia, he doubtless deemed himself responsible more than any other person for the Saxon faith so extensively confided to him. His conscience was struck: if he spoke, he ran great risks; if he remained silent, he believed he should incur damnation.

"It was in the year 1517, when the profligate monk Tetzel, a worthy servant of the pope and the devil—for I am certain that the pope is the agent of the devil on earth—came among us selling indulgences, maintaining their efficacy, and impudently practicing on the credulity of the people. When I beheld this unholy and detestable traffic taking place in open day, and thereby sanctioning the most villainous crimes, I could not, though I was then but a young doctor of divinity, refrain from protesting against it in the strongest manner, not only as directly contrary to the Scriptures, but as opposed to the canons of the church itself. Accordingly, in my place at Wittemberg—in which university, by the favor of God and the kindness of the illustrious elector of Saxony, I was honored with the office of professor of divinity—I resolved to oppose the career of this odious monk, and to put the people on their guard against the revival of this infamous imposition on their credulity. When I put this resolution into practice, instead of being abused and condemned, as I have been, by these worthless tyrants and impostors, the pope and his mercenaries, I expected to be warmly encouraged and commended, for I did little more than make use of the pope's own language, as set forth in the decretals, against the rapacity and extortion of the collectors. I cautioned my hearers against the snares which were laid for them, showing them that this was a scheme altogether opposed to religion, and only intended as a source of emolument by these unprincipled men. It was on the festival of All-Hallows Eve that I first drew their attention to the gross errors touching indulgences; and about the same time I wrote two letters, one to the most reverend prelate Jerome, bishop of Brandenburg, within whose jurisdiction Tetzel and his associates were carrying on their scandalous traffic; the other to the most reverend prelate and prince, Albert, archbishop of Magdeburg, pointing out to them the consequences of this imposition, and praying them to silence Tetzel. My letter to the archbishop was in these terms:

> " 'To the most reverend father in Christ, my most illustrious lord, prince Albert, archbishop of Magdeburg and Mayence, marquis of Brandenburg, &c. Luther to his lord and pastor in Christ, in all submission and reverence.

> JESUS

> " 'The grace and mercy of God, and whatever can be and is. Pardon me, most reverend father in Christ, illustrious prince, that I have the temerity, I who am the lees of mankind, to raise my eyes to your sublimity, and address a letter to you. Jesus, my Lord and Savior, is witness for me, that, long restrained by the consciousness of my own turpitude and weakness, I have long delayed commencing the work which I now undertake with open and upraised brow, impelled by the fidelity I owe to Jesus Christ; deign then, your grace, to cast a look upon the grain of sand who now approaches you, and to receive my prayer with paternal clemency.

> " 'Persons are now hawking about papal indulgences, under the name and august title of your lordship, for the construction of St. Peter's at Rome. I say nothing about the vaporings of the preachers, which I have not myself heard; but I complain bitterly of the fatal errors in which they are involving the common people, men of weak understanding, whom, foolish as they are, these men persuade that they will be sure of salvation if they only buy their letters of plenary indulgence. They believe that souls will fly out of purgatory, the moment that the money paid for their redemption is thrown into the preacher's bag, and that such virtue belongs to these indulgences, that there is no sin, howsoever great, even the violation, which is impossible, of the Mother of God, which the indulgences will not absolutely and at once efface.

> " 'Great God! And is it thus that men dare to teach unto death, those who are entrusted to your care, oh reverend father, and make more difficult the account which will be demanded from you in the great day! When I saw these

things I could remain silent no longer. No; there is no episcopal power which can insure to man his salvation; even the
infused grace of our Lord cannot wholly render him secure;
our apostle commands us to wash out our salvation in fear and
trembling: *The righteous scarcely shall be saved,* so narrow
is the way which leads to life. Those who are saved are called
in the Scripture, brands saved from the burning; everywhere
the Lord reminds us of the difficulty of salvation. How,
then, dare these men seek to render poor souls fatally confident of salvation, on the mere strength of purchased indulgences and futile promises? The chiefest work of bishops
should be to take care that the people learn truly the gospel,
and be full of Christian charity. Never did Christ preach
indulgences, nor command them to be preached: what he
preached and commanded to be preached, was the gospel.
. . . I would implore you to silence these ill preachers, ere
some one shall arise, and utterly confuting them and their
preachings, cast discredit upon your sublimity, a thing to be
avoided, but which I fear must needs occur, unless you take
measures for silencing these men. . . . I entreat your grace
to read and consider the propositions, wherein I have demon-
strated the vanity of these indulgences, which the preachers
thereof call all-powerful.'

"To this letter I received no answer, and indeed I knew
not at the time that the archbishop had bargained with the
pope to receive one-half of the money raised from these indulgences, and to remit the other half to Rome. These, then,
were my first steps in the matter, until the increased insolence and the lying representations of Tetzel, which seemed
to be fully sanctioned by the silence of his superiors, as well
as my determination to maintain the truth at all hazards,
induced me to adopt more decisive measures than a mere personal remonstrance, in a series of cautions to those with whom
I was more particularly connected, to beware of these arch
impostors and blasphemers. So finding all my remonstrances
disregarded, on the festival of All Saints, in November, 1517,
I read, in the great church of Wittemberg, a series of propositions against these infamous indulgences, in which, while I
set forth their utter inefficiency and worthlessness, I expressly declared in my protest, that I would submit on all

occasions to the word of God and the decisions of the church. At the same time I was not so presumptuous as to imagine that my opinion would be preferred above all others, nor yet so blind as to set the fables and decrees of man above the written word of God. I took occasion to express these opinions rather as subjects of doubt than of positive assertion, but I held it to be my duty to print and circulate them throughout the country, for the benefit of all classes—for the learned, that they might detect inaccuracies—for the ignorant, that they might be put on their guard against the villainies and impositions of Tetzel, until the matter was properly determined."

These famous propositions were affixed to the outer pillars of the gate of the church of All Saints at midday, on the 31st October, 1517.

"Some copies of my propositions," continues Luther, "having found their way to Frankfort-on-the-Oder, where Tetzel was then acting as inquisitor and selling indulgences under the archbishop-elector of Mayence, he, foaming with rage and alarm at the propositions I had set forth, published a set of counter-resolutions in reply, to the number of one hundred and six, in which he maintained the most insolent and blasphemous doctrines respecting the pretended power and infallibility of the pope; and in a second series of propositions, he assumed the office of general interpreter of the Scripture, and railed against heretics and heresiarchs, by which name he designated myself and my friends, and he concluded his insolence by burning my themes publicly in the city of Frankfort. When the news of this madman's proceedings reached Wittemberg, a number of persons collected together, and having procured Tetzel's productions, retaliated upon him by burning them in the great square, amid the cheers and derision of a large proportion of the inhabitants. I was not sorry that such a mass of absurdity and extravagance should meet with the fate it really merited; but, at the same time, I regretted the manner in which it was done, and solemnly affirm that I knew nothing of it at the time, and that it was done without the knowledge either of the elector or of the magistrates.

"I soon found that Tetzel was not the only opponent

resolved to take the field against me, although I had maintained nothing in my propositions inconsistent with the avowed doctrines of these hirelings; and had, indeed, advanced my propositions more by way of doubt than in a positive manner. John Eck made his appearance in a violent attack upon me: but as his observations were more in the nature of mere abuse than of conclusive argument, that person did a vast deal of harm to his own party, while he rendered me unintentional service. Another antagonist also entered the lists against me, in the person of Silvestro Prierio, a Dominican, who with the pedantry peculiar to his office of censor in the metropolis of popery, chose to answer all my propositions in a way most convenient to himself, by declaring, in a manner altogether begging the question, that they were all heretical. In my reply, I exposed the absurdity of this method of proceeding, which, however, is the usual style of argument adopted by the Romish tyrants and their slaves. Prierio again attacked me; but when I found the man asserting that the authority of the pope was superior to the councils and canons of the church, and that even the sacred Scriptures depended for their interpretation on the mere dictum of that representative of Antichrist, I thought it unnecessary to reply further, than by simply declaring my conviction, that the said Prierio's book, being a compound of blasphemies and lies, must certainly have been the work of the devil; and that if the pope and cardinals sanctioned such writings, which I did not then believe, although I now know it well, Rome must be the seat of Antichrist, the center of abomination, and the synagogue of Satan. Who is Antichrist, if the pope is not Antichrist? O Satan, Satan, how long wilt thou be suffered to abuse the patience of God by thy great wickedness? Unhappy, abandoned, blasphemous Rome! the wrath of God is upon thee, and thou richly deservest it, for thou art the habitation of all that is impure and disgusting! a very pantheon of impiety!

"In this way passed the year 1517, I maintaining the truth, and these apologists for impiety railing against me with their false accusations; for hitherto pope Leo had taken no notice of the matter, not wishing, as I was afterwards informed, to interfere at all, thinking that the zeal of both parties would soon subside. Meantime I began to consider what measures to adopt, for I knew that no reasonings of mine would have any weight with such obstinate and insolent disputants as Tetzel, Eck, and Prierio, bigoted slaves of that system of iniquity and licentiousness which I myself had witnessed when at Rome."

The publication of these theses and the sermon in German, which Luther delivered in support of them, struck upon the whole of Germany like a huge thunderbolt. This sacrifice of liberty to grace, of man to God, of the finite to the infinite, was at once recognized by the German people as the true national religion, as the faith which Gottschalk proclaimed in the time of Charlemagne, from the very cradle of German Christianity, the faith of Tauler and of all the mystical preachers of the Low Countries. The people, accordingly, threw themselves with the most hungry avidity upon this religious pasture, from which they had been shut out ever since the fourteenth century. The propositions were printed in thousands, devoured, spread abroad, diffused in every direction. Luther himself was alarmed at his success. "I am sorry," said he, "to see them so extensively printed and distributed; this is not a good way wherein to set about the instruction of the people. I myself feel some doubts upon points. There are things I should more closely have investigated and ascertained, others which I should have altogether omitted, had I foreseen this result."

And he at this juncture seemed exceedingly disposed to throw up the whole matter, and to submit without further caviling. "I will obey, implicitly," said he; "I had rather so than perform miracles, even though I had the gift of performing miracles."

Tetzel himself shook this pacific resolution by burning, as has been seen, Luther's propositions in public, whereupon the students of Wittemberg forthwith made reprisals upon Tetzel's own propositions. Though this circumstance was one, as Luther has informed us, which he regretted, he followed it up by sending forth his *Resolutions,* in support of his first propositions. "You will see," he wrote to a friend, "my *Resolutiones et responsiones.* Perhaps, in certain passages, you will find them more free than was absolutely necessary;

and if they seem so to you, they will *à fortiori,* appear perfectly intolerable to the flatterers of Rome. They were published before I was aware, or I would have modified them in some respects.''

The report of this controversy spread beyond the confines of Germany, and in due course reached Rome.

''While I was attacked and misrepresented, beloved reader, I knew well the malevolence of Tetzel, Eck, and the rest of them. Nor in this feeling was I mistaken, for I found that everywhere they were assiduously inculcating among the people that I was not only an obstinate heretic, but the enemy of all religion whatever. By disseminating these and other lies, unnecessary for me to mention, they hoped to excite the prejudices of the people against me, and while they carried on their detestable traffic of indulgences, retain the poor souls in the chains of that disgusting and odious despotism under which the pope and his satellites blind and overwhelm their unfortunate and superstitious slaves. So to show the whole world the characters of these men, and how unscrupulous they are in publishing daring lies to serve their own purposes—a common practice in that mystery of iniquity called popedom, of which, I verily believe, the devil is the agent—I wrote to the pope Leo the following most submissive letter, for at that time my eyes were not fully open to the abominations of Rome.

''To the most holy father, Leo X., Martin Luther, of the Augustin order of monks at Wittemberg, wishes eternal salvation.

''I have heard, most holy father, that some most idle charges have been made against me to you, which bring me under your holiness' censure, as though I had contrived a plot to undermine the authority of the church, and the power of the supreme pontiff. I am called a heretic, an apostate, a traitor, and no end of odious names. My ears are shocked, my mind is lost in amazement, at these accusations. One testimony to my upright conduct is with me, however, the testimony of a good and quiet conscience. I do not mention these circumstances as if I had never heard of them before, for the men to whom I refer, who pretend to be most trustworthy and honest, have cast such names upon me in my own country; and, conscious of their falsehood, have imputed to me the most ignominious conduct, that they may justify their own villainies. But you, most holy father, are the best judge of the matter in dispute; you only, impartial and unprejudiced, are worthy to hear it from me.

"At the time that the jubilee of the apostolic indulgences was announced, certain persons, under the sanction of your authority, imagining they might say and do what they pleased, publicly taught the most blasphemous heresies, to the serious scandal and contempt of the church, as if the decretals contained nothing in them condemning the impositions of these extortioners. Not content with the unwarrantable language which they used in propagating their poison, they moreover published little pamphlets, and circulated them among the common people, in which—proving that I say nothing unjust of the insatiable and monstrous imposition of their conduct—they themselves maintained these same blasphemies and heretical doctrines, and so determinedly, that they bound themselves by oath to inculcate them fixedly on the people.

"If these men deny the facts I speak of, their pamphlets are in existence to prove their conduct to have been what I say. They carried on this traffic prosperously, and the poor people were thoroughly deceived by false hopes; as the prophet says, *the very flesh was taken from their bones,* the impostors themselves living meantime in all luxury and gluttony.

"One argument they oftenest put forwards was the authority of your name, threatening summary punishment upon all who differed from them, and branding them as heretics. The language they used is indescribable, nor shall I say how fiercely they resented opposition, and even the merest doubt respecting them. If this mode of propagating error be sanctioned, schisms and seditions cannot fail to appear.

"Soon stories began to get abroad, in the shops and public places, concerning the avarice of these indulgence-hawkers, and prejudicial to the authority of the holy see; this is well known throughout the country. I confess that I myself, for the sake of Christ, as I believed, burned with indignation at the preposterous proceedings of these men, though I did not for a while make up my mind what to do. I privately sent intimations to certain prelates of the church as to what was going on. Some treated me with utter silence, others wrote to me slightingly; the influence of your alleged authority prevailing with them. At last, finding humble remonstrance of no avail, I resolved to challenge these indulgence-sellers to prove their dogmas in disputation with me. I published a list of propositions, inviting only the doctors, if they were so disposed, to discuss with me, as may be seen in the preamble to my propositions.

"And this is partly why they rage so, being furious that I, only a master of theology, should claim to discuss in the public school, though after the custom of all universities and of the whole church, not only concerning indulgences, but also concerning the power of remission of sin, the divine authority of indulgences, and other important matters. Now though I resent their denying me the privilege conceded by your most holy license, 'tis with reluctance I take up the controversy with them, and declare against their proceedings, wherein they mix up the dreams of Aristotle with theology, and set forth silly matters concerning the divine majesty above and beyond the power vested in them. Now what shall I do? I cannot recall that which I have done, and I perceive a determined hatred bursting forth against me. I am publicly discussed, according to the various views people take. By some I am called ignorant, stupid, unlearned, in this most refined and illustrious age, which even, as to learning and the arts, eclipses the age of Cicero. Others call me a paltry imitator. But I am compelled to answer geese in their own language.

"Therefore, that I may mitigate the anger of honest enemies, and satisfy the doubts of many, I forward to your holiness my humble propositions, and I do so, secure in your protection and authority, by which all may understand how entirely and implicitly I reverence and respect the ecclesiastical power and authority, and at the same time how falsely, how infamously, my opponents have maligned me. Were I what they call me, it is not probable the illustrious prince Frederick, duke of Saxony and elector of the empire, a prince devotedly attached to the catholic and apostolic truth, would tolerate such a pest in his own university, nor should I have the support of our own learned and virtuous body. I put forward these things in my favor, knowing they will carefully be suppressed by those who seek unjustly to embitter you against me.

"Wherefore, most holy father, I prostrate myself at the feet of your clemency, with all which I have and am. Bid me live, or slay me, call, recall, approve, disapprove, as it pleases you; I acknowledge in your voice the voice of Christ speaking and presiding in you. If I am worthy of death, I shall not refuse to die; for 'the earth is the Lord's, and the fullness thereof, who is blessed forevermore. Amen.' May he preserve you to all eternity! Trinity Sunday, 1518."

"Protest of the reverend father, Martin Luther, of the
      Augustin order at Wittemberg.

"Because this is a theological disputation, touching which some individuals inclined to peace may peradventure take offense, by reason of the recondite nature of the subject, I protest:

"First, that I have never held or taught anything but what is contained in the sacred Scriptures, in the writings of the fathers of the church, and acknowledged by the Roman church in the canons and pontifical decretals. Yet, if any opinion of mine cannot be refuted or proved by these authorities, I shall hold it for the sake of discussion only, for the exercise of reason, and for the promotion of knowledge and inquiry, always having respect to the judgment of my superiors.

"Further, I venture to challenge, by the law of Christian liberty, what were the acknowledged opinions of St. Thomas, Buonaventure, and the other casuists and schoolmen, without any gloss or interpretation. I am resolved to refute or to admit, as circumstances may render necessary, according to the advice of St. Paul, 'Prove all things: hold fast that which is good.' I know the opinion of certain Thomists, that St. Thomas should be approved in all things from the church, but St. Thomas, at all events, is sufficiently acknowledged for an authority. I have shown enough in what I may be wrong. but I am no heretic, though my enemies roar and rage in their vociferations that I am so."

And Luther here inserts his ninety-five propositions for the pope's perusal, occupying seventy-two folio pages.

"Moreover," proceeds Luther, "I thought it necessary to write to several noble and reverend prelates, in justification of my conduct; and to refute the calumnies of those scandalous monks who were deceiving the people and ensnaring their souls, and more especially to the illustrious prince and most reverend father, Albert, archbishop of Magdeburg, to whom I also sent my disputations."

Rome began to put itself in motion. The master of the ceremonies to the sacred palace, the old Dominican, Sylvestro de Prierio, wrote in support of the doctrine of St. Thomas against the Augustin monk, and drew down upon himself a crushing reply, (towards the end of August, 1518). Luther immediately received orders to appear at Rome within sixty days. The emperor Maximilian had in vain called upon them not to precipitate matters, undertaking himself to do all the pope might order to be done with respect to Luther. But the zeal of Maximilian himself had begun to be somewhat distrusted at Rome. There had reached the holy city certain expressions of his which sounded disagreeably in the ears of the pope.

Luther's main hope was in the protection of the elector. This prince, whether out of the interest he took in his new university, or from a personal attachment to Luther, had always shown him peculiar favor. He had proposed to take upon himself the expenses attending his protégé's obtaining his doctor's degree. In 1517, Luther thanks him, in a letter, for having sent him, at the beginning of winter, cloth to make him a gown. He felt pretty sure, too, that the elector by no means owed him any grudge for getting up an excitement of a nature to annoy the archbishop of Mayence and Magdeburg, a prince of the house of Brandeburg, and consequently an enemy to that of Saxony. Finally, the elector had announced that he recognized no other rule of faith than the words of Scripture themselves; and this afforded Luther a powerful argument for deeming himself secure in that quarter. Luther reminds the elector of this circumstance in the following passage of a letter, dated 27th March, 1519. "Doctor Staupitz, my true father in Christ, has related to me that conversing one day with your electoral highness respecting these preachers who, instead of giving forth the pure word of God, preached to the people nothing but miserable quirks or human traditions, you said to him, that the Holy Scripture speaks with so imposing a majesty, with such completeness of proof, that it has no need of all this adventitious aid of polemics, and that it places in one's mouth, involuntarily, these words: 'Never man spoke thus: this is the finger of God; this teaches not as the scribes and pharisees teach, but as the direct organ and mouthpiece of Almighty Power.' Staupitz approving these words, you went on: 'Give me your hand, and promise me, I entreat, that henceforth you will follow the new doctrine!' "

Yet it would be an entire misconception to understand from the above passages that Staupitz and his disciple were merely the instruments of the elector. The Reformation of Luther was evidently a spontaneous principle of his own. The prince, as we shall have occasion to observe elsewhere, was rather alarmed at the daring of Luther. He embraced, he loved, he profited by the initiated Reformation: he would never himself have commenced it.

Luther had written on the 15th February, 1518, to his prudent friend Spalatin, the chaplain, secretary and confidant of the elector: "Here are bawlers who go about saying, to my infinite vexation, that all this is the work of our illustrious prince, that it is he who has urged me on to it, for the sake of spiting the archbishop of Magdeburg and Mayence. I wish you maturely to consider whether or no it is desirable to mention the matter to his highness. I am truly afflicted to see him suspected on my account. To be a cause of discord between such mighty lords, is an awful thing." He holds the same language to the elector himself, in his account of the conference at Augsburg. On the 21st March, writing to M. Lange, afterwards archbishop of Saltzburg, he says: "Our prince has taken Carlstadt and myself under his protection, and without any solicitation on our part. He will not permit them to drag me to Rome. This they know, and it is this vexes them so;" which would obviously lead us to suppose that Luther had already received from the elector definite promises. Yet, on the 21st August, 1518, in a letter, still more confidential, to Spalatin, he says: "I do not at all see at present how I can escape the censures with which I am threatened, if the prince does not come forward to my succor, though I would rather undergo the censure of the whole world, than have his highness blamed for my sake. This, therefore, is the course which it appears to our learned friends best for me to pursue, that I should demand of the prince a safe-conduct (salvum, ut vocant, conductum, per meum dominum). He will refuse it me, I am certain, and I shall then, say our friends, have a valid excuse for not appearing at Rome. I would ask you, then, to obtain from our illustrious prince, a rescript setting forth that he refuses me the safe-conduct, and makes me responsible, if I persist in setting out, for all the dangers I may incur. By so doing, you will render me an important service. But the thing must be done at once: time presses, the assigned day is near at hand."

Luther might have saved himself this letter. The prince, without having communicated with him on the point, had been taking measures for his security. He had managed that Luther should be examined by a legate in Germany, in the free town of Augsburg; where he himself was at this time, and where he had doubtless come to an understanding with the magistrates to guarantee the safety of Luther during the dangerous conference. It was, we may be pretty sure, to this invisible Providence hovering over Luther, that we are to assign the almost painful anxiety evinced by these magistrates to preserve the reformer from the snares that might be laid for him by the Italians. As to him, he went straightforward on, strong in courage and in simple faith, quite uncertain to what extent the prince was disposed to act in his favor.

"I have said, and I repeat it, I would not in this business have our prince, who is throughout blameless, take the least step towards defending my propositions. If he can do it without compromising himself, let him guard me against actual violence; but if he cannot safely do this, I am ready to meet the utmost peril that may threaten me."

"In the year 1518, the 9th of October," says Luther, "when I was cited to Augsburg, I came and appeared: Frederick, prince-elector of Saxony, having appointed me a strong con-

voy and safe-conduct; and recommended me to the people of
the city, who were very attentive, and warned me in no case
to have conversation with the Italians, nor to repose any trust
or confidence in them, for I knew not, they said, what sort
of wretches they were. I was three whole days in Augsburg
without the emperor's safe-conduct. In the meantime, an
Italian [Urban di Serra Longa] came to me, invited me to
go to the cardinal, and earnestly persuaded me to recant.
I should (said he) need to speak but only one word before
the cardinal, *Revoco;* and then the cardinal would recommend me to the pope's favor, so that with honor I might
return safely again to my master, the prince-elector. He
quoted several examples, among others, that of the famous
Joachim de Flores, who had submitted, and was consequently
no heretic, though he had advanced heretical propositions.
When he urged me no longer to delay waiting on the cardinal,
I replied that certain excellent individuals to whom I had
been recommended by the elector Frederick, had urged me
first to procure the emperor's safe-conduct. Thereupon he
replied, with much warmth: 'What! do you think the elector
will take up arms on your account?' 'I should be unwilling,'
said I, 'to be the occasion of such an extremity.' 'But if
you had the pope and cardinals in your power,' returned he,
'what would you do with them?' 'I would show them all
reverence and honor,' I replied. He paused, snapped his
fingers after the Italian manner, and cried *Hem!* after which
he departed, and I saw him no more.

"At the expiration of three days, the bishop of Trent
came, who, in the emperor's name, showed and declared to
the cardinal my safe-conduct. Then I went unto him in
all humility, fell down first upon my knees, then prostrate
upon the ground, where I remained at his feet, till after the
cardinal had three times bade me rise; thereupon I stood up.
This pleased him well, hoping I would consider, and better
bethink myself.

"The next day, when I came before him again, and would
absolutely revoke nothing at all, he said to me, 'What!
thinkest thou the pope cares much for Germany? his little
finger is more powerful than all Germany. Or dost thou
think the princes will raise arms and armies to defend thee?

Oh, no! where, then, wilt thou remain in safety?' I replied,
'Under heaven.'

"After this the pope lowered his tone, and wrote to our
church, even to the prince-elector's chaplain, and to one
of his counselors, Pfeffinger, that they would surrender me
into his hands, and procure that his commands might be
put in execution. And the pope wrote also to the prince-
elector himself as thus:

"'Although, as touching thy person, thou art to me unknown, yet I have seen thy father (prince Ernest) at Rome,
who was altogether an obedient son to the church; he visited
and frequented our religion with great devotion, and held
the same in highest honor. I wish that thy illustrious seren-
ity would tread in his footsteps,' &c.

"But the prince-elector well marked the pope's unaccustomed humility, and his evil conscience; he was also acquainted with the power and operation of the holy Scriptures.
Therefore he remained where he was, and merely returned
thanks to the pope for his affection towards him.

"My books and resolutions in a short time went, or rather
flew throughout Europe, therefore the prince-elector was
confirmed and strengthened, insomuch that he utterly refused to execute the pope's commands, and subjected himself
fully to the acknowledgment of the Scriptures.

"If the cardinal had handled me with more discretion at
Augsburg, and had received me when I fell at his feet, things
would never have come thus far; for at that time I saw very
few of the pope's errors which now I see; had he been silent,
so had I held my peace. It was at that time the style and
custom of the Romish court, in dark and confused cases, for
the pope to say: *We, by virtue of our papal power, do take
these causes unto us, we annul them and destroy them;* and
the parties had nothing left for it but to weep.

"I am persuaded that the pope willingly would give three
cardinals to have the matter where it was, before he began to
meddle with me."

Let us add some other details from a letter of Luther's to
Spalatin, that is to say, to the elector. It is dated the 14th
of October.

"On the day I was first admitted to an audience, I was

received by the most reverend cardinal legate, not only with kindness but with marked deference and respect; for he is a very different man from some of the more violent of his brethren. He had no inclination, he said, to debate with me, but he mildly and feelingly proposed to compromise the matter, by submitting to me three conditions sanctioned by the pope:—1. That I should alter my opinions, and retract my erroneous propositions; 2. That I should engage to abstain from propagating such doctrines in future; and, 3. That I should not circulate any opinions opposed to the authority of the church. I immediately desired to be informed in what respect I had erred, as I was not conscious of inculcating any error, for that the opinions I had set forth at Wittemberg had occasioned me no trouble or opposition there, and I was not aware I had changed any of my sentiments since I had arrived in Augsburg. This went on for four days, the prelate still refusing to have any controversy with me publicly or privately; all he did was to repeat, over and over and over again, 'Retract!—acknowledge thy error, whether thou believest it an error or not. The pope commands thee to do this.' At length, he was induced to consent that I might explain myself in writing, which I accordingly did, in presence of the seigneur de Feilitzch, the elector's representative. But when I had done, the legate refused to receive what I had written, and renewed his cry of *Retract! retract!* Next he hurled out some long harangue' or other in the romance of St. Thomas, with which he fancied he would utterly crush me, and reduce me to silence. Ten times did I essay to speak, and ten times did he stop me short; raging and tyrannizing over me throughout the whole affair. At last he referred me to the Extravagant of pope Clement VI., entitled *Unigenitus,* and objected on the strength of it to my 58th proposition: 'That the merits of Christ were not the treasure of the *indulgences.*' He strenuously urged me to retract the proposition, and he paused for a little, in confidence of my submission, for he flattered himself, nay seemed almost certain, that I was ignorant of the Extravagant referred to, and he was the more confident about this, in that it is not inserted in all the collections.

"I then, in my turn, took to raising my voice somewhat.

'Come,' said I, 'if you can show me that your decretal of Clement VI. says expressly that the merits of Christ *are* the treasure of the indulgences, I retract.' Lord, what a laugh there was at this! The legate snatched the book, and ran over the pages in breathless haste, till he came to the place where it is written that 'Christ by his passion *acquired* the treasures,' &c. I stopped him at the word 'acquired.'

"By and by, upon my asserting that the pope had no power except *salvâ Scriptura,* the cardinal laughed, and said: 'Do you not know that the pope is above all councils? Has he not recently condemned and punished the council of Bâle?' 'Yes,' I replied; 'but the university of Paris has appealed from his decision.' The cardinal: 'The university of Paris will be punished too.' After a while, I spoke of Gerson. The cardinal said: 'What are the Gersonists to me?' I asked him, who the Gersonists were? 'Bah!' said he; 'let's speak no more about them,' and so he turned the conversation to something else.

"After dinner, the legate sent for the reverend father Staupitz, and endeavored to cajole him into bringing me to a retractation, adding, that I should have a difficulty in finding any one who had a more friendly feeling towards me than he had."

The disputants pursued courses diametrically opposed the one to the other: conciliation was impossible. The friends of Luther feared a snare for him on the part of the Italians: he accordingly quitted Augsburg, leaving behind him an *Appeal to the Pope better informed,* and at the same time addressed a long narrative of the conference to the elector. In it he entreats that prince not to deliver him up to the pope: "I call upon your illustrious highness to follow the dictates of honor and conscience, and not to send me to the pope. The legate certainly has not in his instructions any guarantee for my security at Rome. For them to demand of you to send me thither, is to ask you to spill Christian blood, to become a homicide. To Rome! why the pope himself does not live in security there! They have plenty of pens and ink in the Eternal City, plenty of scribes, scribes innumerable. They can easily put down in writing what my errors are. It will cost them less money to draw up an indictment against me absent, than to have me to Rome, and destroy me there by treachery.

"What affects me most especially is, that my lord the legate speaks ill of your electoral grace, as though it were upon you that I relied in undertaking all these things. There are even liars, who go about saying that it was your grace's exhortation that induced me to commence discussing the question of indulgences; whereas, in point of fact, even among my dearest friends, there was no one who knew beforehand of my intention, except the archbishop of Magdeburg, and the bishop of Mayence."

His fears were well grounded; the court of Rome was at the time making direct application to the elector of Saxony. It insisted upon having Luther at any rate. The legate had already complained bitterly to Frederic of the audacity of Luther, entreating him either to send him back to Augsburg, or to expel him from his dominions, if he did not desire to sully his glory and that of his ancestors, by protecting this miserable monk. "I heard yesterday, at Nuremberg, that Charles von Miltitz is on his way, armed (as I am assured from an eye-witness worthy of implicit credit) with no fewer than three briefs from the pope, to take me bodily and deliver me over to the pontiff. But I have appealed from him and his briefs to the future council." It was, indeed, necessary for him thus to repudiate the pope, for, as the legate had communicated to Frederic, Luther was already condemned at Rome. He, however, put forth this new protest, with all the regular forms, declared he would submit readily to the judgment of the pope, well informed of the whole matter, but that the pope was fallible, as St. Peter himself had been fallible; and he therefore appealed to a general council, superior to the pope, with respect to all that the pope might decree against him. Meantime, he feared some sudden violence; he might perhaps be carried off from Wittemberg. "They have misled you," he writes to Spalatin: "I have not bid farewell to the people of Wittemberg. All that I said to them was this: You every one know that I am a preacher, somewhat given to moving about from place to place. How many times have I quitted you abruptly, without saying farewell. Should the same thing happen again, and

I should not return, you must assume that I have bid you adieu beforehand.''

On the 2nd December he writes: ''I am advised to request the prince to shut me up, as though I were a prisoner, in some castle, and then that he should write to the legate, that he holds me in sure custody, where I shall be compelled to answer all that the pope may put to me.

''There cannot be a moment's doubt that the prince and the university are for me. I have had related to me a conversation that passed on the subject at the court of the bishop of Brandenburg. Some one observed that Erasmus, Fabricius, and other learned personages supported Luther. 'The pope would not humble himself much for that,' replied the bishop, 'if it were not that the university of Wittemberg and the elector are also on his side.' '' Still Luther passed the autumn of 1518 in constant alarm. He even thought of quitting Germany. ''In order not to involve your highness in any danger, I will leave your territory; I will go whither the mercy of God shall lead me, confiding myself, in all things, to his divine will. I therefore now humbly offer my respects to your highness. Among whatsoever people I may retire I shall preserve an eternal recollection, an undying gratitude for all the good you have done me,'' (19 November). Saxony, in truth, might well appear to Luther a somewhat insecure retreat. The pope was seeking to gain over the elector. Charles von Miltitz, a Saxon nobleman, canon of Mayence, named by Leo his agent in the matter, was commissioned to offer him the consecrated Golden Rose, a distinction which the court of Rome seldom accorded to other than kings, as a recompense for peculiar filial piety towards the church. This was putting the elector to a severe trial. It became necessary for him to make a definite explanation, one way or the other, and thus perhaps to involve himself in very considerable danger. The elector's hesitation on this occasion appears from a letter of Luther: ''The prince at first altogether dissuaded me from publishing the proceedings of the conference of Augsburg; then he permitted me to publish them, and they are at this moment being printed. In his anxiety for me he would prefer I were anywhere else. He sent for me to Lichtenberg, where I had a long conversation with Spalatin on the subject; 'If the censures come,' I said, 'I will remain not a day longer.' He told me, however, not to be premature in setting out for France.''

This was written on the 13th December. On the 20th, Luther was quite re-assured. The elector had replied to the pope, with truly diplomatic coolness, that he acknowledged himself an obedient son of holy mother church; that he entertained very great respect for his pontifical holiness, but that he wished the affair to be examined by judges not liable to suspicion. This was an infallible means of delaying the business, and, meantime, some circumstance or other might arise to lessen, or, at all events, put off the danger. The great point was to gain time: and the expectation was fulfilled. In January, 1519, the emperor died; and during the interregnum which followed, Frederic, by the express choice of Maximilian, acted as regent of the empire.

On the 3rd March, 1519, Luther, thus restored to confidence, wrote to the pope a letter, high in its spirit, though respectful in its form. It ran thus:

"Most holy father, necessity once more compels me, refuse of society and dust of the earth that I am, to address your exalted majesty; and I implore your holiness to listen to the bleatings of the poor lamb that now approaches you.

"Charles von Miltitz, private chancellor to your holiness, a just and worthy man, has, in your name, accused me to the illustrious prince Frederic of presumption, of irreverence towards the Roman church, and demanded, in your name, satisfaction; and I have been filled with grief at the misfortune of being suspected of disrespect towards the column of the church—I, who have never had any other wish than to assert and defend its honor.

"What am I to do, holy father? I have none to counsel me, on the one hand; on the other, I dare not expose myself to the effects of your resentment. Yet how avoid them? I know not. Retract, you say. Were the retractation demanded from me possible, it should be made. Thanks to my adversaries, to their fierce resistance, and to their rabid hostility, my writings have spread abroad far more widely than I had anticipated; my doctrines have penetrated too deeply into men's hearts for them now to be effaced. Ger-

many is at this time flourishing in men of learning, of judgment, of genius: if I desire to do honor to the Roman
church, it will be by revoking nothing. A retractation
would only injure her in the estimation of the people, and
expose her to ill representations.

"They whom I oppose, most holy father, are the men who
have really injured and disgraced the holy Roman church;
those adorers of filthy lucre, who have gone about, in your
name, involving the very name of repentance in discredit and
opprobrium, and seeking to throw the whole weight of their
iniquities upon me, the man who struggled against their
monstrosities.

"Ah, holy father, before God, before the whole creation,
I affirm that I have never once had it in my thought to
weaken or shake the authority of the holy see. I fully
admit that the power of the Roman church is superior to all
things under God; neither in heaven nor on earth is there
aught above it, our Lord Jesus excepted. Let no credit be
given by your holiness to any who seek to represent Luther
to you in any other light.

"As to indulgences, I promise your holiness to occupy
myself no further with them, to keep silence respecting them
for the future, provided my adversaries, on their side, remain
silent; to recommend the people, in my sermons, to love
Rome, and not to impute to her the faults of others; not to
give implicit faith to all the severe things I have abusively
said of her, in the excitement of combating these mounte-
banks; so that, by God's help, these dissensions may, in brief
time, be appeased; for my whole desire has been, that the
Roman church, our common mother, should not be dishon-
ored by the base lies and jargon of these lucre-hunters, and
that men should learn to prefer charity to indulgences."

Luther had formed his determination. Already, a month
or two previously, he had written: "The pope has not
chosen to allow me a just judge, and I will not admit the
judgment of the pope. He then will be the text, and I the
commentary."

Whatever progress Luther might make in violence, the
pope had thenceforward but very little chance of wresting
from a powerful prince, to whom the majority of electors had

delegated the empire, that prince's favorite theologian. Miltitz accordingly modified his tone.

On the arrival of Miltitz in Germany, Luther had said he would hold his peace, provided his opponents did the same; but they themselves released him from his engagement.

Meantime, the principal adversary of Luther, Dr. Eck, had proceeded to Rome, to solicit the condemnation of the reformer, and Luther was judged and sentenced beforehand. All that was left to him to do, was to judge his judge, and repudiate his authority in the face of the world, and this he accordingly did in his terrible book On the Captivity of Babylon, wherein he maintained that the church was captive, that Jesus Christ, constantly profaned in the idolatry of the mass, set aside in the dogma of transubstantiation, was the pope's prisoner.

He explains in the preface, with daring freedom, the manner in which he found himself daily driven more and more to extremities by the conduct of his adversaries: "Whether I will or no, I become each day more learned and expert, driven about as I am, and kept in active exercise by so many antagonists at once. I wrote on the indulgences two years ago, but in a way that makes me repent I sent forth what I had written to the public. At that time I was still prodigiously attached to the papal power, so that I dared not, altogether reject the indulgences. I saw them, moreover, sanctioned by great numbers of intelligent persons—in fact, I was left to roll the great stone by myself. But since then, thanks to Sylvestro and the other brothers who so warmly defended them, I have found that they were nothing more than mere impostures invented by the flatterers of Rome, to ruin men's faith and their pockets. Would to God I could induce the booksellers, and all those who have my writings on the indulgences, to put them into the fire, and replace them by this single proposition:—*Indulgences are delusive trash, invented by the parasites of Rome.*

"After that, Eck, Emser, and their gang came to tackle me on the question of the pope's supremacy. I am bound to admit, in gratitude towards these learned personages, that the trouble they took in this matter was not without its effect, and that a considerable effect, on my advancement. Previously,

I merely denied that popery was founded on right divine, admitting that it had human right on its side. But, after having heard and read the ultra-subtle subtleties on which these poor people found the rights of their idols, I have arrived at a sounder conclusion, and am convinced that the reign of the pope is that of Babylon, and of *Nimrod the mighty hunter.* And so I request all booksellers and readers (that nothing may be wanting to the success of my good friends) to burn, also, whatever I have written hitherto on this matter, and to stick to this simple proposition: *the pope is the mighty hunter, the hunter of Roman episcopacy.*

At the same time, in order that it might be clearly understood that he was attacking popery rather than the pope, he wrote a long letter, both in German and in Latin, to Leo X., wherein he repudiated any personal ill will to himself.

When the bull of condemnation arrived in Germany, it found a whole nation in a state of ebullition. At Erfurt, the students took it from the booksellers' shops, tore it in pieces, and threw it into the water, saying, with more vehemence than point—"It is a bull; let us see if it can swim." Luther at once sent forth a pamphlet, *Against the execrable Bull of Antichrist.* On the 10th December, 1520, he publicly burnt the Pope's anathema at the gates of the town, amid the exulting shouts of the people; and on the same day wrote to Spalatin, his ordinary medium of communication with the Elector: "This day, the tenth of December, in the year 1520, at nine o'clock in the morning, were burnt at Wittemberg, at the east gate, opposite the church of the Holy Cross, all the pope's books, the rescripts, the decretals of Clement VI., the extravagants, the new bull of Leo X., the *Somma Angelica,* the *Chrysopasus* of Eck, and some other productions of his, and of Emser's. This is something new, I wot." He adds, in the report he drew up on the subject: "if any one asks me why I act thus, I will answer him, that it is an old custom to burn bad books. The apostles burned books to the value of five thousand deniers."

According to the tradition, he said, on throwing the book of the decretals into the flames—"Thou hast afflicted the holy of the Lord: may eternal fire afflict thee, and consume thee."

He writes, on the 29th November, to the Augustines of Wittemberg—"I feel more and more every day, how difficult it is to lay aside the scruples which one has had so long within one. Oh, how much pain it has cost me, though I had the Scripture on my side, to justify it to myself that I should dare to make a stand alone against the pope, and hold him forth as antichrist. What have the tribulations of my heart not been! How many times have I not asked myself with bitterness the same question which the papists put to me— *Art thou alone wise?* Can everybody else be so mistaken? Can so many ages have been mistaken? How will it be, if, after all, thou thyself it is who art wrong, and art thus involving in thy error so many souls, who will then be eternally damned? 'Twas so I fought with myself, till Jesus Christ, by his own infallible word, fortified my heart against these doubts, till it became as a coast of rocks, defying the waves which impotently dash against it."

The excitement was immense. The nobles and the people, the castles and the free towns, rivaled each other in zeal and enthusiasm for Luther. At Nuremberg, at Strasburg, even at Mayence, there was a constant struggle for his least pamphlets. The sheet, yet wet, was brought from the press under some one's cloak, and passed from shop to shop. The pedantic bookmen of the German trades' unions, the poetical tinmen, the literary shoemakers, devoured the good news. Worthy Hans Sachs raised himself above his wonted commonplace; he left his shoe half made, and wrote his most high-flown verses, his best productions. He sang, in under tones, *The Nightingale of Wittemberg,* and the song was taken up, and resounded all over the land.

Luther's principal friends among the nobility were Silvester Von Schauenberg, Franz Von Sickengen, Taubenheim, and Ulrich Von Hutten. Schauenberg had confided the education of his young son to Melancthon, and offered to assist the elector of Saxony with troops, in the event of his becoming involved in any danger from his advocacy of the cause of the Reformation. Taubenheim and others sent money to Luther. "I have received," he says, "a hundred gold pieces, sent me by Taubenheim; Schart has given me fifty more; and I begin to fear lest God should pay me here, instead of hereafter;

but I have already protested, that I must not be thus gorged with money, or I should be fain to throw it all up again.'' The Margrave of Brandenburg had solicited to see him, as a great favor; Sickengen and Hutten promised him their active aid against all and any assailants. ''Hutten,'' says he, ''in September, 1520, sent me a letter, burning with indignation against the Roman pontiff; he wrote me that he was about to fall with pen and with sword upon sacerdotal tyranny; that he was furious at the pope's having tried to use the poniard and poison against him, and had written to the bishop of Mayence, that he would send him, bound hand and foot, to Rome. You see,'' adds Luther, ''what Hutten would have; but I would never consent to aid God's cause by aid of violence and murder, and so I wrote him word.''

Meantime, the emperor had summoned Luther to appear at Worms, before the imperial diet; and the two parties were now about to meet face to face.

We are indebted to Luther himself for a fine narrative of what took place at the diet—a narrative in all essential points conformable with that which has been given of it by his enemies:—

''The herald summoned me on the Tuesday in Holy Week, and brought me safe-conducts from the emperor, and from several princes. On the very next day, Wednesday, these safe conducts were, in effect, violated at Worms, where they condemned and burned my writings. Intelligence of this reached me when I was at Worms. The condemnation, in fact, was already published in every town, so that the herald himself asked me whether I still intended to repair to Worms.

''Though, in truth, I was physically fearful and trembling, I replied to him—'I will repair thither, though I should find there as many devils as there are tiles on the house tops.' When I arrived at Oppenheim, near Worms, Master Bucer came to see me, and tried to dissuade me from entering the city. He told me that Glapion, the emperor's confessor had been to him, and had entreated him to warn me not to go to Worms; for that if I did, I should be burned. I should do well, he added, to stop in the neighborhood, at Franz Von Sickengen's, who would be very glad to entertain me.

''The wretches did this for the purpose of preventing me

from making my appearance within the time prescribed; they knew that if I delayed only three more days, my safe-conduct would have been no longer available, and then they would have shut the gates in my face, and, without hearing what I had to say, have arbitrarily condemned me. I went on, then, in the purity of my heart, and on coming within sight of the city, at once sent forward word to Spalatin that I had arrived, and desired to know where I was to lodge. All were astonished at hearing of my near approach; for it had been generally imagined that, a victim to the trick sought to be practiced on me, my terrors would have kept me away.

"Two nobles, the seigneur Von Hirschfeldt and John Schott, came to me by order of the elector, and took me to the house in which they were staying. No prince came at the time to see me, but several counts and other nobles did, who gazed at me fixedly. These were they who had presented to his majesty the four hundred articles against ecclesiastical abuses, praying that they might be reformed, and intimating that they would take the remedy into their own hands if need were. They had all been entirely freed by my gospel!

"The pope had written to the emperor desiring him not to observe the safe-conduct. The bishops urged his majesty to comply with the pope's request, but the prince and the states would not listen to it; for such conduct would have excited a great disturbance. All this brought me still more prominently into general notice, and my enemies might well have been more afraid of me than I was of them. The landgrave of Hesse, still a young man at that time, desired to have a conference with me, came to my lodgings, and after a long interview said, on going away: 'Dear doctor, if you be in the right, as I think you are, God will aid you.'

"On my arrival, I had written to Glapion, the emperor's confessor, entreating him to come and see me at his first leisure; but he refused, saying it would be useless for him to do so.

"I was then cited, and appeared before the whole council of the imperial diet in the town hall, where the emperor, the electors, and the princes, were assembled. Dr. Eck, official of the archbishop of Treves, opened the business by saying to me, first in Latin, and then in German:

"'Martin Luther, his sacred and invincible majesty, with the advice of the states of the empire, has summoned you hither, that you may reply to the two questions I am now about to put to you: do you acknowledge yourself the author of the writings published in your name, and which are here before me, and will you consent to retract certain of the doctrines which are therein inculcated?' 'I think the books are mine,' replied I. But immediately, Dr. Jerome Schurff added: 'Let the titles of the works be read.' When they had read the titles, I said: 'Yes, the books are mine.'

"Then he asked me: 'Will you retract the doctrines therein?' I replied: 'Gracious emperor,—as to the question whether I will retract the opinions I have given forth, a question of faith in which are directly interested my own eternal salvation, and the free enunciation of the Divine Word—that word which knows no master either on earth or in heaven, and which we are all bound to adore, be we as great as we may—it would be rash and dangerous for me to reply to such a question, until I had meditated thereupon in silence and retreat, lest I incur the anger of our Lord and Savior Jesus Christ, who has said, *He who shall deny me before men, I will deny him before my Father which is in heaven.* I therefore entreat your sacred majesty to grant me the time necessary to enable me to reply with full knowledge of the point at issue, and without fear of blaspheming the word of God, or endangering the salvation of my own soul.' They gave me till the next day at the same hour.

"The following morning I was sent for by the bishops and others who were directed to confer with me, and endeavor to induce me to retract. I said to them: 'The Word of God is not my word: I therefore cannot abandon it. But in all things short of that, I am ready to be docile and obedient.' The margrave Joachim then interposed, and said: 'Sir doctor, as I understand it, your desire is to listen to counsel and to instruction on all points that do not trench upon the Word?' 'Yes,' I replied, 'that is my desire.'

"Then they told me that I ought to place myself entirely in the hands of his majesty, but I said, I could not consent to this. They asked me, whether they were not themselves Christians, and entitled to have a voice in deciding the questions between us, as well as I? Whereunto I answered, 'That I was ready to accept their opinions in all points which did not offend against the Word, but that from the Word I would not depart,' repeating, that as it was not my own I could not abandon it. They insisted that I ought to rely upon them, and have full confidence that they would decide rightly. 'I am not,' rejoined I, 'by any means disposed to place my trust in men who have already condemned me without a hearing, although under safe-conduct. But to show you my zeal and sincerity, I tell you what I will do; act with me as you please; I consent to renounce my safe-conduct, and to place it unreservedly in your hands.' At this my lord Frederic de Feilitsch observed, 'Truly this is saying quite enough, or indeed, too much.'

"By and by they said: 'Will you, at all events, abandon some of the articles?' I replied: 'In the name of God I will not defend for a moment any articles that are opposed to the Scripture.' Hereupon two bishops slipped out, and went and told the emperor I was retracting. At this a message came to me, asking whether I really consented to place myself in the hands of the emperor and of the diet? I answered: that I had consented to nothing of the sort, and should never consent to it. So I went on, resisting, alone, the attempts of them all, for Dr. Schurff and my other friends had become angry with me for my obstinacy, as they called it. Some of my disputants said to me, that if I would come over to them, they would in return, give up to me and abandon the articles which had been condemned at the council of Constance. To all which I simply replied: 'Here is my body, here my life: do with them as you will.'

"Then Cochlæus came up to me, and said: 'Martin, if thou wilt renounce the safe-conduct, I will dispute with thee.' I, in my simplicity and good faith, would have consented to this, but Dr. Jerome Schurff replied, with an ironical laugh: 'Aye, truly, that were a good idea—that were a fair bargain, i'faith; you must needs think the doctor a fool.' So I refused to give up the safe-conduct. Several worthy friends of mine, who were present, had already, at the bare mention of the proposition, advanced towards me, as if to protect me, exclaiming to Cochlæus: 'What, you would carry him off a prisoner, then! That shall not be.'

"Meantime, there came a doctor of the retinue of the margrave of Baden, who essayed to move me by fine flourishes: I ought, he said, to do a very great deal, to grant a very great deal, for the love of charity, that peace and union might continue, and no tumult arise.' All, he urged, were called upon to obey his imperial majesty, as being the supreme authority; we ought all to avoid creating unseemly disturbances, and therefore, he concluded, I ought to retract. 'I will,' replied I, 'with all my heart, in the name of charity, do all things, and obey in all things, which are not opposed to the faith and honor of Christ.'

"Then the chancellor of Treves said to me: 'Martin, thou art disobedient to his imperial majesty; wherefore depart hence, under the safe-conduct which has been given thee.' I answered: 'It has been as it pleased the Lord it should be. And you,' I added, 'do all of you, on your part, consider well the position in which you are.' And so I departed, in singleness of heart, without remarking or comprehending their machinations.

"Soon afterwards they put in force their cruel edict—that ban, which gave all ill men an opportunity of taking vengeance with impunity on their personal enemies, under the pretext of their being Lutheran heretics; and yet, in the end, the tyrants found themselves under the necessity of recalling what they had done.

"And this is what happened to me at Worms, where I had no other aid than the Holy Spirit."

Soon after this, the official sent for Luther, and in the presence of the arch-chancellor, read to him the imperial sentence.

"Luther," he added, "since you have not chosen to listen to the counsels of his majesty and of the states of the empire, and to confess your errors, it is now for the emperor to act. By his order, I give you twenty days, wherein to return to Wittemberg, secure under the imperial safe-conduct, provided that on your way you excite no disorders by preaching or otherwise."

As the official concluded, Sturm, the herald, inclined his staff, in token of respect.

Luther bowed, and said: "Be it as the Lord pleases; blessed be the name of the Lord." He added the expression of his warm gratitude towards the emperor personally, and towards his ministers, and the states of the empire, for whom, he affirmed, with his hand on his heart, he was ready to sacrifice life, honor, reputation—all, except the word of God.

Next day, 26th April, after a collation given him by his friends, the doctor resumed the route to Wittemberg.

On his arrival at Freyburg, Luther wrote two letters, one to the emperor, the other to the electors and states assembled at Worms. In the first, he expresses his regret at having found himself under the necessity of disobeying his majesty: "But," says he, "God and his word are above man." He laments, further, that he had not been able to obtain a discussion of the evidences he had collected from Scripture, adding that he was ready to present himself before any other assembly that might be convened for the purpose, and to submit himself in all things without exception, provided the word of God received no detriment. The letter to the electors and states is written in the same spirit.

To Spalatin (in a letter, dated 14th May) he says: "You would hardly believe the civility with which I was received by the abbot of Hirschfeldt. He sent forward his chancellor and his treasurer a full mile on the road to meet us, and he himself came to receive us at a short distance from his castle, attended by a troop of cavaliers, who escorted us into the town. The senate received us at the great gate. The abbot entertained us splendidly in his monastery, and assigned me his own bed to sleep in. On the fifth day, they absolutely forced me to preach in the morning, though I represented to them that they ran a risk of losing their privileges, should the imperialist party choose to treat this as a violation of my undertaking not to preach up my doctrines on the way. But then, I added, that I had never pledged myself to chain up the word of God; nor will I.

"I preached also at Eisenach, in presence of the minister, who was in a great fright, and of a notary and his witnesses, who formally protested against what I was doing, but excused themselves privately to me on the ground that, otherwise they dreaded the resentment of their tyrants. So, very likely, you will hear it said at Worms, that I have broken my faith; but I have not broken it. To chain up the word of God is a condition it is not in my power to enter into.

"Our friends met us on foot a little way out of Eisenach, and accompanied us into the town, in the evening. Our companions had set out in the morning with Jerome.

"As to myself, I was proceeding to rejoin my relations through the forest, and was on my way to Walterhausen, when near the fortress of Altenstein, I was taken prisoner. Amsdorf no doubt knew that it was arranged to seize me, but he is not aware to what place they carried me.

"My brother, who saw the horsemen coming up, jumped out of the carriage, and, without saying a word, ran off through the wood, and, as I am told, reached Walterhausen in the evening. As for me, the horsemen took off my robe, and put me on a military garb, desiring me to let my hair and beard grow, and meanwhile put me on a false beard. You would scarcely recognize me; indeed, I hardly knew myself. However, here I am, living *in libertate Christianâ*, free from the chains of the tyrants."

When taken to the castle of Wartburg, Luther was not at all certain to whom it was he owed the pleasant and honorable captivity in which he found himself. He had sent away the imperial herald as soon as they had got a few leagues from Worms, and his enemies have thence concluded that he was aware of the contemplated proceedings; but it fully appears, from his own correspondence, that he was not. Meantime a cry of grief arose throughout Germany. It was believed that he had perished, and the pope and the emperor were accused of his death. In reality, it was the elector of Saxony, Luther's patron, who, alarmed at the imperial sentence fulminated against the reformer, and at once incapable of openly supporting him against his enemies, or of allowing him to fall their victim, had conceived this mode of saving him from the effects of his own daring, and to gain time wherein to strengthen the party. To conceal Luther for awhile was a sure means of augmenting the public excitement in Germany, by arousing its fears for the champion of the reformed faith.

III

1521-1524

WHILST in Worms the Roman party was furious at having allowed the audacious innovator to escape, he himself was securely looking down upon his enemies from the platform of the donjon of Wartburg. In that quiet retreat, he was at full leisure to resume his flute, to sing his German psalms, to translate his Bible, and to thunder forth against the pope and the devil.

"The rumor has gone abroad," writes Luther, "that it was friends from Franconia who took me prisoner." And elsewhere: "They imagined, as I suspect, that Luther had been killed, or condemned to eternal silence, in order that the common weal might once more fall powerless beneath the weight of sophistical tyranny, the downfall of which its abettors so hated me for having commenced." He took care, however, to let his friends know that he was still alive. He writes to Spalatin (June, 1521): "I would not for the world have the letter I now send you fall by any negligence of your own, or of those about you, into the hands of our enemies. . . . I wish you to get the portion of Gospel I send you herewith, copied by some careful person; it is essential that my hand should not be seen in the matter just at present."—"I had fully intended in this, my solitude, to dedicate to my host, a book on the Traditions of Men, for he has asked me to give him some information on that subject; but I have not done so, least I should thereby disclose the place of my retreat."—"It is with great difficulty I have obtained permission to send you this letter, so fearful are they of its becoming known where I am."

"The priests and the monks, who played their gambols while I was at liberty, have become so afraid since my captivity, that they themselves are beginning to modify the preposterous extravangances they were wont to send forth against me. They find they can no longer resist the pressure of the increasing crowd of questioners, and they know not in what direction to make their escape. See you not herein the arm

of the Mighty One of Jacob, all that he is doing for us, while
we hold our peace, while we stand aside, while we pray to
him. Is not this a fulfillment of the sayings of Moses: *The
Lord shall fight for you, and you shall hold your peace.*
One of the fellows at Rome, has written to a Mayence hoo-
poe: 'Luther is quashed just as we wished; but the people
are so excited about him, that I fear we shall run a chance
of losing our lives, if we do not go in search of him, candle
in hand, and bring him back.' "

Luther dates his letters: *from the region of the air; from
the region of birds; or, from amidst the birds which sing
sweetly on the branches of the tall trees, and praise God,
night and day, with all their might;* or, again, *from the
mountains; from the Isle of Patmos.*

On his arrival at Wartburg, Luther had found very few
books there. He applied himself with ardor, as soon as he
had obtained the requisite materials, to the study of Greek
and Hebrew; he drew up an answer to the work of Latonus,
so prolix, he calls it, and so ill written. He translated into
German the Apology of Melancthon against the "blockhead
theologians of Paris," adding a Commentary of his own. It
was here, too, that he commenced his translation of the Bible.
In fact, though he speaks of himself as doing nothing, he
displayed the most extraordinary activity in his Patmos, and
from its height inundated Germany with his writings. "I
have published," he writes, on 1st November, "a little volume
against that of Catharinus on Antichrist; a treatise in German on Confession; a commentary in German on the 67th
Psalm; another, also in German, on the Canticle of Mary; a
third on the 37th Psalm, and a Consolation to the Church of
Wittemberg. Moreover, I have in the press, a commentary
in German, on the Epistles and Gospels for the year; I have
just sent off a public reprimand to the bishop of Mayence,
on the Idol of the Indulgences he has raised up again at Halle,
and I have finished a commentary on the gospel story of the
Ten Lepers. All these writings are in German: I was born
for the good of my dear Germans, and I will never cease to
serve them. While I was at Wittemberg, I commenced a
series of sermons to illustrate in a popular manner the Two
Testaments; I had got in Genesis as far as the xxxii. chap-

ter, and in the New Testament to John the Baptist. Here I stopped."

On the 9th September, he writes: "I am full of trembling, and my conscience troubles me, for that when at Worms, yielding to your advice and that of your friends, I allowed the spirit within me to give way, instead of showing another Elias to those idols. They should find things very different on my part, if I were once again to come in contact with them."

From the depth of his retreat, when he himself could not come forward in the lists, he thus exhorts Melancthon:

"Even though I should perish, the gospel would lose nothing, for thou art far more important to it than I am now; thou art the Elisha on whom the spirit of Elias rests. Suffer not thyself to be cast down, but sing in the night the song of the Lord which I gave you; I will sing it also, having no other care than for the Word. Let him who is ignorant, be ignorant if he will; let him who perishes, perish; our care must be that they have no cause to complain of us that we failed in our duty to them." (26th May, 1521.)

He was at this time urged to resolve an important question he himself had raised, and the discussion of which did not turn upon theological controversies, the question of monastic vows; the monks in every direction were anxious to throw them aside, but Melancthon dared not take the settlement of the question upon himself. Even Luther, when it came to the point, approached the subject with considerable hesitation:

"You have not yet convinced me," he writes, "that we must regard under the same point of view the vow of priests and that of monks. I am strongly impressed with the feeling that the sacerdotal orders instituted by God are free; but it is a great question whether this principle applies to monks, who have chosen their condition, and offered themselves of their own full accord, to God. On the whole, however, I should be very much inclined to decide, that such of the inmates of these cut-throat places as have not yet attained the age of marriage, or who have not exceeded it, should be allowed to recall their vows without scruple; as to those who are past the proper age for conjugal life, and who have grown old in their present state, I am not prepared **to form** the same judgment respecting them.

"As to the priests, St. Paul gives, concerning them, a decision at length, saying that it was devils who forbade them to marry; and as the voice of St. Paul was the voice of divine Majesty, I have no doubt but that we ought to follow it. Accordingly I would say that priests, even though at the time of their professing they bound themselves by this engagement of the devil, now that they know what sort of an engagement it is, are at full liberty without any hesitation to renounce and throw it off. (1 Aug.) As to myself, I have annulled unceremoniously vows made by me before I was twenty years of age, and I would annul them again; for every one must see, who chooses to open his eyes, that such vows as these were made without due deliberation, without adequate knowledge of the matter. But I admit of this dispensation only, with reference to those who have not as yet actually entered upon their office; to them who have administered the functions of their profession in the monasteries, I cannot say, I have as yet made up my mind to extend the same license. Truly my brain is confused and obscured with this matter." (6 Aug. 1521.)

At times he became more confident on the subject, and spoke out plainly: "As to the vows of monks and priests," he writes to Gerbell, 19th May, 1521, "Philip and I have entered into a determination to prosecute a vigorous crusade against them, and not to rest till we have utterly destroyed and annihilated them. That miserable celibacy of young people of both sexes, constantly presents to my eyes such monstrosities of nature, that now nothing sounds more disagreeably in my ears than the words nun, monk, priest; and marriage appears to me a paradise, even though accompanied by the depth of poverty." (1 Nov.)

Acting upon the views he had expressed, he sent word to Wenceslaus Link to give the monks permission to quit their convents, without, however, any attempt to induce them to do so. "I am sure," he says, "you will do nothing yourself, nor suffer anything to be done, contrary to the gospel, even though the safety of all the monasteries in Christendom were at stake. I do not at all approve of the turbulent manner in which, as I understand, whole flocks of monks and nuns have quitted their convents; but though they have acted herein ill and unbecomingly, it would not be well or becoming in us to recall them, now the thing is done. After the example of Cyrus, in Herodotus, I would have you give full liberty to those who desire to leave their seclusion, but by no means compel any to leave it, nor, on the other hand, force any to stay who wish to go."

Towards the end of November 1521, the desire to see and encourage his disciples induced him to make a short excursion to Wittemberg; but he took care the elector should know nothing of the matter. "I conceal from him," he writes to Spalatin, "both my journey and my return; I need not tell you why; you understand my motive."

That motive was the alarming character which the Reformation was assuming in the hands of Carlstadt, and the demagogue theologians, the image-breakers, the anabaptists and others, who were beginning to come forward.

To the inhabitants of Wittemberg he wrote (Dec., 1521): "You are directing your energies against the mass, images, and other unimportant matters, and in doing so, laying aside that faith and charity of which you have so much need. You have afflicted, by your outrageous conduct, many pious men—men perhaps, better than yourselves. You have forgotten what is due to the weak. If the strong run on at the utmost of their speed, regardless of their feebler brethren, who come more slowly after them, the latter, thus left helpless behind, must needs succumb.

"God granted you a great blessing, in giving you the Word pure and undefiled. Yet I see none the more charity in you. You extend no helping hand to those who have never heard the Word. You take no thought for our brothers and sisters of Leipzig, of Meissen, and infinite other places, whom we are bound to save in common with ourselves. You have rushed into your present proceedings, eyes shut, head down, like a bull, looking neither to the left nor to the right. Reckon no longer upon me; I cast you off, I abjure you. You began without me; finish how you may."

Matters, however, assumed such an aspect at Wittemberg,

that Luther could not permit himself to remain any longer in his donjon. He departed accordingly, without asking the elector's consent.

On his way to Wittemberg, he wrote to the elector, who had enjoined him not to quit Wartburg:

"I would have your grace know, that it is not from men, but from Heaven, through our Lord Jesus Christ, that I hold the gospel. I might long since, and I shall do it in future, have called and subscribed myself his servant and apostle. If I have several times asked to be examined, it was not that I doubted the goodness of my cause, but simply to prove my deference and humility. But, as I see that this excess of humility only humbles the gospel, and that the devil, if I yield him an inch of ground, will seek to occupy all, my conscience compels me now to act otherwise. It is surely enough that, to please your electoral grace, I have passed a year in retirement. The devil well knows it was not fear made me do this: he saw my heart when I entered Worms, and knows perfectly well, that, had the city been as full of devils as there are tiles on the house-tops, I would joyfully throw myself among them. Now duke George is even less in my eye than a devil. As the father of infinite mercy has given me power, by his gospel, over all the devils and over death, and has given me the kingdom to come, your electoral grace must see clearly that it were an insult on my part towards my Master not to put my full trust in him, or to forget that I stand far above the anger of duke George. If God called me to Leipzig, as he does to Wittemberg, I would go there, though for nine whole days together it were to rain duke Georges, and every one of them were nine times more furious than this devil of a duke is. He takes my Christ for a straw, a reed; he shall find that neither Christ nor I will permit this any longer. I will not conceal from your electoral grace that I have more than once wept, and prayed that God would enlighten the duke; and I will do so once more, with earnestness, but this shall be the last time. I supplicate your electoral grace also yourself to pray, and to have prayers offered up, that, by our united solicitations, we may turn away, by God's mercy, the terrible judgment which each day more and more nearly menaces the duke. I write

this to let you know that I am going to Wittemberg, under
a protection far higher than that of princes and electors.
I have no need of your help; 'tis you who need mine, which
will be of greater use to you, than yours can be to me. Nay,
if I thought you would persist in offering me your protection,
I would not set out at all. This is a matter which requires
neither sage councils, nor the edge of the sword; God alone,
and without any paraphernalia of visible force, God alone is
my master, and my protector. He among men, who has the
fullest faith, is the best able to protect me; you are too feeble
in the faith for me to regard you as a protector and savior.

"You wish to know, doubtless, what you have to do on
this occasion, persuaded as you are that hitherto you have
not done enough. I will tell you, in all respect, that you
have already done more than was desirable, and that now
you have nothing to do at all. God will not permit you to
share my griefs and my torments; he reserves them to
himself and to his ministers. If your grace really have faith,
you will find it bring you peace and security; but whether
or not that be so, I believe, and I must leave your grace
to undergo the penalties with which God afflicts the in-
credulous.

"In disobeying the directions of your grace, I relieve
you, in the sight of God, from any responsibility should I
be thrown into prison, or be deprived of life by the tyrants.
Let, therefore, the emperor take his own course; do you
obey him respectfully as becomes a prince of the empire; if
he take my life, it will be his business to account for it, and
no longer yours. You will not be angry with me, prince,
for that I do not consent to involve you in my own misery
and danger; Christ has not instructed me to show myself
Christian at the expense of my neighbor. Wanting faith,
I would not have you revolt against power. I hope that they
will act so far consistently with common sense and decency,
as not to call upon a person of your grace's exalted condition
to be my jailer; but should they be mad enough to require
you to lay hands upon me, this is what I would have you do:
obey them, without taking any heed to me, for I would not
desire you to suffer on my account, in mind, body, or estate.

"God be with you, prince! some other time, if necessary,

we will discourse at greater length. I dispatch this letter in haste, fearing lest your electoral grace should be made uneasy at the news of my arrival; for it is my duty, as a good Christian to comfort all men, and to do ill to none. In you, I have to do with a very different man from duke George: I know that duke well, and he knows me not indifferently. If your grace believed, you would see the kingdom of God; as you do not believe, you have as yet seen nothing. Love and honor to God forever. Amen. Given at Borna, by the side of my guide, this Ash-Wednesday, 1522. Your grace's humble servant.

"MARTIN LUTHER."

On hearing of Luther's departure from Wartburg, the elector had dispatched Schurff to meet him, and persuade him to return, or at least to furnish him with an explanation of his conduct, which he might show to the emperor. In his answer to the elector, dated 7th March, Luther gives three reasons for his proceeding; first, that the church of Wittemberg had earnestly solicited his return; secondly, that disorder had crept in among his flock; thirdly, that he wished to avert, as far as in him lay, the insurrection which he regarded as threatening the country.

Towards the middle of this year, Luther broke out with the greatest violence against princes and potentates. A number of secular and ecclesiastical dignitaries (duke George among them) had prohibited the sale of the translation he was then publishing of the Bible, and offered to return the money paid by those who had already purchased the work. Luther unhesitatingly accepted the defiance thus cast at him: "We have triumphed over the papal tyranny which weighed down kings and princes; it will be still easier to demolish the kings and princes themselves. . . . I much fear that if they continue to heed what that blockhead duke George says, there will arise throughout Germany disturbances which will involve in ruin all the princes and magistrates, and drag down at the same time the whole body of the clergy. This is the aspect in which I view coming events. The people on all sides are in a state of excitement; they have opened their eyes, so long closed, and they will not, they cannot, suffer them-

selves to be oppressed any longer. It is the Lord himself who
is bringing this about, and who shuts the eyes of the princes
to the threatening symptoms which all else see; it is He
who will accomplish the inevitable results, by means of the
blindness and violence of these haughty men. I see before
me Germany swimming in blood!

"Why will they not perceive that the sword of civil war
is suspended over their heads? They are exerting all their
efforts to destroy Luther, while Luther is doing his utmost
to save them. It is not for Luther, but for them, that per-
dition approaches; and they, instead of seeking to avert,
advance it. In what I am now saying, I verily believe the
Spirit speaks by my lips. But if the decree of anger is
passed in Heaven, and neither prayer nor prudence can avert
its effects, we will obtain that our Josias shall fall asleep in
peace, and that the world shall be left to itself in its Babylon.
Though exposed every hour to death, in the very midst of
my enemies, without any human aid, I have ever entertained
the most perfect contempt for these stupid menaces of prince
George and his fellows. The Spirit, doubt it not, will
thoroughly master duke George and his emulators in folly.
I write this fasting, quite early in the morning, my heart
filled with a pious confidence. My Christ lives and reigns,
and I too shall live and reign" (19th March).

In the middle of the year appeared the book which
Henry VIII. had got his chaplain, Edward Lee, to draw up
in his name, and in which he put himself forward as the
champion of the Roman church.

"There is, indeed, in this book," observes Luther, (22nd
July,) "a plentiful manifestation of royal ignorance; but its
virulence and mendacity are the exclusive property of Lee."
Luther's reply was not long in making its appearance; its
violence surpassed anything that even his attacks on the pope
might have led us to expect. Never before had a private
man addressed to a sovereign-prince words so contemptuous,
so daring. "Two years ago," he says, "I published a little
book called, *The Captivity of the Church at Babylon*. It
horribly vexed and confounded the papists, who spared
neither lies nor invective in replying to it. I readily forgive
them both the one and the other, neither having hurt me.

There were some who tried to swallow it down with a laugh; but the hook was too hard and too pointed for their throats. And now, quite recently, the lord Henry, not by the grace of God king of England, has written in Latin against my treatise. There are some who believe that this pamphlet of the king's did not emanate from the king's own pen; but whether Henry wrote it, or Hal, or the devil in hell, is nothing to the point. He who lies is a liar; and I fear him not, be he who he may. This is my own notion about the matter: that Henry gave out an ell or two of coarse cloth, and that, then, this pituitous Thomist, Lee, this follower of the Thomist herd, who, in his presumption, wrote against Erasmus, took scissors and needle and made a cape of it. If a king of England spits his impudent lies in my face, I have a right, in my turn, to throw them back down his very throat. If he blasphemes my sacred doctrines; if he casts his filth at the throne of my monarch, my Christ, he need not be astonished at my defiling, in like manner, his royal diadem, and proclaiming him, king of England though he be, a liar and a rascal.

"He thought to himself, doubtless: 'Luther is so hunted about, he will have no opportunity of replying to me; his books are all burnt, so my calumnies will remain unconfuted; I am a king, and people will needs believe me. I need not fear to throw anything that comes first to hand in the poor monk's teeth, to publish what I like, to hunt down his character as I think fit.' Ah! ah! my worthy Henry! you've reckoned without your host in this matter: you have had your say, and I'll have mine; you shall hear truths that won't amuse you at all; I'll make you smart for your tricks. This excellent Henry accuses me of having written against the pope out of personal hatred and ill-will; of being snarlish, quarrelsome, back-biting, proud, and so conceited that I think myself the only man of sense in the world! I ask you, my worthy Hal, what has my being conceited, snappish, cross-grained—supposing I am so—to do with the question? Is the papacy free from blame because I am open to it? Is the king of England a wise man, because I take him to be a fool? Answer me that. The best of it is, that this worthy monarch, who has such a horror of lying and calumny, has assuredly collected together more lies and more slanders in this little book than can be charged upon me, by my worst enemies, in the whole extent of my writings. But, forsooth, in these quarrels, we must be respecters of persons; that is to say, a king, so he fawns upon the pope, may abuse a poor monk to the top of his bent. What most surprises me, is, not the ignorance of this Hal of England, not that he understands less about faith and works than a log of wood, but that the devil should trouble himself to make use of this man against me, when he knows perfectly well that I don't care a straw for either one or the other. King Henry justifies the proverb: *Kings and princes are fools.* Who sees not the hand of God in the blindness and imbecility of this man? I shall say very little more about him at present, for I have the Bible to translate, and other important matters to attend to; on some future occasion, God willing, when I shall be more at leisure, I will reply at greater length to this royal driveler of lies and poison. . . . I imagine that he set about his book by way of penance, for his conscience is ever smiting him for having stolen the crown of England, making way for himself by murdering the last scion of the royal line, and corrupting the blood of the kings of England. He trembles in his skin, lest the blood he has shed be demanded at his hands; and this it is makes him clutch hold of the pope to keep him on his throne, makes him pay court, now to the Emperor, now to the king of France. 'Tis precisely what might have been expected in a conscience-haunted tyrant. Hal and the pope have exactly the same legitimacy: the pope stole his tiara as the king did his crown; and therefore it is they are as thick together as two mules in harness.''

Then turning upon the Thomists, Luther thus defies them: ''Come on, pigs that you are! burn me if you dare! I am here to be seized upon. My ashes shall pursue you after my death, though you throw them to all the winds—into all the seas. Living, I shall be the enemy of popery, dead, I should be doubly its enemy. Pigs of Thomists, do what you can: Luther will be the bear in your path, the lion in your way; he will pursue you wheresoever you go, he will present himself incessantly before you, will leave you not a moment's peace or truce, till he has broken your iron head and your brazen front—for your salvation or your damnation, as you shall then act.''

He was still more violent in the German treatise he sent forth at about the same time on the secular power, and which opens thus:

''God has heated the brains of princes. They think they are fully entitled to follow out their own caprices; they put themselves under the wing of the emperor, and, according to their own account, in what they do, merely execute his orders like obedient subjects, as if they could in this way conceal their iniquity from men's eyes. Knaves that pass themselves off as Christian princes! And these are the hands to which Cæsar has confided the keys of Germany; madmen who would extirpate faith from our land, and establish blasphemy in its place, if we did not resist them by the mighty power of the Word. And resist them I will; I, who feared not to take the pope by the horns, that great idol of Rome, am not likely to be intimidated by his scales and peelings. . . . Princes are of this world, and this world is the enemy of God, so that they live according to the world, and against the law of God. Be not astonished, therefore, at their furious violence against the gospel, for they cannot act counter to their own nature.

''The simple fact is, that God abandons these reprobates to their own perverted courses; he will put an end to them and to the great ones of the church; their reign is over, and they are about to descend into the tomb—the whole mob of scoundrels, princes, bishops, monks, covered with the contempt and hatred of mankind.

''The Holy Scripture says that faith is a rock against which shall not avail the gates of hell, death, the devil, or any other power; that it is a divine power; and that this divine power may be vindicated against all opposing powers by the merest child. Oh, God, how senseless, then, are the worldly princes and potentates, in acting as they do! There is the king of England, entitling himself, in his turn, *Defender of the Faith!* So, too, the Hungarians boast of being the protectors of God, and presumptuously sing in their Litany, *That it may please thee to hear us, thy defenders!* By and by, we shall have some princes putting themselves forward as *defenders of Jesus Christ,* and others as *defenders of the Holy Ghost!* Should this be so, the Trinity, truly, will be fitly guarded!''

These daring freedoms alarmed the elector, and Luther had some difficulty in reassuring him.

That wherein consisted the real security of Luther at this period was the circumstance that a general disorder in the political world seemed close at hand. The populace in every direction were murmuring in a tone not to be mistaken. The gentry and the lower class of the nobility, still more dis-contented and impatient than the people, were taking the initiative in the social changes called for. The wealthy, over-grown ecclesiastical principalities lay spread out before the eyes of all, as a fair prey, in the pillage of which civil war might best be commenced. The catholics themselves called, though in a regular, legal way, for the reformation of those abuses in the church against which Luther had taken his stand. In March, 1523, the diet of Nuremberg suspended the execution of the imperial edict against Luther, and drew up against the Roman clergy the list of grievances and accusa-tions known as the *Centum gravamina.* Already the most ardent of the Rhine nobles, Franz Von Sickingen, had com-menced the struggle of the lesser lords against the princes, by attacking the palatine. ''This,'' observes Luther, ''is a very sad circumstance, and with other presages renders well nigh certain a general disorder in our political system. I have no doubt but that Germany is menaced with a very fearful civil war, if not altogether with destruction.'' (16th Jan. 1523.)

IV

1524-1529

DURING the terrible tragedy of the peasants' war, the theological war upon Luther continued almost without inter-mission. The reformers of Switzerland and of the Rhine—Zwinglius, Bucer, Œcolampadius,—fully participated in the theological principles of Carlstadt, differing from him only in their submission to the civil authority. In all other respects, not one of them was prepared to remain within the limits

which Luther had assigned to the Reformation. Cold, un-
bending logicians, they, bit by bit, sternly demolished what
he had sought to preserve of the old poetry of Christianity.
Less daring than they, but infinitely more dangerous, the
king of the men of letters of that period, the phlegmatic but
infinitely spiritual Erasmus, dealt doctor Martin, from time
to time, some terrible blows.

He was more especially exasperated at the apparent moderation of Erasmus, who, not daring to assail the edifice of
Christianity at its base, seemed desirous of overturning it
gradually, stone by stone. This maneuvering, this ambiguous
method of proceeding did not at all suit Luther's straightforward energy. "Erasmus," says he, "that amphibolous
being, sitting calmly and unmoved on the throne of amphi-
bology, cheats and deludes us by his double-meaning, covert
phraseology, and claps his hands when he sees us involved
in his insidious figures of speech, as a spider rejoices over a
captured fly. Then, seeing the occasion arrived for the display of his rhetoric, he comes thundering down upon us,
tearing us, flagellating us, crucifying us, throwing all hell at
our heads, because we have, as he says, apprehended in a
calumnious, infamous, and diabolical manner, words which,
though he says not, he all the while meant we should understand in the sense wherein we have understood them. See
him in another direction, crawling on like a viper to ensnare
simple souls, after the manner of the serpent of old, which
whispered in the ear of Mother Eve, and made her doubt the
precepts of God." The quarrel, in point of fact, caused
Luther, whatever he may say to the contrary, so much annoyance and embarrassment, that at last he refused to continue the discussion, and even forbade his people to take the
matter up for him. "If I fight against mud, whether I get
the better of it or no, I am all the same covered with mud,
and so the best way is to let mud pass on."

"I would not," he writes to his son John, "I would not for
ten thousand florins ready money, take upon myself the peril
in which Jerome, and still more Erasmus, will be, when they
find themselves in the presence of Christ.

"If ever I get well and strong again, I will fully and publicly assert my God against Erasmus. I will not sell my

dear Jesus. I am daily approaching the grave—nearer and nearer—and I am, therefore, anxious to lose no time in once more, and emphatically asserting my God in the face of all, against this bad man. Hitherto I have hesitated; I said to myself, if you kill him, what will happen? I killed Munzer, and his death at times weighs upon me, but I killed him because he sought to kill my Christ.''

One Trinity Sunday, again, Dr. Martin said: ''I entreat all you present, with whom the honor of Christ and the gospel is felt to be a serious matter—I pray you all to vow enmity to Erasmus.''

On another occasion he said to Dr. Jonas and Dr. Pomeramus, with peculiar and manifestly heartfelt emphasis: ''I recommend it to you as my last will, to be terrible and unflinching towards that serpent.—If I myself am restored to health, by God's help I will write against him and kill him. We have suffered him to insult us, and to take us by the throat; but now that he seeks to do so to Christ, we will array ourselves determinedly against him. It is true that to crush Erasmus is like crushing a bug, but he has mocked and insulted my Christ, and he shall be punished.''

''If I live, I will, God aiding, purge the church of this vile creature. It is he who sowed and cultivated Crotus, Egranus, Witzeln, Œcolampadius, Campanus, and other visionaries and epicureans. He shall be expelled the church, I tell him.''

On seeing a portrait of Erasmus, one day, Luther burst out—''That fellow, as his face manifestly proves, is full of trick and underhand malice—a very fox—a knave who has mocked God and religion. He makes use, indeed, of finesounding words: 'The dear Lord Christ, the Word of Salvation, the Holy Sacraments,' and so on, but as to the truth, he cares not a straw for it. When he preaches, it rings false, like a cracked pitcher. He once attacked Popery, and now he is trying to pull its head out of the mud.''

The strongest mind could not be expected to resist so many shocks, and Luther's had been visibly giving way ever since the crisis in the year 1525.

The part in which he had so long and so prominently appeared before the world, had been changed, and in a manner most painful to his own feelings. The opposition instituted by Erasmus was a clear manifestation of the estrangement from Luther of the men of letters, who had so powerfully aided his cause in the outset. This, in itself, had a very depressing effect; and the book, *De Libero Arbitrio,* was allowed to remain without any earnest answer. Again, the great innovator, the leader of the people against Rome, had since found himself left behind by the people, cursed by the people, in the war of the peasants. We need not, therefore, feel any surprise at the dejection of mind into which he fell at this period. As the intellectual man grew weaker, the empire of the flesh became stronger; and, yielding to its impulse, Luther married. The next two or three years are a sort of eclipse of the sun of Luther; whenever, during their course, we catch sight of him, we find him generally engaged in the material cares of life, which, as may have been expected, did not serve to fill up the void in a mind like his. Accordingly, he, at last, gave way: a grand physical crisis marked the close of this period of atony. He was aroused from his lethargy by the double danger of Germany—menaced from without by the arms of Soliman (1529), and within, as to its liberty and faith, by Charles V., at the diet of Augsburg, (1530).

"Since from the very nature of woman as created by God, she necessarily requires the support and society of man, we need inquire no further: God is on our side: let us then honor marriage, as a thing honorable and divine.

"This mode of life was ordained by the Almighty from the very beginning of the world; he has been pleased to continue it from that time to the present, and he will glorify it to the last. Where were the kingdoms and empires of this earth, when Adam, when the patriarchs, their sons, and their daughters married and were given in marriage? From what other state of life does empire itself descend, from generation to generation? The wickedness of man has caused it to be necessary for the magistrate to take the institution of marrage under his control to a great extent; and has occasioned itself to become, as it were, an empire of war, but, in its early purity and simplicity, marriage was the empire of peace." (17th Jan., 1525.)

"You tell me, in your last letter, my dear Spalatin, that

you are desirous of resigning your office and of retiring from
the court. My advice is, that you remain there; unless, indeed, your intention, in retiring, is to marry. . . . For myself, I am in the hands of God, as a creature whose heart
he may change and change again, whom he may kill, or
vivify at any hour, at any moment. Yet, in the state wherein
my heart always has been, and still is, I shall not take a wife;
not, God knows, that I have no consciousness of the flesh,
not that I am a stock or a stone, but because my mind is
not turned towards marriage at a period when every day I
am in expectation of encountering torture and death as a
heretic.'' (30th November, 1524.)

"Be not surprised that I do not marry, I who am *sic
famosus amator*. And yet, perhaps, it is matter of wonder
that one who has so constantly written in favor of marriage,
and who has been so much in the society of women, should
not himself, ere this, have been woman enough to marry. If
you would regulate yourself by my example, here it is: I
have had with me at one and the same time no fewer than
three women, whom I loved and whom I should have liked
to marry, but I have let two of them pass on and wed other
husbands. The third is still with me, and I am holding on
to her with my left hand; but, if I take not care, she too will
escape me.'' (16th April, 1525.)

To Amsdorf he writes thus, on the 21st June, 1525: "I
am a married man. Hoping yet to live some time, I can no
longer refuse to my father the desire he has so long expressed
of leaving behind him a posterity through me. Moreover, I
am anxious to be myself an example of what I have taught;
and the more so, that many around me fail to practice that
which is clearly commanded in the gospel. It is the will of
God I follow in this matter; I do not feel towards my wife
any burning passion, any lawless love, but simply affection.''

The person whom Luther married was a young woman of
noble family, an escaped nun, twenty-four years old, and
remarkably handsome. Her name was Catherine de Bora.
It seems that she had previously been attached to Jerome
Baumgærtner, a young doctor and senator of Nuremberg;
for we find Luther writing to the latter on the 12th October,
1524: "If you are anxious to have your Ketha, come here

at once, or she will become the property of another, who has already got her with him in this house. However, she has not as yet conquered her love for you; and, after all, I should be perhaps better pleased that you, having a prior title, should be united to her.''

On the 12th August, 1526, a year after his marriage, he writes thus to Stiefel: ''Catherine, my dear rib, salutes you. She is quite well, thank God; gentle, obedient, and kind in all things, far beyond my hopes. I would not exchange my poverty with her, for all the riches of Crœsus without her.''

His poverty, indeed, at this period was extreme; and anxious to provide for his wife, and the family he saw reason to anticipate, he determined to have recourse to some occupation for a livelihood: ''If the world will not support us for the sake of the Word, let us learn to support ourselves by the labor of our hands.'' As a matter of choice, doubtless, had the matter been open to him, he would have selected one of the arts he so loved—that of Albert Durer and of his friend Lucas Cranach, or music, which he was wont to call the first science after theology; but, unprovided with a master to teach him either of these, he became a turner. ''Since amongst us barbarians there is no man of art to instruct us in better things, I and my servant, Wolfgang, have set ourselves to turning.'' In one of his letters, we find him directing Wenceslaus Link to purchase the necessary instruments for him at Nuremberg. He also applied himself to gardening and building. ''I have laid out a garden,'' he writes to Spalatin, (December, 1525,) ''and I have constructed a fountain, and have succeeded excellently well in both undertakings.''

In April, 1527, writing to an abbot at Nuremberg, who had made him a present of a clock, he says: ''I must put myself to school with some mechanician, so that I may understand the wonderful details of the clock you have sent me, for I never saw anything like it before.'' And, a month after, he writes: ''I have received the turning tools, and the dial, and the cylinder, and the wooden clock. You omitted to mention how much more I have to pay you. For the present, I have got tools enough, unless, indeed, you have any instruments newly discovered that will turn of them-

selves, while that idle knave of mine is snoring or gaping
about him. I have made considerable progress in clock-
making, and I am very much delighted at it, for these
drunken Saxons need to be constantly reminded of what the
real time is; not that they themselves care much about it, for
so long as their glasses are kept filled, they trouble themselves very little as to whether clocks or clockmakers, or the
time itself, go right." (19th May, 1527.) "My melons,"
he writes, on the 5th July, "as well as my gourds and
pumpkins are getting up famously; so you see the seeds
you sent me were not thrown away."

Melons, gourds, and pumpkins, however, are but a miserable resource, and Luther soon found himself in a situation
as singular as it was afflicting. Here was the man who had
defied and fought popes and sovereign-princes, compelled to
depend for his daily subsistence upon the precarious and
scanty aid of the elector. The new church, in throwing off
the thrall of popery, had placed itself in subjection to the
civil authority, and the civil authority had left it, from its
very birth, to starve.

In 1523, Luther wrote to Spalatin, proposing to resign
the revenue of his convent into the hands of the elector:
"Since we no longer read, nor sing, nor say mass, nor do
anything our founder contemplated that we should do, we
have no business to live upon his money, and we ought,
therefore, to hand over the property to whomsoever may
show a better title to it." (November.)

"Staupitz has not sent us our money yet, and meantime
we are becoming more and more involved in debt. I don't
know what to do; whether to send once more to the elector,
or to let things take their course, from bad to worse, until
absolute misery and starvation compel me, for aught I know,
to quit Wittemberg, and make it up with the pope and the
emperor." (November, 1523.) "Here we are expected to
pay everybody, and yet nobody pays us. Things are come
to a fine pass, truly!" (1 February, 1524.) "I am becoming day by day more and more overwhelmed with debt;
I shall be compelled to solicit alms, by and by." (24th
April, 1524.) "This sort of thing cannot possibly continue.
These delays on the part of the prince necessarily give rise

to great suspicions in our minds. As to myself, I should long since have quitted the convent, to live elsewhere by the labor of my hands (though here, God knows, I labor hard enough,) had I not feared thereby to compromise the gospel and my prince.'' (December, 1524.)

''You ask me for eight florins: where on earth am I to get eight florins? As you know, I am compelled to live with the strictest economy, and yet my want of means, perhaps my want of care, has necessitated me to contract, during the past year, debts amounting to more than a hundred florins, which I must, somehow or other, and at some time or other, repay to various persons. I have been obliged to pawn three goblets, presents from different people, for fifty florins, and absolutely to sell one for twelve.'' (He writes elsewhere, with reference to this debt: ''The Lord, who punished me so long for this imprudence of mine, has at length relieved me from its effects.'') ''Neither Lucas nor Christian will any longer accept me as security, for they have found that by doing so, they either lose all the money, or that my poor purse is drained of its last penny.'' (2nd February, 1527.)

''Tell Nicholas Endrissus to send to me for some copies of my works. I have retained certain claims upon my publishers in this respect, as is just, seeing that, poor as I am, I get no money from them for my labor, nor any other return, except that of, now and then, a copy or two of my productions. This is not too much to expect, I should say, considering that other writers, even mere translators, receive a ducat a sheet for their manuscript.'' (5th July, 1527.)

''What has occurred, my dear Spalatin, that you should write to me in so menacing and imperious a tone? Has not Jonas already undergone enough of your contumely, and that of your prince, that you are still so inveterate against the excellent man. I know the prince's character well, I know with what slights he is in the habit of treating men. . . . Is it, I ask you, honoring the gospel, to refuse to its ministers a small subsistence? I tell you, it is at once gross injustice and treacherous meanness to order him privately to depart, and yet in public to wear an air as though you had given him no such order. Think you that your tricks will pass unobserved by Christ? . . . I don't imagine that we have been the occasion of any pecuniary loss to your prince; on the contrary, I am pretty certain that he has already realized a very handsome balance of the goods of this world by our means, and that he is likely to realize still more. I have no fear but God will provide us with food, if you refuse it us; but for your own sakes, dear Spalatin, I beseech you to treat us poor exiles in Christ with greater consideration and kindness. At all events, I request you to explain yourself distinctly and definitely, in order that we may know what we are about; whether we are to go or stay, and that we may be no longer made fools of by people, who, while they order us to go forth, are afraid of our naming, in our own justification, those who compelled us to take that step." (27th November, 1524.)

"We have received, dear Gerard Lampadarius, the letter and the cloth you have so benevolently bestowed upon us. . . . We burn the lamp you gave us, every night; and both Catherine and myself frequently lament that we have been able to make you no little present in return, at once to mark our gratitude, and that you might have something about you which should retain us in your memory. I am ashamed of myself, that I have hitherto omitted to make you even a present of some printed paper, for that is in my power; but I will not delay to send you a parcel of my books. I would have forwarded you herewith a German Isaiah I have just published, but there has been such an overflowing demand for the work, that I have absolutely not got a copy left." (14th October, 1528.)

To Martin Gorlitz, who had sent him a barrel of beer, he writes: "Thy Cerealian gift from Torgau has been done noble justice to. I assure thee, that it has dispensed happiness in appreciating quarters. My co-visitors seemed as though they would never have done drinking and praising it, praising it and drinking it. They exalted its qualities above those of all the barrels of beer they had ever been at the broaching of. And here have I, lout that I am, omitted till this present moment, to thank thee and thy Emilia for the bounteous gift! But the fact is, I am a poor οιχοδεσποτης (housekeeper), so heedless of domestic affairs, so forgetful, that, until the other day, I had not recalled to mind that thy pleasant donation was in my cellar at all; and then it was my servant who brought it to my recollection. Salute, in my name, all our brethren, and, more especially, salute in my name, thy Emilia and her son, the graceful hind and the young fawn. May the Lord bless thee, and multiply thee a thousand-fold, in the Spirit as in the flesh!'' (15th January, 1529.)

On the 29th March, 1529, Luther sends word to Amsdorf, that he is about to receive into his house the wife of a mutual friend, who is near her confinement: "If my Catherine should be brought to bed at the same time, so much the worse for thy pocket; so come, having first girded on, not a sword, but a bag with silver and gold therein, for I will not let thee off without a handsome present on the occasion.''

To Jonas he writes: "I had read ten lines of your letter when it was announced to me that my Ketha had given me a daughter. *Gloria et laus Patri in Cœlis.* My little John has recovered. Augustin's wife is getting better, and so is Margaret Mochinn, whose escape from death seems an absolute miracle. On the other hand, we have lost five pigs, which is very disagreeable; however, I hope the plague will accept them as our full contribution: *Ego sum, qui sum hactenus, scilicet ut Apostolus, quasi mortuus, et ecce vivo.''*

The plague had broken out in Wittemberg, just as Luther's wife was on the eve of her confinement, and his little son very ill with his teeth. Two women who were on a visit in the house, Hannah and Margaret Mochinn, were attacked with the pestilence, so that he might truly say, as he did in a letter to Amsdorf, (1st Nov., 1527,) "My house has become a regular hospital.''

"The wife of George, our chaplain, died a few days ago of the plague. Everybody seemed afraid to have any intercourse with the poor fellow, so we took him and his children into our house." (4th Nov., 1527.) "Thy little favorite, John, does not salute thee, for he is too ill to speak, but, through me, he solicits your prayers. For the last twelve days he has not eaten a morsel. 'Tis wonderful to see how the poor child keeps up his spirits; he would manifestly be as gay and joyous as ever, were it not for the excess of his physical weakness. Margaret Mochinn's imposthume was opened yesterday, and she is getting quite round again already; I have put her into our winter bedroom; we ourselves are in the great front room, Jenny in the chamber with the stove, and Augustin's wife in her own room; we are beginning to hope that the plague will soon disappear. Farewell; salute thy daughter and her mother in our name, and remember us all in thy prayers.'' (10th Nov., 1527.)

"My poor son was all but dead, but he has now recovered; he had eaten nothing for twelve days. It has pleased the Lord to increase my family with a daughter. We are all well, except myself, who, though sound in body and apart from the world, still suffer within from the assaults of Satan and all his angels. I am writing, for the second and last time, against the sacramentarians and their futilities.'' (31st Dec., 1527.)

"My little daughter, Elizabeth, is dead; 'tis wonderful how sick at heart her loss has made me; I feel a mere woman, so great is the agitation that has since pervaded me. I could never have dreamed that a man's soul could be filled with such tenderness even towards his child.'' (5th August, 1528.)

"I am now, unhappily, in a condition to explain to you truly what it is to be a parent, *præsertem sexûs, qui ultra filiorum casum etiam habet misericordiam valde moventem.*'' (5th June, 1530.)

Towards the close of the year 1527, Luther was himself several times attacked with illness both of body and of mind. On the 27th October, he thus closes a letter to Melancthon: "I have not yet read Erasmus' new work, and indeed, how should I read it—I, a poor sick servant of Christ, who can hardly keep life within him. This is no time for me to read, or write, or do anything at all. Yet it is hard: it would really seem as though God had resolved to overwhelm me with all the waves of his displeasure at once. Men who ought to have compassion upon me, are selecting the very moment of my bodily and mental prostration, to come and give me a final thrust. God mend them and enlighten them! Amen.''

"For nearly three months,'' he writes on the 8th Oct. 1527, "I have been languishing not so much in body as in mind, so that I have scarce been able in that whole time to pen as many lines. These are the persecutions of Satan.

"I want to answer the sacramentarians, but if my soul does not acquire greater strength, I shall not be capable of doing that or anything else." (1 Nov., 1527.) "I have not yet read Erasmus' recent books, nor the late productions of the sacramentarians, with the exception of a few pages of Zwinglius. It is well done in them to take advantage of my debility to crush me under foot. I alone bear the burden of God's anger, because I have sinned towards him; the pope and the emperor, the princes and bishops, the whole people hate me and assail me; and, as if this were not enough, my own brethren now come to persecute me! My sins, death, the devil and his angels incessantly assail me. And who will guard me, who console me, if Jesus Christ also abandons me; He for whom I have incurred all this hatred! But he will not abandon the miserable sinner in his extremity; not even myself, for I think I shall be the last of all men. Oh, please God! please God, that Erasmus and the sacramentarians may some day, if only for a quarter of an hour, undergo the agonies which my poor heart endures." (10 Nov. 1527.)

"Satan makes me suffer terrible temptations, but the prayers of the saints do not abandon me, though the wounds of my heart are hard to cure. My consolation is that there are many others who have to fight the same internal fights. Doubtless, I have committed sins more than enough to warrant the torments I undergo; but my life and my strength is, the consciousness that I have taught, to the salvation of many, the true and pure Word of God; it is this which so infuriates Satan, who gnashes his teeth at the thought that he has not been able to drown and destroy me and the Word . . . I have not suffered bodily the cruelties which the tyrants of this world have inflicted upon those who have been burned and slaughtered for the sake of Christ; but Satan has made me writhe all the more with the martyrdom of the soul." (21 Aug. 1527.)

"When I try to work, my head becomes filled with all sorts of whizzing, buzzing, thundering noises, and if I did not leave off on the instant, I should faint away. For the last three days, I have not been able even to look at a letter. My head has lessened down to a very short chapter, soon it will be only a paragraph, then only a syllable, then nothing at all. . . . The day your letter came from Nuremberg, I had another visit from the devil. I was alone, Vitus and Cyriacus having gone out, and this time the evil one got the better of me, drove me out of my bed, and compelled me to seek the face of man.'' (12th May, 1530.)

''I am well in health, but sick at heart from the persecutions of Satan, so that I can neither read nor write. The last day, I feel convinced, is near at hand. Farewell, omit not to pray frequently for poor Luther.'' (28th Feb., 1529.) ''One may extinguish the temptations of the flesh; but, oh! how difficult it is to struggle against the temptations of blasphemy and despair! We do not comprehend sin, and we are equally ignorant of the true remedy.'' After a week of constant suffering, we find him writing, on the 2nd August, 1527: ''Having well-nigh lost my Christ, I was beaten about fearfully on the waves and tempests of despair and blasphemy.''

v

1529-1541

LUTHER was raised from the state of depression into which he had sunk, and recalled into active life, by the perils which menaced the Reformation and Germany. When the scourge of God, whom he had awaited with resignation, as the sign of the Day of Judgment, burst over the German states, when the Turks were seen pitching their tents before Vienna, Luther altered his mind, summoned his countrymen to arms, and wrote a book against the Turks, which he dedicated to the landgrave of Hesse. On the 9th of October, 1528, he addressed to this prince an exposition of the motives by which he had been actuated in composing this book.

''I cannot hold my peace. Unhappily there are amongst us, preachers who induce the people to believe that there is no need to trouble themselves about this war with the Turks. There are, on the other hand, fanatics who give out that under all circumstances it is forbidden to Christians to have recourse to temporal weapons. Others, again, who look upon the German people as upon a nation of incorrigible brutes, go to the extreme of hoping that they may become subject to the Turks. These absurdities, these atrocious calumnies, are all imputed to Luther and the Gospel, as three years ago was the revolt of the peasants; and as, in general, every evil that occurs throughout the world. It is therefore now most urgent that I should write publicly upon this subject, as well to confound the calumniators, as to enlighten the consciences of the innocent in respect to that course which it behooves them to take against the Turks.''

Again: ''We heard yesterday that the Turkish host has, by a great miracle of God, left Vienna, and gone towards Hungary. For after having made twenty successive assaults, without effect, the enemy opened a breach in three places by springing a mine: but nothing could induce the Turkish troops to renew the attack—God had struck them with a panic; they preferred being decapitated by their chiefs to the attempt at a last assault. It is believed by some that they retreated from an apprehension of our bombards and of our future army; others think differently. The Almighty has evidently combated for us this year. The Turk has lost twenty-six thousand men, and of our troops there have perished, during their sorties, no more than three thousand soldiers. I have desired to communicate these tidings to you, in order that we may return thanks to the Most High, and that we may render our prayers in unison to Him—for the Turk, become our neighbor, will not allow us to enjoy peace forever.'' (27th October, 1529.)

Although the catholics and protestants united for a moment in order to crush the anabaptists, their mutual hatred was in no degree abated; constant rumors of an approaching general council were no proofs that either of the two parties desired one to be called. In fact, the pope mistrusted such a proceeding, whilst the protestants were forward in denouncing it. ''They write me word from the diet,'' says Luther, in a letter of the 9th July, 1545, ''that the emperor has been urging our people to consent to a council, and that he has been much enraged by their refusal. I cannot comprehend such absurdities. The pope absolutely refuses to heretics like ourselves any standing in a council, whilst the emperor wills that we at once consent to its appointment, and obey its decrees. It is, perhaps, God who has caused them to become foolish; but I think I can fathom their absurd combination.

As, up to the present time, they have not been able, under
the titles of pope, church, emperor, diets, to render their
unjust cause formidable, they now think to clothe themselves
with the name of a council, in order to be able to obtain an
excuse for accusing us of being so utterly lost and without
hope, that he will listen neither to pope, church, emperor,
the edicts of the empire, nor even of the council itself, which
we have so repeatedly called.

"Herein may be discovered the wonderful cleverness displayed by knowing Satan against poor half-witted God, who
doubtless will have great difficulty in escaping from a snare
so aptly contrived. No; it is our Lord who will mock the
designs of those who lay toils for him. If we are now to
consent to the appointment of a council entertaining such intentions towards us, why, let me ask, did we not submit ourselves, twenty-five years ago, to the supreme head of all
councils, the pope, and to his bulls?"

The council thus proposed, might, had it been assembled,
have reunited the bonds of the catholic hierarchy, but it could
in no shape whatever have reëstablished those of the church.
Arms alone could determine that question. The protestants
had already driven the Austrians out of Wittemberg. They
despoiled, likewise, Henry of Brunswick, who was carrying
into effect, for his own behoof, the decrees of the imperial
chamber. They encouraged the archbishop of Cologne to
imitate the example of Albert of Brandenburg, in secularizing
his archbishopric, by which means they would have obtained a
majority in the electoral council. There were not wanting,
however, in the interval, several conciliatory attempts. Conferences were opened at Worms and Ratisbon (1540-1541),
which were equally futile with those that had preceded them.
Luther never attended any of them; and, indeed, he paid little
heed to disputes which every day assumed more decidedly a
political, rather than a religious, character.

"I have received no tidings from Worms," says he in one
of his letters, "save what is told me by Melancthon, who
tells me there is such a swarm of learned persons from France,
Italy, Spain, and Germany, as, as he says, never before were
exhibited by any pontifical synod." (27th November, 1540.)

Shortly after this, Luther again writes: "I have heard

from Worms, where our people are conducting matters with strength and wisdom, whilst our adversaries, like foolish and unskillful people, resort only to barren craft and lies. One would almost think the devil himself could be seen at sunrise, running to and fro, seeking, without avail, some gloomy abode wherein he might shelter himself, and thus escape the flood of light which pursues him.'' (9th January, 1541.)

After another conference of the theologians of both parties, the opinion of Luther upon ten articles of faith, which had been mutually agreed on, was sought by them. Respecting this he writes, ''Our prince learning that they were coming directly to me, without having recourse to him first, went at once to Pontanus, and these two drew up the reply in their own way.''

Had such an interference as this been ventured upon a few years before by the prince, Luther's indignation would have known no bounds. But here he speaks of it without any angry feeling; he was already beginning to flag, owing to the lassitude and disgust that had seized upon him. He clearly saw, that in laboring to restore the gospel to its primitive purity, he was only furnishing the princes of his time with the means of gratifying their earthly ambition; and that every day they sought to make a market of his Christ.

''Our excellent prince,'' says he, on the 4th April, 1541, ''has sent for my perusal the conditions which he is about to propose, in order to bring about a peace with the emperor and our adversaries. I perceive that they all look upon this matter as if it were a comedy which they are acting amongst themselves, whereas it is a solemn tragedy enacted between God and Satan, wherein Satan triumphs and God is humbled. But the catastrophe has yet to come, when the All Powerful, the author of the drama, will assign to us the victory. I am utterly indignant to see matters of such vast moment thus trifled with.''

VI

1543-1546

A MAN was complaining one day of the itch; said Luther: ''I should be very glad to change with you, and to give you ten florins into the bargain. You don't know what a horrible thing this vertigo of mine is. Here, all to-day, I have not been able to read a letter through, nor even two or three lines of the Psalms consecutively. I have not got beyond more than three or four words, when, buzz, buzz! the noise begins again, and often I am very near falling off my chair with the pain. But the itch, that's nothing; nay, it is rather a beneficial complaint.''

One day, when he had been preaching at Schmalkald, he had, after dinner, a severe attack of the stone, whereupon he knelt down and prayed fervently: ''O my God, my Lord Jesus! thou knowest with what zeal I have preached thy word; *if it be for the glory of thy name,* come to my succor; if not, close my eyes. I will die the enemy of thy enemies, I will die full of hatred of that villain pope, who has essayed to exalt himself above thee, O Christ.'' And he composed forthwith four Latin verses on the subject.

''My head is so weak, so unsteady, that I can neither read nor write, especially when fasting.'' (9th Feb. 1543.)

''I am feeble, and weary of life; I would fain bid adieu to the world, which is now given over to the evil one. God grant me a favorable hour for my departure, and a prosperous journey. Amen.'' (14th March.)

To Amsdorff he says, on the 18th August, in the same year: ''I write this to thee after supper, for when fasting, I cannot, without geat danger, even look at a book or at paper. I don't understand this wretched malady at all; whether it is one of Satan's blows at me, or the effect of nature's decay.''

''I take it that my malady is made up, first of the ordinary weakness of advanced age; secondly, of the results of my long labors, and habitual tension of thought; thirdly, above all, of the blows of Satan; if this be so, there is no medicine in the world will cure me.'' (7 Nov. 1543.)

To Spalatin he writes (30th Jan. 1544): ''I confess to thee, that in my whole life, throughout our whole struggle, I have never spent a more unpleasant year than the last has been to me. I have had a most terrible business with the lawyers, on the subject of secret marriages; I have found in those whom I regarded as devoted friends to the church, most bitter enemies. This is enough to plague me, is it not?

''I am indolent, weary, indifferent, in other words, old and useless. I have finished my journey, and nought remains but for the Lord to reunite me to my fathers, and give the worms and rottenness their due. I am weary of life, if this can be called life. Pray for me, that the hour of my departure may be pleasing to God and salutary for myself. I think no more about the emperor and the empire, except to recommend the one and the other to God in my prayers. The world seems to me to have reached its last hour, to be grown old like unto a garment, as the Psalmist expresses it; 'tis time it were changed." (5th Dec. 1544.)

"If I had known in the beginning that men were so hostile to the word of God, I should certainly have held my peace, and kept myself quiet. I imagined that they sinned merely through ignorance."

On one occasion he said, "Nobles, citizens, peasants, everybody, anybody, knows the gospel better than Dr. Luther, or even St. Paul himself. They all despise the pastors of God, or rather, the God and master of pastors.

"Our nobles want to govern, but they don't know how to set about it; the pope does. The least papist of them all is more capable of governing than ten of our court nobles put together. They may rely upon that."

Some one told Luther that in the diocese of Wurtzburg there were six hundred rich livings vacant. "There will no good come of that," replied he; "and it will be the same with us, if we persist in despising the word of God and his servants. . . . If I wanted to become rich, all I need do were to abstain from preaching. . . . The ecclesiastical visitors asked the peasantry in several places, why they did not support their pastors? Oh, returned they, we've enough to do to keep our shepherds and pigherds, and we can't do without them. They thought they could very well dispense with their soul-herds."

Luther, during six months that he did not preach in the church, used to read the services and deliver sermons on the Sabbath in his own house. "I do this," said he to Dr. Jonas, "to acquit my own conscience by fulfilling my duty as father of this family; but as to any other result, I see very clearly that the Word of God will be no more heeded here than it is in the church.

"It is you, Dr. Jonas, who will succeed me in my pulpit; I hope you will acquit yourself of the duty conscientiously."

He one day came out of the church in disgust, at seeing some people talking. (1545.)

On the 16th Feb., 1546, Luther observed: "The best thing Aristotle ever wrote was the fifth book of the Ethics, where he pays a fine and well-merited homage to moderation, wherein I entirely concur." (This tribute in favor of moderation is very remarkable, given, as it was, in the last year of Luther's life.)

The count of Mansfeldt's chancellor, dining with Luther at Eisleben, on his way from the diet of Frankfort, mentioned that the pope and the emperor were proceeding sharply against Hermann, bishop of Cologne, and were even thinking of expelling him from his electorate. Luther said: "They won't be able to do anything; they find that God and the holy gospel will not aid them against us, so they are resolved to see whether world wisdom, violence, cunning, will stand them in stead; but they will fail, for our Lord is with us. Do they think that God will suffer himself and his Son to be always regarded as nobodies? Even were they to kill me, they must, to do themselves any good, utterly destroy and extinguish all I have taught. I have the advantage over them. My Lord has said, *I will raise you up at the last day;* and when the last day comes, he will say, *Dr. Martin, Dr. Jonas, Maître Michael Cælius, come to me;* for he will call you by your names, as he has promised in 1 John: *I will call my own sheep by name.* Be not afraid, then.

"God has now and then a fine game at cards, all of them court cards—kings, princes, and so on. He deals them out, and plays them against one another—the pope against Luther, for instance; and, by and by, as children do when they've been fighting at beggar-my-neighbor for a long time without result, gets tired, and throws the cards under the table.

"The world is like a drunken peasant: put him on his horse on one side, and he tumbles over on the other. Take him in what way you may, you cannot help him; he won't let you. The world is bent upon going to the devil."

Luther used often to say, that if he died in his bed, it would be a great disgrace to the pope: "You, all of you,

pope, devil, kings, princes, and lords—you are all of you
enemies to Luther, and yet you can't do him any harm. It
was not so with John Huss. I am persuaded that, for the
last hundred years, there has not existed a man whom the
world at large hated more than it hates me. I, in my turn,
am hostile to the world; there is nothing, *in tota vitâ*, which
gives me any pleasure: I am utterly weary of life. I pray
the Lord will come forthwith, and carry me hence. Let him
come, above all, with his Last Judgment: I will stretch out
my neck, the thunder will burst forth, and I shall be at rest.''
He subsequently consoles himself for the ingratitude of the
world by calling to mind the example of Moses, Samuel,
St. Paul, and Christ.

One of his guests observed, that if the world were to subsist another fifty years, a great many things would happen
which they could not then foresee. ''Pray God it may not
exist so long,'' cried Luther; ''matters would be even worse
than they have been. There would rise up infinite sects and
schisms, which are at present hidden within men's hearts,
not yet mature. No; may the Lord come at once! let him
cut the whole matter short with the Day of Judgment, for
there is no amendment to be expected.''

The conversation one day having turned upon eclipses, and
the little influence they in reality exercised over the death of
kings and princes, the doctor said: ''No; eclipses no longer
have any influence over such matters, and the reason I take
to be that the Lord is shortly about to bring matters to a real
crisis, to settle everything with the Judgment. I was meditating upon this the other afternoon, as I went to sleep, and I
said to myself, soon I shall *go to rest in the Lord*. The Judgment must needs be at hand, for what help is there for the
world? The papal church will not reform itself; that is out
of the question; and the Turks and the Jews are as little inclined to amendment. Our empire makes no progress towards improvement: here have we been for the last thirty
years assembling diets from time to time, yet nothing is done.
When I am meditating, I often ask myself, what prayer I
ought to offer up for the Diet. The bishop of Mayence is
naught, the pope is worse than naught. I see no other prayer
that is fitting but only this: *Thy kingdom come.*

"Poor creatures that we are! We gain our bread even in sin. Up to seven years old, we do nothing but eat, drink, play, and sleep. Thence, up to twenty-one, we go to our studies, perhaps, three or four hours a day, and the rest of our time follow out our own caprices, running about, drinking, and what not. After that, we begin to work, and go on working till we are fifty, and then we become children once more. All along, we sleep out one-half of our lives. Ah, shame upon us! we do not give to God even a tenth of the time; and yet we imagine that with our good works, forsooth, we merit Heaven! What have I myself done? chattered two hours, been at my meals three, sat quite idle four. Ah! *enter not into judgment with thy servant, O Lord!*"

In a letter to Melancthon, dated 18th April, 1541, after relating his sufferings, he says: "Please Christ to remove my soul into the peace of the Lord. By the grace of God, I am ready and desirous to go. I have lived out and finished the course assigned me by God. O, may my soul, wearied with so long a journey on earth, now ascend to Heaven!"

"I have no time to write to thee at any length, my dear Probst, for though I am overwhelmed with age and weariness: *old, cold, and half blind,* as the saying is, yet I am not permitted as yet to take my repose, besieged as I am by circumstances which compel me to write on, on, on. I know more than thou dost about the destiny of our world: that destiny is destruction; it is inevitably so—seeing how triumphantly the devil walks about, and how mankind grow daily worse and worse. There is one consolation, that the Day of Judgment is quite close at hand. The word of God has become a wearisome thing to man, a thing viewed with disgust. The very circumstance that no new false prophets have arisen up amongst us of late, is in itself an unfavorable symptom; there is no occasion, no place for new heresies, where the universal sentiment is an epicurean contempt for the word of God altogether. Germany has been: and it will never be again what it has been. The nobles are solely intent upon grasping what they can from other people; the towns are only thinking of themselves (and so far, are very much in the right of it); the effect of all this is that the nation is divided against itself, which ought to be firmly united for the purpose of making head against that army of devils let loose, the Turks. We trouble ourselves very little as to whether God is for us or against us; for we imagine we are to conquer, by our own strength, against Turks, and devils, against God himself. The self-confidence of this poor dying Germany amounts to sheer insanity. Yet we can do nothing for her. Lamentations are vain, tears are vain, exhortations are vain. Nothing remains but to pray: *thy will be done.*" (26th March, 1542.)

"All around me I observe an unconquerable cupidity prevalent; this is another of the signs which convince me that the last day is at hand; it seems as though the world in its old age, its last paroxysm, was growing delirious, as sometimes happens to dying people." (8th March, 1544.)

"I consider that we are the last trumpet which is to prepare and precede the coming of Christ. However weak we ourselves are, however low the note we sound in the ear of the world, yet the sound we give forth in the ears of heaven's angels is loud and telling, and they, aiding our weakness here, will take it up, prolong, and give it out in full blast. Amen." (6th August, 1545.)

During the last two or three years of his life, his enemies from time to time spread abroad a rumor that he was dead, coloring the rumor, moreover, with circumstances of a most extraordinary and tragical description. To put an end to this annoyance, Luther, in 1545, printed in German and Italian, a pamphlet entitled: *Lies of the Italians, touching the alleged death of Martin Luther.*

"I said long ago to Dr. Pomer, that he who after my death shall slight the authority of this school and this church, must be regarded in no other light than as a perverse-minded man and a heretic. For it was in this school that God purified his word, and made a new revelation of it. Twenty-five years ago, who could do anything at all in the way of freedom and faith? Twenty-one years ago, how many were there standing at my side? None."

"I reckon up the progress of things from time to time, and I find that we are getting very near to the close of the forty years, at the expiration of which, according to my calculations, all this will have a final end. St. Paul preached only forty years, and 'twas the same with Jeremiah and

St. Augustine. In all these cases, on the termination of the forty years respectively during which the word of God had been preached, the word ceased to be heard, and great calamities immediately ensued.''

The electress dowager, one day when Luther was dining with her, said to him: "Doctor, I wish you may live forty years to come.'' "Madam,'' replied he, "rather than live forty years more, I would give up my chance of Paradise. I have ceased consulting the physicians. They tell me I am to live another year—so, meantime, I shall get on as well as I may, and make myself as comfortable, eating and drinking whatever I fancy.

"I would to God our adversaries would kill me by some violence, for my death at their hands would be far more useful to the church than my life.''

It was destined that Luther's should be a life of labor and excitement to its very close; well nigh his last days were occupied in the difficult and delicate task of bringing about a reconciliation between the counts of Mansfeldt, of whom, by birth he was the vassal. "A week, more or less,'' he writes to count Albert, who had asked him to come to Eisleben, as arbiter, "a week, more or less, will not stop me from coming, though truly I am very much occupied with other affairs. But I feel that I shall lie down on my death-bed with joy, when I have seen my dear lords reconciled and once more friends.'' (6th December, 1545.)

On his arrival he wrote thus to his wife: "To the very learned and deeply profound dame Catherine Luther, my most gracious spouse.—Dear Catherine, we are terribly annoyed here in one way and another, and would willingly return home, but I think we shall have to remain a full week longer. You may tell Maître Philip from me, that he would do well to revise his notes on the Gospel; for he does not seem, in writing them, to have rightly understood why our Lord, in the parable, calls riches thorns. This is the school in which we really learn these things. The Scripture throughout menaces thorns with the eternal fire; this at once alarms me, and gives me patience with life; for I must exercise my utmost powers in settling this matter, by God's aid.'' . . . (6th February, 1546.)

"To the gracious dame Catherine Luther, my dear spouse, who is tormenting herself quite unnecessarily. Grace and peace in our Lord Jesus Christ.—Dear Catherine, thou shouldst read St. John, and what the catechism says respecting the confidence we ought to have in God. Thou afflictest thyself just as though God were not all-powerful, and able to raise up new doctor Martins by dozens, if the old doctor Martin were to be drowned in the Saale, or perish in any other way. There is One who takes care of me in his own manner, better than thou and all the angels could ever do: He sits by the side of the almighty Father. Tranquilize thyself, then. Amen. . . . I had intended this very day to depart *in my anger*, but the affliction in which I see my native place involved, still detains me. Would you believe it? I am become a lawyer! I doubt, however, whether I shall do much good in that line; they had much better let me exercise my own profession. It were a great blessing for these people, if I could succeed in humbling their arrogant pride. They speak and act as though they were gods, but I fear they will rather become devils, if they continue in their present course. They should bear in mind that it was by pride the angels fell. Hand this letter to Philip; I have no time to write separately to him." (7th February, 1546.)

"To my sweet wife, Catherine Luther Von Bora. Grace and peace in the Lord. Dear Catherine,—we hope to be with you again this week, if it please God. The Almighty has manifested the power of his grace in this affair. The lords have come to an agreement upon all the points in dispute, except two or three; and, among other great ends achieved, counts Gebhard and Albert are reconciled. I am to dine with them to-day, and will endeavor, before we separate, to make them once more brothers. They have written against each other with great bitterness, and, during the conferences, have not as yet interchanged a single word. . . . Our young nobles are all gayety now; they drive the ladies out in sledges, and make the horses' bells jingle to a pretty tune. God has fulfilled our prayers.

"I send thee some trout that countess Albert has given me. This lady is full of joy at seeing peace reëstablished in her family. There is a rumor current here, that the emperor is advancing towards Westphalia, and that the French are enlisting lanzknecht, as well as the landgrave, &c., &c. Let them go on with their news,—true or false, it matters little which: we await in patience God's declaration of his will. I commend thee to his protection. Martin Luther. 14th February, 1546.''

Luther had arrived at Eisleben on 28th January, and, although very ill, he took part in the conferences which ensued, up to 17th February. He also preached four times, and revised the ecclesiastical regulations for the territory of Mansfeldt. On the 17th he was so ill that the counts entreated him not to quit his house. At supper, on the same day, he spoke a great deal about his approaching death; and some one having asked him whether we should recognize one another in the next world, he said he thought we should. On retiring to his chamber, accompanied by maître Cælius and his two sons, he went to the window, and remained there for a considerable time, engaged in silent prayer. Aurifaber then entered the chamber, to whom he said: ''I feel very weak, and my pains are worse than ever.'' They gave him a soothing draft, and endeavored to increase the circulation by friction. He then addressed a few words to count Albert, who had joined him, and lay down on the bed, saying ''If I could manage to sleep for a half hour, I think it would do me good.'' He did fall asleep, and remained in gentle slumber for an hour and a half. On awaking about eleven, he said to those present, ''What! are you still there? will you not go, dear friends, and rest yourselves?'' On their replying that they would remain with him, he began to pray, saying with fervor: *In manus tuas commendo spiritum meum; redemisti me, Domine, Deus veritatis.''* He then said to those present, ''Pray, all of you, dear friends, for the gospel of our Lord; pray that its reign may extend, for the Council of Trent and the pope menace it round about.'' He then fell asleep again for about an hour. When he awoke, Dr. Jonas asked him how he felt. ''O my God!'' he replied, ''I feel very ill. My dear Jonas, I think I shall remain here at Eisleben, here, where I was born.'' He took a turn or two in the room, and then lay down again, and had a number of clothes and cushions placed upon him to produce perspiration. Two physicians, with the count and his wife, entered the chamber. Luther said to them, feebly: "Friends, I am dying; I shall remain with you here at Eisleben." Doctor Jonas expressing a hope that perspiration would, perhaps, supervene, and relieve him: "No, dear Jonas," he replied, "I feel no wholesome perspiration, but a cold, dry sweat; I get worse and worse every instant." He then began praying again: "O my father, thou, the God of our Lord Jesus Christ, thou, the source of all consolation, I thank thee for having revealed unto me thy well beloved Son, in whom I believe, whom I have preached, and acknowledged, and made known; whom I have loved and celebrated, and whom the pope and the impious persecute. I commend my soul to thee, O my Lord Jesus Christ! I am about to quit this terrestrial body, I am about to be removed from this life, but I know that I shall abide eternally with thee." He then thrice repeated: *In manus tuas commendo spiritum meum; redemisti me, Domine, Deus veritatis!* All at once his eyes closed, and he fell back in a swoon. Count Albert, and his wife, and the physicians, made every effort to restore him to life, but for some time, altogether in vain. When he was somewhat revived, Dr. Jonas said to him: "Reverend father, do you die firm in the faith you have taught?" He opened his eyes, which were half closed, looked fixedly at Jonas, and replied, firmly and distinctly: "YES." He then fell asleep; soon after, those nearest him saw him grow paler and paler; he became cold, his breathing was more and more faint: at length, he sent forth one deep sigh, and the great Reformer was dead.

His body was conveyed, in a leaden coffin, to Wittemberg, where it was interred on the 22nd February with the greatest honors. He sleeps in the castle church, at the foot of the pulpit.

The following is Luther's will, dated 6th January, 1542:—

"I, the undersigned Martin Luther, doctor of divinity, do hereby give and grant unto my dear and faithful wife, Catherine, as dower to be enjoyed by her during her life, at her own will and pleasure, the farm of Zeilsdorf, with all the improvements and additions I have made thereto; the house called *Brun*, which I purchased under the name of Wolff; and all my silver goblets, and other valuables, such as rings, chains, gold and silver medals, &c., to the amount of about a thousand florins.

"I make this disposition of my means, in the first place, because my Catherine has always been a gentle, pious, and faithful wife to me, has loved me tenderly, and has, by the blessing of God, given me, and brought up for me, five children, still, I thank God, living, beside others who are now dead. Secondly, that out of the said means she may discharge my debts, amounting to about four hundred and fifty florins, in the event of my not paying them myself before my death. In the third place, and more especially, because I would not have her dependent on her children, but rather that her children should be dependent on her—honoring her, and submissive to her, according to God's command; and that they should not act as I have seen some children act, whom the devil has excited to disobey the ordinance of God in this respect, more particularly in cases when their mother has become a widow, and they themselves have married. I consider, moreover, that the mother will be the best guardian of these means in behalf of her children, and I feel that she will not abuse this confidence I place in her, to the detriment of those who are her own flesh and blood, whom she has borne in her bosom.

"Whatever may happen to her after my death, (for I cannot foresee the designs of God,) I have, I say, full confidence that she will ever conduct herself as a good mother towards her children, and will conscientiously share with them whatever she possesses.

"And here I beg all my friends to testify the truth, and to defend my dear Catherine, should it happen as is very possible, that ill tongues should charge her with retaining for her own private use, separate from the children, any money they may say I left concealed. I hereby certify that we have no ready money, no treasure of coin of any description. Nor will it appear surprising to any who shall consider that I have had no income beyond my salary, and a few presents now and then, and that, yet, with this limited revenue, we have built a good deal, and maintained a large establishment. I consider it, indeed, a special favor of God, and I thank him daily, therefore, that we have been able to manage as we have done, and that our debts are not greater than they are. . . .

"I pray my gracious lord, duke John Frederick, elector, to confirm and maintain the present deed, even though it should not be exactly in the form required by the law.

"Signed, MARTIN LUTHER.

"*Witnesses,* MELANCTHON, CRUCIGER, BUGENHAGEN."

FREDERICK
THE GREAT

FREDERICK THE GREAT

1712-1786

INTRODUCTORY NOTE

Frederick II of Prussia, commonly called the Great, was the leading European sovereign of those days of arbitrary kingly power which preceded the French Revolution. There can be no question of the military abilities of Frederick, of his daring, his persistency, his coldly cynical and successful statecraft. Almost without allies Prussia faced the chief kingdoms of continental Europe in the great Seven Years' War, and held her own against their united forces. No man but Frederick could have carried his country through the dangers into which he himself had plunged her.

As Frederick himself tells us, he was in his early days possessed by that impulse toward authorship so characteristic of his century. Hence we have from his own pen the history of his early but not of his later wars. The history however is almost wholly military and impersonal, merely describing the course of campaigns and speaking of himself in the third person. Only in the opening of his work and again at the very close does he discourse of himself, explaining in clear and most self-revealing fashion his theories of statecraft and of life.

THE HISTORY OF MY OWN TIME

MOST of our historians are compilers of falsehood interspersed occasionally with truth. Among the prodigious number of events which are transmitted to posterity, none may be perfectly relied on except those which concern some historical epoch, whether of the rise or of the fall of empires. It appears indubitable that the battle of Salamis was fought, and that the Persians were vanquished. There can be no doubt but that Alexander the Great conquered the empire of Darius, that the Romans subjected the Carthaginians, and that Antiochus vanquished Persia. Such evidence is confirmed by the

223

conquerors' having taken possession of the countries. History acquires additional credit in what relates to the civil wars between Marius and Sylla, Pompey and Cæsar, Anthony and Augustus, by the authenticity of contemporary authors, who have described these events. The fall of the western and eastern empires cannot be disputed, for kingdoms have arisen and been formed from the dismemberment of the Roman domains. But when invited by curiosity we would examine circumstantially facts which happened in times so remote, we lose ourselves in a labyrinth abounding in obscurities and contradictions, without any clew to guide us in research. The love of the marvelous, the prejudices of historians, their ill-placed zeal for their own nation, and their hatred to its enemies, have each inspired passions which have influenced their opinions; and the ages that have passed away, since they have written, have so much altered, by disguising, facts that to develop them at present would be impossible, even did we possess the eyes of the lynx.

Nevertheless among the multitude of ancient authors we distinguish with pleasure the description which Xenophon has given of the retreat of the ten thousand, commanded by himself, and brought back into Greece. Thucydides enjoys nearly the same advantages. We are delighted to find in the fragments we possess of Polybius, who was the friend and companion of Scipio Africanus, events recorded of which the writer was himself a witness. The letters of Cicero to his friend Atticus bear the same stamp. He was an actor in the grand scenes which he delineates. I shall not forget the Commentaries of Cæsar, written with the noble simplicity of a great man, and, whatever may be affirmed by Hirtius, the narratives of other historians are conformable in all respects to the incidents described in his Commentaries. But from the time of Cæsar history contains nothing but panegyric or satire. The barbarism of succeeding times has made the history of the lower empire a chaos, in which not anything interesting is to be found, except the memoirs written by the daughter of the emperor Alexis Comnenes, a princess who relates what she herself beheld.

The monks, who alone possessed some knowledge, have left annals found in their convents which appertain to the history of Germany. But what materials are these for history! The French also have had their bishop of Tours, their Joinville, and their Journalist de l'Etoile; compilers who wrote what they learned by chance, but who must have written feebly, for they scarcely could have been well informed. Since the revival of letters, the passion for writing is become ungovernable; we have now but too many memoirs, anecdotes and narratives. Among the authors of these we must select the few who have held employments, who have been themselves in action, who have resided at courts, or who have had the permission of sovereigns to search the archives; such as the state president de Thou; Philip de Comines; Vargas, fiscal of the council of Trent; Mademoiselle d'Orleans; the cardinal de Retz, &c. To these let us add the letters of d'Estrades, and the memoirs of de Torcy, well worthy of curiosity, especially the latter, for they develop the truth of the will of Charles II., king of Spain, concerning which there has been such diversity of opinions.

Reflections like these on the incertitude of history, which I have often made, gave birth to the idea of transmitting to posterity the principal events in which I have taken part, or of which I have been a witness, in order that those who hereafter shall govern the kingdom may know the true situation of affairs, when I came to the crown; the reasons that compelled me to act; what were my means; what the snares of our enemies; what the various negotiations, wars, and particularly what the heroic actions of our officers were, by which they have justly acquired immortality.

Since the revolutions which overthrew first the empire of the west, afterward that of the east; since the wonderful success attendant on Charlemagne; since the famous reign of Charles V. since the troubles which were excited by the reformation in Germany, and which were of thirty years continuance; and lastly, since the war which arose for the Spanish succession, there have been no events more remarkable or more interesting than those produced by the death of the emperor Charles VI. the last male descendant of the house of Hapsburg.

The court of Vienna saw itself attacked by a prince whom it could not suppose sufficiently strong to undertake so difficult an enterprise. A conspiracy of kings and sovereigns was soon after formed, all determined to have some part of that immense succession. The imperial crown passed into the house of Bavaria; and, when every incident seemed to concur in the ruin of the youthful queen of Hungary, that princess by her fortitude and address extricated herself from a situation thus dangerous, and supported her monarchy by sacrificing Silesia, and a small part of the Milanese. This was all which could be expected from so young a princess who, scarcely a queen, was imbued with the spirit of government, and became the soul of her council.

This work being destined for posterity, I am relieved from that restraint which bids us respect the living, and observe certain delicacies incompatible with the freedom of truth. I am permitted to speak without reserve, and aloud, what might otherwise only be thought: I shall paint princes as they are, without prejudice in favor of my allies, or hatred for my enemies; I shall mention myself only when obliged by necessity, and must be permitted, after the example of Cæsar, to speak of what relates to myself in the third person, to avoid the disagreeable effects of egotism. By posterity we must be judged; but if we are prudent we shall anticipate posterity by rigorously judging ourselves. The true merit of an excellent prince is to have a sincere love of the public good, of his country, and of fame; I say of fame, for that happy instinct which animates men with the desire of acquiring fame is the true principle of heroic actions. It is that impulse of the soul which raises it from its lethargy, inciting it to useful, necessary and worthy enterprises.

Whatever is affirmed in these memoirs, whether it respects negotiations, letters of sovereign princes, or treaties signed, is affirmed from proofs preserved in the archives. Concerning military facts I may be credited, as an ocular witness. Accounts of battles were deferred two or three days to render them more exact and conformable to truth.

Posterity, perhaps, will see with surprise, in these memoirs, a recital of treaties concluded and broken. Numerous as such examples are, example would not really justify the author of this work, if he had not better reason to excuse and explain his conduct.

The interest of the state ought to serve as the rule to the monarch.

Cases in which alliances may be broken are, (1) When the ally fails in fulfilling his engagements; (2) When the ally meditates deceit, and there is no other resource than that of being the first to deceive; (3) When a superior force oppresses and renders the breaking of a treaty an act of necessity; (4), and lastly, The want of means to continue the war. That despicable thing called money, by I know not what fatality, influences all affairs. Princes are slaves to their means; the interest of the state prescribes law to them, and that law is inviolable. If the prince is under an obligation even to sacrifice his life for the safety of his subjects, how much more ought he to sacrifice those connections the continuation of which would to them become prejudicial! Examples of treaties in like manner broken are frequent. It is not our intention to justify them all, yet dare we affirm there are some treaties which either necessity, wisdom, prudence, or the good of the nation, oblige us to transgress; for kings only possess these means of avoiding ruin. Had Francis I. fulfilled the treaty of Madrid, he would, by the loss of Burgandy, have established an enemy in the heart of his dominions. This would have reduced France to the unhappy condition in which she was in the reign of Louis XI. and Louis XII.

If after the battle of Muhlberg, won by Charles V. the Protestant league in Germany had not strengthened itself by the support of France, it could not but have worn those chains which the emperor had long been forging. Had not the English broken the alliance, so contrary to their interests, by which Charles II. was united with Louis XIV. a diminution of their power would have been risked, and the more so because France would have had greatly the advantage over England in the political balance of Europe. Sages, who predict effects from causes, ought early to resist all such causes as are thus diametrically opposed to their interests. Suffer me to explain myself exactly, on so delicate a subject, which has seldom been otherwise than dogmatically treated. To me it appears evident that a private person ought to be scrupulously tenacious of his promise, though he should have made it inconsiderately. If he is injured he can have recourse to the protection of the laws, and be the issue what it may, an individual only suffers. But where is the tribunal that can redress a monarch's wrongs, should another monarch forfeit his engagement? The word of an individual can only involve an individual in misfortune, while that of a sovereign may draw down calamities on nations. The question then will be reduced to this, must the people perish or must the prince infringe a treaty? And where is the man weak enough to hesitate a moment concerning his answer? Hence, from the case we have supposed, is deduced the necessity of first carefully examining the circumstances under which the monarch acts, the conduct of his allies, the resources he may be able to obtain, or his incapacity to fulfill his engagements, before any decisive judgment ought to be passed upon his proceedings. For, as we have already said, the good or ill state of the finances is the pulse of the kingdom, which has a greater influence than is either known or believed on political and military operations. Ignorant of this, the public judges only from appearances, and consequently is deceived in its judgments. Prudence will not admit that they should be better informed, for it would be the excess of frenzy to vain-gloriously publish the weak side of a nation. Delighted by such a discovery, its enemies would not fail to profit by the intelligence. Wisdom therefore requires we should leave to the public the rash liberty of deciding, and, unable to justify ourselves, while we live, without danger to the state, we must rest satisfied with that justification which may be obtained from disinterested posterity.

No one perhaps will take offense if I add some general reflections on what I have said, concerning events which happened in my own times. I have seen small states able to maintain themselves against the greatest monarchies, when these states possessed industry and great order in their affairs. I find that large empires, fertile in abuses, are full of confusion, and only are maintained by their vast resources, and the intrinsic weight of the body. Those intrigues which exist in such courts would bring destruction on less powerful princes. They always injure, but they do not prevent numerous armies from preserving their preponderance. I observe that all wars carried far from the frontiers of the people by whom they are undertaken, have not equal success with those which are made nearer home. Is not this the result of a sentiment natural to man, who feels it is more just to defend himself than to rob his neighbor? It may be indeed that the physical reason is too mighty for the moral, because of the difficulty of finding provisions when the distance from the frontiers is great, and of furnishing recruits, horses, clothing, ammunition, &c. Let us add, also, that the farther troops have adventured into distant countries the more they fear lest retreat should be cut off, or rendered difficult.

I view the undoubted superiority of the English fleets over those of France and Spain united, and I wonder how it could happen that the naval force of Philip II. which formerly had so much the ascendant over that of the English and the Dutch, did not preserve advantages so great: I further remark, with surprise, that all these naval armaments are rather for ostentation than effect, and that instead of protecting commerce they do not impede its destruction. Here we behold the king of Spain, sovereign of Postosi, overwhelmed by debt in Europe, and accepting credit at Madrid from his officers and domestics; there the King of England profusely scattering his guineas, which thirty years of industry had accumulated in Great Britain to sustain the queen of Hungary and the Pragmatic sanction; independent of which this same queen is obliged to sacrifice some provinces that she may preserve those that remain. The capital of the Christian world receives the first invader; and the Pope, not daring to utter anathemas on those who lay it under contribution, is obliged to give them his benediction. Foreigners inundate Italy, who combat each other to accomplish its subjection. The example of the English, like a torrent, draws the Dutch into a war with which they have no concern; and those republicans, who, when the heroes Eugene and Marlborough commanded their armies, sent their deputies to regulate military operations, no longer send any when a duke of Cumberland finds himself at the head of their troops.

The brand is kindled in the north, and a war fatal to Sweden is the consequence. Denmark awakes, is agitated, and is calmed; Saxony twice changes its party, and gains

nothing with either: on the contrary the Prussians are introduced into the country, and it is ruined. Conflicting events
alter the cause of dispute; effects however continue, though
the motive has ceased; fortune rapidly flies from side to side,
but ambition and the desire of vengeance feed and maintain
the flames of war. We seem to view an assembly of gamblers
who demand their revenge, and who refuse to quit play till
they are totally ruined. If an English minister be asked
what madness induces him to prolong the war, he replies,
because France cannot furnish the expenses of the next campaign. Should a similar question be put to the French minister, the answer would be much the same. The most deplorable effect of such policy is that the lives of men are
sported with, and human blood is ineffectually and profusely
shed.

Could war fix any certain limits to the frontiers of states,
and preserve that balance of power so necessary among the
nations of Europe, we might regard those who have perished
as victims sacrificed to the tranquillity and safety of the
public. But American provinces are objects of cupidity, and
soon we see all Europe engaged, on different sides, to combat
by sea and land. The ambitious ought never to forget that
arms and military discipline, being nearly the same throughout Europe, and that alliances having the general effect of
producing equality between the forces of the belligerent
parties, all that princes may hope from the greatest advantages, in these times, is to acquire, after accumulated success,
either some small town on the frontiers, or some suburb
which will not pay interest for the debts incurred by war, and
the population of which is far inferior to the number of inhabitants which have perished in the field.

Whoever has a heart capable of compassion, when he coolly
examines such objects, must be agitated at the remembrance
of evils which statesmen, either from the want of wisdom, or
hurried on by their passions, have brought upon nations.
Reason prescribes a rule on this subject from which it appears to me that no statesman ought to depart: which is to
seize occasion, and when that is favorable to be enterprising;
but neither to force occasion, nor leave everything to chance.
There are moments which require us to exert all our activity,

in order to profit by them; but there are others in which prudence requires we should remain inactive. This is an affair worthy of the most profound reflection; for, it is requisite, not only perfectly to examine the present state of things, but, to foresee all the consequences of any undertaking, and to weigh the means we ourselves possess, in opposition to those of our enemies, in order to find which must ultimately preponderate. If reason alone does not decide, and if passion takes any part, it is impossible that success should be the result.

State politics exact patience; and the height of wisdom in a great man is to do all things in their proper season. History supplies us with too many examples of wars inconsiderately undertaken. To be convinced of this we have only to read the life of Francis I. and what Brantome tells us was the cause of the unhappy expedition into the Milanese, where this king was made prisoner at Pavia. We have but to cast a retrospect on all the advantages Charles V. derived from the opportunity he had, after the battle of Muhlberg, to subjugate Germany. We have but to examine the history of Frederic V. the elector Palatine, and the precipitation with which he engaged in a contest so much above his strength. In our own times let us recall to mind the conduct of Maximilian of Bavaria, who, in the war of succession, when his country may be said to have been blockaded by the allies, took part with France, only to see himself stripped of his states. Charles XII. will furnish us with a more recent, and more striking example still, of the fatal consequences which the headlong and false conduct of monarchs entails upon their subjects. History is the school of princes; it is their duty to inform themselves of the errors of past ages, in order to shun them, to learn how essential it is for them to form a system and pursue it step by step; and that he, among them, who best calculates consequences, is the competitor who alone is able to carry the prize from others who act less rationally than himself.

[Here follows a wholly impersonal account of Frederick's early wars, leading up to the following closing paragraph or prayer—if Frederick's sarcasm can be called prayer.]

May Providence grant (if Providence shall deign to look

down on human miseries) that the unalterable and flourishing destiny of this State may raise the monarchs by whom it is governed, superior to the calamities and plagues Prussia has endured in these times of trouble and subversion; and that they never may be obliged to have recourse to remedies so violent and fatal, as were then found necessary to be employed, that the country might be preserved against the ambitious hatred of the sovereigns of Europe, who wished to annihilate the house of Brandenburg and eternally exterminate all who bore the name of Prussia.

THOMAS JEFFERSON

THOMAS JEFFERSON

1743-1826

INTRODUCTORY NOTE

We have here a picture of Thomas Jefferson sitting down at the close of his long and tremendously useful life to point out to his descendants which among his splendid deeds he himself regarded as having been of most value to mankind. This picture is one of the most impressive in American history. Jefferson was second only to Washington in his services to the cause of American Independence; he became the Secretary of State to the first President, and then resigned to head the opposition against what he regarded as the too aristocratic inclinations of Washington. Jefferson thus became the founder and chief leader of the Democratic Party in the United States. His enemies called him a demagogue, accused him of merely pretending to trust in the combined wisdom of the masses so as to secure their support for his political career. But few readers of his profoundly thoughtful, earnestly democratic writings will accept this superficial view. His autobiography in particular shows him from the very beginning of his public career a resolute seeker after justice, an enthusiastic believer in universal brotherhood, and yet withal a man of such calm and all pervading common-sense as we might wish to find more frequently among his antagonists.

His autobiography deals chiefly with his public deeds; his private life he scorned either to explain or to defend. He was, like his great leader Washington, a Virginian of the wealthy landed gentry, of Welsh ancestry on his father's side, but on his mother's a descendant of the noted English colonial family of the Randolphs. To them he partly owed his early prominence.

It is deeply to be regretted that increasing age led him to abandon his autobiography when the narrative had only reached the year 1790. The richest part of his great career was still to follow, and we thus remain without his own analysis of his greatest triumphs. Yet what we possess is in itself invaluable; no man of his times saw more of the world or saw with keener eyes than Jefferson. His analysis of the opening days and deeds of the French Revolution should be known to every reader. He watched the outbreak as the Minister of the United States in France, as an American profoundly grateful for French assistance in 1778, and as the foremost democrat of the world, eagerly hopeful for the future of mankind's experiments in self-government; keenly, watchfully observant of every blunder.

He himself asked to have inscribed upon his tombstone "Here lies buried Thomas Jefferson, author of the Declaration of American Independence, and of the Statute of Virginia for Religious Freedom, and Father of the University of Virginia." Could there be a prouder or more broad-minded record?

AUTOBIOGRAPHY

JANUARY 6, 1821. At the age of 77, I begin to make some memoranda, and state some recollections of dates and facts concerning myself, for my own more ready reference, and for the information of my family.

The tradition in my father's family was, that their ancestor came to this country from Wales, and from near the mountain of Snowdon, the highest in Great Britain. I noted once a case from Wales, in the law reports, where a person of our name was either plaintiff or defendant; and one of the same name was secretary to the Virginia Company. These are the only instances in which I have met with the name in that country. I have found it in our early records; but the first particular information I have of any ancestor was of my grandfather, who lived at the place in Chesterfield called Ozborne's, and owned the lands afterwards the glebe of the parish. He had three sons: Thomas, who died young; Field, who settled on the waters of Roanoke and left numerous descendants; and Peter, my father, who settled on the lands I still own, called Shadwell, adjoining my present residence. He was born February 29, 1707-8, and intermarried, 1739, with Jane Randolph, of the age of 19, daughter of Isham Randolph, one of the seven sons of that name and family, settled at Dungeoness in Goochland. They trace their pedigree far back in England and Scotland, to which let every one ascribe the faith and merit he chooses.

My father's education had been quite neglected; but being of a strong mind, sound judgment, and eager after information, he read much and improved himself, insomuch that he was chosen, with Joshua Fry, Professor of Mathematics in

William and Mary college, to continue the boundary line between Virginia and North Carolina, which had been begun by Colonel Byrd; and was afterwards employed with the same Mr. Fry, to make the first map of Virginia which had ever been made, that of Captain Smith being merely a conjectural sketch. They possessed excellent materials for so much of the country as is below the blue ridge; little being then known beyond that ridge. He was the third or fourth settler, about the year 1737, of the part of the country in which I live. He died, August 17th, 1757, leaving my mother a widow, who lived till 1776, with six daughters and two sons, myself the elder. To my younger brother he left his estate on James River, called Snowdon, after the supposed birth-place of the family; to myself, the lands on which I was born and live.

He placed me at the English school at five years of age; and at the Latin at nine, where I continued until his death. My teacher, Mr. Douglas, a clergyman from Scotland, with the rudiments of the Latin and Greek languages, taught me the French; and on the death of my father, I went to the Reverend Mr. Maury, a correct classical scholar, with whom I continued two years; and then, to wit, in the spring of 1760, went to William and Mary college, where I continued two years. It was my great good fortune, and what probably fixed the destinies of my life, that Dr. William Small of Scotland was then professor of mathematics, a man profound in most of the useful branches of science, with a happy talent of communication, correct and gentlemanly manners, and an enlarged and liberal mind. He, most happily for me, became soon attached to me, and made me his daily companion when not engaged in the school; and from his conversation I got my first views of the expansion of science, and of the system of things in which we are placed. Fortunately, the philosophical chair became vacant soon after my arrival at college, and he was appointed to fill it *per interim;* and he was the first who ever gave, in that college, regular lectures in Ethics, Rhetoric, and Belles lettres. He returned to Europe in 1762, having previously filled up the measure of his goodness to me, by procuring for me, from his most intimate friend, George Wythe, a reception as a student of law, under his direction, and introduced me to the acquaintance and familiar table of

Governor Fauquier, the ablest man who had ever filled that office. With him, and at his table, Dr. Small and Mr. Wythe, his *amici omnium horarum,* and myself, formed a *partie quarree,* and to the habitual conversations on these occasions I owed much instruction. Mr. Wythe continued to be my faithful and beloved mentor in youth, and my most affectionate friend through life. In 1767, he led me into the practice of the law at the bar of the General court, at which I continued until the Revolution shut up the courts of justice.

In 1769, I became a member of the legislature by the choice of the county in which I live, and so continued until it was closed by the Revolution. I made one effort in that body for the permission of the emancipation of slaves, which was rejected; and indeed, during the regal government, nothing liberal could expect success. Our minds were circumscribed within narrow limits, by an habitual belief that it was our duty to be subordinate to the mother country in all matters of government, to direct all our labors in subservience to her interests, and even to observe a bigoted intolerance for all religions but hers. The difficulties with our representatives were of habit and despair, not of reflection and conviction. Experience soon proved that they could bring their minds to rights, on the first summons of their attention. But the King's Council, which acted as another house of legislature, held their places at will, and were in most humble obedience to that will. The Governor too, who had a negative on our laws, held by the same tenure, and with still greater devotedness to it; and, last of all, the Royal negative closed the last door to every hope of amelioration.

On the 1st of January, 1772, I was married to Martha Skelton, widow of Bathurst Skelton, and daughter of John Wayles, then twenty-three years old. Mr. Wayles was a lawyer of much practice, to which he was introduced more by his great industry, punctuality, and practical readiness, than by eminence in the science of his profession. He was a most agreeable companion, full of pleasantry and good humor, and welcomed in every society. He acquired a handsome fortune, and died in May, 1773, leaving three daughters. The portion which came on that event to Mrs. Jefferson, after the debts should be paid, which were very considerable, was about equal to my own patrimony, and consequently doubled the ease of our circumstances.

When the famous Resolutions of 1765, against the Stamp-act, were proposed, I was yet a student of law in Williams-burgh. I attended the debate, however, at the door of the lobby of the House of Burgesses, and heard the splendid display of Mr. Henry's talents as a popular orator. They were great indeed; such as I have never heard from any other man. He appeared to me to speak as Homer wrote. Mr. Johnson, a lawyer, and member from the Northern Neck, seconded the resolutions, and by him the learning and the logic of the case were chiefly maintained. My recollections of these transactions may be seen, page 60 of the life of Patrick Henry, by Wirt, to whom I furnished them.

In May, 1769, a meeting of the General Assembly was called by the Governor, Lord Botetourt. I had then become a member; and to that meeting became known the joint resolutions and address of the Lords and Commons, of 1768-9, on the proceedings in Massachusetts. Counter-resolutions, and an address to the King by the House of Burgesses, were agreed to with little opposition, and a spirit manifestly displayed itself of considering the cause of Massachusetts as a common one. The Governor dissolved us; but we met the next day in the Apollo [1] of the Raleigh tavern, formed ourselves into a voluntary convention, drew up articles of association against the use of any merchandise imported from Great Britain, signed and recommended them to the people, repaired to our several counties, and were reëlected without any other exception than of the very few who had declined assent to our proceedings.

Nothing of particular excitement occurring for a considerable time, our countrymen seemed to fall into a state of insensibility to our situation; the duty on tea, not yet repealed, and the declaratory act of a right in the British Parliament to bind us by their laws in all cases whatsoever, still suspended over us. But a court of inquiry held in Rhode Island in 1762, with a power to send persons to England to be tried for offenses committed here, was considered, at our session of the spring of 1773, as demanding attention. Not thinking

[1] The name of a public room in the Raleigh.

our old and leading members up to the point of forwardness and zeal which the times required, Mr. Henry, Richard Henry Lee, Francis L. Lee, Mr. Carr, and myself agreed to meet in the evening, in a private room of the Raleigh, to consult on the state of things. There may have been a member or two more whom I do not recollect. We were all sensible that the most urgent of all measures was that of coming to an understanding with all the other colonies, to consider the British claims as a common cause to all, and to produce a unity of action; and, for this purpose, that a committee of correspondence in each colony would be the best instrument for intercommunication; and that their first measure would probably be to propose a meeting of deputies from every colony, at some central place, who should be charged with the direction of the measures which should be taken by all. We, therefore, drew up the resolutions which may be seen in Wirt, page 87. The consulting members proposed to me to move them, but I urged that it should be done by Mr. Carr, my friend and brother-in-law, then a new member, to whom I wished an opportunity should be given of making known to the house his great worth and talents. It was so agreed; he moved them, they were agreed to *nem. con.*, and a committee of correspondence appointed, of whom Peyton Randolph, the speaker, was chairman. The Governor (then Lord Dunmore) dissolved us, but the committee met the next day, prepared a circular letter to the speakers of the other colonies, inclosing to each a copy of the resolutions, and left it in charge with their chairman to forward them by expresses.

The origination of these committees of correspondence between the colonies has been since claimed for Massachusetts; and Marshall has given into this error, although the very note of his appendix to which he refers, shows that their establishment was confined to their own towns. This matter will be seen clearly stated in a letter of Samuel Adams Wells to me of April 2, 1819, and my answer of May 12th. I was corrected by the letter of Mr. Wells in the information I had given Mr. Wirt, as stated in his note, page 87, that the messengers of Massachusetts and Virginia crossed each other on the way, bearing similar propositions; for Mr. Wells shows that Massachusetts did not adopt the measure, but, on the receipt of our proposition, delivered at their next session. Their message, therefore, which passed ours, must have related to something else, for I well remember Peyton Randolph's informing me of the crossing of our messengers.

The next event which excited our sympathies for Massachusetts was the Boston port bill, by which that port was to be shut up on the 1st of June, 1774. This arrived while we were in session in the spring of that year. The lead in the House, on these subjects, being no longer left to the old members, Mr. Henry, R. H. Lee, Fr. L. Lee, three or four other members, whom I do not recollect, and myself, agreeing that we must boldly take an unequivocal stand in the line with Massachusetts, determined to meet and consult on the proper measures, in the council-chamber, for the benefit of the library in that room. We were under conviction of the necessity of arousing our people from the lethargy into which they had fallen, as to passing events; and thought that the appointment of a day of general fasting and prayer would be most likely to call up and alarm their attention. No example of such a solemnity had existed since the days of our distresses in the war of '55, since which a new generation had grown up. With the help, therefore, of Rushworth, whom we rummaged over for the revolutionary precedents and forms of the Puritans of that day, preserved by him, we cooked up a resolution, somewhat modernizing their phrases, for appointing the 1st day of June, on which the port-bill was to commence, for a day of fasting, humiliation, and prayer, to implore Heaven to avert from us the evils of civil war, to inspire us with firmness in support of our rights, and to turn the hearts of both the King and Parliament to moderation and justice.

To give greater emphasis to our proposition, we agreed to wait the next morning on Mr. Nicholas, whose grave and religious character was more in unison with the tone of our resolution, and to solicit him to move it. We accordingly went to him in the morning. He moved it the same day; the 1st of June was proposed; and it passed without opposition. The Governor dissolved us, as usual. We retired to the Apollo, as before, agreed to an association, and instructed the committee of correspondence to propose to the corresponding

committees of the other colonies, to appoint deputies to meet
in Congress at such place, *annually*, as should be convenient,
to direct, from time to time, the measures required by the
general interest; and we declared that an attack on any one
colony, should be considered as an attack on the whole. This
was in May. We further recommended to the several counties
to elect deputies to meet at Williamsburg, the 1st of August
ensuing, to consider the state of the colony, and particularly
to appoint delegates to a general congress, should that measure be acceded to by the committees of correspondence generally. It was acceded to; Philadelphia was appointed for
the place, and the 5th of September for the time of meeting.
We returned home, and in our several counties invited the
clergy to meet assemblies of the people on the 1st of June,
to perform the ceremonies of the day, and to address to them
discourses suited to the occasion. The people met generally,
with anxiety and alarm in their countenances, and the effect
of the day, through the whole colony, was like a shock of
electricity, arousing every man, and placing him erect and
solidly on his center. They chose, universally, delegates for
the convention.

Being elected for my own county, I prepared a draft of
instructions to be given to the delegates whom we should
send to the Congress, which I meant to propose at our meeting. In this I took the ground that, from the beginning, I
had thought the only one orthodox or tenable, which was, that
the relation between Great Britain and these colonies was
exactly the same as that of England and Scotland, after the
accession of James, and until the union, and the same as her
present relations with Hanover, having the same executive
chief, but no other necessary political connection; and that
our emigration from England to this country gave her no
more rights over us, than the emigrations of the Danes and
Saxons gave to the present authorities of the mother country,
over England. In this doctrine, however, I had never been
able to get any one to agree with me but Mr. Wythe. He
concurred in it from the first dawn of the question, What
was the political relation between us and England? Our
other patriots, Randolph, the Lees, Nicholas, Pendleton,
stopped at the half-way house of John Dickinson, who ad-

mitted that England had a right to regulate our commerce, and to lay duties on it for the purposes of regulation, but not of raising revenue. But for this ground there was no foundation in compact, in any acknowledged principles of colonization, nor in reason: expatriation being a natural right, and acted on as such, by all nations, in all ages.

I set out for Williamsburg some days before that appointed for our meeting, but was taken ill of a dysentery on the road, and was unable to proceed. I sent on, therefore, to Williamsburg, two copies of my draft, the one under cover to Peyton Randolph, who I knew would be in the chair of the convention, the other to Patrick Henry. Whether Mr. Henry disapproved the ground taken, or was too lazy to read it (for he was the laziest man in reading I ever knew) I never learned; but he communicated it to nobody. Peyton Randolph informed the convention he had received such a paper from a member, prevented by sickness from offering it in his place, and he laid it on the table for perusal. It was read generally by the members, approved by many, though thought too bold for the present state of things; but they printed it in pamphlet form, under the title of "A Summary View of the Rights of British America." It found its way to England, was taken up by the opposition, interpolated a little by Mr. Burke so as to make it answer opposition purposes, and in that form ran rapidly through several editions. This information I had from Parson Hurt, who happened at the time to be in London, whither he had gone to receive clerical orders; and I was informed afterwards by Peyton Randolph, that it had procured me the honor of having my name inserted in a long list of proscriptions, enrolled in a bill of attainder commenced in one of the Houses of Parliament, but suppressed in embryo by the hasty step of events, which warned them to be a little cautious. Montague, agent of the House of Burgesses in England, made extracts from the bill, copied the names, and sent them to Peyton Randolph. The names, I think, were about twenty, which he repeated to me, but I recollect those only of Hancock, the two Adamses, Peyton Randolph himself, Patrick Henry, and myself. The convention met on the 1st of August, renewed their association, appointed delegates to the Congress, gave them instructions very temperately and properly expressed, both as to style and matter; and they repaired to Philadelphia at the time appointed. The splendid proceedings of that Congress, at their first session, belong to general history, are known to every one, and need not therefore be noted here. They terminated their session on the 26th of October, to meet again on the 10th of May ensuing.

The convention, at their ensuing session of March, '75, approved of the proceedings of Congress, thanked their delegates, and reappointed the same persons to represent the colony at the meeting to be held in May; and foreseeing the probability that Peyton Randolph, their president, and speaker also of the House of Burgesses, might be called off, they added me, in that event, to the delegation. Mr. Randolph was, according to expectation, obliged to leave the chair of Congress, to attend the General Assembly summoned by Lord Dunmore, to meet on the 1st day of June, 1775. Lord North's conciliatory propositions, as they were called, had been received by the Governor, and furnished the subject for which this assembly was convened. Mr. Randolph accordingly attended, and the tenor of these propositions being generally known, as having been addressed to all the governors, he was anxious that the answer of our Assembly, likely to be the first, should harmonize with what he knew to be the sentiments and wishes of the body he had recently left. He feared that Mr. Nicholas, whose mind was not yet up to the mark of the times, would undertake the answer, and therefore pressed me to prepare it. I did so, and, with his aid, carried it through the House, with long and doubtful scruples from Mr. Nicholas and James Mercer, and a dash of cold water on it here and there, enfeebling it somewhat, but finally with unanimity, or a vote approaching it. This being passed, I repaired immediately to Philadelphia, and conveyed to Congress the first notice they had of it. It was entirely approved there. I took my seat with them on the 21st of June. On the 24th, a committee which had been appointed to prepare a declaration of the causes of taking up arms, brought in their report (drawn I believe by J. Rutledge) which, not being liked, the House recommitted it, on the 26th, and added Mr. Dickinson and myself to the committee.

On the rising of the House, the committee having not yet met, I happened to find myself near Governor W. Livingston, and proposed to him to draw the paper. He excused himself and proposed that I should draw it. On my pressing him with urgency, "We are as yet but new acquaintances, sir," said he, "why are you so earnest for my doing it?" "Because," said I, "I have been informed that you drew the Address to the people of Great Britain, a production, certainly, of the finest pen in America." "On that," says he, "perhaps, sir, you may not have been correctly informed." I had received the information in Virginia from Colonel Harrison on his return from that Congress. Lee, Livingston, and Jay had been the committee for that draft. The first, prepared by Lee, had been disapproved and recommitted. The second was drawn by Jay, but being presented by Governor Livingston, had led Colonel Harrison into the error. The next morning, walking in the hall of Congress, many members being assembled, but the House not yet formed, I observed Mr. Jay speaking to R. H. Lee, and leading him by the button of his coat to me. "I understand, sir," said he to me, "that this gentleman informed you that Governor Livingston drew the Address to the people of Great Britain." I assured him, at once, that I had not received that information from Mr. Lee, and that not a word had ever passed on the subject between Mr. Lee and myself; and after some explanations the subject was dropped. These gentlemen had had some sparrings in debate before, and continued ever very hostile to each other.

I prepared a draft of the declaration committed to us. It was too strong for Mr. Dickinson. He still retained the hope of reconciliation with the mother country, and was unwilling it should be lessened by offensive statements. He was so honest a man, and so able a one, that he was greatly indulged even by those who could not feel his scruples. We therefore requested him to take the paper, and put it into a form he could approve. He did so, preparing an entire new statement, and preserving of the former only the last four paragraphs and half of the preceding one. We approved and reported it to Congress, who accepted it. Congress gave a signal proof of their indulgence to Mr. Dickinson, and of their great desire not to go too fast for any respectable part of our body, in permitting him to draw their second petition to the King according to his own ideas, and passing it with scarcely any amendment. The disgust against this humility was general; and Mr. Dickinson's delight at its passage was the only circumstance which reconciled them to it. The vote being passed, although further observation on it was out of order, he could not refrain from rising and expressing his satisfaction, and concluded by saying, "There is but one word, Mr. President, in the paper which I disapprove, and that is the word *Congress;*" on which Ben Harrison rose and said, "There is but one word in the paper, Mr. President, of which I approve, and that is the word *Congress.*"

On the 22d of July, Dr. Franklin, Mr. Adams, R. H. Lee, and myself, were appointed a committee to consider and report on Lord North's conciliatory resolution. The answer of the Virginia Assembly on that subject having been approved, I was requested by the committee to prepare this report, which will account for the similarity of feature in the two instruments.

On the 15th of May, 1776, the convention of Virginia instructed their delegates in Congress, to propose to that body to declare the colonies independent of Great Britain, and appointed a committee to prepare a declaration of rights and plan of government.

In Congress, Friday, June 7, 1776. The delegates from Virginia moved, in obedience to instructions from their constituents, that the Congress should declare that these United colonies are, and of right ought to be, free and independent states, that they are absolved from all allegiance to the British crown, and that all political connection between them and the state of Great Britain is, and ought to be, totally dissolved; that measures should be immediately taken for procuring the assistance of foreign powers, and a Confederation be formed to bind the colonies more closely together.

The House being obliged to attend at that time to some other business, the proposition was referred to the next day, when the members were ordered to attend punctually at ten o'clock.

Saturday, June 8. They proceeded to take it into consideration, and referred it to a committee of the whole, into which they immediately resolved themselves, and passed that day and Monday, the 10th, in debating on the subject.

It was argued by Wilson, Robert R. Livingston, E. Rutledge, Dickinson, and others:

That, though they were friends to the measures themselves, and saw the impossibility that we should ever again be united with Great Britain, yet they were against adopting them at this time:

That the conduct we had formerly observed was wise and proper now, of deferring to take any capital step till the voice of the people drove us into it:

That they were our power, and without them our declarations could not be carried into effect:

That the people of the middle colonies (Maryland, Delaware, Pennsylvania, the Jerseys and New York) were not yet ripe for bidding adieu to British connection, but that they were fast ripening, and, in a short time, would join in the general voice of America:

That the resolution, entered into by this House on the 15th of May, for suppressing the exercise of all powers derived from the crown, had shown, by the ferment into which it had thrown these middle colonies, that they had not yet accommodated their minds to a separation from the mother country:

That some of them had expressly forbidden their delegates to consent to such a declaration, and others had given no instructions, and consequently no powers to give such consent:

That if the delegates of any particular colony had no power to declare such colony independent, certain they were, the others could not declare it for them; the colonies being as yet perfectly independent of each other:

That the assembly of Pennsylvania was now sitting above stairs, their convention would sit within a few days, the convention of New York was now sitting, and those of the Jerseys and Delaware counties would meet on the Monday following, and it was probable these bodies would take up the question of Independence, and would declare to their delegates the voice of their state:

That if such a declaration should now be agreed to, these delegates must retire, and possibly their colonies might secede from the Union:

That such a secession would weaken us more than could be compensated by any foreign alliance:

That in the event of such a division, foreign powers would either refuse to join themselves to our fortunes, or, having us so much in their power as that desperate declaration would place us, they would insist on terms proportionably more hard and prejudicial:

That we had little reason to expect an alliance with those to whom alone, as yet, we had cast our eyes:

That France and Spain had reason to be jealous of that rising power, which would one day certainly strip them of all their American possessions:

That it was more likely they should form a connection with the British court, who, if they should find themselves unable otherwise to extricate themselves from their difficulties, would agree to a partition of our territories, restoring Canada to France, and the Floridas to Spain, to accomplish for themselves a recovery of these colonies:

That it would not be long before we should receive certain information of the disposition and feelings of the French court, from the agent whom he had sent to Paris for that purpose:

That if this disposition should be favorable, by waiting the event of the present campaign, which we all hoped would be successful, we should have reason to expect an alliance on better terms:

That this would in fact work no delay of any effectual aid from such ally, as, from the advance of the season and distance of our situation, it was impossible we could receive any assistance during this campaign:

That it was prudent to fix among ourselves the terms on which we should form alliance, before we declared we would form one at all events:

And that if these were agreed on, and our Declaration of Independence ready by the time our Ambassador should be prepared to sail, it would be as well as to go into that Declaration at this day.

On the other side, it was urged by J. Adams, Lee, Wythe, and others, that no gentleman had argued against the policy or the right of separation from Britain, nor had supposed it possible we should ever renew our connection; that they had only opposed its being now declared:

That the question was not whether, by a Declaration of Independence, we should make ourselves what we are not; but whether we should declare a fact which already exists:

That, as to the people or parliament of England, we had always been independent of them, their restraints on our trade deriving efficacy from our acquiescence only, and not from any rights they possessed of imposing them, and that so far, our connection had been federal only, and was now dissolved by the commencement of hostilities:

That, as to the King, we had been bound to him by allegiance, but that this bond was now dissolved by his assent to the last act of Parliament, by which he declares us out of his protection, and by his levying war on us, a fact which had long ago proved us out of his protection; it being a certain position in law, that allegiance and protection are reciprocal, the one ceasing when the other is withdrawn:

That James the II. never declared the people of England out of his protection, yet his actions proved it, and the Parliament declared it:

No delegates then can be denied, or ever want, a power of declaring an existing truth:

That the delegates from the Delaware counties having declared their constituents ready to join, there are only two colonies, Pennsylvania and Maryland, whose delegates are absolutely tied up, and that these had, by their instructions, only reserved a right of confirming or rejecting the measure:

That the instructions from Pennsylvania might be accounted for from the times in which they were drawn, near a twelvemonth ago, since which the face of affairs has totally changed:

That within that time, it had become apparent that Britain was determined to accept nothing less than a *carte-blanche*, and that the King's answer to the Lord Mayor, Aldermen and Common Council of London, which had come to hand four days ago, must have satisfied every one of this point:

That the people wait for us to lead the way:

That *they* are in favor of the measure, though the instructions given by some of their *representatives* are not:

That the voice of the representatives is not always consonant with the voice of the people, and that this is remarkably the case in these middle colonies:

That the effect of the resolution of the 15th of May has proved this, which, raising the murmurs of some in the colonies of Pennsylvania and Maryland, called forth the opposing voice of the freer part of the people, and proved them to be the majority even in these colonies:

That the backwardness of these two colonies might be ascribed, partly to the influence of proprietary power and connections, and partly, to their having not yet been attacked by the enemy:

That these causes were not likely to be soon removed, as there seemed no probability that the enemy would make either of these the seat of this summer's war:

That it would be vain to wait either weeks or months for perfect unanimity, since it was impossible that all men should ever become of one sentiment on any question:

That the conduct of some colonies, from the beginning of this contest, had given reason to suspect it was their settled policy to keep in the rear of the confederacy, that their particular prospect might be better, even in the worst event:

That, therefore, it was necessary for those colonies who had thrown themselves forward and hazarded all from the beginning, to come forward now also, and put all again to their own hazard:

That the history of the Dutch Revolution, in which three states only confederated at first, proved that a secession of some colonies would not be so dangerous as some apprehended:

That a declaration of Independence alone could render it consistent with European delicacy, for European powers to treat with us, or even to receive an Ambassador from us:

That till this, they would not receive our vessels into their ports, nor acknowledge the adjudications of our courts of admiralty to be legitimate, in cases of capture of British vessels:

That though France and Spain may be jealous of our rising power, they must think it will be much more formidable with the addition of Great Britain; and will therefore see it their interest to prevent a coalition; but should they refuse, we shall be but where we are; whereas without trying, we shall never know whether they will aid us or not:

That the present campaign may be unsuccessful, and therefore we had better propose an alliance while our affairs wear a hopeful aspect:

That to wait the event of this campaign will certainly work delay, because, during the summer, France may assist us effectually, by cutting off those supplies of provisions from England and Ireland, on which the enemy's armies here are to depend; or by setting in motion the great power they have collected in the West Indies, and calling our enemy to the defense of the possessions they have there:

That it would be idle to lose time in settling the terms of alliance, till we had first determined we would enter into alliance:

That it is necessary to lose no time in opening a trade for our people, who will want clothes, and will want money too, for the payment of taxes:

And that the only misfortune is, that we did not enter into alliance with France six months sooner, as, besides opening her ports for the vent of our last year's produce, she might have marched an army into Germany, and prevented the petty princes there from selling their unhappy subjects to subdue us.

It appearing in the course of these debates that the colonies of New York, New Jersey, Pennsylvania, Delaware, Maryland, and South Carolina were not yet matured for falling from the parent stem, but that they were fast advancing to that state, it was thought most prudent to wait a while for them, and to postpone the final decision to July 1st; but, that this might occasion as little delay as possible, a committee was appointed to prepare a Declaration of Independence. The committee were John Adams, Dr. Franklin, Roger Sherman, Robert R. Livingston, and myself. Committees were also appointed, at the same time, to prepare a plan of confederation for the colonies, and to state the terms proper to be proposed for foreign alliance. The committee for drawing the Declaration of Independence desired me to do it. It was accordingly done, and being approved by them, I reported it to the House on Friday, the 28th of June, when it was read, and ordered to lie on the table. On Monday, the 1st of July, the House resolved itself into a committee of the whole, and resumed the consideration of the original motion made by the delegates of Virginia, which, being again debated through the day, was carried in the affirmative by the votes of New Hampshire, Connecticut, Massachusetts, Rhode Island, New Jersey, Maryland, Virginia, North Carolina and Georgia. South Carolina and Pennsylvania voted against it. Delaware had but two members present, and they were divided. The delegates from New York declared they were for it themselves, and were assured their constituents were for it; but that their instructions having been drawn near a twelvemonth before, when reconciliation was still the general object, they were enjoined by them to do nothing which should impede that object. They, therefore, thought themselves not justifiable in voting on either side, and asked leave to withdraw from the question; which was given them. The committee rose and reported their resolution to the House. Mr. Edward Rutledge, of South Carolina, then requested the determination might be put off to the next day, as he believed his colleagues, though they disapproved of the resolution, would then join in it for the sake of unanimity. The ultimate question, whether the House would agree to the resolution of the committee, was accordingly postponed to the next day, when it was again moved, and South Carolina concurred in voting for it. In the meantime, a third member had come post from the Delaware counties, and turned the vote of that colony in favor of the resolution. Members of a different sentiment attending that morning from Pennsylvania also, her vote was changed, so that the whole twelve colonies who were authorized to vote at all, gave their voices for it; and, within a few days,[2] the convention of New York approved of it, and thus supplied the void occasioned by the withdrawing of her delegates from the vote.

Congress proceeded the same day to consider the Declaration of Independence, which had been reported and lain on the table the Friday preceding, and on Monday referred to a committee of the whole. The pusillanimous idea that we had friends in England worth keeping terms with still haunted

[2] July 9.

the minds of many. For this reason, those passages which conveyed censures on the people of England were struck out, lest they should give them offense. The clause, too, reprobating the enslaving the inhabitants of Africa, was struck out in complaisance to South Carolina and Georgia, who had never attempted to restrain the importation of slaves, and who, on the contrary, still wished to continue it. Our northern brethren also, I believe, felt a little tender under those censures; for though their people had very few slaves themselves, yet they had been pretty considerable carriers of them to others. The debates, having taken up the greater parts of the second, third, and fourth days of July, were, on the evening of the last, closed; the Declaration was reported by the committee, agreed to by the House, and signed by every member present, except Mr. Dickinson.

Our delegation had been renewed for the ensuing year, commencing August 11; but the new government was now organized, a meeting of the legislature was to be held in October, and I had been elected a member by my county. I knew that our legislation, under the regal government, had many very vicious points which urgently required reformation, and I thought I could be of more use in forwarding that work. I therefore retired from my seat in Congress on the 2d of September, resigned it, and took my place in the legislature of my State, on the 7th of October.

On the 11th, I moved for leave to bring in a bill for the establishment of courts of justice, the organization of which was of importance. I drew the bill; it was approved by the committee, reported and passed, after going through its due course.

On the 12th, I obtained leave to bring in a bill declaring tenants in tail to hold their lands in fee simple. In the earlier times of the colony, when lands were to be obtained for little or nothing, some provident individuals procured large grants; and, desirous of founding great families for themselves, settled them on their descendants in fee tail. The transmission of this property from generation to generation, in the same name, raised up a distinct set of families, who, being privileged by law in the perpetuation of their wealth, were thus formed into a Patrician order, distinguished by the splendor and luxury of their establishments. From this order, too, the king habitually selected his counselors of State; the hope of which distinction devoted the whole corps to the interests and will of the crown. To annul this privilege, and instead of an aristocracy of wealth, of more harm and danger, than benefit, to society, to make an opening for the aristocracy of virtue and talent, which nature has wisely provided for the direction of the interests of society, and scattered with equal hand through all its conditions, was deemed essential to a well-ordered republic.—To effect it, no violence was necessary, no deprivation of natural right, but rather an enlargement of it by a repeal of the law. For this would authorize the present holder to divide the property among his children equally, as his affections were divided; and would place them, by natural generation, on the level of their fellow citizens. But this repeal was strongly opposed by Mr. Pendleton, who was zealously attached to ancient establishments; and who, taken all in all, was the ablest man in debate I have ever met with. He had not indeed the poetical fancy of Mr. Henry, his sublime imagination, his lofty and overwhelming diction; but he was cool, smooth and persuasive; his language flowing, chaste and embellished; his conceptions quick, acute and full of resource; never vanquished: for if he lost the main battle, he returned upon you, and regained so much of it as to make it a drawn one, by dexterous maneuvers, skirmishes in detail, and the recovery of small advantages which, little singly, were important all together. You never knew when you were clear of him, but were harassed by his perseverance, until the patience was worn down of all who had less of it than himself. Add to this, that he was one of the most virtuous and benevolent of men, the kindest friend, the most amiable and pleasant of companions, which insured a favorable reception to whatever came from him. Finding that the general principle of entails could not be maintained, he took his stand on an amendment which he proposed, instead of an absolute abolition, to permit the tenant in tail to convey in fee simple, if he chose it; and he was within a few votes of saving so much of the old law. But the bill passed finally for entire abolition.

In that one of the bills for organizing our judiciary system, which proposed a court of Chancery, I had provided for a trial by jury of all matters of fact, in that as well as in the courts of law. He defeated it by the introduction of four words only, "*if either party choose.*" The consequence has been, that as no suitor will say to his judge, "Sir, I distrust you, give me a jury," juries are rarely, I might say, perhaps, never, seen in that court, but when called for by the Chancellor of his own accord.

The first establishment in Virginia which became permanent, was made in 1607. I have found no mention of negroes in the colony until about 1650. The first brought here as slaves were by a Dutch ship; after which the English commenced the trade, and continued it until the revolutionary war. That suspended, *ipso facto*, their further importation for the present, and the business of the war pressing constantly on the legislature, this subject was not acted on finally until the year '78, when I brought in a bill to prevent their further importation. This passed without opposition, and stopped the increase of the evil by importation, leaving to future efforts its final eradication.

The first settlers of this colony were Englishmen, loyal subjects to their king and church, and the grant to Sir Walter Raleigh contained an express proviso that their laws "should not be against the true Christian faith, now professed in the church of England." As soon as the state of the colony admitted, it was divided into parishes, in each of which was established a minister of the Anglican church, endowed with a fixed salary, in tobacco, a glebe house and land with the other necessary appendages. To meet these expenses, all the inhabitants of the parishes were assessed, whether they were or not, members of the established church. Towards Quakers who came here, they were most cruelly intolerant, driving them from the colony by the severest penalties. In process of time, however, other sectarisms were introduced, chiefly of the Presbyterian family; and the established clergy, secure for life in their glebes and salaries, adding to these, generally, the emoluments of a classical school, found employment enough, in their farms and school-rooms, for the rest of the week, and devoted Sunday only to the edification of their flock, by service, and a sermon at their parish church. Their other pastoral functions were little attended to. Against this inactivity, the zeal and industry of sectarian preachers had an open and undisputed field; and by the time of the revolution, a majority of the inhabitants had become dissenters from the established church, but were still obliged to pay contributions to support the pastors of the minority. This unrighteous compulsion, to maintain teachers of what they deemed religious errors, was grievously felt during the regal government, and without a hope of relief. But the first republican legislature, which met in '76, was crowded with petitions to abolish this spiritual tyranny. These brought on the severest contests in which I have ever been engaged. Our great opponents were Mr. Pendleton and Robert Carter Nicholas; honest men, but zealous churchmen.

The petitions were referred to the committee of the whole house on the state of the country; and, after desperate contests in that committee, almost daily from the 11th of October to the 5th of December, we prevailed so far only, as to repeal the laws which rendered criminal the maintenance of any religious opinions, the forbearance of repairing to church, or the exercise of any mode of worship; and further, to exempt dissenters from contributions to the support of the established church; and to suspend, only until the next session, levies on the members of that church for the salaries of their own incumbents. For although the majority of our citizens were dissenters, as has been observed, a majority of the legislature were churchmen. Among these, however, were some reasonable and liberal men, who enabled us, on some points, to obtain feeble majorities. But our opponents carried, in the general resolutions of the committee of November 19, a declaration that religious assemblies ought to be regulated, and that provision ought to be made for continuing the succession of the clergy, and superintending their conduct. And, in the bill now passed, was inserted an express reservation of the question, Whether a general assessment should not be established by law, on every one, to the support of the pastor of his choice; or whether all should be left to voluntary contributions; and on this question, debated at every session, from '76 to '79, (some of our dissenting allies, having now secured their particular object, going over to the advocates of a general assessment,) we could only obtain a suspension from session to session until '79, when the question against a general assessment was finally carried, and the establishment of the Anglican church entirely put down. In justice to the two honest but zealous opponents who have been named, I must add, that although, from their natural temperaments, they were more disposed generally to acquiesce in things as they are, than to risk innovations, yet whenever the public will had once decided, none were more faithful or exact in their obedience to it.

The seat of our government had originally been fixed in the peninsula of Jamestown, the first settlement of the colonists; and had been afterwards removed a few miles inland to Williamsburg. But this was at a time when our settlements had not extended beyond the tide waters. Now they had crossed the Alleghany; and the center of population was very far removed from what it had been. Yet Williamsburg was still the depository of our archives, the habitual residence of the Governor and many other of the public functionaries, the established place for the sessions of the legislature, and the magazine of our military stores; and its situation was so exposed that it might be taken at any time in war, and, at this time particularly, an enemy might in the night run up either of the rivers, between which it lies, land a force above, and take possession of the place, without the possibility of saving either persons or things. I had proposed its removal so early as October, '76; but it did not prevail until the session of May, '79.

Early in the session of May, '79, I prepared, and obtained leave to bring in a bill, declaring who should be deemed citizens, asserting the natural right of expatriation, and prescribing the mode of exercising it. This, when I withdrew from the house, on the 1st of June following, I left in the hands of George Mason, and it was passed on the 26th of that month.

In giving this account of the laws of which I was myself the mover and draftsman, I, by no means, mean to claim to myself the merit of obtaining their passage. I had many occasional and strenuous coadjutors in debate, and one, most steadfast, able and zealous; who was himself a host. This was George Mason, a man of the first order of wisdom among those who acted on the theater of the revolution, of expansive mind, profound judgment, cogent in argument, learned in the lore of our former constitution, and earnest for the republican change on democratic principles. His elocution was neither flowing nor smooth; but his language was strong, his manner most impressive, and strengthened by a dash of biting cynicism, when provocation made it seasonable.

Mr. Wythe, while speaker in the two sessions of 1777, between his return from Congress and his appointment to the Chancery, was an able and constant associate in whatever was before a committee of the whole. His pure integrity, judgment and reasoning powers, gave him great weight. Of him, see more in some notes inclosed in my letter of August 31, 1821, to Mr. John Saunderson.

Mr. Madison came into the House in 1776, a new member and young; which circumstances, concurring with his extreme modesty, prevented his venturing himself in debate before his removal to the Council of State, in November, '77. From thence he went to Congress, then consisting of few members. Trained in these successive schools, he acquired a habit of self-possession, which placed at ready command the rich resources of his luminous and discriminating mind, and of his extensive information, and rendered him the first of every assembly afterwards, of which he became a member. Never wandering from his subject into vain declamation, but pursuing it closely, in language pure, classical and copious, soothing always the feelings of his adversaries by civilities and softness of expression, he rose to the eminent station which he held in the great National Convention of 1787; and in that of Virginia which followed, he sustained the new constitution in all its parts, bearing off the palm against the logic of George Mason, and the fervid declamation of Mr. Henry. With these consummate powers, were united a pure and spotless virtue, which no calumny has ever attempted to sully. Of the powers and polish of his pen, and of the wisdom of his administration in the highest office of the nation, I need say nothing. They have spoken, and will forever speak for themselves.

So far we were proceeding in the details of reformation

only; selecting points of legislation, prominent in character and principle, urgent, and indicative of the strength of the general pulse of reformation. When I left Congress, in '76, it was in the persuasion that our whole code must be reviewed, adapted to our republican form of government; and, now that we had no negatives of Councils, Governors, and Kings to restrain us from doing right, that it should be corrected, in all its parts, with a single eye to reason, and the good of those for whose government it was framed. Early, therefore, in the session of '76, to which I returned, I moved and presented a bill for the revision of the laws, which was passed on the 24th of October; and on the 5th of November, Mr. Pendleton, Mr. Wythe, George Mason, Thomas L. Lee, and myself, were appointed a committee to execute the work.

We agreed to meet at Fredericksburg to settle the plan of operation, and to distribute the work. We met there accordingly, on the 13th of January, 1777. The first question was, whether we should propose to abolish the whole existing system of laws, and prepare a new and complete Institute, or preserve the general system, and only modify it to the present state of things. Mr. Pendleton, contrary to his usual disposition in favor of ancient things, was for the former proposition, in which he was joined by Mr. Lee. To this it was objected, that to abrogate our whole system would be a bold measure, and probably far beyond the views of the legislature; that they had been in the practice of revising, from time to time, the laws of the colony, omitting the expired, the repealed, and the obsolete, amending only those retained, and probably meant we should now do the same, only including the British statutes as well as our own: that to compose a new Institute, like those of Justinian and Bracton, or that of Blackstone, which was the model proposed by Mr. Pendleton, would be an arduous undertaking, of vast research, of great consideration and judgment; and when reduced to a text, every word of that text, from the imperfection of human language, and its incompetence to express distinctly every shade of idea, would become a subject of question and chicanery, until settled by repeated adjudications; and this would involve us for ages in litigation, and render property uncertain, until, like the statutes of old, every word had been tried and settled by numerous decisions, and by new volumes of reports and commentaries; and that no one of us, probably, would undertake such a work, which to be systematical, must be the work of one hand. This last was the opinion of Mr. Wythe, Mr. Mason, and myself. When we proceeded to the distribution of the work, Mr. Mason excused himself, as, being no lawyer, he felt himself unqualified for the work, and he resigned soon after. Mr. Lee excused himself on the same ground, and died, indeed, in a short time. The other two gentlemen, therefore, and myself divided the work among us. The common law and statutes to the 4 James I. (when our separate legislature was established) were assigned to me; the British statutes, from that period to the present day, to Mr. Wythe; and the Virginia laws to Mr. Pendleton.

As the law of Descents, and the criminal law fell of course within my portion, I wished the committee to settle the leading principles of these, as a guide for me in framing them; and, with respect to the first, I proposed to abolish the law of primogeniture, and to make real estate descendible in parcenary to the next of kin, as personal property is, by the statute of distribution Mr. Pendleton wished to preserve the right of primogeniture, but seeing at once that that could not prevail, he proposed we should adopt the Hebrew principle, and give a double portion to the elder son. I observed, that if the eldest son could eat twice as much, or do double work, it might be a natural evidence of his right to a double portion; but being on a par in his powers and wants, with his brothers and sisters, he should be on a par also in the partition of the patrimony; and such was the decision of the other members.

On the subject of the Criminal law, all were agreed, that the punishment of death should be abolished, except for treason and murder; and that, for other felonies, should be substituted hard labor in the public works, and in some cases, the *Lex talionis*. How this last revolting principle came to obtain our approbation, I do not remember. There remained, indeed, in our laws, a vestige of it in a single case of a slave; it was the English law, in the time of the Anglo-Saxons, copied probably from the Hebrew law of "an eye for an eye, a tooth for a tooth," and it was the law of several ancient people; but the modern mind had left it far in the rear of its advances. These points, however, being settled, we repaired to our respective homes for the preparation of the work.

In the execution of my part, I thought it material not to vary the diction of the ancient statutes by modernizing it, nor to give rise to new questions by new expressions. The text of these statutes had been so fully explained and defined, by numerous adjudications, as scarcely ever now to produce a question in our courts. I thought it would be useful, also, in all new drafts, to reform the style of the later British statutes, and of our own acts of Assembly; which, from their verbosity. their endless tautologies, their involutions of case within case, and parenthesis within parenthesis, and their multiplied efforts at certainty, by *saids* and *aforesaids,* by *ors* and by *ands,* to make them more plain, are really rendered more perplexed and incomprehensible, not only to common readers, but to the lawyers themselves. We were employed in this work from that time to February, 1779, when we met at Williamsburg, that is to say, Mr. Pendleton, Mr. Wythe and myself; and meeting day by day, we examined critically our several parts, sentence by sentence, scrutinizing and amending, until we had agreed on the whole.

We then returned home, had fair copies made of our several parts, which were reported to the General Assembly, June 18, 1779, by Mr. Wythe and myself, Mr. Pendleton's residence being distant, and he having authorized us by letter to declare his approbation. We had, in this work, brought so much of the Common law as it was thought necessary to alter, all the British statutes from *Magna Charta* to the present day, and all the laws of Virginia, from the establishment of our legislature, in the 4th Jac. 1. to the present time, which we thought should be retained, within the compass of one hundred and twenty-six bills, making a printed folio of ninety pages only. Some bills were taken out, occasionally, from time to time, and passed; but the main body of the work was not entered on by the legislature until after the general peace, in 1785, when, by the unwearied exertions of Mr. Madison, in opposition to the endless quibbles, chicaneries, perversions, vexations and delays of lawyers and demi-lawyers, most of the bills were passed by the legislature, with little alteration.

The bill for establishing religious freedom, the principles of which had, to a certain degree, been enacted before, I had drawn in all the latitude of reason and right. It still met with opposition; but, with some mutilations in the preamble, it was finally passed; and a singular proposition proved that its protection of opinion was meant to be universal. Where the preamble declares, that coercion is a departure from the plan of the holy author of our religion, an amendment was proposed, by inserting the word "Jesus Christ," so that it should read, "a departure from the plan of Jesus Christ, the holy author of our religion;" the insertion was rejected by a great majority, in proof that they meant to comprehend, within the mantle of its protection, the Jew and the Gentile, the Christian and Mahometan, the Hindoo, and Infidel of every denomination.

Beccaria, and other writers on crimes and punishments, had satisfied the reasonable world of the unrightfulness and inefficacy of the punishment of crimes by death; and hard labor on roads, canals and other public works, had been suggested as a proper substitute. The Revisers had adopted these opinions; but the general idea of our country had not yet advanced to that point. The bill, therefore, for proportioning crimes and punishments, was lost in the House of Delegates by a majority of a single vote. I learned afterwards, that the substitute of hard labor in public, was tried (I believe it was in Pennsylvania) without success. Exhibited as a public spectacle, with shaved heads and mean clothing, working on the high roads, produced in the criminals such a prostration of character, such an abandonment of self-respect, as, instead of reforming, plunged them into the most desperate and hardened depravity of morals and character. To pursue the subject of this law.—I was written to in 1785 (being then in Paris) by directors appointed to superintend the building of a Capitol in Richmond, to advise them as to a plan, and to add to it one of a Prison. Thinking it a favorable opportunity of introducing into the State an example of architecture, in the classic style of antiquity, and the Maison quarrée of Nismes, an ancient Roman temple, being considered as the most perfect model existing of what may be called Cubic architecture, I applied to M. Clerissault, who had published drawings of the Antiquities of Nismes, to have me a model of the building made in stucco, only changing the order from Corinthian to Ionic, on account of the difficulty of the Corinthian capitals. I yielded, with reluctance, to the taste of Clerissault, in his preference of the modern capital of Scamozzi to the more noble capital of antiquity. This was executed by the artist whom Choiseul Gouffier had carried with him to Constantinople, and employed, while Ambassador there, in making those beautiful models of the remains of Grecian architecture which are to be seen at Paris. To adapt the exterior to our use, I drew a plan for the interior, with the apartments necessary for legislative, executive, and judiciary purposes; and accommodated in their size and distribution to the form and dimensions of the building. These were forwarded to the Directors, in 1786, and were carried into execution, with some variations, not for the better, the most important of which, however, admit of future correction and amendment.

With respect to the plan of a Prison, requested at the same time, I had heard of a benevolent society, in England, which had been indulged by the government, in an experiment of the effect of labor, in *solitary confinement,* on some of their criminals; which experiment had succeeded beyond expectation. The same idea had been suggested in France, and an Architect of Lyons had proposed a plan of a well-contrived edifice, on the principle of solitary confinement. I procured a copy, and as it was too large for our purposes, I drew one on a scale less extensive, but susceptible of additions as they should be wanting. This I sent to the Directors, instead of a plan of a common prison, in the hope that it would suggest the idea of labor in solitary confinement, instead of that on the public works, which we had adopted in our Revised Code. Its principle, accordingly, but not its exact form, was adopted by Latrobe in carrying the plan into execution, by the erection of what is now called the Penitentiary, built under his direction. In the meanwhile, the public opinion was ripening, by time, by reflection, and by the example of Pennsylvania, where labor on the highways had been tried, without approbation, from 1786 to '89, and had been followed by their Penitentiary system on the principle of confinement and labor, which was proceeding auspiciously. In 1796, our legislature resumed the subject, and passed the law for amending the Penal laws of the commonwealth.

On the 1st of June, 1779, I was appointed Governor of the Commonwealth, and retired from the legislature. Being elected, also, one of the Visitors of William and Mary College, a self-electing body, I effected, during my residence in Williamsburg that year, a change in the organization of that institution, by abolishing the Grammar school, and the two professorships of Divinity and Oriental languages, and substituting a professorship of Law and Police, one of Anatomy, Medicine and Chemistry, and one of Modern languages; and the charter confining us to six professorships, we added the Law of Nature and Nations, and the Fine Arts to the duties of the Moral professor, and Natural History to those of the professor of Mathematics and Natural Philosophy.

Being now, as it were, identified with the Commonwealth itself, to write my own history, during the two years of my administration, would be to write the public history of that portion of the revolution within this State. This has been done by others, and particularly by Mr. Girardin, who wrote his Continuation of Burke's History of Virginia, while at Milton, in this neighborhood, had free access to all my papers while composing it, and has given as faithful an account as I could myself. For this portion, therefore, of my own life, I refer altogether to his history. From a belief that, under the pressure of the invasion under which we were then laboring, the public would have more confidence in a Military chief, and that the Military commander, being invested with the Civil power also, both might be wielded with more energy, promptitude and effect for the defense of the State, I resigned the administration at the end of my second year, and General Nelson was appointed to succeed me.

Soon after my leaving Congress, in September, '76, to wit, on the last day of that month, I had been appointed, with Dr. Franklin, to go to France, as a Commissioner, to negotiate treaties of alliance and commerce with that government. Silas Deane, then in France, acting as [3] agent for procuring

[3] His ostensible character was to be that of a merchant, his real one that of agent for military supplies, and also for sounding the dispositions of the government of France, and seeing how far they would favor

military stores, was joined with us in commission. But such
was the state of my family that I could not leave it, nor
could I expose it to the dangers of the sea, and of capture
by the British ships, then covering the ocean. I saw, too,
that the laboring oar was really at home, where much was
to be done, of the most permanent interest, in new modeling
our governments, and much to defend our fanes and fire-sides
from the desolations of an invading enemy, pressing on
our country in every point. I declined, therefore, and Dr.
Lee was appointed in my place. On the 15th of June, 1781,
I had been appointed, with Mr. Adams, Dr. Franklin, Mr.
Jay, and Mr. Laurens, a Minister Plenipotentiary for negotiating peace, then expected to be effected through the mediation of the Empress of Russia. The same reasons obliged
me still to decline; and the negotiation was in fact never
entered on. But, in the autumn of the next year, 1782, Congress receiving assurances that a general peace would be concluded in the winter and spring, they renewed my appointment on the 13th of November of that year. I had, two
months before that, lost the cherished companion of my life,
in whose affections, unabated on both sides, I had lived the
last ten years in unchequered happiness. With the public
interests, the state of my mind concurred in recommending
the change of scene proposed; and I accepted the appointment, and left Monticello on the 19th of December, 1782, for
Philadelphia, where I arrived on the 27th. The Minister
of France, Luzerne, offered me a passage in the Romulus
frigate, which I accepted; but she was then lying a few miles
below Baltimore, blocked up in the ice. I remained, therefore, a month in Philadelphia, looking over the papers in
the office of State, in order to possess myself of the general
state of our foreign relations, and then went to Baltimore,
to await the liberation of the frigate from the ice. After
waiting there nearly a month, we received information that
a Provisional treaty of peace had been signed by our Commissioners on the 3d of September, 1782, to become absolute,
on the conclusion of peace between France and Great Britain.
Considering my proceeding to Europe as now of no utility

us, either secretly or openly. His appointment had been by the Committee of foreign correspondence, March, 1776.

to the public, I returned immediately to Philadelphia, to take the orders of Congress, and was excused by them from further proceeding. I, therefore, returned home, where I arrived on the 15th of May, 1783.

On the 6th of the following month, I was appointed by the legislature a delegate to Congress, the appointment to take place on the 1st of November ensuing, when that of the existing delegation would expire. I, accordingly, left home on the 16th of October, arrived at Trenton, where Congress was sitting, on the 3d of November, and took my seat on the 4th, on which day Congress adjourned, to meet at Annapolis on the 26th.

Congress had now become a very small body, and the members very remiss in their attendance on its duties, insomuch, that a majority of the States, necessary by the Confederation to constitute a House even for minor business, did not assemble until the 13th of December.

They, as early as January 7, 1782, had turned their attention to the moneys current in the several States, and had directed the Financier, Robert Morris, to report to them a table of rates, at which the foreign coins should be received at the treasury. That officer, or rather his assistant, Gouverneur Morris, answered them on the 15th, in an able and elaborate statement of the denominations of money current in the several States, and of the comparative value of the foreign coins chiefly in circulation with us. He went into the consideration of the necessity of establishing a standard of value with us, and of the adoption of a money Unit. He proposed for that Unit, such a fraction of pure silver as would be a common measure of the penny of every State, without leaving a fraction. This common divisor he found to be 1-1440 of a dollar, or 1-1600 of the crown sterling. The value of a dollar was, therefore, to be expressed by 1,440 units, and of a crown by 1,600; each Unit containing a quarter of a grain of fine silver. Congress turning again their attention to this subject the following year, the Financier, by a letter of April 30, 1783, further explained and urged the Unit he had proposed; but nothing more was done on it until the ensuing year, when it was again taken up, and referred to a committee, of which I was a member. The general views of the Financier were sound, and the principle was ingenious on which he proposed to found his Unit; but it was too minute for ordinary use, too laborious for computation, either by the head or in figures. The price of a loaf of bread, 1-20 of a dollar, would be 72 units.

A pound of butter, 1-5 of a dollar, 288 units.

A horse or bullock, of eighty dollars' value, would require a notation of six figures, to wit, 115,200, and the public debt, suppose of eighty millions, would require twelve figures, to wit, 115,200,000,000 units. Such a system of money-arithmetic would be entirely unmanageable for the common purposes of society. I proposed, therefore, instead of this, to adopt the Dollar as our Unit of account and payment, and that its divisions and sub-divisions should be in the decimal ratio. I wrote some Notes on the subject, which I submitted to the consideration of the Financier. I received his answer and adherence to his general system, only agreeing to take for his Unit one hundred of those he first proposed, so that a Dollar should be 14 40-100, and a crown 16 units. I replied to this, and printed my notes and reply on a flying sheet, which I put into the hands of the members of Congress for consideration, and the Committee agreed to report on my principle. This was adopted the ensuing year, and is the system which now prevails. I insert, here, the Notes and Reply, as showing the different views on which the adoption of our money system hung. The divisions into dimes, cents, and mills is now so well understood, that it would be easy of introduction into the kindred branches of weights and measures. I use, when I travel, an Odometer of Clarke's invention, which divides the mile into cents, and I find every one comprehends a distance readily, when stated to him in miles and cents; so he would in feet and cents, pounds and cents, &c.

The remissness of Congress, and their permanent session, began to be a subject of uneasiness; and even some of the legislatures had recommended to them intermissions, and periodical sessions. As the Confederation had made no provision for a visible head of the government, during vacations of Congress, and such a one was necessary to superintend the executive business, to receive and communicate with foreign ministers and nations, and to assemble Congress on sudden and extraordinary emergencies, I proposed, early in April, the appointment of a committee, to be called the "Committee of the States," to consist of a member from each State, who should remain in session during the recess of Congress: that the functions of Congress should be divided into executive and legislative, the latter to be reserved, and the former, by a general resolution, to be delegated to that Committee. This proposition was afterwards agreed to; a Committee appointed, who entered on duty on the subsequent adjournment of Congress, quarreled very soon, split into two parties. abandoned their post, and left the government without any visible head, until the next meeting in Congress. We have since seen the same thing take place in the Directory of France; and I believe it will forever take place in any Executive consisting of a plurality. Our plan, best, I believe, combines wisdom and practicability, by providing a plurality of Counselors, but a single Arbiter for ultimate decision.

I was in France when we heard of this schism, and separation of our Committee, and, speaking with Dr. Franklin of this singular disposition of men to quarrel, and divide into parties, he gave his sentiments, as usual, by way of Apologue. He mentioned the Eddystone lighthouse, in the British channel, as being built on a rock, in the mid-channel, totally inaccessible in winter, from the boisterous character of that sea, in that season; that, therefore, for the two keepers employed to keep up the lights, all provisions for the winter were necessarily carried to them in autumn, as they could never be visited again till the return of the milder season; that, on the first practicable day in the spring, a boat put off to them with fresh supplies. The boatmen met at the door one of the keepers, and accosted him with a "How goes it, friend?" "Very well." "How is your companion?" "I do not know." "Don't know? Is not he here?" "I can't tell." "Have not you seen him to-day?" "No." "When did you see him?" "Not since last fall." "You have killed him?" "Not I, indeed." They were about to lay hold of him, as having certainly murdered his companion; but he desired them to go up stairs and examine for themselves. They went up, and there found the other keeper.

They had quarreled, it seems, soon after being left there, had divided into two parties, assigned the cares below to one, and those above to the other, and had never spoken to, or seen, one another since.

But to return to our Congress at Annapolis. The definitive treaty of peace which had been signed at Paris on the 3d of September, 1783, and received here, could not be ratified without a House of nine States. On the 23d of December, therefore, we addressed letters to the several Governors, stating the receipt of the definitive treaty; that seven States only were in attendance, while nine were necessary to its ratification; and urging them to press on their delegates the necessity of their immediate attendance. And on the 26th, to save time, I moved that the Agent of Marine (Robert Morris) should be instructed to have ready a vessel at this place, at New York, and at some Eastern port, to carry over the ratification of the treaty when agreed to. It met the general sense of the House, but was opposed by Dr. Lee, on the ground of expense, which it would authorize the Agent to incur for us; and, he said, it would be better to ratify at once, and send on the ratification. Some members had before suggested, that seven States were competent to the ratification.

My motion was therefore postponed, and another brought forward by Mr. Read, of South Carolina, for an immediate ratification. This was debated the 26th and 27th. Read, Lee, Williamson and Jeremiah Chase, urged that ratification was a mere matter of form, that the treaty was conclusive from the moment it was signed by the ministers; that, although the Confederation requires the assent of *nine States* to *enter into* a treaty, yet, that its conclusion could not be called *entrance into it;* that supposing nine States requisite, it would be in the power of five States to keep us always at war; that nine States had virtually authorized the ratification, having ratified the provisional treaty, and instructed their ministers to agree to a definitive one in the same terms, and the present one was, in fact, substantially, and almost verbatim, the same; that there now remain but sixty-seven days for the ratification, for its passage across the Atlantic, and its exchange; that there was no hope of our soon having nine States present; in fact, that this was the ultimate point of time to which we could venture to wait; that if the ratification was not in Paris by the time stipulated, the treaty would become void; that if ratified by seven States, it would go under our seal, without its being known to Great Britain that only seven had concurred; that it was a question of which they had no right to take cognizance, and we were only answerable for it to our constituents; that it was like the ratification which Great Britain had received from the Dutch, by the negotiations of Sir William Temple.

On the contrary, it was argued by Monroe, Gerry, Howel, Ellery and myself, that by the modern usage of Europe, the ratification was considered as the act which gave validity to a treaty, until which, it was not obligatory. That the commission to the ministers reserved the ratification to Congress; that the treaty itself stipulated that it should be ratified; that it became a second question, who were competent to the ratification? That the Confederation expressly required nine States to enter into any treaty; that, by this, that instrument must have intended, that the assent of nine States should be necessary, as well to the *completion* as to the *commencement* of the treaty, its object having been to guard the rights of the Union in all those important cases where nine States are called for; that by the contrary construction, seven States, containing less than one-third of our whole citizens, might rivet on us a treaty, commenced indeed under commission and instructions from nine States, but formed by the minister in express contradiction to such instructions, and in direct sacrifice of the interests of so great a majority; that the definitive treaty was admitted not to be a verbal copy of the provisional one, and whether the departures from it were of substance, or not, was a question on which nine States alone were competent to decide; that the circumstances of the ratification of the provisional articles by nine States, the instructions to our ministers to form a definitive one by them, and their actual agreement in substance, do not render us competent to ratify in the present instance; if these circumstances are in themselves a ratification, nothing further is requisite than to give attested copies of them, in exchange for the British ratification; if they are not, we remain where we were, without a ratification by nine States, and incompetent ourselves to ratify; that it was but four days since the seven States, now present, unanimously concurred in a resolution, to be forwarded to the Governors of the absent States, in which they stated, as a cause for urging on their delegates, that nine States were necessary to ratify the treaty; that in the case of the Dutch ratification, Great Britain had courted it, and therefore was glad to accept it as it was; that they knew our Constitution, and would object to a ratification by seven; that, if that circumstance was kept back, it would be known hereafter, and would give them ground to deny the validity of a ratification, into which they should have been surprised and cheated, and it would be a dishonorable prostitution of our seal; that there is a hope of nine States; that if the treaty would become null, if not ratified in time, it would not be saved by an imperfect ratification; but that, in fact, it would not be null, and would be placed on better ground, going in unexceptionable form, though a few days too late, and rested on the small importance of this circumstance, and the physical impossibilities which had prevented a punctual compliance in point of time; that this would be approved by all nations, and by Great Britain herself, if not determined to renew the war, and if so determined, she would never want excuses, were this out of the way. Mr. Read gave notice, he should call for the yeas and nays; whereon those in opposition, prepared a resolution, expressing pointedly the reasons of their dissent from his motion. It appearing, however, that his proposition could not be carried, it was thought better to make no entry at all. Massachusetts alone would have been for it; Rhode Island, Pennsylvania and Virginia against it, Delaware, Maryland and North Carolina, would have been divided.

Our body was little numerous, but very contentious. Day after day was wasted on the most unimportant questions. A member, one of those afflicted with the morbid rage of debate, of an ardent mind, prompt imagination, and copious flow of words, who heard with impatience any logic which was not his own, sitting near me on some occasion of a trifling but wordy debate, asked me how I could sit in silence, hearing so much false reasoning, which a word should refute. I observed to him, that to refute indeed was easy, but to silence was impossible; that in measures brought forward by myself, I took the laboring oar, as was incumbent on me; but that in general, I was willing to listen; that if every sound argument or objection was used by some one or other of the numerous debaters, it was enough; if not, I thought it sufficient to suggest the omission, without going into a repetition of what had been already said by others: that this was a waste and abuse of the time and patience of the House, which could not be justified. And I believe, that if the members of deliberate bodies were to observe this course generally, they would do in a day, what takes them a week; and it is really more questionable, than may at first be thought, whether Bonaparte's dumb legislature, which said nothing, and did much, may not be preferable to one which talks much, and does nothing.

I served with General Washington in the legislature of Virginia, before the revolution, and, during it, with Dr. Franklin in Congress. I never heard either of them speak ten minutes at a time, nor to any but the main point, which was to decide the question. They laid their shoulders to the great points, knowing that the little ones would follow of themselves. If the present Congress errs in too much talking, how can it be otherwise, in a body to which the people send one hundred and fifty lawyers, whose trade it is to question everything, yield nothing, and talk by the hour? That one hundred and fifty lawyers should do business together, ought not to be expected. But to return again to our subject.

Those who thought seven States competent to the ratification, being very restless under the loss of their motion, I proposed, on the third of January, to meet them on middle ground, and therefore moved a resolution, which premised, that there were but seven States present, who were unanimous for the ratification, but that they differed in opinion on the question of competency; that those however in the negative were unwilling that any powers which it might be supposed they possessed, should remain unexercised for the restoration of peace, provided it could be done, saving their good faith, and without importing any opinion of Congress, that seven States were competent, and resolving that the treaty be ratified so far as they had power; that it should be transmitted to our ministers, with instructions to keep it uncommunicated; to endeavor to obtain three months longer for exchange of ratifications; that they should be informed, that so soon as nine States shall be present, a ratification by nine shall be sent them: if this should get to them before the ultimate point of time for exchange, they were to use it, and not the other; if not, they were to offer the act of the seven States in exchange, informing them the treaty had come to hand while Congress was not in session; that but seven States were as yet assembled, and these had unanimously concurred in the ratification. This was debated on the third and fourth; and on the fifth, a vessel being to sail for England, from this port (Annapolis), the House directed the President to write to our ministers accordingly.

January 14. Delegates from Connecticut having attended yesterday, and another from South Carolina coming in this day, the treaty was ratified without a dissenting voice; and three instruments of ratification were ordered to be made out, one of which was sent by Colonel Harmer, another by Colonel Franks, and the third transmitted to the Agent of Marine, to be forwarded by any good opportunity.

Congress soon took up the consideration of their foreign relations. They deemed it necessary to get their commerce placed with every nation, on a footing as favorable as that of other nations; and for this purpose, to propose to each a distinct treaty of commerce. This act too would amount to an acknowledgment, by each, of our independence, and of our reception into the fraternity of nations; which, although as possessing our station of right, and in fact we would not condescend to ask, we were not unwilling to furnish opportunities for receiving their friendly salutations and welcome. With France, the United Netherlands, and Sweden, we had already treaties of commerce; but commissions were given for those countries also, should any amendments be thought necessary. The other States to which treaties were to be proposed, were England, Hamburg, Saxony, Prussia, Denmark, Russia, Austria, Venice, Rome, Naples, Tuscany, Sardinia, Genoa, Spain, Portugal, the Porte, Algiers, Tripoli, Tunis, and Morocco.

On the 7th of May Congress resolved that a Minister Pleni-potentiary should be appointed, in addition to Mr. Adams and Dr. Franklin, for negotiating treaties of commerce with foreign nations, and I was elected to that duty. I accord-ingly left Annapolis on the 11th, took with me my eldest daughter, then at Philadelphia (the two others being too young for the voyage), and proceeded to Boston, in quest of a passage. While passing through the different States, I made a point of informing myself of the state of the commerce of each; went on to New Hampshire with the same view, and returned to Boston. Thence I sailed on the 5th of July, in the Ceres, a merchant ship of Mr. Nathaniel Tracey, bound to Cowes. He was himself a passenger, and, after a pleasant voyage of nineteen days, from land to land, we arrived at Cowes on the 26th. I was detained there a few days by the indisposition of my daughter. On the 30th, we embarked for Havre, arrived there on the 31st, left it on the 3d of August, and arrived at Paris on the 6th. I called immedi-ately on Dr. Franklin, at Passy, communicated to him our charge, and we wrote to Mr. Adams, then at the Hague, to join us at Paris.

Before I had left America, that is to say, in the year 1781, I had received a letter from M. de Marbois, of the French legation in Philadelphia, informing me, he had been instructed by his government to obtain such statistical ac-counts of the different States of our Union, as might be useful for their information; and addressing to me a num-ber of queries relative to the State of Virginia. I had always made it a practice, whenever an opportunity occurred of ob-taining any information of our country, which might be of use to me in any station, public or private, to commit it to writing. These memoranda were on loose papers, bundled up without order, and difficult of recurrence, when I had occa-sion for a particular one. I thought this a good occasion to embody their substance, which I did in the order of Mr. Marbois' queries, so as to answer his wish, and to arrange them for my own use. Some friends, to whom they were occasionally communicated, wished for copies; but their vol-ume rendering this too laborious by hand, I proposed to get a few printed, for their gratification. I was asked such a price, however, as exceeded the importance of the object. On my arrival at Paris, I found it could be done for a fourth of what I had been asked here. I therefore corrected and enlarged them, and had two hundred copies printed, under the title of "Notes on Virginia." I gave a very few copies to some particular friends in Europe, and sent the rest to my friends in America. An European copy, by the death of the owner, got into the hands of a bookseller, who engaged its translation, and when ready for the press, communicated his intentions and manuscript to me, suggesting that I should correct it, without asking any other permission for the publication. I never had seen so wretched an attempt at translation. Interverted, abridged, mutilated, and often reversing the sense of the original, I found it a blotch of errors, from beginning to end. I corrected some of the most material, and, in that form, it was printed in French. A London bookseller, on seeing the translation, requested me to permit him to print the English original. I thought it best to do so, to let the world see that it was not really so bad as the French translation had made it appear. And this is the true history of that publication.

Mr. Adams soon joined us at Paris, and our first employment was to prepare a general form, to be proposed to such nations as were disposed to treat with us. During the negotiations for peace with the British Commissioner, David Hartley, our Commissioners had proposed, on the suggestion of Dr. Franklin, to insert an article, exempting from capture by the public or private armed ships, of either belligerent, when at war, all merchant vessels and their cargoes, employed merely in carrying on the commerce between nations. It was refused by England, and unwisely, in my opinion. For, in the case of a war with us, their superior commerce places infinitely more at hazard on the ocean, than ours; and, as hawks abound in proportion to game, so our privateers would swarm, in proportion to the wealth exposed to their prize, while theirs would be few, for want of subjects of capture. We inserted this article in our form, with a provision against the molestation of fishermen, husbandmen, citizens unarmed, and following their occupations in unfortified places, for the humane treatment of prisoners of war, the abolition of contraband of war, which exposes merchant vessels to such vexatious and ruinous detentions and abuses; and for the principle of free bottoms, free goods.

In a conference with the Count de Vergennes, it was thought better to leave to legislative regulation, on both sides, such modifications of our commercial intercourse, as would voluntarily flow from amicable dispositions. Without urging, we sounded the ministers of the several European nations, at the court of Versailles, on their dispositions towards mutual commerce, and the expediency of encouraging it by the protection of a treaty. Old Frederic, of Prussia, met us cordially, and without hesitation, and appointing the Baron de Thulemeyer, his minister at the Hague, to negotiate with us, we communicated to him our Projét, which, with little alteration by the King, was soon concluded. Denmark and Tuscany entered also into negotiations with us. Other powers appearing indifferent, we did not thing it proper to press them. They seemed, in fact, to know little about us, but as rebels, who had been successful in throwing off the yoke of the mother country. They were ignorant of our commerce, which had been always monopolized by England, and of the exchange of articles it might offer advantageously to both parties. They were inclined, therefore, to stand aloof, until they could see better what relations might be usefully instituted with us. The negotiations, therefore, begun with Denmark and Tuscany, we protracted designedly, until our powers had expired; and abstained from making new propositions to others having no colonies; because our commerce being an exchange of raw for wrought materials, is a competent price for admission into the colonies of those possessing them; but were we to give it, without price, to others, all would claim it, without price, on the ordinary ground of *gentis amicissimæ*.

Mr. Adams being appointed Minister Plenipotentiary of the United States, to London, left us in June, and in July, 1785, Dr. Franklin returned to America, and I was appointed his successor at Paris. In February, 1786, Mr. Adams wrote to me, pressingly, to join him in London immediately, as he thought he discovered there some symptoms of better disposition towards us. Colonel Smith, his secretary of legation, was the bearer of his urgencies for my immediate attendance. I, accordingly, left Paris on the 1st of March, and, on my arrival in London, we agreed on a very summary form of treaty, proposing an exchange of citizenship for our citizens, our ships, and our productions generally, except as to office. On my presentation, as usual, to the King and Queen, at their levées, it was impossible for anything to be more ungracious, than their notice of Mr. Adams and myself. I saw, at once, that the ulcerations of mind in that quarter, left nothing to be expected on the subject of my attendance; and, on the first conference with the Marquis of Caermarthen, the Minister for foreign affairs, the distance and disinclination which he betrayed in his conversation, the vagueness and evasions of his answers to us, confirmed me in the belief of their aversion to have anything to do with us. We delivered him, however, our Projét, Mr. Adams not despairing as much as I did, of its effect. We afterwards, by one or more notes, requested his appointment of an interview and conference, which, without directly declining, he evaded, by pretenses of other pressing occupations for the moment. After staying there seven weeks, till within a few days of the expiration of our commission, I informéd the minister, by note, that my duties at Paris required my return to that place, and that I should, with pleasure, be the bearer of any commands to his Ambassador there. He answered, that he had none, and, wishing me a pleasant journey, I left London the 26th, and arrived at Paris the 30th of April.

A dislocated wrist, unsuccessfully set, occasioned advice from my surgeon, to try the mineral waters of Aix, in Provence, as a corroborant. I left Paris for that place therefore, on the 28th of February, and proceeded up the Seine, through Champagne and Burgundy, and down the Rhone through the Beaujolais by Lyons, Avignon, Nismes to Aix; where, finding on trial no benefit from the waters, I concluded to visit the rice country of Piedmont, to see if anything might be learned there, to benefit the rivalship of our Carolína rice with that, and thence to make a tour of the seaport towns of France, along its Southern and Western coast, to inform myself, if anything could be done to favor our commerce with them. From Aix, therefore, I took my route

by Marseilles, Toulon, Hieres, Nice, across the Col de Tende,
by Coni, Turin, Vercelli, Novara, Milan, Pavia, Novi, Genoa.
Thence, returning along the coast of Savona, Noli, Albenga,
Oneglia, Monaco, Nice, Antibes, Frejus, Aix, Marseilles,
Avignon, Nismes, Montpellier, Frontignan, Cette, Agde, and
along the canal of Languedoc, by Bezieres, Narbonne, Cascas-
sonne, Castelnaudari, through the Souterrain of St. Feriol,
and back by Castelnaudari, to Toulouse; thence to Montau-
ban, and down the Garonne by Langon to Bordeaux. Thence
to Rochefort, la Rochelle, Nantes, L'Orient; then back by
Rennes to Nantes, and up the Loire by Angers, Tours, Am-
boise, Blois to Orleans, thence direct to Paris, where I arrived on the 10th of June. Soon after my return from this
journey, to wit, about the latter part of July, I received my
younger daughter, Maria, from Virginia, by the way of London, the youngest having died some time before.

Our first essay, in America, to establish a federative government had fallen, on trial, very short of its object. During
the war of Independence, while the pressure of an external
enemy hooped us together, and their enterprises kept us
necessarily on the alert, the spirit of the people, excited by
danger, was a supplement to the Confederation, and urged
them to zealous exertions, whether claimed by that instrument
or not; but, when peace and safety were restored, and every
man became engaged in useful and profitable occupation,
less attention was paid to the calls of Congress. The fundamental defect of the Confederation was, that Congress was
not authorized to act immediately on the people, and by its
own officers. Their power was only requisitory, and these
requisitions were addressed to the several Legislatures, to be
by them carried into execution, without other coercion than
the moral principle of duty. This allowed, in fact, a negative to every Legislature, on every measure proposed by
Congress; a negative so frequently exercised in practice, as
to benumb the action of the Federal government, and to render it inefficient in its general objects, and more especially
in pecuniary and foreign concerns. The want, too, of a separation of the Legislative, Executive, and Judiciary functions
worked disadvantageously in practice. Yet this state of things
afforded a happy augury of the future march of our Con-

federacy, when it was seen that the good sense and good dispositions of the people, as soon as they perceived the incompetence of their first compact, instead of leaving its correction to insurrection and civil war, agreed, with one voice, to elect deputies to a general Convention, who should peaceably meet and agree on such a Constitution as "would ensure peace, justice, liberty, the common defense and general welfare."

This Convention met at Philadelphia on the 25th of May, '87. It sat with closed doors, and kept all its proceedings secret, until its dissolution on the 17th of September, when the results of its labors were published all together. I received a copy, early in November, and read and contemplated its provisions with great satisfaction. As not a member of the Convention, however, nor probably a single citizen of the Union, had approved it in all its parts, so I, too, found articles which I thought objectionable. The absence of express declarations ensuring freedom of religion, freedom of the press, freedom of the person under the uninterrupted protection of the Habeas corpus, and trial by jury in Civil as well as in Criminal cases, excited my jealousy; and the reëligibility of the President for life, I quite disapproved. I expressed freely, in letters to my friends, and most particularly to Mr. Madison and General Washington, my approbations and objections. How the good should be secured and the ill brought to rights, was the difficulty. To refer it back to a new Convention might endanger the loss of the whole.

My first idea was, that the nine States first acting, should accept it unconditionally, and thus secure what in it was good, and that the four last should accept on the previous condition, that certain amendments should be agreed to; but a better course was devised, of accepting the whole, and trusting that the good sense and honest intentions of our citizens, would make the alterations which should be deemed necessary. Accordingly, all accepted, six without objection, and seven with recommendations of specified amendments. Those respecting the press, religion, and juries, with several others, of great value, were accordingly made; but the Habeas corpus was left to the discretion of Congress, and the amendment against the reëligibility of the President was not proposed. My fears of that feature were founded on the importance of the office, on the fierce contentions it might excite among ourselves, if continuable for life, and the dangers of interference, either with money or arms, by foreign nations, to whom the choice of an American President might become interesting. Examples of this abounded in history; in the case of the Roman Emperors, for instance; of the Popes, while of any significance; of the German Emperors, the Kings of Poland, and the Deys of Barbary. I had observed, too, in the feudal history, and in the recent instance, particularly, of the Stadtholder of Holland, how easily offices, or tenures for life, slide into inheritances. My wish, therefore, was, that the President should be elected for seven years, and be ineligible afterwards. This term I thought sufficient to enable him, with the concurrence of the Legislature, to carry through and establish any system of improvement he should propose for the general good. But the practice adopted, I think, is better, allowing his continuance for eight years, with a liability to be dropped at half way of the term, making that a period of probation. That his continuance should be restrained to seven years, was the opinion of the Convention at an earlier stage of its session, when it voted that term, by a majority of eight against two, and by a simple majority that he should be ineligible a second time. This opinion was confirmed by the House so late as July 26, referred to the Committee of detail, reported favorably by them, and changed to the present form by final vote, on the last day but one only of their session. Of this change, three States expressed their disapprobation; New York, by recommending an amendment, that the President should not be eligible a third time, and Virginia and North Carolina that he should not be capable of serving more than eight, in any term of sixteen years; and though this amendment has not been made in form, yet practice seems to have established it. The example of four Presidents voluntarily retiring at the end of their eighth year, and the progress of public opinion, that the principle is salutary, have given it in practice the force of precedent and usage; insomuch, that, should a President consent to be a candidate for a third election, I trust he would be rejected, on this demonstration of ambitious views.

The States General were opened on the 5th of May, '89, by speeches from the King, the Garde des Sceaux, Lamoignon, and M. Necker. The last was thought to trip too lightly over the constitutional reformations which were expected. His notices of them in this speech, were not as full as in his previous "Rapport au Roi." This was observed, to his disadvantage; but much allowance should have been made for the situation in which he was placed, between his own counsels, and those of the ministers and party of the court. Overruled in his own opinions, compelled to deliver, and to gloss over those of his opponents, and even to keep their secrets, he could not come forward in his own attitude.

The composition of the Assembly, although equivalent, on the whole, to what had been expected, was something different in its elements. It had been supposed, that a superior education would carry into the scale of the Commons a respectable portion of the Noblesse. It did so as to those of Paris, of its vicinity, and of the other considerable cities, whose greater intercourse with enlightened society had liberalized their minds, and prepared them to advance up to the measure of the times. But the Noblesse of the country, which constituted two-thirds of that body, were far in their rear. Residing constantly on their patrimonial feuds, and familiarized, by daily habit, with Seigneurial powers and practices, they had not yet learned to suspect their inconsistence with reason and right. They were willing to submit to equality of taxation, but not to descend from their rank and prerogatives to be incorporated in session with the Tiers etat. Among the Clergy, on the other hand, it had been apprehended that the higher orders of the Hierarchy, by their wealth and connections, would have carried the elections generally; but it turned out, that in most cases, the lower clergy had obtained the popular majorities. These consisted of the Curés, sons of the peasantry, who had been employed to do all the drudgery of parochial services for ten, twenty, or thirty Louis a year; while their superiors were consuming their princely revenues in palaces of luxury and indolence.

The objects for which this body was convened, being of the first order of importance, I felt it very interesting to understand the views of the parties of which it was composed, and especially the ideas prevalent as to the organization contemplated for their government. I went, therefore, daily from Paris to Versailles, and attended their debates, generally till the hour of adjournment. Those of the Noblesse were impassioned and tempestuous. They had some able men on both sides, actuated by equal zeal. The debates of the Commons were temperate, rational, and inflexibly firm. As preliminary to all other business, the awful questions came on, shall the States sit in one, or in distinct apartments? And shall they vote by heads or houses? The opposition was soon found to consist of the Episcopal order among the clergy, and two-thirds of the Noblesse; while the Tiers etat were, to a man, united and determined. After various propositions of compromise had failed, the Commons undertook to cut the Gordian knot. The Abbe Sieyes, the most logical head of the nation, (author of the pamphlet "Qu'est ce que le Tiers etat?" which had electrified that country, as Paine's Common Sense did us,) after an impressive speech on the 10th of June, moved that a last invitation should be sent to the Noblesse and Clergy, to attend in the hall of the States, collectively or individually, for the verification of powers, to which the Commons would proceed immediately, either in their presence or absence. This verification being finished, a motion was made, on the 15th, that they should constitute themselves a National Assembly; which was decided on the 17th, by a majority of four-fifths. During the debates on this question, about twenty of the Curés had joined them, and a proposition was made, in the chamber of the Clergy, that their whole body should join. This was rejected, at first, by a small majority only; but, being afterwards somewhat modified, it was decided affirmatively, by a majority of eleven. While this was under debate, and unknown to the court, to wit, on the 19th, a council was held in the afternoon, at Marly, wherein it was proposed that the King should interpose, by a declaration of his sentiments, in a *seance royale.*

A form of declaration was proposed by Necker, which, while it censured, in general, the proceedings, both of the Nobles and Commons, announced the King's views, such as substantially to coincide with the Commons. It was agreed to in Council, the *seance* was fixed for the 22d, the meetings of the States were till then to be suspended, and everything, in the meantime, kept secret. The members, the next morning (the 20th) repairing to their house, as usual, found the doors shut and guarded, a proclamation posted up for a *seance royale* on the 22d, and a suspension of their meetings in the meantime. Concluding that their dissolution was now to take place, they repaired to a building called the "Jeu de paume" (or Tennis court) and there bound themselves by oath to each other, never to separate, of their own accord, till they had settled a constitution for the nation, on a solid basis, and, if separated by force, that they would reassemble in some other place. The next day they met in the church of St. Louis, and were joined by a majority of the clergy. The heads of the Aristocracy saw that all was lost without some bold exertion. The King was still at Marly. Nobody was permitted to approach him but their friends. He was assailed by falsehoods in all shapes. He was made to believe that the Commons were about to absolve the army from their oath of fidelity to him, and to raise their pay. The court party were now all rage and desperation. They procured a committee to be held, consisting of the King and his Ministers, to which Monsieur and the Count d'Artois should be admitted. At this committee, the latter attacked M. Necker personally, arraigned his declaration, and proposed one which some of his prompters had put into his hands. M. Necker was brow-beaten and intimidated, and the King shaken. He determined that the two plans should be deliberated on the next day, and the *seance royale* put off a day longer. This encouraged a fiercer attack on M. Necker the next day. His draft of a declaration was entirely broken up, and that of the Count d'Artois inserted into it. Himself and Montmorin offered their resignation, which was refused; the Count d'Artois saying to M. Necker, "No sir, you must be kept as the hostage; we hold you responsible for all the ill which shall happen." This change of plan was immediately whispered without doors. The Noblesse were in triumph; the people in consternation.

I was quite alarmed at this state of things. The soldiery had not yet indicated which side they should take, and that which they should support would be sure to prevail. I considered a successful reformation of government in France, as insuring a general reformation through Europe, and the resurrection, to a new life, of their people, now ground to dust by the abuses of the governing powers. I was much acquainted with the leading patriots of the Assembly. Being from a country which had successfully passed through a similar reformation, they were disposed to my acquaintance, and had some confidence in me. I urged, most strenuously, an immediate compromise; to secure what the government was now ready to yield, and trust to future occasions for what might still be wanting. It was well understood that the King would grant, at this time, 1. Freedom of the person by Habeas corpus: 2. Freedom of conscience: 3. Freedom of the press: 4. Trial by jury: 5. A representative Legislature: 6. Annual meetings: 7. The origination of laws: 8. The exclusive right of taxation and appropriation: and 9. The responsibility of Ministers; and with the exercise of these powers they could obtain, in future, whatever might be further necessary to improve and preserve their constitution. They thought otherwise, however, and events have proved their lamentable error. For, after thirty years of war, foreign and domestic, the loss of millions of lives, the prostration of private happiness, and the foreign subjugation of their own country for a time, they have obtained no more, nor even that securely. They were unconscious of (for who could foresee?) the melancholy sequel of their well-meant perseverance; that their physical force would be usurped by a first tyrant to trample on the independence, and even the existence of other nations: that this would afford a fatal example for the atrocious conspiracy of Kings against their people; would generate their unholy and homicide alliance to make common cause among themselves, and to crush, by the power of the whole, the efforts of any part to moderate their abuses and oppressions.

When the King passed, the next day, through the lane formed from the Chateau to the "Hotel des etats," there was a dead silence. He was about an hour in the House, delivering his speech and declaration. On his coming out, a feeble cry of "vive le Roi" was raised by some children, but the people remained silent and sullen. In the close of his speech, he had ordered that the members should follow him, and resume their deliberations the next day. The Noblesse followed him, and so did the Clergy, except about thirty, who, with the Tiers, remained in the room, and entered into deliberation. They protested against what the King had done, adhered to all their former proceedings, and resolved the inviolability of their own persons. An officer came, to order them out of the room in the King's name. "Tell those who sent you," said Mirabeau, "that we shall not move hence but at our own will, or the point of the bayonet." In the afternoon, the people, uneasy, began to assemble in great numbers in the courts, and vicinities of the palace. This produced alarm. The Queen sent for M. Necker. He was conducted, amidst the shouts and acclamations of the multitude, who filled all the apartments of the palace. He was a few minutes only with the Queen, and what passed between them did not transpire. The King went out to ride. He passed through the crowd to his carriage, and into it, without being in the least noticed. As M. Necker followed him, universal acclamations were raised of "vive Monsieur Necker, vive le sauveur de la France opprimée." He was conducted back to his house with the same demonstrations of affection and anxiety. About two hundred deputies of the Tiers, catching the enthusiasm of the moment, went to his house, and extorted from him a promise that he would not resign. On the 25th, forty-eight of the Nobles joined the Tiers, and among them the Duke of Orleans. There were then with them one hundred and sixty-four members of the Clergy, although the minority of that body still sat apart, and called themselves the Chamber of the Clergy. On the 26th, the Archbishop of Paris joined the Tiers, as did some others of the Clergy and of the Noblesse.

These proceedings had thrown the people into violent ferment. It gained the soldiery, first of the French guards, extended to those of every other denomination, except the Swiss, and even to the body guards of the King. They began to quit their barracks, to assemble in squads, to declare they would defend the life of the King, but would not be the murderers of their fellow-citizens. They called themselves the soldiers *of the nation*, and left now no doubt on which side they would be, in case of rupture. Similar accounts came in from the troops in other parts of the kingdom, giving good reason to believe they would side with their fathers and brothers, rather than with their officers. The operation of this medicine at Versailles was as sudden as it was powerful. The alarm there was so complete, that in the afternoon of the 27th, the King wrote, with his own hand, letters to the Presidents of the Clergy and Nobles, engaging them immediately to join the Tiers. These two bodies were debating, and hesitating, when notes from the Count d'Artois decided their compliance. They went in a body, and took their seats with the Tiers, and thus rendered the union of the orders in one chamber complete.

The Assembly now entered on the business of their mission, and first proceeded to arrange the order in which they would take up the heads of their constitution, as follows:

First, and as Preliminary to the whole, a general Declaration of the Rights of Man. Then, specifically, the Principles of the Monarchy; Rights of the Nation; rights of the King; rights of the Citizens; organization and rights of the National Assembly; forms necessary for the enactment of Laws; organization and functions of the Provincial and Municipal Assemblies; duties and limits of the Judiciary power; functions and duties of the Military power.

A Declaration of the Rights of Man, as the preliminary of their work, was accordingly prepared and proposed by the Marquis de La Fayette.

But the quiet of their march was soon disturbed by information that troops, and particularly the foreign troops, were advancing on Paris from various quarters. The King had probably been advised to this, on the pretext of preserving peace in Paris. But his advisers were believed to have other things in contemplation. The Marshal de Broglio was appointed to their command, a high-flying aristocrat, cool and capable of everything. Some of the French guards were soon arrested, under other pretexts, but really, on account of their dispositions in favor of the National cause. The people of Paris forced their prison, liberated them, and sent a deputation to the Assembly to solicit a pardon. The Assembly recommended peace and order to the people of Paris, the pris-

oners to the King, and asked from him the removal of the
troops. His answer was negative and dry, saying they might
remove themselves, if they pleased, to Noyons or Soissons. In
the meantime, these troops, to the number of twenty or thirty
thousand, had arrived, and were posted in, and between Paris
and Versailles. The bridges and passes were guarded. At
three o'clock in the afternoon of the 11th of July, the Count
de La Luzerne was sent to notify M. Necker of his dismission, and to enjoin him to retire instantly, without saying a
word of it to anybody. He went home, dined, and proposed
to his wife a visit to a friend, but went in fact to his country
house at St. Ouen, and at midnight set out for Brussels.
This was not known till the next day (the 12th,) when the
whole Ministry was changed, except Villedeuil, of the domestic department, and Barenton, Garde des sceaux. The
changes were as follows:

The Baron de Breteuil, President of the Council of Fi-
nance; de la Galaisiere, Comptroller General, in the room of
M. Necker; the Marshal de Broglio, Minister of War, and
Foulon under him, in the room of Puy-Segur; the Duke de
la Vauguyon, Minister of Foreign Affairs, instead of the
Count de Montmorin; de La Porte, Minister of Marine, in
place of the Count de La Luzerne; St. Priest was also removed from the Council. Luzerne and Puy-Segur had been
strongly of the Aristocratic party in the Council, but they
were not considered equal to the work now to be done. The
King was now completely in the hands of men, the principal
among whom had been noted, through their lives, for the
Turkish despotism of their characters, and who were associated around the King, as proper instruments for what was
to be executed. The news of this change began to be known
at Paris, about one or two o'clock. In the afternoon, a body
of about one hundred German cavalry were advanced, and
drawn up in the Place Louis XV., and about two hundred
Swiss posted at a little distance in their rear. This drew people to the spot, who thus accidentally found themselves in
front of the troops, merely at first as spectators; but, as their
numbers increased, their indignation rose. They retired a
few steps, and posted themselves on and behind large piles of
stone, large and small, collected in that place for a bridge,

which was to be built adjacent to it. In this position, happening to be in my carriage on a visit, I passed through the lane they had formed, without interruption. But the moment after I had passed, the people attacked the cavalry with stones. They charged, but the advantageous position of the people, and the showers of stones, obliged the horse to retire, and quit the field altogether, leaving one of their number on the ground, and the Swiss in the rear not moving to their aid. This was the signal for universal insurrrection, and this body of cavalry, to avoid being massacred, retired towards Versailles. The people now armed themselves with such weapons as they could find in armorer's shops, and private houses, and with bludgeons; and were roaming all night, through all parts of the city, without any decided object.

The next day (the 13th,) the Assembly pressed on the King to send away the troops, to permit the Bourgeoisie of Paris to arm for the preservation of order in the city, and offered to send a deputation from their body to tranquillize them; but their propositions were refused. A committee of magistrates and electors of the city were appointed by those bodies, to take upon them its government. The people, now openly joined by the French guards, forced the prison of St. Lazare, released all the prisoners, and took a great store of corn, which they carried to the corn-market. Here they got some arms, and the French guards began to form and train them. The city-committee determined to raise forty-eight thousand Bourgeoise, or rather to restrain their numbers to forty-eight thousand. On the 14th, they sent one of their members (Monsieur de Corny) to the Hotel des Invalides, to ask arms for their Garde Bourgeoise. He was followed by, and he found there, a great collection of people. The Governor of the Invalids came out, and represented the impossibility of his delivering arms, without the orders of those from whom he received them. De Corny advised the people then to retire, and retired himself; but the people took possession of the arms. It was remarkable, that not only the Invalids themselves made no opposition, but that a body of five thousand foreign troops, within four hundred yards, never stirred. M. de Corny, and five others, were then sent to ask arms of M. de Launay, Governor of the Bastile. They found a great collection of people already before the place, and they immediately planted a flag of truce, which was answered by a like flag hoisted on the parapet. The deputation prevailed on the people to fall back a little, advanced themselves to make their demand of the Governor, and in that instant, a discharge from the Bastile killed four persons of those nearest to the deputies. The deputies retired.

I happened to be at the house of M. de Corny, when he returned to it, and received from him a narrative of these transactions. On the retirement of the deputies, the people rushed forward, and almost in an instant, were in possession of a fortification of infinite strength, defended by one hundred men, which in other times had stood several regular sieges, and had never been taken. How they forced their entrance has never been explained. They took all the arms, discharged the prisoners, and such of the garrison as were not killed in the first moment of fury; carried the Governor and Lieutenant Governor, to the Place de Grève, (the place of public execution,) cut off their heads, and sent them through the city, in triumph, to the Palais royal. About the same instant, a treacherous correspondence having been discovered in M. de Flesselles, Prevôt des Marchands, they seized him in the Hotel de Ville, where he was in the execution of his office, and cut off his head. These events, carried imperfectly to Versailles, were the subject of two successive deputations from the Assembly to the King, to both of which he gave dry and hard answers; for nobody had as yet been permitted to inform him, truly and fully, of what had passed at Paris. But at night, the Duke de Liancourt forced his way into the King's bed chamber, and obliged him to hear a full and animated detail of the disasters of the day in Paris. He went to bed fearfully impressed.

The decapitation of de Launay worked powerfully through the night on the whole Aristocratic party; insomuch, that in the morning, those of the greatest influence on the Count d'Artois represented to him the absolute necessity that the King should give up everything to the Assembly. This according with the dispositions of the King, he went about eleven o'clock, accompanied only by his brothers, to the Assembly, and there read to them a speech, in which he asked

their interposition to reëstablish order. Although couched
in terms of some caution, yet the manner in which it was delivered, made it evident that it was meant as a surrender at
discretion. He returned to the Chateau a foot, accompanied
by the Assembly. They sent off a deputation to quiet Paris,
at the head of which was the Marquis de La Fayette, who
had, the same morning, been named Commandant en chef
of the Milice Bourgeoise; and Monsieur Bailly, former President of the States General, was called for as Prevôt des Marchands. The demolition of the Bastile was now ordered and
begun. A body of the Swiss guards, of the regiment of Ven-
timille, and the city horse guards joined the people. The
alarm at Versailles increased. The foreign troops were ordered off instantly. Every Minister resigned. The King confirmed Bailly as Prevôt des Marchands, wrote to M. Necker,
to recall him, sent his letter open to the Assembly, to be
forwarded by them, and invited them to go with him to Paris
the next day, to satisfy the city of his dispositions; and that
night, and the next morning, the Count d'Artois, and M. de
Montesson, a deputy connected with him, Madame de Poli-
gnac, Madame de Guiche, and the Count de Vaudreuil, favorites of the Queen, the Abbe de Vermont, her confessor, the
Prince of Conde, and Duke of Bourbon fled.

The King came to Paris, leaving the Queen in consternation
for his return. Omitting the less important figures of the
procession, the King's carriage was in the center; on each side
of it, the Assembly, in two ranks a foot; at their head the
Marquis de La Fayette, as Commander-in-chief, on horseback,
and Bourgeois guards before and behind. About sixty thousand citizens, of all forms and conditions, armed with the conquests of the Bastile and Invalids, as far as they would go,
the rest with pistols, swords, pikes, pruning-hooks, scythes,
&c., lined all the streets through which the procession passed,
and with the crowds of people in the streets, doors, and windows, saluted them everywhere with the cries of "vive la
nation," but not a single "vive le Roi" was heard. The
King stopped at the Hotel de Ville. There M. Bailly presented, and put into his hat, the popular cockade, and addressed him. The King being unprepared, and unable to
answer, Bailly went to him, gathered from him some scraps

of sentences, and made out an answer, which he delivered to the audience, as from the King. On their return, the popular cries were "vive le Roi et la nation." He was conducted by a garde Bourgeoise to his palace at Versailles, and thus concluded an "amende honorable," as no sovereign ever made, and no people ever received.

And here, again, was lost another precious occasion of sparing to France the crimes and cruelties through which she has since passed, and to Europe, and finally America, the evils which flowed on them also from this mortal source. The King was now become a passive machine in the hands of the National Assembly, and had he been left to himself, he would have willingly acquiesced in whatever they should devise as best for the nation. A wise constitution would have been formed, hereditary in his line, himself placed at its head, with powers so large as to enable him to do all the good of his station, and so limited as to restrain him from its abuse. This he would have faithfully administered, and more than this, I do not believe, he ever wished. But he had a Queen of absolute sway over his weak mind and timid virtue, and of a character the reverse of his in all points. This angel, as gaudily painted in the rhapsodies of Burke, with some smartness of fancy, but no sound sense, was proud, disdainful of restraint, indignant at all obstacles to her will, eager in the pursuit of pleasure, and firm enough to hold to her desires, or perish in their wreck. Her inordinate gambling and dissipations, with those of the Count d'Artois, and others of her *clique,* had been a sensible item in the exhaustion of the treasury, which called into action the reforming hand of the nation; and her opposition to it, her inflexible perverseness, and dauntless spirit, led herself to the Guillotine, drew the King on with her, and plunged the world into crimes and calamities which will forever stain the pages of modern history. I have ever believed, that had there been no Queen, there would have been no revolution. No force would have been provoked, nor exercised. The King would have gone hand in hand with the wisdom of his sounder counselors, who, guided by the increased lights of the age, wished only, with the same pace, to advance the principles of their social constitution.

The deed which closed the mortal course of these sovereigns, I shall neither approve nor condemn. I am not prepared to say, that the first magistrate of a nation cannot commit treason against his country, or is unamenable to its punishment; nor yet, that where there is no written law, no regulated tribunal, there is not a law in our hearts, and a power in our hands, given for righteous employment in maintaining right, and redressing wrong. Of those who judged the King, many thought him willfully criminal; many, that his existence would keep the nation in perpetual conflict with the horde of Kings who would war against a generation which might come home to themselves, and that it were better that one should die than all. I should not have voted with this portion of the legislature. I should have shut up the Queen in a convent, putting harm out of her power, and placed the King in his station, investing him with limited powers, which, I verily believe, he would have honestly exercised, according to the measure of his understanding. In this way, no void would have been created, courting the usurpation of a military adventurer, nor occasion given for those enormities which demoralized the nations of the world, and destroyed, and is yet to destroy, millions and millions of its unfortunate inhabitants.

There are three epochs in history, signalized by the total extinction of national morality. The first was of the successors of Alexander, not omitting himself: The next, the successors of the first Cæsar: The third, our own age. This was begun by the partition of Poland, followed by that of the treaty of Pilnitz; next the conflagration of Copenhagen; then the enormities of Bonaparte, partitioning the earth at his will, and devastating it with fire and sword; now the conspiracy of Kings, the successors of Bonaparte, blasphemously calling themselves the Holy Alliance, and treading in the footsteps of their incarcerated leader; not yet, indeed, usurping the government of other nations, avowedly and in detail, but controlling by their armies the forms in which they will permit them to be governed; and reserving, *in petto*, the order and extent of the usurpations further meditated. But I will return from a digression, anticipated, too, in time, into which I have been led by reflection on the criminal passions which refused to the world a favorable occasion of saving it from the afflictions it has since suffered.

M. Necker had reached Basle before he was overtaken by the letter of the King, inviting him back to resume the office he had recently left. He returned immediately, and all the other Ministers having resigned, a new administration was named, to wit: St. Priest and Montmorin were restored; the Archbishop of Bordeaux was appointed Garde des sceaux, La Tour du Pin, Minister of War; La Luzerne, Minister of Marine. This last was believed to have been effected by the friendship of Montmorin; for although differing in politics, they continued firm in friendship, and Luzerne, although not an able man, was thought an honest one. And the Prince of Bauvau was taken into the Council.

Seven Princes of the blood Royal, six ex-Ministers, and many of the high Noblesse, having fled, and the present Ministers, except Luzerne, being all of the popular party, all the functionaries of government moved, for the present, in perfect harmony.

In the evening of August the 4th, and on the motion of the Viscount de Noailles, brother in law of La Fayette, the Assembly abolished all titles of rank, all the abusive privileges of feudalism, the tithes and casuals of the Clergy, all Provincial privileges, and, in fine, the Feudal regimen generally. To the suppression of tithes, the Abbe Sieyes was vehemently opposed; but his learned and logical arguments were unheeded, and his estimation lessened by a contrast of his egoism (for he was beneficed on them), with the generous abandonment of rights by the other members of the Assembly.

Many days were employed in putting into the form of laws, the numerous demolitions of ancient abuses; which done, they proceeded to the preliminary work of a Declaration of rights. There being much concord of sentiment on the elements of this instrument, it was liberally framed, and passed with a very general approbation. They then appointed a Committee for the "reduction of a projet" of a constitution, at the head of which was the Archbishop of Bordeaux. I received from him, as chairman of the Committee, a letter of July 20th, requesting me to attend and assist at their deliberations; but

I excused myself, on the obvious considerations, that my mission was to the King as Chief Magistrate of the nation, that my duties were limited to the concerns of my own country, and forbade me to intermeddle with the internal transactions of that, in which I had been received under a specific character only. Their plan of a constitution was discussed in sections, and so reported from time to time, as agreed to by the Committee. The first respected the general frame of the government; and that this should be formed into three departments, Executive, Legislative and Judiciary, was generally agreed. But when they proceeded to subordinate developments, many and various shades of opinion came into conflict, and schism, strongly marked, broke the Patriots into fragments of very discordant principles. The first question, Whether there should be a King? met with no open opposition; and it was readily agreed, that the government of France should be monarchial and hereditary. Shall the King have a negative on the laws? Shall that negative be absolute, or suspensive only? Shall there be two Chambers of Legislation? or one only? If two, shall one of them be hereditary? or for life? or for a fixed term? and named by the King? or elected by the people? These questions found strong differences of opinion, and produced repulsive combinations among the Patriots. The Aristocracy was cemented by a common principle, of preserving the ancient regime, or whatever should be nearest to it. Making this their polar star, they moved in phalanx, gave preponderance on every question to the minorities of the Patriots, and always to those who advocated the least change. The features of the new constitution were thus assuming a fearful aspect, and great alarm was produced among the honest Patriots by these dissensions in their ranks.

In this uneasy state of things, I received one day a note from the Marquis de La Fayette, informing me that he should bring a party of six or eight friends to ask a dinner of me the next day. I assured him of their welcome. When they arrived, they were La Fayette himself, Duport, Barnave, Alexander la Meth, Blacon, Mounier, Maubourg, and Dagout. These were leading Patriots, of honest but differing opinions, sensible of the necessity of effecting a coalition by mutual sacrifices, knowing each other, and not afraid, therefore, to unbosom themselves mutually. This last was a material principle in the selection. With this view, the Marquis had invited the conference, and had fixed the time and place inadvertently, as to the embarrassment under which it might place me. The cloth being removed, and wine set on the table, after the American manner, the Marquis introduced the objects of the conference, by summarily reminding them of the state of things in the Assembly, the course which the principles of the Constitution were taking, and the inevitable result, unless checked by more concord among the Patriots themselves. He observed, that although he also had his opinion, he was ready to sacrifice it to that of his brethren of the same cause; but that a common opinion must now be formed, or the Aristocracy would carry everything, and that, whatever they should now agree on, he, at the head of the National force, would maintain.

The discussions began at the hour of four, and were continued till ten o'clock in the evening; during which time, I was a silent witness to a coolness and candor of argument, unusual in the conflicts of political opinion; to a logical reasoning, and chaste eloquence, disfigured by no gaudy tinsel of rhetoric or declamation, and truly worthy of being placed in parallel with the finest dialogues of antiquity, as handed to us by Xenophon, by Plato and Cicero. The result was, that the King should have a suspensive veto on the laws, that the legislature should be composed of a single body only, and that to be chosen by the people. This Concordate decided the fate of the constitution. The Patriots all rallied to the principles thus settled, carried every question agreeably to them, and reduced the Aristocracy to insignificance and impotence. But duties of exculpation were now incumbent on me.

I waited on Count Montmorin the next morning, and explained to him, with truth and candor, how it had happened that my house had been made the scene of conferences of such a character. He told me, he already knew everything which had passed, that so far from taking umbrage at the use made of my house on that occasion, he earnestly wished I would habitually assist at such conferences, being sure I should be useful in moderating the warmer spirits, and promoting a wholesome and practicable reformation only. I told him, I knew too well the duties I owed to the King, to the nation, and to my own country, to take any part in councils concerning their internal government, and that I should persevere, with care, in the character of a neutral and passive spectator, with wishes only, and very sincere ones, that those measures might prevail which would be for the greatest good of the nation. I have no doubts, indeed, that this conference was previously known and approved by this honest Minister, who was in confidence and communication with the Patriots, and wished for a reasonable reform of the Constitution.

Here I discontinue my relation of the French Revolution. The minuteness with which I have so far given its details, is disproportioned to the general scale of my narrative. But I have thought it justified by the interest which the whole world must take in this Revolution. As yet, we are but in the first chapter of its history. The appeal to the rights of man, which had been made in the United States, was taken up by France, first of the European nations. From her, the spirit has spread over those of the South. The tyrants of the North have allied indeed against it; but it is irresistible. Their opposition will only multiply its millions of human victims; their own satellites will catch it, and the condition of man through the civilized world, will be finally and greatly ameliorated. This is a wonderful instance of great events from small causes. So inscrutable is the arrangement of causes and consequences in this world, that a two-penny duty on tea, unjustly imposed in a sequestered part of it, changes the condition of all its inhabitants. I have been more minute in relating the early transactions of this regeneration, because I was in circumstances peculiarly favorable for a knowledge of the truth. Possessing the confidence and intimacy of the leading Patriots, and more than all, of the Marquis Fayette, their head and Atlas, who had no secrets from me, I learned with correctness the views and proceedings of that party; while my intercourse with the diplomatic missionaries of Europe at Paris, all of them with the court, and eager in prying into its councils and proceedings, gave me a knowledge of these also. My information was always, and immediately committed to writing, in letters to Mr. Jay, and often to my friends, and a recurrence to these letters now insures me against errors of memory.

These opportunities of information ceased at this period, with my retirement from this interesting scene of action. I had been more than a year soliciting leave to go home, with a view to place my daughters in the society and care of their friends, and to return for a short time to my station at Paris. But the metamorphosis through which our government was then passing from its Chrysalid to its Organic form suspended its action in a great degree; and it was not till the last of August, that I received the permission I had asked. And here, I cannot leave this great and good country, without expressing my sense of its preëminence of character among the nations of the earth. A more benevolent people I have never known, nor greater warmth and devotedness in their select friendships. Their kindness and accommodation to strangers is unparalleled, and the hospitality of Paris is beyond anything I had conceived to be practicable in a large city. Their eminence, too, in science, the communicative dispositions of their scientific men, the politeness of the general manners, the ease and vivacity of their conversation, give a charm to their society, to be found nowhere else. In a comparison of this, with other countries, we have the proof of primacy, which was given to Themistocles, after the battle of Salamis. Every general voted to himself the first reward of valor, and the second to Themistocles. So, ask the traveled inhabitant of any nation, in what country on earth would you rather live?—Certainly, in my own, where are all my friends, my relations, and the earliest and sweetest affections and recollections of my life. Which would be your second choice? France.

On the 26th of September I left Paris for Havre, where I was detained by contrary winds until the 8th of October. On that day, and the 9th, I crossed over to Cowes, where I had engaged the Clermont, Capt. Colley, to touch for me. She did so; but here again we were detained by contrary winds, until the 22d, when we embarked, and landed at Norfolk on the 23d of November. On my way home, I passed some days at Eppington, in Chesterfield, the residence of my friend and connection, Mr. Eppes; and, while there, I received a letter from the President, General Washington, by express, covering an appointment to be Secretary of State. I received it with real regret. My wish had been to return to Paris, where I had left my household establishment, as if there myself, and to see the end of the Revolution, which I then thought would be certainly and happily closed in less than a year. I then meant to return home, to withdraw from political life, into which I had been impressed by the circumstances of the times, to sink into the bosom of my family and friends, and devote myself to studies more congenial to my mind. In my answer of December 15th, I expressed these dispositions candidly to the President, and my preference of a return to Paris; but assured him, that if it was believed I could be more useful in the administration of the government, I would sacrifice my own inclinations without hesitation, and repair to that destination; this I left to his decision. I arrived at Monticello on the 23d of December, where I received a second letter from the President, expressing his continued wish that I should take my station there, but leaving me still at liberty to continue in my former office, if I could not reconcile myself to that now proposed. This silenced my reluctance, and I accepted the new appointment.

In the interval of my stay at home, my eldest daughter had been happily married to the eldest son of the Tuckahoe branch of Randolphs, a young gentleman of genius, science, and honorable mind, who afterwards filled a dignified station in the General Government, and the most dignified in his own State. I left Monticello on the first of March, 1790, for New York. At Philadelphia I called on the venerable and beloved Franklin. He was then on the bed of sickness from which he never rose. My recent return from a country in which he had left so many friends, and the perilous convulsions to which they had been exposed, revived all his anxieties to know what part they had taken, what had been their course, and what their fate. He went over all in succession, with a rapidity and animation almost too much for his strength. When all his inquiries were satisfied, and a pause took place,

I told him I had learned with much pleasure that, since his return to America, he had been occupied in preparing for the world the history of his own life. "I cannot say much of that," said he; "but I will give you a sample of what I shall leave;" and he directed his little grandson (William Bache) who was standing by the bedside, to hand him a paper from the table, to which he pointed. He did so; and the Doctor putting it into my hands, desired me to take it and read it at my leisure. It was about a quire of folio paper, written in a large and running hand, very like his own. I looked into it slightly, then shut it, and said I would accept his permission to read it, and would carefully return it. He said, "No, keep it." Not certain of his meaning, I again looked into it, folded it for my pocket, and said again, I would certainly return it. "No," said he, "keep it." I put it into my pocket, and shortly after took leave of him.

He died on the 17th of the ensuing month of April; and as I understood that he had bequeathed all his papers to his grandson, William Temple Franklin, I immediately wrote to Mr. Franklin, to inform him I possessed this paper, which I should consider as his property, and would deliver to his order. He came on immediately to New York, called on me for it, and I delivered it to him. As he put it into his pocket, he said carelessly, he had either the original, or another copy of it, I do not recollect which. This last expression struck my attention forcibly, and for the first time suggested to me the thought that Dr. Franklin had meant it as a confidential deposit in my hands, and that I had done wrong in parting from it. I have not yet seen the collection he published of Dr. Franklin's works, and, therefore, know not if this is among them. I have been told it is not. It contained a narrative of the negotiations between Dr. Franklin and the British Ministry, when he was endeavoring to prevent the contest of arms which followed. The negotiation was brought about by the intervention of Lord Howe and his sister, who, I believe, was called Lady Howe, but I may misremember her title. Lord Howe seems to have been friendly to America, and exceedingly anxious to prevent a rupture. His intimacy with Dr. Franklin, and his position with the Ministry, induced him to undertake a mediation between them; in which his sister seemed to have been associated. They carried from one to the other, backwards and forwards, the several propositions and answers which passed, and seconded with their own intercessions, the importance of mutual sacrifices, to preserve the peace and connection of the two countries.

I remember that Lord North's answers were dry, unyielding, in the spirit of unconditional submission, and betrayed an absolute indifference to the occurrence of a rupture; and he said to the mediators distinctly, at last, that "a rebellion was not to be deprecated on the part of Great Britain; that the confiscations it would produce would provide for many of their friends." This expression was reported by the mediators to Dr. Franklin, and indicated so cool and calculated a purpose in the Ministry, as to render compromise hopeless, and the negotiation was discontinued. If this is not among the papers published, we ask, what has become of it? I delivered it with my own hands, into those of Temple Franklin. It certainly established views so atrocious in the British government, that its suppression would, to them, be worth a great price. But could the grandson of Dr. Franklin be, in such degree, an accomplice in the parricide of the memory of his immortal grandfather? The suspension for more than twenty years of the general publication, bequeathed and confided to him, produced, for awhile, hard suspicions against him; and if, at last, all are not published, a part of these suspicions may remain with some.

I arrived at New York on the 21st of March, where Congress was in session.

ALEXANDER HAMILTON

ALEXANDER HAMILTON

1757-1804

INTRODUCTORY NOTE

That amazing boy genius of the American Revolution, Alexander Hamilton, lived through a career, the splendor and romance of which have scarcely ever been excelled. From his tragic birth and youth among the islands of the West Indies, through his spectacular boyish championing of the Revolution in New York City, his ardent friendship ~nd support of the two great generals, Washington and Schuyler, down to his supremely able leadership in statecraft, and his sudden, tragic death, the career of Hamilton was brilliant almost beyond the telling. It should be read and studied by every American.

Unfortunately we learn but little of that life from Hamilton's own pen, the pen which best of all possessed the skill to make its master known. Hamilton, supreme in so many things, was perhaps the ablest writer of his time, as his papers in the ''Federalist'' so strongly evidence. Of himself, however, he seems only once to have written at any length. In 1797, a distant relative in Scotland wrote to the now celebrated statesman claiming kinship with him, a kinship which had been neglected in the days of his impoverished youth and his father's disgrace. Hamilton accepted the advance with genial courtesy, and at the request of his correspondent briefly outlined his own career in the following letter.

AN AUTOBIOGRAPHICAL SKETCH

ALBANY, New York, May 2, 1797.

SOME days since I received with great pleasure your letter of the 10th of March. The mark it affords of your kind attention, and the particular account it gives me of so many relations in Scotland are extremely gratifying to me. You, no doubt, have understood that my father's affairs at a very early day went to wreck, so as to have rendered his situation during the greatest part of his life far from eligible. This state of things occasioned a separation between him and me, when I was very young, and threw me upon the bounty of my mother's relatives, some of whom were then wealthy, though by vicissitudes to which human affairs are so liable, they have been since much reduced and broken up. Myself, at about sixteen, came to this country. Having always had a strong propensity to literary pursuits, by a course of study and laborious exertion, I was able, by the age of nineteen, to qualify myself for the degree of Bachelor of Arts in the (Columbia) College of New York, and to lay the foundation by preparatory study for the future profession of the law.

The American Revolution supervened. My principles led me to take part in it; at nineteen, I entered into the American army as captain of artillery. Shortly after I became, by his invitation, aide-de-camp to General Washington, in which station I served until the commencement of that campaign which ended with the siege of York in Virginia, and the capture of Cornwallis's army. The campaign I made at the head of a corps of light infantry, with which I was present at the siege of York, and engaged in some interesting operations.

At the period of peace with Great Britain I found myself a member of Congress, by appointment of the legislature of this state.

After the peace I settled in the city of New York, in the practice of the law, and was in a very lucrative course of practice, when the derangement of our public affairs, by the feebleness of the general Confederation, drew me again reluctantly into public life. I became a member of the Convention which framed the present constitution of the United States; and having taken part in this measure, I conceived myself to be under an obligation to lend my aid toward putting the machine in some regular motion. Hence, I did not hesitate to accept the offer of President Washington to undertake the office of Secretary of the Treasury.

In that office I met with many intrinsic difficulties, and many artificial ones, proceeding from passions, not very worthy, common to human nature, and which act with peculiar force in republics. The object, however, was effected of establishing public credit and introducing order in the finances.

Public office in this country, has few attractions. The pecuniary emolument is so inconsiderable as to amount to a sacrifice to any man who can employ his time with advantage in any liberal profession. The opportunity of doing good, from the jealousy of power and the spirit of faction, is too small in any station to warrant a long continuance of private sacrifices. The enterprises of party had so far succeeded as materially to weaken the necessary influence and energy of the executive authority, and so far diminish the power of doing good in that department, as greatly to take away the motives which a virtuous man might have for making sacrifices. The prospect was even bad for gratifying in future the love of fame, if that passion was to be the spring of action.

The union of these motives, with the reflections of prudence in relation to a growing family, determined me as soon as my plan had attained a certain maturity, to withdraw from office. This I did by a resignation about two years since, when I resumed the profession of the law in the city of New York under every advantage I could desire.

It is a pleasant reflection to me that since the commencement of my connection with General Washington to the present time, I have possessed a flattering share of his confidence and friendship.

Having given you a brief sketch of my political career, I proceed to some further family details.

In the year 1780 I married the second daughter of General Schuyler, a gentleman of one of the best families of this country, of large fortune, and no less personal and political consequence. It is impossible to be happier than I am in a wife; and I have five children, four sons and a daughter, the eldest a son somewhat past fifteen, who all promise as well as their years permit, and yield me much satisfaction. Though I have been too much in public life to be wealthy, my situation is extremely comfortable, and leaves me nothing to wish for but a continuance of health. With this blessing, the profits of my profession and other prospects authorize an expectation of such additions to my resources, as will render the eve of my life easy and agreeable, so far as may depend upon this consideration.

It is now several months since I have heard from my father, who continued at the island of St. Vincent's. My anxiety at this silence would be greater than it is, were it not for the considerable interruption and precariousness of intercourse which is produced by the war.

I have strongly pressed the old gentleman to come and reside with me, which would afford him every enjoyment of which his advanced age is capable; but he has declined it on the ground that the advice of his physicians leads him to fear that the change of climate would be fatal to him. The next thing for me is, in proportion to my means, to endeavor to increase his comforts where he is.

It will give me the greatest pleasure to receive your son Robert at my house in New York, and still more to be of use to him; to which end my recommendation and interest will not be wanting, and I hope not unavailing. It is my intention to embrace the opening which your letter affords me to extend my intercourse with my relations in your country, which will be a new source of satisfaction to me.

ROBERT BURNS

ROBERT BURNS

1759-1796

INTRODUCTORY NOTE

The world is fortunate, indeed, in possessing Burns' own sketch of his life and estimate of his labors, even though the sketch be but a brief one. Burns wrote this outline in a letter to a friend, Dr. Moore, who had requested it. It was written in the first full tide of his success in Edinburgh, when he was hailed as the greatest of all poets, and life promised fair indeed.

The grim tragedy of Burns' life is too well known to need repeating. Born a peasant lad in an age when peasants were still regarded as being of different clay from the upper classes, Burns amazed the whole Scottish world by his genius. The gentry of Edinburgh welcomed him at first with open arms; but soon found that the problem of supporting him was a difficult one. Poetry did not yet pay as a profession, and Burns was of far too independent a spirit to accept charity. Moreover, the democratic spirit of his verse was scarcely likely to endear him to the aristocratic government. A government position was at length found for him; but it was such a mean one as to indicate that the government authorities thought of him as a peasant rather than as a poet. He was made a ''gauger,'' or revenue officer, in charge of testing liquors and preventing the brewing or buying of these in secret among the countryfolk. This made of Burns a sort of spy upon his own people; and he accepted the position with disgust, and only under pressure of extreme necessity. He had married Jean Armour and had children. Shamed now and embittered, feeling his life a failure, Burns turned more and more to drink, as the only remaining source of pleasure or forgetfulness.

AN AUTOBIOGRAPHICAL SKETCH

Mauchline, August 2, 1787.

FOR some months past I have been rambling over the country, but I am now confined with some lingering complaints, originating, as I take it, in the stomach. To divert my spirits a little in this miserable fog of ennui, I have taken a whim to give you a history of myself. My name has made some little noise in this country; you have done me the honor to interest yourself very warmly in my behalf; and I think a faithful account of what character of a man I am, and how I came by that character, may perhaps amuse you in an idle moment. I will give you an honest narrative, though I know it will be, often at my own expense; for I assure you, sir, I have, like Solomon, whose character, excepting in the trifling affair of wisdom, I sometimes think I resemble—I have, I say, like him, turned my eyes to behold madness and folly, and like him, too, frequently shaken hands with their intoxicating friendship. After you have perused these pages, should you think them trifling and impertinent, I only beg leave to tell you that the poor author wrote them under some twitching qualms of conscience, arising from a suspicion that he was doing what he ought not to do; a predicament he has more than once been in before.

I have not the most distant pretensions to assume that character with the pye-coated guardians of escutcheons call a gentleman. When at Edinburgh last winter, I got acquainted in the Herald's office; and, looking through that granary of honors, I there found almost every name in the kingdom; but for me,

My ancient but ignoble blood
Has crept thro' scoundrels ever since the flood.

Gules, purpure, argent, etc., quite disowned me.

My father was of the north of Scotland, the son of a farmer, and was thrown by early misfortunes on the world at large; where, after many years' wanderings and sojournings, he picked up a pretty large quantity of observation and experience, to which I am indebted for most of my little pretensions to wisdom. I have met with few who understood men, their manners and their ways, equal to him; but stubborn, ungainly integrity, and headlong, ungovernable irascibility, are disqualifying circumstances; consequently, I was born a very poor man's son. For the first six or seven years of my life, my father was gardener to a worthy gentleman of small estate in the neighborhood of Ayr. Had he continued in that station, I must have marched off to be one of the little underlings about a farmhouse; but it was his dearest wish and prayer to have it in his power to keep his children under his own eye, till they could discern between good and evil; so with the assistance of his generous master, my father ventured on a small farm on his estate.

At those years, I was by no means a favorite with anybody. I was a good deal noted for a retentive memory, a stubborn sturdy something in my disposition, and an enthusiastic idiotic piety. I say idiotic piety, because I was then but a child. Though it cost the schoolmaster some thrashings, I made an excellent English scholar; and by the time I was ten or eleven years of age, I was a critic in substantives, verbs, and particles. In my infant and boyish days, too, I owe much to an old woman who resided in the family, remarkable for her ignorance, credulity, and superstition. She had, I suppose, the largest collection in the country of tales and songs concerning devils, ghosts, fairies, brownies, witches, warlocks, spunkies, kelpies, elf-candles, dead-lights, wraiths, apparitions, cantraips, giants, enchanted towers, dragons, and other trumpery. This cultivated the latent seeds of poetry; but had so strong an effect on my imagination, that to this hour, in my nocturnal rambles, I sometimes keep a sharp lookout in suspicious places; and though nobody can be more skeptical than I am in such matters, yet it often takes an effort of philosophy to shake off these idle terrors.

The earliest composition that I recollect taking pleasure in, was "The Vision of Mirza," and a hymn of Addison's beginning, "How are thy servants blest, O Lord!" I particularly remember one half-stanza which was music to my boyish ear—

> For though on dreadful whirls we hung
> High on the broken wave—

I met with these pieces in Mason's English Collection, one of my schoolbooks. The first two books I ever read in private, and which gave me more pleasure than any two books I ever read since, were "The Life of Hannibal," and "The History of Sir William Wallace." Hannibal gave my young ideas such a turn, that I used to strut in raptures up and down after the recruiting drum and bagpipe, and wish myself tall enough to be a soldier; while the story of Wallace poured a Scottish prejudice into my veins, which will boil along there till the floodgates of life shut in eternal rest.

Polemical divinity about this time was putting the country half mad, and I, ambitious of shining in conversation parties on Sundays, between sermons, at funerals, etc., used a few years afterward to puzzle Calvinism with so much heat and indiscretion, that I raised a hue and cry of heresy against me, which has not ceased to this hour.

My vicinity to Ayr was of some advantage to me. My social disposition, when not checked by some modifications of spirited pride, was like our catechism definition of infinitude, without bounds or limits. I formed several connections with other younkers, who possessed superior advantages; the youngling actors who were busy in the rehearsal of parts, in which they were shortly to appear on the stage of life, where, alas! I was destined to drudge behind the scenes. It is not commonly at this green age, that our young gentry have a just sense of the immense distance between them and their ragged playfellows. It takes a few dashes into the world to give the young great man that proper, decent, unnoticing disregard for the poor, insignificant, stupid devils, the mechanics and peasantry around him, who were, perhaps, born in the same village. My young superiors never insulted the clouterly appearance of my plow-boy carcass, the two extremes of which were often exposed to all the inclemencies of all the seasons. They would give me stray volumes of books; among them, even then, I could pick up some observations, and one, whose heart, I am sure, not even the "Munny Begum" scenes have tainted, helped me to a little French.

Parting with these my young friends and benefactors, as they occasionally went off for the East or West Indies, was often to me a sore affliction; but I was soon called to more serious evils. My father's generous master died, the farm proved a ruinous bargain; and to clinch the misfortune, we fell into the hands of a factor, who sat for the picture I have drawn of one in my tale of "Twa Dogs." My father was advanced in life when he married; I was the eldest of seven children, and he, worn out by early hardships, was unfit for labor. My father's spirit was soon irritated, but not easily broken. There was a freedom in his lease in two years more, and to weather these two years, we retrenched our expenses. We lived very poorly; I was a dexterous plowman for my age; and the next eldest to me was a brother (Gilbert), who could drive the plow very well, and help me to thrash the corn. A novel-writer might, perhaps, have viewed these scenes with some satisfaction, but so did not I; my indignation yet boils at the recollection of the scoundrel factor's insolent threatening letters, which used to set us all in tears.

This kind of life—the cheerless gloom of a hermit, with the unceasing moil of a galley slave, brought me to my sixteenth year; a little before which period I first committed the sin of rime. You know our country custom of coupling a man and woman together as partners in the labors of harvest. In my fifteenth autumn, my partner was a bewitching creature, a year younger than myself. My scarcity of English denies me the power of doing her justice in that language, but you know the Scottish idiom: she was a "bonnie, sweet, sonsie (engaging) lass." In short, she, altogether unwittingly to herself, initiated me in that delicious passion, which, in spite of acid disappointment, gin-horse prudence, and bookworm philosophy, I hold to be the first of human joys, our dearest blessing here below! How she caught the contagion I cannot tell; you medical people talk much of infection from breathing the same air, the touch, etc., but I never expressly said I loved her. Indeed I did not know myself why I liked so much to loiter behind with her, when returning in the evening from our labors; why the tones of her voice made my heartstrings thrill like an Æolian harp; and particularly why my pulse beat such a furious ratan, when I looked and fingered over her little hand to pick out the cruel nettle-stings and thistles. Among her other love-inspiring qualities, she sung sweetly; and it was her favorite reel to which I attempted giving an embodied vehicle in rime.

I was not so presumptuous as to imagine that I could make

verses like printed ones, composed by men who had Greek and
Latin; but my girl sung a song which was said to be composed by a small country laird's son, on one of his father's
maids, with whom he was in love; and I saw no reason why I
might not rime as well as he; for, excepting that he could
smear sheep, and cast peats, his father living in the moorlands,
he had no more scholar-craft than myself.

Thus with me began love and poetry, which at times have
been my only, and till within the last twelve months, have
been my highest enjoyment. My father struggled on till he
reached the freedom in his lease, when he entered on a larger
farm, about ten miles farther in the country. The nature
of the bargain he made was such as to throw a little ready
money into his hands at the commencement of his lease, otherwise the affair would have been impracticable. For four years
we lived comfortably here, but a difference commencing between him and his landlord as to terms, after three years'
tossing and whirling in the vortex of litigation, my father was
just saved from the horrors of a jail, by a consumption, which,
after two years' promises, kindly stepped in, and carried him
away, to where the wicked cease from troubling, and where
the weary are at rest!

It is during the time that we lived on this farm that my
little story is most eventful. I was, at the beginning of this
period, perhaps the most ungainly, awkward boy in the parish—no hermit was less acquainted with the ways of the world.
What I knew of ancient story was gathered from Salmon's and
Guthrie's Geographical Grammars; and the ideas I had formed
of modern manners, of literature, and criticism, I got from the
Spectator. These, with Pope's Works, some Plays of Shakespeare, Tull and Dickson on Agriculture, the "Pantheon,"
Locke's "Essay on the Human Understanding," Stackhouse's
"History of the Bible," Justice's "British Gardener's Directory," Boyle's "Lectures," Allan Ramsay's Works, Taylor's
"Scripture Doctrine of Original Sin," "A Select Collection
of English Songs," and Hervey's "Meditations," had formed
the whole of my reading. The collection of songs was my
companion, day and night. I pored over them, driving my
cart, or walking to labor, song by song, verse by verse; carefully noting the true, tender, or sublime, from affectation and

fustian. I am convinced I owe to this practice much of my critic-craft, such as it is.

In my seventeenth year, to give my manners a brush, I went to a country dancing-school. My father had an unaccountable antipathy against these meetings, and my going was, what to this moment I repent, in opposition to his wishes. My father, as I said before, was subject to strong passions; from that instance of disobedience in me he took a sort of dislike to me, which, I believe, was one cause of the dissipation which marked my succeeding years. I say dissipation, comparatively with the strictness, and sobriety, and regularity of Presbyterian country life; for though the will-o'-wisp meteors of thoughtless whim were almost the sole lights of my path, yet early ingrained piety and virtue kept me for several years afterward within the line of innocence. The great misfortune of my life was to want an aim. I had felt early some stirrings of ambition, but they were the blind gropings of Homer's Cyclops round the walls of his cave.

I saw my father's situation entailed on me perpetual labor. The only two openings by which I could enter the temple of fortune were the gate of niggardly economy, or the path of little chicaning bargain-making. The first is so contracted an aperture I never could squeeze myself into it; the last I always hated—there was contamination in the very entrance! Thus abandoned of aim or view in life, with a strong appetite for sociability, as well from native hilarity as from a pride of observation and remark; a constitutional melancholy or hypochondriasm that made me fly solitude; add to these incentives to social life, my reputation for bookish knowledge, a certain wild logical talent, and a strength of thought, something like the rudiments of good sense; and it will not seem surprising that I was generally a welcome guest where I visited, or any great wonder that always, where two or three met together, there was I among them. But far beyond all other impulses of my heart, was a leaning toward the adorable half of humankind. My heart was completely tinder, and was eternally lighted up by some goddess or other; and, as in every other warfare in this world, my fortune was various; sometimes I was received with favor, and sometimes I was mortified with a repulse. At the plow, scythe, or reap-hook I feared no competitor, and thus I set absolute want at defiance; and as I never cared further for my labors than while I was in actual exercise, I spent the evenings in the way after my own heart.

Another circumstance in my life which made some alteration in my mind and manners, was, that I spent my nineteenth summer on a smuggling coast, a good distance from home, at a noted school, to learn mensuration, surveying, dialing, etc., in which I made a pretty good progress. But I made a greater progress in the knowledge of mankind. The contraband trade was at that time very successful, and it sometimes happened to me to fall in with those who carried it on. Scenes of swaggering riot and roaring dissipation were, till this time, new to me; but I was no enemy to social life.

My reading meantime was enlarged with the very important addition of Thomson's and Shenstone's Works. I had séen human nature in a new phase; and I engaged several of my schoolfellows to keep up a literary correspondence with me. This improved me in composition. I had met with a collection of letters by the wits of Queen Anne's reign, and pored over them most devoutly. I kept copies of any of my own letters that pleased me, and a comparison between them and the composition of most of my correspondents flattered my vanity. I carried this whim so far that, though I had not three-farthings' worth of business in the world, yet almost every post brought me as many letters as if I had been a broad plodding son of the day-book and ledger.

My life flowed on much in the same course till my twenty-third year. The addition of two more authors to my library gave me great pleasure; Sterne and Mackenzie—"Tristram Shandy" and the "Man of Feeling"—were my bosom favorites. Poesy was still a darling walk for my mind, but it was only indulged in according to the humor of the hour. I had usually half a dozen or more pieces on hand; I took up one or other, as it suited the momentary tone of the mind, and dismissed the work as it bordered on fatigue. My passions, when once lighted up, raged like so many devils, till they got vent in rime; and then the conning over my verses, like a spell, soothed all into quiet! None of the rimes of those days are in print, except, "Winter, a Dirge," the eldest of my printed pieces; "The Death of Poor Maillie," "John

Barleycorn,'' and Songs First, Second and Third. Song Second was the ebullition of that passion which ended the forementioned school-business.

My twenty-third year, was to me an important era. Partly through whim, and partly that I wished to set about doing something in life, I joined a flax-dresser in a neighboring town (Irvine), to learn the trade. This was an unlucky affair. As we were giving a welcome carousal to the new year, the shop took fire and burned to ashes, and I was left, like a true poet, not worth a sixpence.

I was obliged to give up this scheme, the clouds of misfortune were gathering thick round my father's head; and, what was worst of all, he was visibly far gone in a consumption; and to crown my distresses, a beautiful girl, whom I adored, and who had pledged her soul to meet me in the field of matrimony, jilted me, with peculiar circumstances of mortification. The finishing evil that brought up the rear of this infernal file, was my constitutional melancholy being increased to such a degree, that for three months I was in a state of mind scarcely to be envied by the hopeless wretches who have got their mittimus—depart from me, ye cursed!

From this adventure I learned something of a town life; but the principal thing which gave my mind a turn, was a friendship I formed with a young fellow, a very noble character, but a hapless son of misfortune. He was the son of a simple mechanic; but a great man in the neighborhood taking him under his patronage, gave him a genteel education, with a view of bettering his situation in life. The patron dying just as he was ready to launch out into the world, the poor fellow in despair went to sea; where, after a variety of good and ill fortune, a little before I was acquainted with him he had been set on shore by an American privateer, on the wild coast of Connaught, stripped of everything. I cannot quit this poor fellow's story without adding, that he is at this time master of a large West Indiaman belonging to the Thames.

His mind was fraught with independence, magnanimity, and every manly virtue. I loved and admired him to a degree of enthusiasm, and of course strove to imitate him. In some measure I succeeded; I had pride before, but he taught it to flow in proper channels. His knowledge of the world was

vastly superior to mine, and I was all attention to learn. . . .
My reading only increased while in this town by two stray
volumes of "Pamela," and one of "Ferdinand Count
Fathom," which gave me some idea of novels. Rime, except
some religious pieces that are in print, I had given up; but
meeting with Fergusson's Scottish Poems, I strung anew my
wildly sounding lyre with emulating vigor. When my father
died, his all went among the hell-hounds that growl in the
kennel of justice; but we made a shift to collect a little money
in the family amongst us, with which to keep us together, my
brother and I took a neighboring farm. My brother wanted
my hare-brained imagination, as well as my social and amorous
madness; but in good sense, and every sober qualification, he
was far my superior.

I entered on this farm with a full resolution, "Come, go to,
I will be wise!" I read farming books, I calculated crops;
I attended markets; and in short, in spite of the devil, and
the world, and the flesh, I believe I should have been a wise
man; but the first year, from unfortunately buying bad seed,
the second from a late harvest, we lost half our crops. This
overset all my wisdom, and I returned, "like the dog to his
vomit, and the sow that was washed, to her wallowing in the
mire."

I now began to be known in the neighborhood as a maker of
rimes. The first of my poetic offspring that saw the light
was a burlesque lamentation on a quarrel between two reverend Calvinists, both of them figuring in my "Holy Fair."
I had a notion myself that the piece had some merit; but, to
prevent the worst, I gave a copy of it to a friend, who was
very fond of such things, and told him that I could not guess
who was the author of it, but that I thought it pretty clever.
With a certain description of the clergy, as well as laity, it
met with a roar of applause. "Holy Willie's Prayer" next
made its appearance, and alarmed the kirk-session so much,
that they held several meetings to look over their spiritual
artillery, if happily any of it might be pointed against profane
rimers. Unluckily for me, my wanderings led me on another
side, within point-blank shot of their heaviest metal. This is
the unfortunate story that gave rise to my printed poem, "The
Lament." This was a most melancholy affair, which I cannot

yet bear to reflect on, and had very nearly given me one or two of the principal qualifications for a place among those who have lost the chart, and mistaken the reckoning of rationality. I gave up my part of the farm to my brother; in truth it was only nominally mine; and made what little preparation was in my power for Jamaica.

But before leaving my native country forever, I resolved to publish my poems. I weighed my productions as impartially as was in my power; I thought they had merit; and it was a delicious idea that I should be called a clever fellow, even though it should never reach my ears—a poor Negro driver— or perhaps a victim to that inhospitable clime, and gone to the world of spirits! I can truly say that, poor and unknown as I then was, I had pretty nearly as high an idea of myself and of my works as I have at this moment, when the public has decided in their favor. It ever was my opinion that the mistakes and blunders, both in a rational and religious point of view, of which we see thousands daily guilty, are owing to their ignorance of themselves. To know myself had been all along my constant study. I weighed myself alone; I balanced myself with others. I watched every means of information, to see how much ground I occupied as a man and as a poet; I studied assiduously Nature's design in my formation—where the lights and shades in my character were intended. I was pretty confident my poems would meet with some applause; but at the worst, the roar of the Atlantic would deafen the voice of censure, and the novelty of West Indian scenes make me forget neglect. I threw off six hundred copies, of which I had got subscriptions for about three hundred and fifty. My vanity was highly gratified by the reception I met with from the public; and besides I pocketed, all expenses deducted, nearly twenty pounds. This sum came very seasonably, as I was thinking of indenting myself for want of money to procure my passage. As soon as I was master of nine guineas, the price of wafting me to the torrid zone, I took a steerage passage in the first ship that was to sail from the Clyde, for

Hungry ruin had me in the wind.

I had been for some days skulking from covert to covert, under all the terrors of a jail; as some ill-advised people had uncoupled the merciless pack of the law at my heels. I had taken the last farewell of my few friends; my chest was on the road to Greenock; I had composed the last song I should ever measure in Caledonia—"The Gloomy Night Is Gathering Fast," when a letter from Dr. Blacklock to a friend of mine, overthrew all my schemes, by opening new prospects to my poetic ambition. The doctor belonged to a set of critics for whose applause I had not dared to hope. His opinion, that I would meet with encouragement in Edinburgh for a second edition, fired me so much, that away I posted for that city, without a single acquaintance, or a single letter of introduction. The baneful star that had so long shed its blasting influence in my zenith for once made a revolution to the nadir; and a kind Providence placed me under the patronage of one of the noblest of men, the Earl of Glencairn. *Oublie moi, grand Dieu, si jamais je l'oublie.*[1]

I need relate no further. At Edinburgh I was in a new world; I mingled among many classes of men, but all of them new to me, and I was all attention to "catch" the characters and "the manners living as they rise." Whether I have profited, time will show.

---

[1] Forget me, Great God, if I ever forget him!

NAPOLEON
BONAPARTE

NAPOLEON BONAPARTE

1768-1821

INTRODUCTORY NOTE

Napoleon had always an inclination toward autobiography. Several times he spoke of writing a full narrative of his own career; but he never actually reached the point of doing so. A few days before his death, however, he seemed suddenly impressed with the need of leaving to his son a personal statement of self-explanation and advice; and he dictated the celebrated "Legacy to my Son," which is given here. The fact that it was Napoleon's last work, composed when he knew death was close at hand, lends it a peculiar weight and dignity.

Outside of this remarkable statement, we find our clearest glimpses of the man Napoleon in his letters to his wife, the Empress Josephine. Though he divorced Josephine for the sake of having a son and founding a dynasty, there has never been any question of his genuine devotion to her. She was a young widow when Napoleon first met her, the widow of General Beauharnais, with two children, Eugene and Hortense; and Napoleon seems to have opened his heart to the children also, watching over them affectionately and directing their careers. The first letters to Josephine that have been preserved are those written immediately after their marriage, when the young general, not yet thirty years of age, left his bride so as to take command of the Army of Italy. In this campaign he won his first great military triumph, and his letters to his bride breathe equally of battle and of love. The first such letter that is longer than a mere hurried note, is given here. We include also the first letter written after their divorce, and the letter sent to announce the Emperor's downfall, his retirement to Elba. The contrasted tone of these three addresses to the ever faithful wife of his heart must impress every reader.

323

NAPOLEON'S FIRST LOVE LETTER TO JOSEPHINE

[Written shortly after the marriage, this is the first surviving letter which contains any personal message beyond a word or two.]

MARMIROLO, July 17, 1796, 9 o'clock, P. M.

I HAVE received your letter, my adorable friend. It has filled my heart with joy. I am grateful to you for the trouble you have taken to send me the news. I hope that you are better to-day. I am sure that you have recovered. I earnestly desire that you should ride on horseback: it can not fail to benefit you.

Since I left you, I have been constantly depressed. My happiness is to be near you. Incessantly I live over in my memory your caresses, your tears, your affectionate solicitude. The charms of the incomparable Josephine kindle continually a burning and a glowing flame in my heart. When, free from all solicitude, all harassing care, shall I be able to pass all my time with you, having only to love you, and to think only of the happiness of so saying, and of proving it to you? I will send you your horse, but I hope you will soon join me. I thought that I loved you months ago, but since my separation from you I feel that I love you a thousand fold more. Each day since I knew you, have I adored you yet more and more. This proves the maxim of Bruyère, that "love comes all of a sudden," to be false. Everything in nature has its own course, and different degrees of growth.

Ah! I entreat you to permit me to see some of your faults. Be less beautiful, less gracious, less affectionate, less good, especially be not over-anxious, and never weep. Your tears rob me of reason, and inflame my blood. Believe me it is not in my power to have a single thought which is not of thee, or a wish which I could not reveal to thee.

Seek repose. Quickly reëstablish your health. Come and join me, that at least. before death, we may be able to say, "We were many days happy." A thousand kisses, and one even to Fortuna, notwithstanding his spitefulness.

BONAPARTE.

THE FIRST LETTER AFTER THE DIVORCE

December, 1809; 8 o'clock in the evening.

My Love—I found you more feeble to-day than you ought to be. You have exhibited much fortitude, and it is necessary that you should still continue to sustain yourself. You must not yield to funereal melancholy. Strive to be tranquil, and above all to preserve your health, which is so precious to me. If you are attached to me, if you love me, you must maintain your energy, and strive to be cheerful. You can not doubt my constancy, and my tender affection. You know too well all the sentiments with which I regard you, to suppose that I can be happy if you are unhappy, that I can be serene if you are agitated. Adieu, my love. May you have peaceful sleep. Believe that I wish it. NAPOLEON.

THE ANNOUNCEMENT OF DEFEAT

[Written after Napoleon's first overthrow, when he had agreed to retire to the Island of Elba.]

FONTAINEBLEAU, April 16, 1814.

DEAR JOSEPHINE—I wrote to you on the 8th of this month (it was a Friday), and perhaps you have not received my letter. Hostilities still continued; possibly it may have been intercepted. At present, communications must be reëstablished. I have formed my resolution. I have no doubt that this billet will reach you. I will not repeat what I said to you. There I lamented my situation; now I congratulate myself thereon. My head and spirit are freed from an enormous weight. My fall is great, but at least it is useful, as men say. In my retreat, I shall substitute the pen for the sword. The history of my reign will be curious. The world has yet seen me only in profile; I shall show myself in full.

How many things have I to disclose! how many are the men of whom a fatal estimate is entertained! I have heaped benefits upon millions of wretches. What have they done in the end for me? They have all betrayed me; yes, all. I except from the number the good Eugene, so worthy of you and of me. Adieu, my dear Josephine. Be resigned, as I am, and ever remember him who never forgets, and never will forget you. Farewell Josephine. NAPOLEON.

LEGACY TO MY SON

[NAPOLEON'S REVIEW OF HIS CAREER,
WRITTEN A FEW DAYS BEFORE HIS DEATH]

My son should not think of avenging my death. He should profit by it. Let the remembrance of what I have done never leave his mind. Let him always be like me, every inch a Frenchman. The aim of all his efforts should be to reign by peace. If he should recommence my wars out of pure love of imitation, and without any absolute necessity, he would be a mere ape. To do my work over again would be to suppose that I had done nothing. To complete it, on the contrary, would be to show the solidity of the basis, and explain the whole plan of an edifice which I had only roughly sketched. The same thing is not done twice in a century. I was obliged to daunt Europe by my arms. In the present day the way is to convince her. I saved the revolution which was about to perish. I raised it from its ruins and showed it to the world beaming with glory. I have implanted new ideas in France and in Europe. They cannot retrograde. Let my son bring into blossom all that I have sown. Let him develop all the elements of prosperity enclosed in the soil of France, and by these means he may yet be a great sovereign.

The Bourbons will not maintain their position after my death. A reaction in my favor will take place everywhere, even in England. This reaction will be a fine inheritance for my son. It is possible that the English, in order to efface the remembrance of their persecutions, will favor my son's return to France. But in order to live in a good understanding with England, it is necessary at any cost to favor her commercial interests. This necessity leads to one of these two consequences—war with England, or a sharing of the commerce of the world with her. This second condition is the only one possible in the present day. The exterior question will long take precedence in France of the interior. I bequeath to my son sufficient strength and sympathy to enable him to continue my work with the single aid of an elevated and conciliatory diplomacy.

His position at Vienna is deplorable. Will Austria set him at liberty unconditionally? But after all, Francis I. was once in a more critical position, and yet his French nationality was nothing impaired by it. Let not my son ever mount the throne by the aid of foreign influence. His aim should be not to fulfill a desire to reign, but to deserve the approbation of posterity. Let him cherish an intimacy with my family, whenever it shall be in his power. My mother is a woman of the old school. Joseph and Eugene are able to give him good counsel. Hortense and Catherine are superior women. If he remains in exile, let him marry one of my nieces. If France recalls him, let him seek the hand of a Princess of Russia. This court is the only one where family ties rule policy. The alliance which he may contract should tend to increase the exterior influence of France, and not to introduce a foreign influence into its councils. The French nation, when it is not taken the wrong way, is more easily governed than any other. Its prompt and easy comprehension is unequaled. It immediately discerns who labors for and who against it. But then it is necessary always to speak to its senses, otherwise its uneasy spirit gnaws; it explodes and ferments. My son will arrive after a time of civil troubles. He has but one party to fear, that of the Duke of Orleans. This party has been germinating for a long time. Let him despise all parties, and only see the mass of the people. Excepting those who have betrayed their country, he ought to forget the previous conduct of all men, and reward talent, merit, and services wherever he finds them. Chateaubriand, notwithstanding his libel, is a good Frenchman.

France is the country where the chiefs of parties have the least influence. To rest for support on them is to build on sand. Great things can only be done in France by having the support of the *mass of the people*. Besides, a government should always seek support where it is really to be found. There are moral laws as inflexible and imperious as the physical ones. The Bourbons can only rely for support on the nobles and the priest, whatever may be the constitution which they are made to adopt. The water will descend again to its level, in spite of the machine which has raised it for a moment. I, on the contrary, relied on the whole mass of the people without exception. I set the example of a government which favored the interests of all. I did not govern by the help of, or solely for either the nobles, the priests, the citizens, or tradesmen. I governed for the whole community, for the whole family of the French nation.

My nobility will afford no support to my son. I required more than one generation to succeed in making them assume my color, and preserve, by tradition, the sacred deposit of my moral conquests. From the year 1815, all the grandees openly espoused the opposite party. I felt no reliance either on my marshals or my nobility, not even on my colonels; but the whole mass of the people, and the whole army, up to the grade of captain, were on my side. I was not deceived in feeling this confidence. They owe much to me. I was their true representative. My dictatorship was indispensable. The proof of this is, that they always offered me more power than I desired. In the present day there is nothing possible in France but what is necessary. It will not be the same with my son. His power will be disputed. He must anticipate every desire for liberty. It is, besides, easier in ordinary times to reign with the help of the Chambers than alone. The Assemblies take a great part of your responsibility, and nothing is more easy than always to have the majority on your side; but care must be taken not to demoralize the country. The influence of the government in France is immense; and if it understands the way, it has no need of employing corruption in order to find support on all sides. The aim of a sovereign is not only to reign, but to diffuse instruction, morality, and well-being. Anything false is but a bad aid.

In my youth, I too entertained some illusions; but I soon recovered from them. The great orators who rule the assemblies by the brilliance of their eloquence, are, in general, men of the most mediocre political talents. They should not be opposed in their own way, for they have always more noisy words at command than you. Their eloquence should be opposed by a serious and logical argument. Their strength lies in vagueness. They should be brought back to the reality of facts. Practical arguments destroy them. In the Council there were men possessed of much more eloquence than I was. I always defeated them by this simple argument—*two and two make four.*

France possesses very clever practical men. The only thing necessary is to find them, and to give them the means of reaching the proper station. One is at the plow, who ought to be in the council, and another is minister who ought to be at the plow. Let not my son be astonished to hear men, the most reasonable to all appearance, propose to him the most absurd plans. From the agrarian law to the despotism of the Grand Turk, every system finds an apologist in France. Let him listen to them all; let him take everything at its just value, and surround himself by all the real capacity of the country. The French people are influenced by two powerful passions—the love of liberty and the love of distinction. These, though seemingly opposed, are derived from one and the same feeling, a government can only satisfy these two wants by the most exact justice. The law and action of the government must be equal towards all. Honors and rewards must be conferred on the men who seem in the eyes of all to be most worthy of them. Merit may be pardoned, but not intrigue. The order of the Legion of Honor has been an immense and powerful incitement to virtue, talent, and courage. If ill employed, it would become a great evil by alienating the whole army, if the spirit of court intrigue and coterie presided at its nominations or in its administrations.

My son will be obliged to allow the liberty of the press. This is a necessity in the present day. In order to govern, it is not necessary to pursue a more or less perfect theory, but to build with the materials which are under one's hand; to submit to necessities and profit by them. The liberty of the press ought to become, in the hands of the government, a powerful auxiliary in diffusing, through all the most distant corners of the empire, sound doctrines and good principles. To leave it to itself would be to fall asleep on the brink of a danger. On the conclusion of a general peace, I would have instituted a Directory of the Press, composed of the ablest men of the country; and I would have diffused, even to the most distant hamlet, my ideas and my intentions. In the present day it is impossible to remain as one might have done three hundred years ago—a quiet spectator of the transformations of society. Now one must, under the pain of death, either direct or hinder everything.

My son ought to be a man of new ideas, and of the cause which I have made triumphant everywhere. He ought to establish institutions which shall efface all traces of the feudal law, secure the dignity of man, and develop those germs of prosperity which have been budding for centuries. He should propagate in all those countries uncivilized and barbarous, the benefits of Christianity and civilization. Such should be the aim of all my son's thoughts. Such is the cause for which I die a martyr to the hatred of the oligarchs, of which I am the object. Let him consider the holiness of my cause. Look at the regicides! They were formerly in the councils of a Bourbon. To-morrow they will return to their country, and I and mine expiate in torture the blessings which I desired to bestow on nations. My enemies are the enemies of humanity. They desire to fetter the people, whom they regard as a flock of sheep. They endeavor to oppress France, and to make the stream re-ascend towards its source. Let them take care that it does not burst its bounds.

With my son, all opposite interests may live in peace; new ideas be diffused and gather strength, without any violent shock, or the sacrifice of any victims, and humanity be spared dreadful misfortunes. But if the blind hatred of kings still pursues my blood after my death, I shall then be avenged, but cruelly avenged. Civilization will suffer in every way, if nations burst their bounds, and rivers of blood will be shed throughout the whole of Europe; the lights of science and knowledge will be extinguished amid civil and foreign warfare. More than three hundred years of troubles will be required in order to destroy in Europe that royal authority which has, but for a day, represented the interests of all classes of men, but which struggled for several centuries before it could throw off all the restraints of the Middle Ages. If, on the other hand, the North advances against civilization, the struggle will be of shorter duration, but the blows more fatal. The well-being of nations, all the results which it has taken so many years to obtain, will be destroyed, and none can foresee the disastrous consequences. The accession of my son is for the interest of nations, as well as kings. Beyond the circle of ideas and principles for which we have fought, and which I have carried triumphantly through all difficulties, I see nought but slavery and confusion for France and for the whole of Europe.

You will publish all that I have dictated or written, and you will engage my son to read and reflect upon it. You will tell him to protect all those who have served me well, and their number is large. My poor soldiers, so devoted, so magnanimous, are now, perhaps, in want of bread! What buried riches, which will, perhaps, never again see the light of day! Europe is progressing toward an inevitable transformation. To endeavor to retard this progress would be but to lose strength by a useless struggle. To favor it is to strengthen the hopes and wishes of all.

There are desires of nationality which must be satisfied sooner or later. It is towards this end that continual progress should be made. My son's position will not be exempt from immense difficulties. Let him do by general consent what I was compelled by circumstances to effect by force of arms. When I was victorious over Russia, in 1812, the problem of a peace of a hundred years' duration was solved. I cut the Gordian knot of nations. In the present day it must be untied. The remembrance of the thrones which I raised up, when it was for the general interest of my policy so to do, should be effaced. In the year 1815, I exacted from my brothers that they should forget their royalty, and only take the title of French princes. My son should follow this example. An opposite course would excite just alarm.

It is no longer in the North that great questions will be resolved, but in the Mediterranean. There, there is enough to content all the ambition of the different powers; and the happiness of civilized nations may be purchased with fragments of barbarous lands. Let the kings listen to reason. Europe will no longer afford matter for maintaining international hatreds. Prejudices are dissipated and intermingled. Routes of commerce are becoming multiplied. It is no longer possible for one nation to monopolize it. As a means by which my son may see whether his administration be good or the contrary, whether his laws are in accordance with the manners of the country, let him have an annual and particular report presented to him of the number of condemnations pronounced by the tribunals. If crimes and delinquencies increase in number, it is a proof that misery is on the increase, and that society is ill governed. Their diminution, on the other hand, is a proof of the contrary.

Religious ideas have more influence than certain narrow-minded philosophers are willing to believe. They are capable of rendering great services to humanity. By standing well with the Pope an influence is still maintained over the consciences of a hundred millions of men. Pius VII. will be always well-disposed towards my son. He is a tolerant and enlightened old man. Fatal circumstances embroiled our cabinets; I regret this deeply. Cardinal Fesch did not understand me. He upheld the party of the *Ultramontanes,* the enemies of true religion in France. If you are permitted to return to France, you will still find many who have remained faithful to my memory. The best monuments which they could raise to me would be to make a collection of all the ideas which I expressed in the Council of State for the administration of the empire; to collect all my instructions to my ministers, and to make a list of the works which I undertook, which I raised in France and Italy. In what I have said in the Council of State, a distinction must be made, between the measures good only for the moment, and those the application of which is eternally true.

Let my son often read and reflect on history. This is the only true philosophy. Let him read and meditate on the wars of the greatest captains. This is the only means of rightly learning the science of war. But all that you say to him, or all that he learns will be of little use to him if he has not in the depth of his heart that sacred fire and love of good which alone can effect great things. I will hope, however, that he will be worthy of his destiny.

SIR WALTER SCOTT

SIR WALTER SCOTT

1771-1832

INTRODUCTORY NOTE

When we turn to biography rather than autobiography, probably the most remarkable and valuable work of that class, next to Boswell's Johnson, is the life of Scott written by his son-in-law, J. G. Lockhart. This most attractive biography opens with an autobiographical section furnished by Scott himself. It is incomplete, dealing only with the author's early life, but this lack is partly made up by the fact that Scott went over the sketch a second time, in 1826, and added copious notes supplying his later viewpoint on events.

Scott's autobiography is interesting for its simplicity and gay humor, and also for giving us yet another sidelight on the noble nature of the man. Few human beings have ever existed so admirable in every way, so splendidly and gallantly heroic as Sir Walter Scott. He has often been compared to the heroes of his own novels; and every student of human nature has delighted to linger with this magnificent specimen of our race. He was certainly the most loved man of his day, and this wide public appreciation was given him even more as a man than as a writer. He first won celebrity as a critic, an antiquarian, and a poet. His ''story-telling'' poems were in fact the means of first attracting the masses of people to reading poetry, and so securing for it an extensive sale. Then, in 1814, Scott began to win his even greater reputation as a novelist.

SCOTT'S UNFINISHED AUTOBIOGRAPHY

Ashestiel, April 26th, 1808.

THE·present age has discovered a desire, or rather a rage, for literary anecdote and private history, that may be well permitted to alarm one who has engaged in a certain degree the attention of the public. That I have had more than my own share of popularity, my contemporaries will be as ready to admit as I am to confess that its measure has exceeded not only my hopes, but my merits, and even wishes. I may be therefore permitted, without an extraordinary degree of vanity, to take the precaution of recording a few leading circumstances (they do not merit the name of events) of a very quiet and uniform life—that, should my literary reputation survive my temporal existence, the public may know from good authority all that they are entitled to know of an individual who has contributed to their amusement.

From the lives of some poets a most important moral lesson may doubtless be derived, and few sermons can be read with so much profit as the Memoirs of Burns, of Chatterton, or of Savage. Were I conscious of anything peculiar in my own moral character which could render such development necessary or useful, I would as readily consent to it as I would bequeath my body to dissection, if the operation could tend to point out the nature and the means of curing any peculiar malady. But as my habits of thinking and acting, as well as my rank in society, were fixed long before I had attained, or even pretended to any poetical reputation,[1] and as it produced, when acquired, no remarkable change upon either, it is hardly to be expected that much information can be derived from minutely investigating frailties, follies, or vices, not very different in number or degree from those of other men in my situation. As I have not been blessed with the talents of Burns or Chatterton, I have been happily exempted from the influence of their violent passions, exasperated by the struggle of feelings which rose up against the unjust decrees of fortune. Yet, although I cannot tell of difficulties vanquished, and distance of rank annihilated by the strength of genius, those who

[1] I do not mean to say that my success in literature has not led me to mix familiarly in society much above my birth and original pretensions, since I have been readily received in the first circles in Britain. But there is a certain intuitive knowledge of the world, to which most well-educated Scotchmen are early trained, that prevents them from being much dazzled by this species of elevation. A man who to good nature adds the general rudiments of good breeding, provided he rest contented with a simple and unaffected manner of behaving and expressing himself, will never be ridiculous in the best society, and, so far as his talents and information permit, may be an agreeable part of the company. I have therefore never felt much elevated, nor did I experience any violent change in situation, by the passport which my poetical character afforded me into higher company than my birth warranted.—1826.

shall hereafter read this little Memoir may find in it some
hints to be improved, for the regulation of their own minds, or
the training those of others.

Every Scotchman has a pedigree. It is a national prerogative, as unalienable as his pride and his poverty. My birth
was neither distinguished nor sordid. According to the prejudices of my country, it was esteemed *gentle,* as I was connected, though remotely, with ancient families both by my
father's and mother's side. My father's grandfather was
Walter Scott, well known in Teviotdale by the surname of
Beardie. He was the second son of Walter Scott, first Laird
of Raeburn, who was third son of Sir William Scott, and the
grandson of Walter Scott, commonly called in tradition *Auld
Watt* of Harden. I am therefore lineally descended from that
ancient chieftain, whose name I have made to ring in many
a ditty, and from his fair dame, the Flower of Yarrow—no
bad genealogy for a Border minstrel.

Beardie, my great-grandfather aforesaid, derived his cognomen from a venerable beard, which he wore unblemished
by razor or scissors, in token of his regret for the banished
dynasty of Stuart. It would have been well that his zeal had
stopped there. But he took arms, and intrigued in their cause,
until he lost all he had in the world, and, as I have heard,
run a narrow risk of being hanged, had it not been for the
interference of Anne, Duchess of Buccleuch and Monmouth.
Beardie's elder brother, William Scott of Raeburn, my great-
granduncle, was killed about the age of twenty-one, in a duel
with Pringle of Crichton, grandfather of the present Mark
Pringle of Clifton. They fought with swords, as was the
fashion of the time, in a field near Selkirk, called from the
catastrophe the *Raeburn Meadowspot.* Pringle fled from Scotland to Spain, and was long a captive and slave in Barbary.
Beardie became, of course, *Tutor of Raeburn,* as the old Scottish phrase called him—that is, guardian to his infant nephew,
father of the present Walter Scott of Raeburn. He also managed the estates of Makerstoun, being nearly related to that
family by his mother, Isobel MacDougal. I suppose he had
some allowance for his care in either case, and subsisted upon
that and the fortune which he had by his wife, a Miss Campbell of Silvercraigs, in the west, through which connection my

father used to *call cousin,* as they say, with the Campbells of Blythswood. Beardie was a man of some learning, and a friend of Dr. Pitcairn, to whom his politics probably made him acceptable. They had a Tory or Jacobite club in Edinburgh, in which the conversation is said to have been maintained in Latin.

He left three sons. The eldest, Walter, had a family, of which any that now remain have been long settled in America:—the male heirs are long since extinct. The third was William, father of James Scott, well known in India as one of the original settlers of Prince of Wales island. The second, Robert Scott, was my grandfather. He was originally bred to the sea; but, being shipwrecked near Dundee in his trial-voyage, he took such a sincere dislike to that element, that he could not be persuaded to a second attempt. This occasioned a quarrel between him and his father, who left him to shift for himself. Robert was one of those active spirits to whom this was no misfortune. He turned Whig upon the spot, and fairly abjured his father's politics, and his learned poverty. His chief and relative, Mr. Scott of Harden, gave him a lease of the farm of Sandy-Knowe, comprehending the rocks in the center of which Smailholm or Sandy-Knowe Tower is situated. He took for his shepherd an old man called Hogg, who willingly lent him, out of respect to his family, his savings, about £30, to stock the new farm.

With this sum, which it seems was at the time sufficient for the purpose, the master and servant set off to purchase a stock of sheep at Whitsun-Tryste, a fair held on a hill near Wooler in Northumberland. The old shepherd went carefully from drove to drove, till he found a *hirsel* likely to answer their purpose, and then returned to tell his master to come up and conclude the bargain. But what was his surprise to see him galloping a mettled hunter about the race-course, and to find he had expended the whole stock in this extraordinary purchase!—Moses's bargain of green spectacles did not strike more dismay into the Vicar of Wakefield's family, than my grandfather's rashness into the poor old shepherd. The thing, however, was irretrievable, and they returned without the sheep. In the course of a few days, however, my grandfather, who was one of the best horsemen of his time, attended

John Scott of Harden's hounds on this same horse, and displayed him to such advantage that he sold him for double the original price. The farm was now stocked in earnest; and the rest of my grandfather's career was that of successful industry. He was one of the first who were active in the cattle trade, afterwards carried to such extent between the Highlands of Scotland and the leading counties in England, and by his droving transactions acquired a considerable sum of money. He was a man of middle stature, extremely active, quick, keen, and fiery in his temper, stubbornly honest, and so distinguished for his skill in country matters, that he was the general referee in all points of dispute which occurred in the neighborhood. His birth being admitted as *gentle,* gave him access to the best society in the county, and his dexterity in country sports, particularly hunting, made him an acceptable companion in the field as well as at the table.[2]

Robert Scott of Sandy-Knowe married, in 1728, Barbara Haliburton, daughter of Thomas Haliburton of Newmains, an ancient and respectable family in Berwickshire. Among other patrimonial possessions, they enjoyed the part of Dryburgh, now the property of the Earl of Buchan, comprehending the ruins of the Abbey. My granduncle, Robert Haliburton, having no male heirs, this estate, as well as the representation of the family, would have devolved upon my father, and indeed Old Newmains had settled it upon him; but this was prevented by the misfortunes of my granduncle, a weak silly man, who engaged in trade, for which he had neither stock nor talents, and became bankrupt. The ancient patrimony was sold for a trifle (about £3000), and my father, who might have purchased it with ease, was dissuaded by my grandfather, who at that time believed a more advantageous purchase might have been made of some lands which Raeburn thought of selling. And thus we have nothing left of Dryburgh, although my father's maternal inheritance, but the right of stretching our bones where mine may perhaps be laid ere any eye but my own glances over these pages.

Walter Scott, my father, was born in 1729, and educated

[2] The present Lord Haddington, and other gentlemen conversant with the south country, remember my grandfather well. He was a fine alert figure, and wore a jockey cap over his gray hair.—1826.

to the profession of a Writer to the Signet. He was the eldest of a large family, several of whom I shall have occasion to mention with a tribute of sincere gratitude. My father was a singular instance of a man rising to eminence in a profession for which nature had in some degree unfitted him. He had indeed a turn for labor, and a pleasure in analyzing the abstruse feudal doctrines connected with conveyancing, which would probably have rendered him unrivaled in the line of a special pleader, had there been such a profession in Scotland; but in the actual business of the profession which he embraced, in that sharp and intuitive perception which is necessary in driving bargains for himself and others, in availing himself of the wants, necessities, caprices, and follies of some, and guarding against the knavery and malice of others, Uncle Toby himself could not have conducted himself with more simplicity than my father. Most attorneys have been suspected, more or less justly, of making their own fortune at the expense of their clients—my father's fate was to vindicate his calling from the stain in one instance, for in many cases his clients contrived to ease him of considerable sums. Many worshipful and be-knighted names occur to my memory, who did him the honor to run in his debt to the amount of thousands, and to pay him with a lawsuit, or a commission of bankruptcy, as the case happened. But they are gone to a different accounting, and it would be ungenerous to visit their disgrace upon their descendants.

My father was wont also to give openings, to those who were pleased to take them, to pick a quarrel with him. He had a zeal for his clients which was almost ludicrous: far from coldly discharging the duties of his employment towards them, he thought for them, felt for their honor as for his own, and rather risked disobliging them than neglecting anything to which he conceived their duty bound them. If there was an old mother or aunt to be maintained, he was, I am afraid, too apt to administer to their necessities from what the young heir had destined exclusively to his pleasures. This ready discharge of obligations which the Civilians tell us are only natural and not legal, did not, I fear, recommend him to his employers. Yet his practice was, at one period of his life, very extensive. He understood his business theoretically, and was early introduced to it by a partnership with George Chalmers, Writer to the Signet, under whom he had served his apprenticeship.

His person and face were uncommonly handsome, with an expression of sweetness of temper, which was not fallacious; his manners were rather formal, but full of genuine kindness, especially when exercising the duties of hospitality. His general habits were not only temperate, but severely abstemious; but upon a festival occasion, there were few whom a moderate glass of wine exhilarated to such a lively degree. His religion, in which he was devoutly sincere, was Calvinism of the strictest kind, and his favorite study related to church history. I suspect the good old man was often engaged with Knox and Spottiswoode's folios, when, immured in his solitary room, he was supposed to be immersed in professional researches. In his political principles he was a steady friend to freedom, with a bias, however, to the monarchical part of our constitution, which he considered as peculiarly exposed to danger during the later years of his life. He had much of ancient Scottish prejudice respecting the forms of marriages, funerals, christenings, and so forth, and was always vexed at any neglect of etiquette upon such occasions. As his education had not been upon an enlarged plan, it could not be expected that he should be an enlightened scholar, but he had not passed through a busy life without observation; and his remarks upon times and manners often exhibited strong traits of practical though untaught philosophy. Let me conclude this sketch, which I am unconscious of having overcharged, with a few lines written by the late Mrs. Cockburn upon the subject. They made one among a set of poetical characters which were given as toasts among a few friends, and we must hold them to contain a striking likeness, since the original was recognized so soon as they were read aloud:—

"To a thing that's uncommon—a youth of discretion,
  Who, though vastly handsome, despises flirtation:
  To the friend in affliction, the heart of affection,
  Who may hear the last trump without dread of detection."

In April 1758, my father married Anne Rutherford, eldest daughter of Dr. John Rutherford, professor of medicine in

the University of Edinburgh. He was one of those pupils of
Boerhaave, to whom the school of medicine in our northern
metropolis owes its rise, and a man distinguished for professional talent, for lively wit, and for literary acquirements.
Dr. Rutherford was twice married. His first wife, of whom
my mother is the sole surviving child, was a daughter of Sir
John Swinton of Swinton, a family which produced many
distinguished warriors during the middle ages, and which, for
antiquity and honorable alliances, may rank with any in Britain. My grandfather's second wife was Miss Mackay, by
whom he had a second family, of whom are now (1808) alive,
Dr. Daniel Rutherford, professor of botany in the University
of Edinburgh, and Misses Janet and Christian Rutherford,
amiable and accomplished women.

My father and mother had a very numerous family, no
fewer, I believe, than twelve children, of whom many were
highly promising, though only five survived very early youth.
My eldest brother Robert was bred in the King's service, and
was in most of Rodney's battles. His temper was bold and
haughty, and to me was often checkered with what I felt to
be capricious tyranny. In other respects I loved him much,
for he had a strong turn for literature, read poetry with
taste and judgment, and composed verses himself, which had
gained him great applause among his messmates. Witness
the following elegy upon the supposed loss of the vessel, composed the night before Rodney's celebrated battle of April the
12th, 1782. It alludes to the various amusements of his
mess :—

> "No more the geese shall cackle on the poop,
>   No more the bagpipe through the orlop sound,
> No more the midshipmen, a jovial group,
>   Shall toast the girls, and push the bottle round.
> In death's dark road at anchor fast they stay,
>   Till Heaven's loud signal shall in thunder roar;
> Then starting up, all hands shall quick obey,
>   Sheet home the topsail, and with speed unmoor."

Robert sang agreeably—(a virtue which was never seen in
me)—understood the mechanical arts, and when in good
humor, could regale us with many a tale of bold adventure

and narrow escapes. When in bad humor, however, he gave us a practical taste of what was then man-of-war's discipline, and kicked and cuffed without mercy. I have often thought how he might have distinguished himself had he continued in the navy until the present times, so glorious for nautical exploit. But the peace of 1783 cut off all hopes of promotion for those who had not great interest; and some disgust which his proud spirit had taken at harsh usage from a superior officer, ·combined to throw poor Robert into the East India Company's service, for which his habits were ill adapted. He made two voyages to the East, and died a victim to the climate.

John Scott, my second brother, is about three years older than I. He addicted himself to the military service, and is now brevet-major in the 73d regiment.[3]

I had an only sister, Anne Scott, who seemed to be from her cradle the butt for mischance to shoot arrows at. Her childhood was·marked by perilous escapes from the most extraordinary accidents. Among others, I remember an iron-railed door leading into the area in the center of George's Square being closed by the wind, while her fingers were betwixt the hasp and staple. Her hand was thus locked in, and must have been smashed to pieces, had not the bones of her fingers been remarkably slight and thin. As it was, the hand was cruelly mangled. On another occasion, she was nearly drowned in a pond, or old quarry-hole, in what was then called Brown's Park, on the south side of the square. But the most unfortunate accident, and which, though it happened while she was only six years old, proved the remote cause of her death, was her cap accidentally taking fire. The child was alone in the room, and before assistance could be obtained, her head was dreadfully scorched. After a lingering and dangerous illness, she recovered—but never to enjoy perfect health. The slightest cold occasioned swellings in her face, and other indications of a delicate constitution. At length [in 1801], poor Anne was taken ill, and died after a very short interval. Her temper, like that of her brothers,

[3] He was this year made major of the second battalion by the kind intercession of Mr. Canning at the War-Office—1809. He retired from the army, and kept house with my mother. His health was totally broken, and he died, yet a young man, on 8th May 1816.—1826.

was peculiar, and in her, perhaps, it showed more odd, from the habits of indulgence which her nervous illness had formed. But she was at heart an affectionate and kind girl, neither void of talent nor of feeling, though living in an ideal world which she had framed to herself by the force of imagination. Anne was my junior by about a year.

A year lower in the list was my brother Thomas Scott, who is still alive.[4]

Last, and most unfortunate of our family, was my youngest brother, Daniel. With the same aversion to labor, or rather, I should say, the same determined indolence that marked us all, he had neither the vivacity of intellect which supplies the want of diligence, nor the pride which renders the most detested labor better than dependence or contempt. His career was as unfortunate as might be augured from such an unhappy combination; and, after various unsuccessful attempts to establish himself in life, he died on his return from the West Indies, in July 1806.

Having premised so much of my family, I return to my own story. I was born, as I believe, on the 15th August 1771, in a house belonging to my father, at the head of the College Wynd. It was pulled down, with others, to make room for the northern front of the new College. I was an uncommonly healthy child, but had nearly died in consequence of my first nurse being ill of a consumption, a circumstance which she chose to conceal, though to do so was murder to both herself and me. She went privately to consult Dr. Black, the celebrated professor of chemistry, who put my father on his guard. The woman was dismissed, and I was consigned to a healthy peasant, who is still alive to boast of her *laddie* being what she calls *a grand gentleman*. I showed every sign of health and strength until I was about eighteen months old.

[4] Poor Tom, a man of infinite humor and excellent parts, pursued for some time my father's profession; but he was unfortunate, from engaging in speculations respecting farms and matters out of the line of his proper business. He afterwards became paymaster of the 70th regiment, and died in Canada. Tom married Elizabeth, a daughter of the family of M'Culloch of Ardwell, an ancient Galwegian stock, by whom he left a son, Walter Scott, now second lieutenant of Engineers in the East India Company's service, Bombay—and three daughters, Jessie, married to Lieutenant-Colonel Huxley; 2, Anne; 3, Eliza—the two last still unmarried.—1826.

One night, I have been often told, I showed great reluctance to be caught and put to bed; and after being chased about the room, was apprehended and consigned to my dormitory with some difficulty. It was the last time I was to show such personal agility. In the morning, I was discovered to be affected with the fever which often accompanies the cutting of large teeth. It held me three days. On the fourth, when they went to bathe me as usual, they discovered that I had lost the power of my right leg. My grandfather, an excellent anatomist as well as physician, the late worthy Alexander Wood, and many others of the most respectable of the faculty, were consulted. There appeared to be no dislocation or sprain; blisters and other topical remedies were applied in vain. When the efforts of regular physicians had been exhausted, without the slightest success, my anxious parents, during the course of many years, eagerly grasped at every prospect of cure which was held out by the promise of empirics, or of ancient ladies or gentlemen who conceived themselves entitled to recommend various remedies, some of which were of a nature sufficiently singular. But the advice of my grandfather, Dr. Rutherford, that I should be sent to reside in the country, to give the chance of natural exertion, excited by free air and liberty, was first resorted to; and before I have the recollection of the slightest event, I was, agreeably to this friendly counsel, an inmate in the farm-house of Sandy-Knowe.

An odd incident is worth recording. It seems my mother had sent a maid to take charge of me, that I might be no inconvenience in the family. But the damsel sent on that important mission had left her heart behind her, in the keeping of some wild fellow, it is likely, who had done and said more to her than he was like to make good. She became extremely desirous to return to Edinburgh, and as my mother made a point of her remaining where she was she contracted a sort of hatred at poor me, as the cause of her being detained at Sandy-Knowe. This rose, I suppose, to a sort of delirious affection, for she confessed to old Alison Wilson, the housekeeper, that she had carried me up to the Craigs, meaning, under a strong temptation of the Devil, to cut my throat with her scissors, and bury me in the moss. Alison instantly took possession of my person, and took care that her confidant should not be subject to any farther temptation, so far as I was concerned. She was dismissed, of course, and I have heard became afterwards a lunatic.[5]

It is here at Sandy-Knowe, in the residence of my paternal grandfather, already mentioned, that I have the first consciousness of existence; and I recollect distinctly that my situation and appearance were a little whimsical. Among the odd remedies recurred to to aid my lameness, some one had

[5] The epistle prefixed to the 6th canto of Marmion, contains a charming picture of the infant poet's feelings amidst the scenery and associations of Smailholm Tower and Sandy-Knowe.

"It was a barren scene and wild,
   Where naked cliffs were rudely piled," &c., &c.

There are still (1836) living in that neighborhood two old women, who were in the domestic service of Sandy-Knowe, when the lame child was brought thither in the third year of his age. One of them, Tibby Hunter, remembers his coming well; and that "he was a sweet-tempered bairn, a darling with all about the house." The young ewe-milkers delighted, she says, to carry him about on their backs among the crags; and he was "very gleg (quick) at the uptake, and soon kenned every sheep and lamb by head-mark as well as any of them." His great pleasure, however, was in the society of the "aged hind" recorded in the epistle to Erskine, "Auld Sandy Ormiston," called, from the most dignified part of his function, "the Cow-bailie," who had the chief superintendence of the flocks that browsed upon "the velvet tufts of loveliest green." If the child saw him in the morning, he could not be satisfied unless the old man would set him astride on his shoulder, and take him to keep him company as he lay watching his charge.

The Cow-bailie blew a particular note on his whistle, which signified to the maid servants in the house below when the little boy wished to be carried home again. He told his friend, Mr. Skene of Rubislaw, when spending a summer day in his old age among these well-remembered crags, that he delighted to roll about on the grass all day long in the midst of the flock, and that "the sort of fellowship he thus formed with the sheep and lambs had impressed his mind with a degree of affectionate feeling towards them which had lasted throughout life." There is a story of his having been forgotten one day among the knolls when a thunder storm came on; and his aunt, suddenly recollecting his situation, and running out to bring him home, is said to have found him lying on his back, clapping his hands at the lightning, and crying out, "Bonny! bonny!" at every flash.—J. G. Lockhart.

recommended, that so often as a sheep was killed for the use of the family, I should be stripped, and swathed up in the skin, warm as it was flayed from the carcass of the animal. In this Tartar-like habiliment I well remember lying upon the floor of the little parlor in the farm-house, while my grandfather, a venerable old man with white hair, used every excitement to make me try to crawl. I also distinctly remember the late Sir George MacDougal of Mackerstoun, father of the present Sir Henry Hay MacDougal, joining in this kindly attempt. He was, God knows how,[6] a relation of ours, and I still recollect him in his old-fashioned military habit (he had been colonel of the Greys), with a small cocked hat, deeply laced, an embroidered scarlet waistcoat, and a light-colored coat, with milk-white locks tied in a military fashion, kneeling on the ground before me, and dragging his watch along the carpet to induce me to follow it. The benevolent old soldier and the infant wrapped in his sheepskin would have afforded an odd group to uninterested spectators. This must have happened about my third year, for Sir George MacDougal and my grandfather both died shortly after that period.

My grandmother continued for some years to take charge of the farm, assisted by my father's second brother, Mr. Thomas Scott, who resided at Crailing, as factor or land-steward for Mr. Scott of Danesfield, then proprietor of that estate.[7] This was during the heat of the American war, and I remember being as anxious on my uncle's weekly visits (for we heard news at no other time) to hear of the defeat of Washington, as if I had had some deep and personal cause of

[6] He was a second-cousin of my grandfather's. Isobel MacDougal, wife of Walter, the first Laird of Raeburn, and mother of Walter Scott, called Beardie, was grandaunt, I take it, to the late Sir George MacDougal. There was always great friendship between us and the Mackerstoun family. It singularly happened, that at the burial of the late Sir Henry MacDougal, my cousin William Scott, younger of Raeburn, and I myself, were the nearest blood-relations present, although our connection was of so old a date, and ranked as pall-bearers accordingly.—1826.

[7] My uncle afterwards resided at Elliston, and then took from Mr. Cornelius Elliot the estate of Woollee. Finally he retired to Monklaw, in the neighborhood of Jedburgh, where he died, 1823, at the advanced age of ninety years, and in full possession of his faculties. It was a fine thing to hear him talk over the change of the country which he had witnessed.—1826.

antipathy to him. I know not how this was combined with a very strong prejudice in favor of the Stuart family, which I had originally imbibed from the songs and tales of the Jacobites. This latter political propensity was deeply confirmed by the stories told in my hearing of the cruelties exercised in the executions at Carlisle, and in the Highlands, after the battle of Culloden. One or two of our own distant relations had fallen on that occasion, and I remember of detesting the name of Cumberland with more than infant hatred. Mr. Curle, farmer at Yetbyre, husband of one of my aunts, had been present at their execution; and it was probably from him that I first heard these tragic tales which made so great an impression on me. The local information, which I conceive had some share in forming my future taste and pursuits, I derived from the old songs and tales which then formed the amusement of a retired country family. My grandmother, in whose youth the old Border depredations were matter of recent tradition, used to tell me many a tale of Watt of Harden, Wight Willie of Aikwood, Jamie Telfer of the fair Dodhead, and other heroes—merrymen all of the persuasion and calling of Robin Hood and Little John. A more recent hero, but not of less note, was the celebrated *Diel of Littledean,* whom she well remembered, as he had married her mother's sister. Of this extraordinary person I learned many a story, grave and gay, comic and warlike. Two or three old books which lay in the window-seat were explored for my amusement in the tedious winter days. Automathes, and Ramsay's Tea-table Miscellany, were my favorites, although at a later period an odd volume of Josephus's Wars of the Jews divided my partiality.

My kind and affectionate aunt, Miss Janet Scott, whose memory will ever be dear to me, used to read these works to me with admirable patience, until I could repeat long passages by heart. The ballad of Hardyknute I was early master of, to the great annoyance of almost our only visitor, the worthy clergyman of the parish, Dr. Duncan, who had not patience to have a sober chat interrupted by my shouting forth this ditty. Methinks I now see his tall thin emaciated figure, his legs cased in clasped gambadoes, and his face of a length that would have rivaled the Knight of La Mancha's, and hear him exclaiming, "One may as well speak in the mouth of a cannon as where that child is." With this little acidity, which was natural to him, he was a most excellent and benevolent man, a gentleman in every feeling, and altogether different from those of his order who cringe at the tables of the gentry, or domineer and riot at those of the yeomanry. In his youth he had been chaplain in the family of Lord Marchmont—had seen Pope—and could talk familiarly of many characters who had survived the Augustan age of Queen Anne. Though valetudinary, he lived to be nearly ninety, and to welcome to Scotland his son, Colonel William Duncan, who, with the highest character for military and civil merit, had made a considerable fortune in India. In [1795], a few days before his death, I paid him a visit, to inquire after his health. I found him emaciated to the last degree, wrapped in a tartan night-gown, and employed with all the activity of health and youth in correcting a history of the Revolution, which he intended should be given to the public when he was no more. He read me several passages with a voice naturally strong, and which the feelings of an author then raised above the depression of age and declining health. I begged him to spare this fatigue, which could not but injure his health. His answer was remarkable. "I know," he said, "that I cannot survive a fortnight—and what signifies an exertion that can at worst only accelerate my death a few days?" I marveled at the composure of this reply, for his appearance sufficiently vouched the truth of his prophecy, and rode home to my uncle's (then my abode), musing what there could be in the spirit of authorship that could inspire its votaries with the courage of martyrs. He died within less than the period he assigned—with which event I close my digression.

I was in my fourth year when my father was advised that the Bath waters might be of some advantage to my lameness. My affectionate aunt, although such a journey promised to a person of her retired habits anything but pleasure or amusement, undertook as readily to accompany me to the wells of Bladud, as if she had expected all the delight that ever the prospect of a watering-place held out to its most impatient visitants. My health was by this time a good deal confirmed by the country air, and the influence of that imperceptible and unfatiguing exercise to which the good sense of my grandfather had subjected me; for when the day was fine, I was usually carried out and laid down beside the old shepherd, among the crags or rocks round which he fed his sheep. The impatience of a child soon inclined me to struggle with my infirmity, and I began by degrees to stand, to walk, and to run. Although the limb affected was much shrunk and contracted, my general health, which was of more importance, was much strengthened by being frequently in the open air; and, in a word, I who in a city had probably been condemned to hopeless and helpless decrepitude, was now a healthy, high-spirited, and, my lameness apart, a sturdy child—*non sine diis animosus infans.*

We went to London by sea, and it may gratify the curiosity of minute biographers to learn that our voyage was performed in the *Duchess of Buccleuch,* Captain Beatson, master. At London we made a short stay, and saw some of the common shows exhibited to strangers. When, twenty-five years afterwards, I visited the Tower of London and Westminster Abbey, I was astonished to find how accurate my recollections of those celebrated places of visitation proved to be, and I have ever since trusted more implicitly to my juvenile reminiscences. At Bath, where I lived about a year, I went through all the usual discipline of the pump-room and baths, but I believe without the least advantage to my lameness. During my residence at Bath, I acquired the rudiments of reading at a day-school, kept by an old dame near our lodgings, and I had never a more regular teacher, although I think I did not attend her a quarter of a year. An occasional lesson from my aunt supplied the rest. Afterwards, when grown a big boy, I had a few lessons from Mr. Stalker of Edinburgh, and finally from the Rev. Mr. Cleeve. But I never acquired a just pronunciation, nor could I read with much propriety.

In other respects my residence at Bath is marked by very pleasing recollections. The venerable John Home, author of Douglas, was then at the watering-place, and paid much attention to my aunt and to me. His wife, who has survived him, was then an invalid, and used to take the air in her carriage on the Downs, when I was often invited to accompany her. But the most delightful recollections of Bath are dated after the arrival of my uncle, Captain Robert Scott, who introduced me to all the little amusements which suited my age, and above all, to the theater. The play was As You Like It; and the witchery of the whole scene is alive in my mind at this moment. I made, I believe, noise more than enough, and remember being so much scandalized at the quarrel between Orlando and his brother in the first scene, that I screamed out, "A'n't they brothers?" A few weeks' residence at home convinced me, who had till then been an only child in the house of my grandfather, that a quarrel between brothers was a very natural event.

The other circumstances I recollect of my residence in Bath are but trifling, yet I never recall them without a feeling of pleasure. The beauties of the parade (which of them I know not), with the river of Avon winding around it, and the lowing of the cattle from the opposite hills, are warm in my recollection, and are only rivaled by the splendors of a toy-shop somewhere near the Orange Grove. I had acquired, I know not by what means, a kind of superstitious terror for statuary of all kinds. No ancient Iconoclast or modern Calvinist could have looked on the outside of the Abbey church (if I mistake not, the principal church at Bath is so called) with more horror than the image of Jacob's Ladder, with all its angels, presented to my infant eye. My uncle effectually combated my terrors, and formally introduced me to a statue of Neptune, which perhaps still keeps guard at the side of the Avon, where a pleasure boat crosses to Spring Gardens.

After being a year at Bath, I returned first to Edinburgh, and afterwards for a season to Sandy-Knowe;—and thus the time whiled away till about my eighth year, when it was thought sea-bathing might be of service to my lameness.

For this purpose, still under my aunt's protection, I remained some weeks at Prestonpans; a circumstance not worth mentioning, excepting to record my juvenile intimacy with an old military veteran, Dalgetty by name, who had pitched his tent in that little village, after all his campaigns, subsisting upon an ensign's half-pay, though called by courtesy a Captain. As this old gentleman, who had been in all the German wars, found very few to listen to his tales of military feats, he formed a sort of alliance with me, and I used invariably to attend him for the pleasure of hearing those communications. Sometimes our conversation turned on the American war, which was then raging. It was about the time of Burgoyne's unfortunate expedition, to which my Captain and I augured different conclusions. Somebody had showed me a map of North America, and, struck with the rugged appearance of the country, and the quantity of lakes, I expressed some doubts on the subject of the General's arriving safely at the end of his journey, which were very indignantly refuted by the Captain. The news of the Saratoga disaster, while it gave me a little triumph, rather shook my intimacy with the veteran.[8]

From Prestonpans I was transported back to my father's house in George's Square, which continued to be my most established place of residence, until my marriage in 1797.

[8] Besides this veteran, I found another ally at Prestonpans, in the person of George Constable, an old friend of my father's, educated to the law, but retired upon his independent property, and generally residing near Dundee. He had many of those peculiarities of temper which long afterwards I tried to develop in the character of Jonathan Oldbuck. It is very odd, that though I am unconscious of anything in which I strictly copied the *manners* of my old friend, the resemblance was nevertheless detected by George Chalmers, Esq., solicitor, London, an old friend, both of my father and Mr. Constable, and who affirmed to my late friend, Lord Kinedder, that I must needs be the author of The Antiquary, since he recognized the portrait of George Constable. But my friend George was not so decided an enemy to womankind as his representative Monkbarns. On the contrary, I rather suspect that he had a *tendresse* for my aunt Jenny, who even then was a most beautiful woman, though somewhat advanced in life. To the close of her life, she had the finest eyes and teeth I ever saw, and though she could be sufficiently sharp when she had a mind, her general behavior was genteel and ladylike. However this might be, I derived a great deal of curious information from George Constable, both at this early period, and afterwards. He was constantly philandering about my aunt, and of course very kind to me. He was the first person who told me about Falstaff and Hotspur, and other characters in Shakespeare. What idea I annexed to them I know not, but I must have annexed some, for I remember quite well being interested on the subject. Indeed, I rather suspect that children derive impulses of a powerful and important kind in hearing things which they cannot entirely comprehend; and therefore, that to write *down* to children's understanding is a mistake: set them on the scent, and let them puzzle it out. To return to George Constable: I knew him well at a much later period. He used always to dine at my father's house

I felt the change from being a single indulged brat, to becoming a member of a large family, very severely; for under the gentle government of my kind grandmother, who was meekness itself, and of my aunt, who, though of an higher temper, was exceedingly attached to me, I had acquired a degree of license which could not be permitted in a large family. I had sense enough, however, to bend my temper to my new circumstances; but such was the agony which I internally experienced, that I have guarded against nothing more in the education of my own family, than against their acquiring habits of self-willed caprice and domination. I found much consolation during this period of mortification, in the partiality of my mother. She joined to a light and happy temper of mind a strong turn to study poetry and works of imagination. She was sincerely devout, but her religion was, as became her sex, of a cast less austere than my father's. Still, the discipline of the Presbyterian Sabbath was severely strict, and I think injudiciously so. Although Bunyan's Pilgrim, Gesner's Death of Abel, Rowe's Letters, and one or two other books, which, for that reason, I still have a favor for, were admitted to relieve the gloom of one dull sermon succeeding to another—there was far too much tedium annexed to the duties of the day; and in the end it did none of us any good.

of a Sunday, and was authorized to turn the conversation out of the austere and Calvinistic tone, which it usually maintained on that day, upon subjects of history or auld lang syne. He remembered the forty-five, and told many excellent stories, all with a strong dash of a peculiar caustic humor.

George's sworn ally as a brother antiquary was John Davidson, then Keeper of the Signet; and I remember his flattering and compelling me to go to dine there. A writer's apprentice with the Keeper of the Signet, whose least officer kept us in order!—It was an awful event. Thither, however, I went with some secret expectation of a scantling of good claret. Mr. D. had a son whose taste inclined him to the army, to which his father, who had designed him for the bar, gave a most unwilling consent. He was at this time a young officer, and he and I, leaving the two seniors to proceed in their chat as they pleased, never once opened our mouths either to them or each other. The Pragmatic Sanction happened unfortunately to become the theme of their conversation, when Constable said in jest, "Now, John, I'll wad you a plack that neither of these two lads ever heard of the Pragmatic Sanction."—"Not heard of the Pragmatic Sanction!" said John Davidson; "I would like to see that;" and with a voice of thunder, he asked his son the fatal question. As young D. modestly allowed he knew nothing about it, his father drove him from the table in a rage, and I absconded during the confusion; nor could Constable ever bring me back again to his friend Davidson's.—1826.

My week-day tasks were more agreeable. My lameness and my solitary habits had made me a tolerable reader, and my hours of leisure were usually spent in reading aloud to my mother Pope's translation of Homer, which, excepting a few traditionary ballads, and the songs in Allan Ramsay's Evergreen, was the first poetry which I perused. My mother had good natural taste and great feeling: she used to make me pause upon those passages which expressed generous and worthy sentiments, and if she could not divert me from those which were descriptive of battle and tumult, she contrived at least to divide my attention between them. My own enthusiasm, however, was chiefly awakened by the wonderful and the terrible—the common taste of children, but in which I have remained a child even unto this day. I got by heart, not as a task, but almost without intending it, the passages with which I was most pleased, and used to recite them aloud, both when alone and to others—more willingly, however, in my hours of solitude, for I had observed some auditors smile, and I dreaded ridicule at that time of life more than I have ever done since.

In [1778] I was sent to the second class of the Grammar School, or High School of Edinburgh, then taught by Mr. Luke Fraser, a good Latin scholar and a very worthy man. Though I had received, with my brothers, in private, lessons of Latin from Mr. James French, now a minister of the Kirk of Scotland, I was nevertheless rather behind the class in which I was placed both in years and in progress. This was a real disadvantage, and one to which a boy of lively temper and talents ought to be as little exposed as one who might be less expected to make up his lee-way, as it is called. The situation has the unfortunate effect of reconciling a boy of the former character (which in a posthumous work I may claim for my own) to holding a subordinate station among his classfellows—to which he would otherwise affix disgrace. There is also, from the constitution of the High School, a certain danger not sufficiently attended to. The boys take precedence in their *places,* as they are called, according to their merit, and it requires a long while, in general, before even a clever boy, if he falls behind the class, or is put into one for which he is not quite ready, can force his way to the situation which his abilities really entitle him to hold. But, in the meanwhile, he is necessarily led to be the associate and companion of those inferior spirits with whom he is placed; for the system of precedence, though it does not limit the general intercourse among the boys, has nevertheless the effect of throwing them into clubs and coteries, according to the vicinity of the seats they hold. A boy of good talents, therefore, placed even for a time among his inferiors, especially if they be also his elders, learns to participate in their pursuits and objects of ambition, which are usually very distinct from the acquisition of learning; and it will be well if he does not also imitate them in that indifference which is contented with bustling over a lesson so as to avoid punishment, without affecting superiority or aiming at reward. It was probably owing to this circumstance, that, although at a more advanced period of life I have enjoyed considerable facility in acquiring languages, I did not make any great figure at the High School—or, at least, any exertions which I made were desultory and little to be depended on.

Our class contained some very excellent scholars. The first *Dux* was James Buchan, who retained his honored place, almost without a day's interval, all the while we were at the High School. He was afterwards at the head of the medical staff in Egypt, and in exposing himself to the plague infection, by attending the hospitals there, displayed the same well-regulated and gentle, yet determined perseverance, which placed him most worthily at the head of his school-fellows, while many lads of livelier parts and dispositions held an inferior station. The next best scholars *(sed longo intervallo)* were my friend David Douglas, the heir and *élève* of the celebrated Adam Smith, and James Hope, now a Writer to the Signet, both since well known and distinguished in their departments of the law. As for myself, I glanced like a meteor from one end of the class to the other, and commonly disgusted my kind master as much by negligence and frivolity, as I occasionally pleased him by flashes of intellect and talent. Among my companions, my good-nature and a flow of ready imagination rendered me very popular. Boys are uncommonly just in their feelings, and at least equally generous. My lameness, and the efforts which I made to supply that disadvantage, by making up in address what I wanted in activity, engaged the latter principle in my favor; and in the winter play hours, when hard exercise was impossible, my tales used to assemble an admiring audience round Lucky Brown's fireside, and happy was he that could sit next to the inexhaustible narrator. I was also, though often negligent of my own task, always ready to assist my friends; and hence I had a little party of staunch partisans and adherents, stout of hand and heart, though somewhat dull of head—the very tools for raising a hero to eminence. So, on the whole, I made a brighter figure in the *yards* than in the *class.*[9]

My father did not trust our education solely to our High School lessons. We had a tutor at home [Mr. James Mitchell], a young man of an excellent disposition, and a laborious student. He was bred to the Kirk, but unfortunately took such a very strong turn to fanaticism, that he afterwards resigned an excellent living in a seaport town, merely because he could not persuade the mariners of the guilt of setting sail of a Sabbath,—in which, by the by, he was less likely to be successful, as, *cæteris paribus,* sailors, from an opinion that it is a fortunate omen, always choose to weigh anchor on that day. The caliber of this young man's understanding may be judged of by this anecdote; but in other respects, he was a faithful and active instructor; and from him chiefly I learned writing and arithmetic. I repeated to him my French lessons, and studied with him my themes in the classics, but not classically. I also acquired, by disputing with him (for this he readily permitted), some knowledge of school-divinity and church-history, and a great acquaintance in particular with the old books describing the early history of the Church of Scotland, the wars and sufferings of the Covenanters, and so forth. I, with a head on fire for chivalry, was a Cavalier; my friend was a Roundhead:

[9] I read not long since, in that authentic record called the *Percy Anecdotes,* that I had been educated at Musselburgh school, where I had been distinguished as an absolute dunce; only Dr. Blair, seeing farther into the mill-stone, had pronounced there was fire in it. I never was at Musselburgh school in my life, and though I have met Dr. Blair at my father's and elsewhere, I never had the good fortune to attract his notice, to my knowledge. Lastly, I was never a dunce, nor thought to be so, but an incorrigibly idle imp, who was always longing to do something else than what was enjoined him.—1826.

I was a Tory, and he was a Whig. I hated Presbyterians, and admired Montrose with his victorious Highlanders; he liked the Presbyterian Ulysses, the dark and politic Argyle: so that we never wanted subjects of dispute; but our disputes were always amicable. In all these tenets there was no real conviction on my part, arising out of acquaintance with the views or principles of either party; nor had my antagonist address enough to turn the debate on such topics. I took up my politics at that period, as King Charles II. did his religion, from an idea that the Cavalier creed was the more gentlemanlike persuasion of the two.

After having been three years under Mr. Fraser, our class was, in the usual routine of the school, turned over to Dr. Adam, the Rector. It was from this respectable man that I first learned the value of the knowledge I had hitherto considered only as a burdensome task. It was the fashion to remain two years at his class, where we read Cæsar, and Livy, and Sallust, in prose; Virgil, Horace, and Terence, in verse. I had by this time mastered, in some degree, the difficulties of the language, and began to be sensible of its beauties. This was really gathering grapes from thistles; nor shall I soon forget the swelling of my little pride when the Rector pronounced, that though many of my school-fellows understood the Latin better, *Gualterus Scott* was behind few in following and enjoying the author's meaning. Thus encouraged, I distinguished myself by some attempts at poetical versions from Horace and Virgil.[10] Dr. Adam used to invite his scholars

[10] One of these little pieces, written in a weak boyish scrawl within penciled marks still visible, had been carefully preserved by his mother; it was folded up in a cover inscribed—"*My Walter's first lines,* 1782." These read:

"In awful ruins Ætna thunders nigh,
And sends in pitchy whirlwinds to the sky
Black clouds of smoke, which, still as they aspire,
From their dark sides there bursts the glowing fire;
At other times huge balls of fire are toss'd,
That lick the stars, and in the smoke are lost:
Sometimes the mount, with vast convulsions torn,
Emits huge rocks, which instantly are borne
With loud explosions to the starry skies,
The stones made liquid as the huge mass flies,
Then back again with greater weight recoils,
While Ætna thundering from the bottom boils."

to such essays, but never made them tasks. I gained some distinction upon these occasions, and the Rector in future took much notice of me; and his judicious mixture of censure and praise went far to counterbalance my habits of indolence and inattention. I saw I was expected to do well, and I was piqued in honor to vindicate my master's favorable opinion. I climbed, therefore, to the first form; and, though I never made a first-rate Latinist, my school-fellows, and what was of more consequence, I myself, considered that I had a character for learning to maintain. Dr. Adam, to whom I owed so much, never failed to remind me of my obligations when I had made some figure in the literary world. He was, indeed, deeply imbued with that fortunate vanity which alone could induce a man who has arms to pare and burn a muir, to submit to the yet more toilsome task of cultivating youth. As Catholics confide in the imputed righteousness of their saints, so did the good old Doctor plume himself upon the success of his scholars in life, all of which he never failed (and often justly) to claim as the creation, or at least the fruits, of his early instructions. He remembered the fate of every boy at his school during the fifty years he had superintended it, and always traced their success or misfortunes entirely to their attention or negligence when under his care. His "noisy mansion," which to others would have been a melancholy bedlam, was the pride of his heart; and the only fatigues he felt, amidst din and tumult, and the necessity of reading themes, hearing lessons, and maintaining some degree of order at the same time, were relieved by comparing himself to Cæsar, who could dictate to three secretaries at once;— so ready is vanity to lighten the labors of duty.

It is a pity that a man so learned, so admirably adapted for his station, so useful, so simple, so easily contented, should have had other subjects of mortification. But the magistrates of Edinburgh, not knowing the treasure they possessed in Dr. Adam, encouraged a savage fellow, called Nicol, one of the undermasters, in insulting his person and authority. This man was an excellent classical scholar, and an admirable convivial humorist (which latter quality recommended him to the friendship of Burns); but worthless, drunken, and inhumanly cruel to the boys under his charge. He carried his feud against the Rector within an inch of assassination, for he waylaid and knocked him down in the dark. The favor which this worthless rival obtained in the town-council led to other consequences, which for some time clouded poor Adam's happiness and fair fame. When the French Revolution broke out, and parties ran high in approving or condemning it, the Doctor incautiously joined the former. This was very natural, for as all his ideas of existing governments were derived from his experience of the town-council of Edinburgh, it must be admitted they scarce brooked comparison with the free states of Rome and Greece, from which he borrowed his opinions concerning republics. His want of caution in speaking on the political topics of the day lost him the respect of the boys, most of whom were accustomed to hear very different opinions on those matters in the bosom of their families. This, however (which was long after my time), passed away with other heats of the period, and the Doctor continued his labors till about a year since, when he was struck with palsy while teaching his class. He survived a few days, but becoming delirious before his dissolution, conceived he was still in school, and after some expressions of applause or censure, he said, "But it grows dark—the boys may dismiss,"—and instantly expired.

From Dr. Adam's class I should, according to the usual routine, have proceeded immediately to college. But, fortunately, I was not yet to lose, by a total dismission from constraint, the acquaintance with the Latin which I had acquired. My health had become rather delicate from rapid growth, and my father was easily persuaded to allow me to spend half-a-year at Kelso with my kind aunt, Miss Janet Scott, whose inmate I again became. It was hardly worth mentioning that I had frequently visited at her home during our short vacations.

At this time she resided in a small house, situated very pleasantly in a large garden, to the eastward of the churchyard of Kelso, which extended down to the Tweed. It was then my father's property, from whom it was afterwards purchased by my uncle. My grandmother was now dead, and my aunt's only companion, besides an old maid servant, was my cousin, Miss Barbara Scott, now Mrs. Meik. My time was here left entirely to my own disposal excepting for about four hours in the day, when I was expected to attend the Grammar School of the village. The teacher, at that time, was Mr. Lancelot Whale, an excellent classical scholar, a humorist, and a worthy man. He had a supreme antipathy to the puns which his very uncommon name frequently gave rise to; insomuch, that he made his son spell the word *Wale*, which only occasioned the young man being nicknamed *the Prince of Wales* by the military mess to which he belonged. As for Whale, senior, the least allusion to Jonah, or the terming him an odd fish, or any similar quibble, was sure to put him beside himself. In point of knowledge and taste, he was far too good for the situation he held, which only required that he should give his scholars a rough foundation in the Latin language. My time with him, though short, was spent greatly to my advantage and his gratification. He was glad to escape to Persius and Tacitus from the eternal Rudiments and Cornelius Nepos; and as perusing these authors with one who began to understand them was to him a labor of love, I made considerable progress under his instructions. I suspect, indeed, that some of the time dedicated to me was withdrawn from the instruction of his more regular scholars; but I was as grateful as I could. I acted as usher, and heard the inferior classes, and I spouted the speech of Galgacus at the public examination, which did not make the less impression on the audience that few of them probably understood one word of it.

In the meanwhile my acquaintance with English literature was gradually extending itself. In the intervals of my school hours I had always perused with avidity such books of history or poetry or voyages and travels as chance presented to me—not forgetting the usual, or rather ten times the usual, quantity of fairy tales, eastern stories, romances, &c. These studies were totally unregulated and undirected. My tutor thought it almost a sin to open a profane play or poem; and my mother, besides that she might be in some degree trammeled by the religious scruples which he suggested, had no longer the opportunity to hear me read poetry as formerly. I found, however, in her dressing-room (where I slept at one time) some odd volumes of Shakespeare, nor can I easily

forget the rapture with which I sat up in my shirt reading
them by the light of a fire in her apartment, until the
bustle of the family rising from supper warned me it was time
to creep back to my bed, where I was supposed to have
been safely deposited since nine o'clock. Chance, however,
threw in my way a poetical preceptor. This was no other
than the excellent and benevolent Dr. Blacklock, well known
at that time as a literary character. I know not how I attracted his attention, and that of some of the young men
who boarded in his family; but so it was that I became a
frequent and favored guest. The kind old man opened to me
the stores of his library, and through his recommendation
I became intimate with Ossian and Spenser. I was delighted
with both, yet I think chiefly with the latter poet. The
tawdry repetitions of the Ossianic phraseology disgusted me
rather sooner than might have been expected from my age.
But Spenser I could have read for ever. Too young to
trouble myself about the allegory, I considered all the knights
and ladies and dragons and giants in their outward and
exoteric sense, and God only knows how delighted I was to
find myself in such society. As I had always a wonderful
facility in retaining in my memory whatever verses pleased
me, the quantity of Spenser's stanzas which I could repeat
was really marvelous. But this memory of mine was a very
fickle ally, and has through my whole life acted merely upon
its own capricious motion, and might have enabled me to
adopt old Beattie of Meikledale's answer, when complimented
by a certain reverend divine on the strength of the same
faculty:—"No, sir," answered the old Borderer, "I have no
command of my memory. It only retains what hits my fancy,
and probably, sir, if you were to preach to me for two hours,
I would not be able when you finished to remember a word
you had been saying." My memory was precisely of the
same kind: it seldom failed to preserve most tenaciously a
favorite passage of poetry, a play-house ditty, or, above all,
a Border-raid ballad; but names, dates, and the other techni-
calities of history, escaped me in a most melancholy degree.
The philosophy of history, a much more important subject,
was also a sealed book at this period of my life; but I gradually assembled much of what was striking and picturesque

in historical narrative; and when, in riper years, I attended more to the deduction of general principles, I was furnished with a powerful host of examples in illustration of them. I was, in short, like an ignorant gamester, who kept up a good hand until he knew how to play it.

I left the High School, therefore, with a great quantity of general information, ill arranged, indeed, and collected without system, yet deeply impressed upon my mind; readily assorted by my power of connection and memory, and gilded, if I may be permitted to say so, by a vivid and active imagination. If my studies were not under any direction at Edinburgh, in the country, it may be well imagined, they were less so. A respectable subscription library, a circulating library of ancient standing, and some private book-shelves, were open to my random perusal, and I waded into the stream like a blind man into a ford, without the power of searching my way, unless by groping for it. My appetite for books was as ample and indiscriminating as it was indefatigable, and I since have had too frequent reason to repent that few ever read so much, and to so little purpose.

Among the valuable acquisitions I made about this time, was an acquaintance with Tasso's Jerusalem Delivered, through the flat medium of Mr. Hoole's translation. But above all, I then first became acquainted with Bishop Percy's Reliques of Ancient Poetry. As I had been from infancy devoted to legendary lore of this nature, and only reluctantly withdrew my attention, from the scarcity of materials and the rudeness of those which I possessed, it may be imagined, but cannot be described, with what delight I saw pieces of the same kind which had amused my childhood, and still continued in secret the Delilahs of my imagination, considered as the subject of sober research, grave commentary, and apt illustration, by an editor who showed his poetical genius was capable of emulating the best qualities of what his pious labor preserved. I remember well the spot where I read these volumes for the first time. It was beneath a huge platanus-tree, in the ruins of what had been intended for an old-fashioned arbor in the *garden* I have mentioned. The summer-day sped onward so fast, that notwithstanding the sharp appetite of thirteen, I forgot the hour of dinner, was sought for with anxiety, and was still found entranced in my intellectual banquet. To read and to remember was in this instance the same thing, and henceforth I overwhelmed my school-fellows, and all who would hearken to me, with tragical recitations from the ballads of Bishop Percy. The first time, too, I could scrape a few shillings together, which were not common occurrences with me, I bought unto myself a copy of these beloved volumes; nor do I believe I ever read a book half so frequently, or with half the enthusiasm. About this period also I became acquainted with the works of Richardson, and those of Mackenzie—(whom in later years I became entitled to call my friend)—with Fielding, Smollet, and some others of our best novelists.

To this period also I can trace distinctly the awaking of that delightful feeling for the beauties of natural objects which has never since deserted me. The neighborhood of Kelso, the most beautiful, if not the most romantic village in Scotland, is eminently calculated to awaken these ideas. It presents objects, not only grand in themselves, but venerable from their association. The meeting of two superb rivers, the Tweed and the Teviot, both renowned in song—the ruins of an ancient Abbey—the more distant vestiges of Roxburgh Castle—the modern mansion of Fleurs, which is so situated as to combine the ideas of ancient baronial grandeur with those of modern taste—are in themselves objects of the first class; yet are so mixed, united, and melted among a thousand other beauties of a less prominent description, that they harmonize into one general picture, and please rather by unison than by concord. I believe I have written unintelligibly upon this subject, but it is fitter for the pencil than the pen. The romantic feelings which I have described as predominating in my mind, naturally rested upon and associated themselves with these grand features of the landscape around me; and the historical incidents, or traditional legends connected with many of them, gave to my admiration a sort of intense impression of reverence, which at times made my heart feel too big for its bosom. From this time the love of natural beauty, more especially when combined with ancient ruins, or remains of our fathers' piety or splendor, became with me an insatiable passion, which, if circumstances had permitted, I would willingly have gratified by traveling over half the globe.

I was recalled to Edinburgh about the time when the College meets, and put at once to the Humanity class, under Mr. Hill, and the first Greek class, taught by Mr. Dalzell. The former held the reins of discipline very loosely, and though beloved by his students—for he was a good-natured man as well as a good scholar—he had not the art of exciting our attention as well as liking. This was a dangerous character with whom to trust one who relished labor as little as I did; and amid the riot of his class I speedily lost much of what I had learned under Adam and Whale. At the Greek class, I might have made a better figure, for Professor Dalzell maintained a great deal of authority, and was not only himself an admirable scholar, but was always deeply interested in the progress of his students. But here lay the villainy. Almost all my companions who had left the High School at the same time with myself, had acquired a smattering of Greek before they came to College. I, alas! had none; and finding myself far inferior to all my fellow-students, I could hit upon no better mode of vindicating my equality than by professing my contempt for the language, and my resolution not to learn it. A youth who died early, himself an excellent Greek scholar, saw my negligence and folly with pain, instead of contempt. He came to call on me in George's Square, and pointed out in the strongest terms the silliness of the conduct I had adopted, told me I was distinguished by the name of the *Greek Blockhead,* and exhorted me to redeem my reputation while it was called to-day. My stubborn pride received this advice with sulky civility; the birth of my Mentor (whose name was Archibald, the son of an inn-keeper) did not, as I thought in my folly, authorize him to intrude upon me his advice. The other was not sharp-sighted, or his consciousness of a generous intention overcame his resentment. He offered me his daily and nightly assistance, and pledged himself to bring me forward with the foremost of my class. I felt some twinges of conscience, but they were unable to prevail over my pride and self-conceit. The poor lad left me more in sorrow than in anger, nor did we ever meet again. All hopes of my progress in the Greek were now over; insomuch that when we were required to write essays on the authors we had studied, I had the audacity to produce a composition in which I weighed Homer against Ariosto, and pronounced him wanting in the balance. I supported this heresy by a profusion of bad reading and flimsy argument. The wrath of the Professor was extreme, while at the same time he could not suppress his surprise at the quantity of out-of-the-way knowledge which I displayed. He pronounced upon me the severe sentence—that dunce I was, and dunce was to remain—which, however, my excellent and learned friend lived to revoke over a bottle of Burgundy, at our literary Club at Fortune's, of which he was a distinguished member.

Meanwhile, as if to eradicate my slightest tincture of Greek, I fell ill during the middle of Mr. Dalzell's second class, and migrated a second time to Kelso—where I again continued a long time reading what and how I pleased, and of course reading nothing but what afforded me immediate entertainment. The only thing which saved my mind from utter dissipation, was that turn for historical pursuit, which never abandoned me even at the idlest period. I had forsworn the Latin classics for no reason I know of, unless because they were akin to the Greek; but the occasional perusal of Buchanan's history, that of Mathew of Paris, and other monkish chronicles, kept up a kind of familiarity with the language even in its rudest state. But I forgot the very letters of the Greek alphabet; a loss never to be repaired, considering what that language is, and who they were who employed it in their compositions.

About this period—or soon afterwards—my father judged it proper I should study mathematics; a study upon which I entered with all the ardor of novelty. My tutor was an aged person, Dr. MacFait, who had in his time been distinguished as a teacher of this science. Age, however, and some domestic inconveniences, had diminished his pupils, and lessened his authority amongst the few who remained. I think, that had I been more fortunately placed for instruction, or had I had the spur of emulation, I might have made some progress in this science, of which, under the circumstances I have mentioned, I only acquired a very superficial smattering.

In other studies I was rather more fortunate. I made some progress in Ethics under Professor John Bruce, and was selected as one of his students whose progress he approved, to read an essay before Principal Robertson. I was farther instructed in Moral Philosophy at the class of Mr. Dugald Stewart, whose striking and impressive eloquence riveted the attention even of the most volatile student. To sum up my academical studies, I attended the class of History, then taught by the present Lord Woodhouselee, and, as far as I remember, no others, excepting those of the Civil and Municipal Law. So that, if my learning be flimsy and inaccurate, the reader must have some compassion even for an idle workman who had so narrow a foundation to build upon. If, however, it should ever fall to the lot of youth to peruse these pages—let such a reader remember, that it is with the deepest regret that I recollect in my manhood the opportunities of learning which I neglected in my youth; that through every part of my literary career I have felt pinched and hampered by my own ignorance; and that I would at this moment give half the reputation I have had the good fortune to acquire, if by doing so I could rest the remaining part upon a sound foundation of learning and science.

I imagine my father's reason for sending me to so few classes in the College, was a desire that I should apply myself particularly to my legal studies. He had not determined whether I should fill the situation of an Advocate or a Writer; but judiciously considering the technical knowledge of the latter to be useful at least, if not essential, to a barrister. he resolved I should serve the ordinary apprenticeship of five years to his own profession. I accordingly entered into indentures with my father about 1785-6, and entered upon the dry and barren wilderness of forms and conveyances.

I cannot reproach myself with being entirely an idle apprentice—far less, as the reader might reasonably have expected,

"A clerk foredoom'd my father's soul to cross."

The drudgery, indeed, of the office I disliked, and the confinement I altogether detested; but I loved my father, and I felt the rational pride and pleasure of rendering myself useful to him. I was ambitious also; and among my companions in labor, the only way to gratify ambition was to labor hard and well. Other circumstances reconciled me in some measure to the confinement. The allowance for copy-money furnished a little fund for the *menus plaisirs* of the circulating library and the Theater, and this was no trifling incentive to labor. When actually at the oar, no man could pull it harder than I; and I remember writing upwards of 120 folio pages with no interval either for food or rest. Again, the hours of attendance on the office were lightened by the power of choosing my own books, and reading them in my own way, which often consisted in beginning at the middle or the end of a volume. A deceased friend, who was a fellow-apprentice with me, used often to express his surprise that, after such a hop-step-and-jump perusal, I knew as much of the book as he had been able to acquire from reading it in the usual manner. My desk usually contained a store of most miscellaneous volumes, especially works of fiction of every kind, which were my supreme delight. I might except novels, unless those of the better and higher class; for though I read many of them, yet it was with more selection than might have been expected. The whole Jemmy and Jenny Jessamy tribe I abhorred; and it required the art of Burney, or the feeling of Mackenzie, to fix my attention upon a domestic tale. But all that was adventurous and romantic I devoured without much discrimination, and I really believe I have read as much nonsense of this class as any man now living. Everything which touched on knight-errantry was particularly acceptable to me, and I soon attempted to imitate what I·so greatly admired. My efforts, however, were in the manner of the tale-teller, not of the bard.

My greatest intimate, from the days of my school-tide, was Mr. John Irving, now a Writer to the Signet. We lived near each other, and by joint agreement were wont, each of us, to compose a romance for the other's amusement. These legends, in which the martial and the miraculous always predominated, we rehearsed to each other during our walks, which were usually directed to the most solitary spots about Arthur's Seat and Salisbury Crags. We naturally sought seclusion, for we were conscious no small degree of ridicule would have attended our amusement, if the nature of it had become known. Whole holidays were spent in this singular pastime, which continued for two or three years, and had, I believe, no small effect in directing the turn of my imagination to the chivalrous and romantic in poetry and prose.

Meanwhile, the translations of Mr. Hoole having made me acquainted with Tasso and Ariosto, I learned from his notes on the latter, that the Italian language contained a fund of romantic lore. A part of my earnings was dedicated to an Italian class which I attended twice a-week, and rapidly acquired some proficiency. I had previously renewed and extended my knowledge of the French language, from the same principle of romantic research. Tressan's romances, the Bibliothèque Bleue, and Bibliothèque de Romans, were already familiar to me; and I now acquired similar intimacy with the works of Dante, Boiardo, Pulci, and other eminent Italian authors. I fastened also, like a tiger, upon every collection of old songs or romances which chance threw in my way, or which my scrutiny was able to discover on the dusty shelves of James Sibbald's circulating library in the Parliament Square. This collection, now dismantled and dispersed, contained at that time many rare and curious works, seldom found in such a collection. Mr. Sibbald himself, a man of rough manners but of some taste and judgment, cultivated music and poetry, and in his shop I 'had a distant view of some literary characters, besides the privilege of ransacking the stores of old French and Italian books, which were in little demand among the bulk of his subscribers. Here I saw the unfortunate Andrew Macdonald, author of Vimonda; and here, too, I saw at a distance, the boast of Scotland, Robert Burns. Of the latter I shall presently have occasion to speak more fully.

I am inadvertently led to confound dates while I talk of this remote period, for, as I have no notes, it is impossible for me to remember with accuracy the progress of studies, if they deserve the name, so irregular and miscellaneous.

But about the second year of my apprenticeship, my health, which from rapid growth and other causes had been hitherto rather uncertain and delicate, was affected by the breaking of a blood-vessel. The regimen I had to undergo on this occasion was far from agreeable. It was spring, and the weather raw and cold, yet I was confined to bed with a single blanket, and bled and blistered till I scarcely had a pulse left. I had all the appetite of a growing boy, but was prohibited any sustenance beyond what was absolutely necessary for the support of nature, and that in vegetables alone. Above all, with a considerable disposition to talk, I was not permitted to open my lips without one or two old ladies who watched my couch being ready at once to souse upon me, "Imposing silence with a stilly sound." My only refuge was reading and playing at chess. To the romances and poetry, which I chiefly delighted in, I had always added a study of history, especially as connected with military events. I was encouraged in this latter study by a tolerable acquaintance with geography, and by the opportunities I had enjoyed while with Mr. MacFait to learn the meaning of the more ordinary terms of fortification. While, therefore, I lay in this dreary and silent solitude, I fell upon the resource of illustrating the battles I read of by the childish expedient of arranging shells, and seeds, and pebbles, so as to represent encountering armies. Diminutive cross-bows were contrived to mimic artillery, and with the assistance of a friendly carpenter, I contrived to model a fortress, which, like that of uncle Toby, represented whatever place happened to be uppermost in my imagination. I fought my way thus through Vertot's Knights of Malta —a book which, as it hovered between history and romance, was exceedingly dear to me; and Orme's interesting and beautiful History of Indostan, whose copious plans, aided by the clear and luminous explanations of the author, rendered my imitative amusement peculiarly easy. Other moments of these weary weeks were spent in looking at the Meadow Walks, by assistance of a combination of mirrors so arranged that, while lying in bed, I could see the troops march out to exercise, or any other incident which occurred on that promenade.

After one or two relapses, my constitution recovered the injury it had sustained, though for several months afterwards I was restricted to a severe vegetable diet. And I must say, in passing, that though I gained health under this necessary restriction, yet it was far from being agreeable to me, and I was affected whilst under its influence with a nervousness which I never felt before or since. A disposition to start upon slight alarms—a want of decision in feeling and acting, which has not usually been my failing, an acute sensibility to trifling inconveniences—and an unnecessary apprehension of contingent misfortunes, rise to my memory as connected with my vegetable diet, although they may very possibly have been entirely the result of the disorder, and not of the cure. Be this as it may, with this illness I bade farewell both to disease and medicine; for since that time, till the hour I am now writing, I have enjoyed a state of the most robust health, having only had to complain of occasional headaches or stomachic affections when I have been long without taking exercise, or have lived too convivially— the latter having been occasionally, though not habitually, the error of my youth, as the former has been of my advanced life.

My frame gradually became hardened with my constitution, and being both tall and muscular, I was rather disfigured than disabled by my lameness. This personal disadvantage did not prevent me from taking much exercise on horseback, and making long journeys on foot, in the course of which I often walked from twenty to thirty miles a day. A distinct instance occurs to me. I remember walking with poor James Ramsay, my fellow-apprentice, now no more, and two other friends, to breakfast at Prestonpans. We spent the forenoon in visiting the ruins at Seton and the field of battle at Preston—dined at Prestonpans on *tiled haddocks* very sumptuously—drank half a bottle of port each, and returned in the evening. This could not be less than thirty miles, nor do I remember being at all fatigued upon the occasion.

These excursions on foot or horseback formed by far my most favorite amusement. I have all my life delighted in traveling, though I have never enjoyed that pleasure upon a large scale. It was a propensity which I sometimes indulged so unduly as to alarm and vex my parents. Wood, water, wilderness itself, had an inexpressible charm for me, and I had a dreamy way of going much further than I intended, so that unconsciously my return was protracted, and my parents had sometimes serious cause of uneasiness. For ex-

ample, I once set out with Mr. George Abercromby [11] (the son
of the immortal General), Mr. William Clerk, and some others,
to fish in the lake above Howgate, and the stream which de-
scends from it into the Esk. We breakfasted at Howgate,
and fished the whole day; and while we were on our return
next morning, I was easily seduced by William Clerk, then
a great intimate, to visit Pennycuik-House, the seat of his
family. Here he and John Irving, and I for their sake, were
overwhelmed with kindness by the late Sir John Clerk and his
lady, the present Dowager Lady Clerk. The pleasure of looking at fine pictures, the beauty of the place, and the flattering
hospitality of the owners, drowned all recollection of home
for a day or two. Meanwhile our companions, who had
walked on without being aware of our digression, returned
to Edinburgh without us, and excited no small alarm in my
father's household. At length, however, they became accustomed to my escapades. My father used to protest to me on
such occasions that he thought I was born to be a strolling
peddler; and though the prediction was intended to mortify
my conceit, I am not sure that I altogether disliked it. I was
now familiar with Shakespeare, and thought of Autolycus's
song—

> "Jog on, jog on, the foot-path way,
>   And merrily hent the stile-a;
> A merry heart goes all the day,
>   Your sad tires in a mile-a."

My principal object in these excursions was the pleasure
of seeing romantic scenery, or what afforded me at least
equal pleasure, the places which had been distinguished by
remarkable historical events. The delight with which I regarded the former, of course had general approbation, but I
often found it difficult to procure sympathy with the interest
I felt in the latter. Yet to me, the wandering over the field
of Bannockburn was the source of more exquisite pleasure
than gazing upon the celebrated landscape from the battlements of Stirling castle. I do not by any means infer that
I was dead to the feeling of picturesque scenery; on the
contrary, few delighted more in its general effect. But I was

---

[11] Now Lord Abercromby.—1826.

unable with the eye of a painter to dissect the various parts
of the scene, to comprehend how the one bore upon the
other, to estimate the effect which various features of the
view had in producing its leading and general effect. I
have never, indeed, been capable of doing this with precision
or nicety, though my latter studies have led me to amend
and arrange my original ideas upon the subject. Even the
humble ambition, which I long cherished, of making sketches
of those places which interested me, from a defect of eye or
of hand was totally ineffectual. After long study and many
efforts, I was unable to apply the elements of perspective
or of shade to the scene before me, and was obliged to relinquish in despair an art which I was most anxious to
practice. But show me an old castle or a field of battle, and
I was at home at once, filled it with its combatants in their
proper costume, and overwhelmed my hearers by the enthusiasm of my description. In crossing Magus Moor, near St.
Andrews, the spirit moved me to give a picture of the assassination of the Archbishop of St. Andrews to some fellow-
travelers with whom I was accidentally associated, and one of
them, though well acquainted with the story, protested my
narrative had frightened away his night's sleep. I mention
this to show the distinction between a sense of the picturesque
in action and in scenery. If I have since been able in
poetry to trace with some success the principles of the latter,
it has always been with reference to its general and leading
features, or under some alliance with moral feeling and even
this proficiency has cost me study.—Meanwhile I endeavored
to make amends for my ignorance of drawing by adopting a sort of technical memory respecting the scenes I visited.
Wherever I went I cut a piece of a branch from a tree—these
constituted what I called my log-book; and I intended to
have a set of chessmen out of them, each having reference
to the place where it was cut—as the kings from Falkland
and Holy-Rood; the queens from Queen Mary's yew tree at
Crookston; the bishops from abbeys or episcopal palaces; the
knights from baronial residences; the rooks from royal for-
tresses; and the pawns generally from places worthy of historical note. But this whimsical design I never carried into
execution.

With music it was even worse than with painting. My mother was anxious we should at least learn Psalmody, but the incurable defects of my voice and ear soon drove my teacher to despair.[12] It is only by long practice that I have acquired the power of selecting or distinguishing melodies; and although now few things delight or affect me more than a simple tune sung with feeling, yet I am sensible that even this pitch of musical taste has only been gained by attention and habit, and, as it were, by my feeling of the words being associated with the tune. I have therefore been usually unsuccessful in composing words to a tune, although my friend Dr. Clarke, and other musical composers, have sometimes been able to make a happy union between their music and my poetry.

In other points, however, I began to make some amends for the irregularity of my education. It is well known that in Edinburgh one great spur to emulation among youthful students is in those associations called *literary societies*, formed not only for the purpose of debate, but of composition. These undoubtedly have some disadvantages, where a bold, petulant, and disputatious temper happens to be combined with considerable information and talent. Still, however, in order to such a person being actually spoiled by his mixing in such debates, his talents must be of a very rare nature, or his effrontery must be proof to every species of assault; for there is generally, in a well-selected society of this nature, talent sufficient to meet the forwardest, and satire enough to penetrate the most undaunted. I am particularly obliged to this

[12] The late Alexander Campbell, a warm-hearted man, and an enthusiast in Scottish music, which he sang most beautifully, had this ungrateful task imposed on him. He was a man of many accomplishments, but dashed with a *bizarrerie* of temper which made them useless to their proprietor. He wrote several books—as a Tour in Scotland, &c.;—and he made an advantageous marriage, but fell nevertheless into distressed circumstances, which I had the pleasure of relieving, if I could not remove. His sense of gratitude was very strong, and showed itself oddly in one respect. He would never allow that I had a bad ear; but contended, that if I did not understand music, it was because I did not choose to learn it. But when he attended us in George's Square, our neighbor, Lady Cumming, sent to beg the boys might not be all flogged precisely at the same hour, as, though she had no doubt the punishment was deserved, the noise of the concord was really dreadful. Robert was the only one of our family who could sing, though my father was musical, and a performer on the violoncello at the *gentlemen's concerts.*—1826.

sort of club for introducing me about my seventeenth year into the society which at one time I had entirely dropped; for, from the time of my illness at college, I had had little or no intercourse with any of my class-companions, one or two only excepted. Now, however, about 1788, I began to feel and take my ground in society. A ready wit, a good deal of enthusiasm, and a perception that soon ripened into tact and observation of character, rendered me an acceptable companion to many young men whose acquisitions in philosophy and science were infinitely superior to anything I could boast.

In the business of these societies—for I was a member of more than one successively—I cannot boast of having made any great figure. I never was a good speaker, unless upon some subject which strongly animated my feelings; and, as I was totally unaccustomed to composition, as well as to the art of generalizing my ideas upon any subject, my literary essays were but very poor work. I never attempted them unless when compelled to do so by the regulations of the society, and then I was like the Lord of Castle Rackrent, who was obliged to cut down a tree to get a few faggots to boil the kettle; for the quantity of ponderous and miscellaneous knowledge which I really possessed on many subjects, was not easily condensed, or brought to bear upon the object I wished particularly to become master of. Yet there occurred opportunities when this odd lumber of my brain, especially that which was connected with the recondite parts of history, did me, as Hamlet says, "yeoman's service." My memory of events was like one of the large, old-fashioned stone-cannons of the Turks—very difficult to load well and discharge, but making a powerful effect when by good chance any object did come within range of its shot. Such fortunate opportunities of exploding with effect maintained my literary character among my companions, with whom I soon met with great indulgence and regard. The persons with whom I chiefly lived at this period of my youth were William Clerk, already mentioned; James Edmonstoune, of Newton; George Abercromby; Adam Fergusson, son of the celebrated Professor Fergusson, and who combined the lightest and most airy temper with the best and kindest disposition; John Irving, already mentioned; the Honorable Thomas Douglas, now Earl

of Selkirk; David Boyle,—and two or three others, who sometimes plunged deeply into politics and metaphysics, and not
unfrequently "doffed the world aside, and bid it pass."

Looking back on these times, I cannot applaud in all respects the way in which our days were spent. There was too
much idleness, and sometimes too much conviviality; but our
hearts were warm, our minds honorably bent on knowledge
and literary distinction; and if I, certainly the least informed
of the party, may be permitted to bear witness, we were not
without the fair and creditable means of attaining the distinction to which we aspired. In this society I was naturally
led to correct my former useless course of reading; for—
feeling myself greatly inferior to my companions in metaphysical philosophy and other branches of regular study—I
labored, not without some success, to acquire at least such a
portion of knowledge as might enable me to maintain my
rank in conversation. In this I succeeded pretty well; but
unfortunately then, as often since through my life, I incurred
the deserved ridicule of my friends from the superficial nature of my acquisitions, which being, in the mercantile phrase,
got up for society, very often proved flimsy in the texture;
and thus the gifts of an uncommonly retentive memory and
acute powers of perception were sometimes detrimental to
their possessor, by encouraging him to a presumptuous reliance upon them.[13]

Amidst these studies, and in this society, the time of my
apprenticeship elapsed; and in 1790, or thereabouts, it became
necessary that I should seriously consider to which department of the law I was to attach myself. My father behaved
with the most parental kindness. He offered, if I preferred
his own profession, immediately to take me into partnership

[13] Scott was admitted into the most celebrated of the Edinburgh debating Societies, *The Speculative,* in January 1791. Soon after he was
elected their librarian; and in the November following, he became also
their secretary and treasurer:—all which appointments indicate the reliance placed on his careful habits of business, the fruit of his chamber
education. The minutes kept in his hand-writing attest the strict regularity of his attention to the affairs of the club; but they show also, as
do all his early letters, a strange carelessness in spelling. His constant
good temper softened the asperities of debate, while his multifarious
lore, and the quaint humor with which he enlivened its display, made him
more a favorite as a speaker than some whose powers of rhetoric were
far above his.—J. G. Lockhart.

with him, which, though his business was much diminished, still afforded me an immediate prospect of a handsome independence. But he did not disguise his wish that I should relinquish this situation to my younger brother, and embrace the more ambitious profession of the bar. I had little hesitation in making my choice—for I was never very fond of money; and in no other particular do the professions admit of a comparison. Besides, I knew and felt the inconveniences attached to that of a Writer; and I thought (like a young man) many of them were "ingenio non subeunda meo." The appearance of personal dependence which that profession requires was disagreeable to me; the sort of connection between the client and the attorney seemed to render the latter more subservient than was quite agreeable to my nature; and, besides, I had seen many sad examples, while overlooking my father's business, that the utmost exertions, and the best meant services, do not secure the *man of business*, as he is called, from great loss, and most ungracious treatment on the part of his employers. The bar, though I was conscious of my deficiencies as a public speaker, was the line of ambition and liberty; it was that also for which most of my contemporary friends were destined. And, lastly, although I would willingly have relieved my father of the labors of his business, yet I saw plainly we could not have agreed on some particulars if we had attempted to conduct it together, and that I should disappoint his expectations if I did not turn to the bar. So to that object my studies were directed with great ardor and perseverance during the years 1789, 1790, 1791, 1792.

In the usual course of study, the Roman or Civil Law was the first object of my attention—the second, the Municipal Law of Scotland. In the course of reading on both subjects, I had the advantage of studying in conjunction with my friend William Clerk, a man of the most acute intellect and powerful apprehension, and who, should he ever shake loose the fetters of indolence by which he has been hitherto trammeled, cannot fail to be distinguished in the highest degree. We attended the regular classes of both laws in the University of Edinburgh. The Civil Law chair, now worthily filled by Mr. Alexander Irving, might at that time be considered as in *abeyance,* since the person by whom it was occupied had never been fit for the situation, and was then almost in a state of dotage. But the Scotch Law lectures were those of Mr. David Hume, who still continues to occupy that situation with as much honor to himself as advantage to his country. I copied over his lectures twice with my own hand, from notes taken in the class, and when I have had occasion to consult them, I can never sufficiently admire the penetration and clearness of conception which were necessary to the arrangement of the fabric of law, formed originally under the strictest influence of feudal principles, and innovated, altered, and broken in upon by the change of times, of habits, and of manners, until it resembles some ancient castle, partly entire, partly ruinous, partly dilapidated, patched and altered during the succession of ages by a thousand additions and combinations, yet still exhibiting, with the marks of its antiquity, symptoms of the skill and wisdom of its founders, and capable of being analyzed and made the subject of a methodical plan by an architect who can understand the various styles of the different ages in which it was subjected to alteration. Such an architect has Mr. Hume been to the law of Scotland, neither wandering into fanciful and abstruse disquisitions, which are the more proper subject of the antiquary, nor satisfied with presenting to his pupils a dry and undigested detail of the laws in their present state, but combining the past state of our legal enactments with the present, and tracing clearly and judiciously the changes which took place, and the causes which led to them.

Under these auspices, I commenced my legal studies. A little parlor was assigned me in my father's house, which was spacious and convenient, and I took the exclusive possession of my new realms with all the feelings of novelty and liberty. Let me do justice to the only years of my life in which I applied to learning with stern, steady, and undeviating industry. The rule of my friend Clerk and myself was, that we should mutually qualify ourselves for undergoing an examination upon certain points of law every morning in the week, Sundays excepted. This was at first to have taken place alternately at each other's houses, but we soon discovered that my friend's resolution was inadequate to severing him from his couch at the early hour fixed for this exercitation. Accordingly, I agreed to go every morning to his house, which, being at the extremity of Prince's Street, New Town, was a walk of two miles. With great punctuality, however, I beat him up to his task every morning before seven o'clock, and in the course of two summers, we went, by way of question and answer, through the whole of Heineccius's Analysis of the Institutes and Pandects, as well as through the smaller copy of Erskine's Institutes of the Law of Scotland. This course of study enabled us to pass with credit the usual trials, which, by the regulations of the Faculty of Advocates, must be undergone by every candidate for admission into their body. My friend William Clerk and I passed these ordeals on the same days—namely, the Civil Law trial on the [30th June 1791], and the Scots Law trial on the [6th of July 1792]. On the [11th July 1792], we both assumed the gown with all its duties and honors.

My progress in life during these two or three years had been gradually enlarging my acquaintance, and facilitating my entrance into good company. My father and mother, already advanced in life, saw little society at home, excepting that of near relations, or upon particular occasions, so that I was left to form connections in a great measure for myself. It is not difficult for a youth with a real desire to please and be pleased, to make his way into good society in Edinburgh—or indeed anywhere; and my family connections, if they did not greatly further, had nothing to embarrass my progress. I was a gentleman, and so welcome anywhere, if so be I could behave myself, as Tony Lumpkin says, "in a concatenation accordingly."

ABRAHAM LINCOLN

ABRAHAM LINCOLN

1809-1865

INTRODUCTORY NOTE

Lincoln wrote the following brief autobiography in 1860 when he had been nominated by the Republican party as their candidate for the presidency of the United States. The sketch of his life was written for a friend who was preparing a biography of the party's candidate to be used for the election. This will explain why Lincoln speaks of himself throughout in the third person, and why the account stops abruptly on a small political point before reaching the great Lincoln-Douglas debates of 1858. Those debates were then fresh in all men's minds. They had won Lincoln the nomination, and they won him the election. The four following years of his gallant and splendid presidency, his inspired leadership and tragic death, will be forever fresh in the mind of every reader of the English language.

LIFE OF ABRAHAM LINCOLN

ABRAHAM LINCOLN was born February 12, 1809, then in Hardin, now in the more recently formed county of La Rue, Kentucky. His father, Thomas, and grandfather, Abraham, were born in Rockingham County, Virginia, whither their ancestors had come from Berks County, Pennsylvania. His lineage has been traced no farther back than this. The family were originally Quakers, though in later times they have fallen away from the peculiar habits of that people. The grandfather, Abraham, had four brothers—Isaac, Jacob, John, and Thomas. So far as known, the descendants of Jacob and John are still in Virginia. Isaac went to a place near where Virginia, North Carolina, and Tennessee join; and his descendants are in that region. Thomas came to Kentucky, and after many years died there, whence his descendants went to Missouri. Abraham, grandfather of the subject of this sketch, came to Kentucky, and was killed by Indians about the year 1784. He left a widow, three sons, and two daughters. Thomas, the youngest son, and father of the present subject, by the early death of his father and very narrow circumstances of his mother, even in childhood was a wandering laboring boy and grew up literally without education. He never did more in the way of writing than to bunglingly write his own name. Before he was grown he passed one year as a hired hand with his uncle Isaac on Watauga, a branch of the Holston River. Getting back into Kentucky, and having reached his twenty-eighth year, he married Nancy Hanks—mother of the present subject—in the year 1806. She also was born in Virginia; and relatives of hers of the name of Hanks, and of other names, now reside in Coles, in Macon, and in Adams counties, Illinois, and also in Iowa. The present subject has no brother or sister of the whole or half blood. He had a sister, older than himself, who was grown and married, but died many years ago, leaving no child; also a brother, younger than himself, who died in infancy. Before leaving Kentucky, he and his sister were sent, for short periods, to A B C schools, the first kept by Zachariah Riney, and the second by Caleb Hazel.

At this time his father resided on Knob Creek, on the road from Bardstown, Kentucky, to Nashville, Tennessee, at a point three or three and a half miles south or southwest of Atherton's Ferry, on the Rolling Fork. From this place he removed to what is now Spencer County, Indiana, in the autumn of 1816, Abraham then being in his eighth year. This removal was partly on account of slavery, but chiefly on account of the difficulty in land titles in Kentucky. He settled in an unbroken forest, and the clearing away of surplus wood was the great task ahead. Abraham, though very young, was large for his age, and had an ax put into his hands at once; and from that till within his twenty-third year he was almost constantly handling that most useful instrument—less, of course, in plowing and harvesting seasons.

At this place Abraham took an early start as a hunter, which was never much improved afterward. A few days before the completion of his eighth year, in the absence of his father, a flock of wild turkeys approached the new log cabin, and Abraham with a rifle-gun, standing inside, shot through a crack and killed one of them. He has never since pulled a trigger on any larger game. In the autumn of 1818 his mother died; and a year afterward his father married Mrs. Sally Johnston, at Elizabethtown, Kentucky, a widow with three children of her first marriage. She proved a good and kind mother to Abraham, and is still living in Coles County, Illinois. There were no children of this second marriage. His father's residence continued at the same place in Indiana till 1830.

While here Abraham went to A B C schools by littles, kept successively by Andrew Crawford, — Sweeney, and Azel W. Dorsey. He does not remember any other. The family of Mr. Dorsey now resides in Schuyler County, Illinois. Abraham now thinks that the aggregate of all his schooling did not amount to one year. He was never in a college or academy as a student, and never inside a college or academy building till since he had a law license. What he has in the way of education he has picked up. After he was twenty-three and had separated from his father, he studied English grammar—imperfectly, of course, but so as to speak and write as well as he now does. He studied and nearly mastered the six books of Euclid since he was a member of Congress. He regrets his want of education, and does what he can to supply the want.

In his tenth year he was kicked by a horse, and apparently killed for a time. When he was nineteen, still residing in Indiana, he made his first trip upon a flatboat to New Orleans. He was a hired hand merely, and he and a son of the owner, without other assistance, made the trip. The nature of part of the "cargo-load," as it was called, made it necessary for them to linger and trade along the sugar-coast; and one night they were attacked by seven Negroes with intent to kill and rob them. They were hurt some in the mêlée, but succeeded in driving the Negroes from the boat, and then "cut cable," "weighed anchor," and left.

March 1, 1830, Abraham having just completed his twenty-first year, his father and family, with the families of the two daughters and sons-in-law of his stepmother, left the old homestead in Indiana and came to Illinois. Their mode of conveyance was wagons drawn by ox-teams, and Abraham drove one of the teams. They reached the county of Macon, and stopped there some time within the same month of March. His father and family settled a new place on the north side of the Sangamon River, at the junction of the timber-land and prairie, about ten miles westerly from Decatur. Here they built a log cabin, into which they removed, and made sufficient of rails to fence ten acres of ground, fenced and broke the ground, and raised a crop of sown corn upon it the same year.

The sons-in-law were temporarily settled in other places in the county. In the autumn all hands were greatly afflicted with ague and fever, to which they had not been used, and by which they were greatly discouraged, so much so that they determined on leaving the county. They remained, however, through the succeeding winter, which was the winter of the very celebrated "deep snow" of Illinois. During that winter Abraham, together with his stepmother's son, John D. Johnston, and John Hanks, yet residing in Macon County, hired themselves to Denton Offutt to take a flatboat from Beardstown, Illinois, to New Orleans; and for that purpose were to join him—Offutt—at Springfield, Illinois, so soon as the snow should go off. When it did go off, which was about the first of March, 1831, the county was so flooded as to make traveling by land impracticable; to obviate which difficulty they purchased a large canoe, and came down the Sangamon River in it. This is the time and manner of Abraham's first entrance into Sangamon County. They found Offutt at Springfield, but learned from him that he had failed in getting a boat at Beardstown. This led to their hiring themselves to him for twelve dollars per month each, and getting the timber out of the trees and building a boat at Old Sangamon town on the Sangamon River, seven miles northwest of Springfield, which boat they took to New Orleans, substantially upon the old contract.

During this boat-enterprise acquaintance with Offutt, who was previously an entire stranger, he conceived a liking for Abraham, and believing he could turn him to account, he contracted with him to act as clerk for him, on his return from New Orleans, in charge of a store and mill at New Salem, then in Sangamon, now in Menard County. Hanks had not gone to New Orleans, but having a family, and being likely to be detained from home longer than at first expected, had turned

back from St. Louis. . . . Abraham's father, with his own
family and others mentioned, had, in pursuance of their intention, removed from Macon to Coles County. John D. Johnston, the stepmother's son, went to them, and Abraham
stopped indefinitely and for the first time, as it were, by himself at New Salem, before mentioned. This was in July, 1831.
Here he rapidly made acquaintances and friends.

In less than a year Offutt's business was failing—had almost failed—when the Black Hawk war of 1832 broke out.
Abraham joined a volunteer company, and, to his own surprise, was elected captain of it. He says he has not since
had any success in life which gave him so much satisfaction.
He went to the campaign, served nearly three months, met
the ordinary hardships of such an expedition, but was in no
battle. He now owns, in Iowa, the land upon which his own
warrants for the service were located. Returning from the
campaign, and encouraged by his great popularity among his
immediate neighbors, he the same year ran for the legislature, and was beaten—his own precinct, however, casting its
votes 277 for and 7 against him—and that, too, while he was an
avowed Clay man, and the precinct the autumn afterward
giving a majority of 115 to General Jackson over Mr. Clay.
This was the only time Abraham was ever beaten on a direct
vote of the people.

He was now without means and out of business, but was
anxious to remain with his friends who had treated him with
so much generosity, especially as he had nothing elsewhere to go to. He studied what he should do—thought
of learning the blacksmith trade—thought of trying to
study law—rather thought he could not succeed at that
without a better education. Before long, strangely enough,
a man offered to sell, and did sell, to Abraham and another as
poor as himself, an old stock of goods, upon credit. They
opened as merchants; and he says that was *the* store. Of
course they did nothing but get deeper and deeper in debt.
He was appointed postmaster at New Salem—the office being
too insignificant to make his politics an objection. The store
winked out. The surveyor of Sangamon offered to depute
to Abraham that portion of his work which was within his
part of the county. He accepted, procured a compass and

chain, studied Flint and Gibson a little, and went at it. This procured bread, and kept soul and body together.

The election of 1834 came, and he was then elected to the legislature by the highest vote cast for any candidate. Major John T. Stuart, then in full practice of the law, was also elected. During the canvass, in a private conversation he encouraged Abraham [to] study law. After the election he borrowed books of Stuart, took them home with him, and went at it in good earnest. He studied with nobody. He still mixed in the surveying to pay board and clothing bills. When the legislature met, the law-books were dropped, but were taken up again at the end of the session. He was reëlected in 1836, 1838, and 1840. In the autumn of 1836 he obtained a law license, and on April 15, 1837, removed to Springfield, and commenced the practice—his old friend Stuart taking him into partnership. March 3, 1837, by a protest entered upon the "Illinois House Journal" of that date, at pages 817 and 818, Abraham, with Dan Stone, another representative of Sangamon, briefly defined his position on the slavery question; and so far as it goes, it was then the same that it is now. The protest is as follows:

"Resolutions upon the subject of domestic slavery having passed both branches of the General Assembly at its present session, the undersigned hereby protest against the passage of the same.

"They believe that the institution of slavery is founded on both injustice and bad policy, but that the promulgation of Abolition doctrines tends rather to increase than abate its evils.

"They believe that the Congress of the United States has no power under the Constitution to interfere with the institution of slavery in the different states.

"They believe that the Congress of the United States has the power, under the Constitution, to abolish slavery in the District of Columbia, but that the power ought not to be exercised unless at the request of the people of the District.

"The difference between these opinions and those contained in the above resolutions is their reason for entering this protest.   "DAN STONE,
                                            "A. LINCOLN,
        "Representatives from the County of Sangamon."

In 1838 and 1840, Mr. Lincoln's party voted for him as Speaker, but being in the minority he was not elected. After 1840 he declined a reëlection to the legislature. He was on the Harrison electoral ticket in 1840, and on that of Clay in 1844, and spent much time and labor in both those canvasses. In November, 1842, he was married to Mary, daughter of Robert S. Todd, of Lexington, Kentucky. They have three living children, all sons, one born in 1843, one in 1850, and one in 1853. They lost one, who was born in 1846.

In 1846 he was elected to the lower house of Congress, and served one term only, commencing in December, 1847, and ending with the inauguration of General Taylor, in March, 1849. All the battles of the Mexican war had been fought before Mr. Lincoln took his seat in Congress, but the American army was still in Mexico, and the treaty of peace was not fully and formally ratified till the June afterward. Much has been said of his course in Congress in regard to this war. A careful examination of the "Journal" and "Congressional Globe" shows that he voted for all the supply measures that came up, and for all the measures in any way favorable to the officers, soldiers, and their families, who conducted the war through: with the exception that some of these measures passed without yeas and nays, leaving no record as to how particular men voted. The "Journal" and "Globe" also show him voting that the war was unnecessarily and unconstitutionally begun by the President of the United States. This is the language of Mr. Ashmun's amendment, for which Mr. Lincoln and nearly or quite all other Whigs of the House of Representatives voted.

Mr. Lincoln's reasons for the opinion expressed by this vote were briefly that the President had sent General Taylor into an inhabited part of the country belonging to Mexico, and not to the United States, and thereby had provoked the first act of hostility, in fact the commencement of the war; that the place, being the country bordering on the east bank of the Rio Grande, was inhabited by native Mexicans born there under the Mexican Government, and had never submitted to, nor been conquered by, Texas or the United States, nor transferred to either by treaty; that although Texas claimed the Rio Grande as her boundary, Mexico had never recognized it, and neither Texas nor the United States had ever enforced it; that there was a broad desert between that and the country over which Texas had actual control; that the country where hostilities commenced, having once belonged to Mexico, must remain so until it was somehow legally transferred, which had never been done.

Mr. Lincoln thought the act of sending an armed force among the Mexicans was unnecessary, inasmuch as Mexico was in no way molesting or menacing the United States or the people thereof; and that it was unconstitutional, because the power of levying war is vested in Congress, and not in the President. He thought the principal motive for the act was to divert public attention from the surrender of "Fifty-four, forty, or fight" to Great Britain, on the Oregon boundary question.

Mr. Lincoln was not a candidate for reëlection. This was determined upon and declared before he went to Washington, in accordance with an understanding among Whig friends, by which Colonel Hardin and Colonel Baker had each previously served a single term in this same district.

In 1848, during his term in Congress, he advocated General Taylor's nomination for the presidency, in opposition to all others, and also took an active part for his election after his nomination, speaking a few times in Maryland, near Washington, several times in Massachusetts, and canvassing quite fully his own district in Illinois, which was followed by a majority in the district of over fifteen hundred for General Taylor.

Upon his return from Congress he went to the practice of the law with greater earnestness than ever before. In 1852 he was upon the Scott electoral ticket, and did something in the way of canvassing, but owing to the hopelessness of the cause in Illinois he did less than in previous presidential canvasses.

In 1854 his profession had almost superseded the thought of politics in his mind, when the repeal of the Missouri Compromise aroused him as he had never been before.

In the autumn of that year he took the stump with no broader practical aim or object than to secure, if possible, the reëlection of Hon. Richard Yates to Congress. His speeches at once attracted a more marked attention than they had ever before done. As the canvass proceeded he was drawn to different parts of the State outside of Mr. Yates's district. He did not abandon the law, but gave his attention by turns to that and politics. The state agricultural fair was at Springfield that year, and Douglas was announced to speak there.

In the canvass of 1856 Mr. Lincoln made over fifty speeches, no one of which, so far as he remembers, was put in print. One of them was made at Galena, but Mr. Lincoln has no recollection of any part of it being printed; nor does he remember whether in that speech he said anything about a Supreme Court decision. He may have spoken upon that subject, and some of the newspapers may have reported him as saying what is now ascribed to him; but he thinks he could not have expressed himself as represented.

CHARLES DARWIN

CHARLES DARWIN

1809-1882

INTRODUCTORY NOTE

"The Life and Letters of Charles Darwin," edited by his son Francis Darwin, has been widely accepted as among the best of modern biographies. It aims, as do most recent biographies, to let the subject speak for himself as much as possible through his own letters and remembered conversations. In accordance with this plan Mr. Francis Darwin incorporated into his book an account of his father's life written by Charles Darwin's own hand and intended only for his family. We are told that the elder Darwin had never expected this narrative to be published. The son, however, recognizing its unique value, gave it to the world. It is this autobiography which is here reprinted in full. Nothing could exceed its homely naturalness, simplicity and keenness of insight. Its honesty and self-understanding show us the ideal of what autobiography might be, but unfortunately seldom is.

Charles Robert Darwin will go down to future ages as the discoverer, or at least as the scientific establisher, of the doctrine of "natural selection," more fully described as the principle that all forms of life develop and change and produce new species of life because of the tendency of the stronger individuals, those which are better fitted for life, to survive where weak or merely average individuals would perish. This is the stern doctrine of "the survival of the more fit" in the struggle for existence. Darwin's book, "The Origin of Species," explaining his theories, was published in 1859 and revolutionized the scientific world. For many years, however, a most bitter controversy raged about the new teaching and Darwin himself was widely misunderstood and misrepresented. We know him now to have been a man as remarkable for his high moral and spiritual character as he was for his intellect.

393

RECOLLECTIONS OF THE DEVELOPMENT OF MY MIND AND CHARACTER

A German Editor having written to me for an account of the development of my mind and character with some sketch of my autobiography, I have thought that the attempt would amuse me, and might possibly interest my children or their children. I know that it would have interested me greatly to have read even so short and dull a sketch of the mind of my grandfather, written by himself, and what he thought and did, and how he worked. I have attempted to write the following account of myself, as if I were a dead man in another world looking back at my own life. Nor have I found this difficult, for life is nearly over with me. I have taken no pains about my style of writing.

I was born at Shrewsbury on February 12th, 1809, and my earliest recollection goes back only to when I was a few months over four years old, when we went to near Abergele for sea-bathing, and I recollect some events and places there with some little distinctness.

My mother died in July 1817, when I was a little over eight years old, and it is odd that I can remember hardly anything about her except her death-bed, her black velvet gown, and her curiously constructed work-table. In the spring of this same year I was sent to a day-school in Shrewsbury, where I stayed a year. I have been told that I was much slower in learning than my younger sister Catherine, and I believe that I was in many ways considered a rather naughty boy.

By the time I went to this day-school my taste for natural history, and more especially for collecting, was well developed. I tried to make out the names of plants, and collected all sorts of things, shells, seals, franks, coins, and minerals. The passion for collecting which leads a man to be a systematic naturalist, a virtuoso, or a miser, was very strong in me, and was clearly innate, as none of my sisters or brother ever had this taste.

One little event during this year has fixed itself very firmly in my mind, and I hope that it has done so from my conscience having been afterwards sorely troubled by it; it is curious as showing that apparently I was interested at this early age in the variability of plants! I told another little boy (I believe it was Leighton, who afterwards became a well-known lichenologist and botanist), that I could produce variously colored polyanthuses and primroses by watering them with certain colored fluids, which was of course a monstrous fable, and had never been tried by me. I may here also confess that as a little boy I was much given to inventing deliberate falsehoods, and this was always done for the sake of causing excitement. For instance, I once gathered much valuable fruit from my father's trees and hid it in the shrubbery, and then ran in breathless haste to spread the news that I had discovered a hoard of stolen fruit.

I must have been a very simple little fellow when I first went to the school. A boy of the name of Garnett took me into a cake shop one day, and bought some cakes for which he did not pay, as the shopman trusted him. When we came out I asked him why he did not pay for them, and he instantly answered, "Why, do you not know that my uncle left a great sum of money to the town on condition that every tradesman should give whatever was wanted without payment to any one who wore his old hat and moved [it] in a particular manner?" and he then showed me how it was moved. He then went into another shop where he was trusted, and asked for some small article, moving his hat in the proper manner, and of course obtained it without payment. When we came out he said, "Now if you like to go by yourself into that cakeshop (how well I remember its exact position) I will lend you my hat, and you can get whatever you like if you move the hat on your head properly." I gladly accepted the generous offer, and went in and asked for some cakes, moved the old hat and was walking out of the shop, when the shopman made a rush at me, so I dropped the cakes and ran for dear life, and was astonished by being greeted with shouts of laughter by my false friend Garnett.

I can say in my own favor that I was as a boy humane, but I owed this entirely to the instruction and example of my sisters. I doubt indeed whether humanity is a natural or innate quality. I was very fond of collecting eggs, but I never took more than a single egg out of a bird's nest, except on one single occasion, when I took all, not for their value, but from a sort of bravado.

I had a strong taste for angling, and would sit for any number of hours on the bank of a river or pond watching the float; when at Maer [1] I was told that I could kill the worms with salt and water, and from that day I never spitted a living worm, though at the expense probably of some loss of success.

Once as a very little boy whilst at the day school, or before that time, I acted cruelly, for I beat a puppy, I believe, simply from cnjoying the sense of power; but the beating could not have been severe, for the puppy did not howl, of which I feel sure, as the spot was near the house. This act lay heavily on my conscience, as is shown by my remembering the exact spot where the crime was committed. It probably lay all the heavier from my love of dogs being then, and for a long time afterwards, a passion. Dogs seemed to know this, for I was an adept in robbing their love from their masters.

I remember clearly only one other incident during this year whilst at Mr. Case's daily school,—namely, the burial of a dragoon soldier; and it is surprising how clearly I can still see the horse with the man's empty boots and carbine suspended to the saddle, and the firing over the grave. This scene deeply stirred whatever poetic fancy there was in me.

In the summer of 1818 I went to Dr. Butler's great school in Shrewsbury, and remained there for seven years till Midsummer 1825, when I was sixteen years old. I boarded at this school, so that I had the great advantage of living the life of a true schoolboy; but as the distance was hardly more than a mile to my home, I very often ran there in the longer intervals between the callings over and before locking up at night. This, I think, was in many ways advantageous to me by keeping up home affections and interests. I remember in the early part of my school life that I often had to run very quickly to be in time, and from being a fleet runner was generally successful; but when in doubt I prayed earnestly to God to help me, and I well remember that I attributed my success to the prayers and not to my quick running, and marveled how generally I was aided.

[1] The house of his uncle, Josiah Wedgwood.

I have heard my father and elder sister say that I had, as a very young boy, a strong taste for long solitary walks; but what I thought about I know not. I often became quite absorbed, and once, whilst returning to school on the summit of the old fortifications round Shrewsbury, which had been converted into a public foot-path with no parapet on one side, I walked off and fell to the ground, but the height was only seven or eight feet. Nevertheless the number of thoughts which passed through my mind during this very short, but sudden and wholly unexpected fall, was astonishing, and seem hardly compatible with what physiologists have, I believe, proved about each thought requiring quite an appreciable amount of time.

Nothing could have been worse for the development of my mind than Dr. Butler's school, as it was strictly classical, nothing else being taught, except a little ancient geography and history. The school as a means of education to me was simply a blank. During my whole life I have been singularly incapable of mastering any language. Especial attention was paid to verse-making, and this I could never do well. I had many friends, and got together a good collection of old verses, which by patching together, sometimes aided by other boys, I could work into any subject. Much attention was paid to learning by heart the lessons of the previous day; this I could effect with great facility, learning forty or fifty lines of Virgil or Homer, whilst I was in morning chapel; but this exercise was utterly useless, for every verse was forgotten in forty-eight hours. I was not idle, and with the exception of versification, generallly worked conscientiously at my classics, not using cribs. The sole pleasure I ever received from such studies, was from some of the odes of Horace, which I admired greatly.

When I left the school I was for my age neither high nor low in it; and I believe that I was considered by all my masters and by my father as a very ordinary boy, rather below the common standard in intellect. To my deep mortification my father once said to me, "You care for nothing but shooting, dogs, and rat-catching, and you will be a disgrace to yourself and all your family." But my father, who was the kindest man I ever knew and whose memory I love with all my heart, must have been angry and somewhat unjust when he used such words.

Looking back as well as I can at my character during my school life, the only qualities which at this period promised well for the future, were, that I had strong and diversified tastes, much zeal for whatever interested me, and a keen pleasure in understanding any complex subject or thing. I was taught Euclid by a private tutor, and I distinctly remember the intense satisfaction which the clear geometrical proofs gave me. I remember, with equal distinctness, the delight which my uncle gave me (the father of Francis Galton) by explaining the principle of the vernier of a barometer. With respect to diversified tastes, independently of science, I was fond of reading various books, and I used to sit for hours reading the historical plays of Shakespeare, generally in an old window in the thick walls of the school. I read also other poetry, such as Thomson's "Seasons," and the recently published poems of Byron and Scott. I mention this because later in life I wholly lost, to my great regret, all pleasure from poetry of any kind, including Shakespeare. In connection with pleasure from poetry, I may add that in 1822 a vivid delight in scenery was first awakened in my mind, during a riding tour on the borders of Wales, and this has lasted longer than any other æsthetic pleasure.

Early in my school days a boy had a copy of the "Wonders of the World," which I often read, and disputed with other boys about the veracity of some of the statements; and I believe that this book first gave me a wish to travel in remote countries, which was ultimately fulfilled by the voyage of the *Beagle*. In the latter part of my school life I became passionately fond of shooting; I do not believe that any one could have shown more zeal for the most holy cause than I did for shooting birds. How well I remember killing my first snipe, and my excitement was so great that I had much difficulty in reloading my gun from the trembling of my hands. This taste long continued, and I became a very good shot. When at Cambridge I used to practice throwing up my gun to my shoulder before a looking-glass to see that I threw it up straight. Another and better plan was to get a friend to wave about a lighted candle, and then to fire at it with a cap on the nipple, and if the aim was accurate the little puff of air would blow out the candle. The explosion of the cap caused a sharp crack, and I was told that the tutor of the college remarked, "What an extraordinary thing it is, Mr. Darwin seems to spend hours in cracking a horse-whip in his room, for I often hear the crack when I pass under his windows."

I had many friends amongst the schoolboys, whom I loved dearly, and I think that my disposition was then very affectionate.

With respect to science, I continued collecting minerals with much zeal, but quite unscientifically—all that I cared about was a new-*named* mineral, and I hardly attempted to classify them. I must have observed insects with some little care, for when ten years old (1819) I went for three weeks to Plas Edwards on the sea-coast in Wales, I was very much interested and surprised at seeing a large black and scarlet Hemipterous insect, many moths (Zygæna), and a Cicindela which are not found in Shropshire. I almost made up my mind to begin collecting all the insects which I could find dead, for on consulting my sister I concluded that it was not right to kill insects for the sake of making a collection. From reading White's "Selborne," I took much pleasure in watching the habits of birds, and even made notes on the subject. In my simplicity I remember wondering why every gentleman did not become an ornithologist.

Towards the close of my school life, my brother worked hard at chemistry, and made a fair laboratory with proper apparatus in the tool-house in the garden, and I was allowed to aid him as a servant in most of his experiments. He made all the gases and many compounds, and I read with great care several books on chemistry, such as Henry and Parkes' "Chemical Catechism." The subject interested me greatly, and we often used to go on working till rather late at night. This was the best part of my education at school, for it showed me practically the meaning of experimental science. The fact that we worked at chemistry somehow got known at school, and as it was an unprecedented fact, I was nicknamed "Gas." I was also once publicly rebuked by the head-master, Dr. Butler, for thus wasting my time on such useless subjects; and he called me very unjustly a "poco curante," and as I did not understand what he meant, it seemed to me a fearful reproach.

As I was doing no good at school, my father wisely took me away at a rather earlier age than usual, and sent me (Oct. 1825) to Edinburgh University with my brother, where I stayed for two years or sessions. My brother was completing his medical studies, though I do not believe he ever really intended to practice, and I was sent there to commence them. But soon after this period I became convinced from various small circumstances that my father would leave me property enough to subsist on with some comfort, though I never imagined that I should be so rich a man as I am; but my belief was sufficient to check any strenuous efforts to learn medicine.

The instruction at Edinburgh was altogether by lectures, and these were intolerably dull, with the exception of those on chemistry by Hope; but to my mind there are no advantages and many disadvantages in lectures compared with reading. Dr. Duncan's lectures on Materia Medica at 8 o'clock on a winter's morning are something fearful to remember. Dr. —— made his lectures on human anatomy as dull as he was himself, and the subject disgusted me. It has proved one of the greatest evils in my life that I was not urged to practice dissection, for I should soon have got over my disgust; and the practice would have been invaluable for all my future work. This has been an irremediable evil, as well as my incapacity to draw. I also attended regularly the clinical wards in the hospital. Some of the cases distressed me a good deal, and I still have vivid pictures before me of some of them; but I was not so foolish as to allow this to lessen my attendance. I cannot understand why this part of my medical course did not interest me in a greater degree; for during the summer before coming to Edinburgh I began attending some of the poor people, chiefly children and women in Shrewsbury: I wrote down as full an account as I could of the case with all the symptoms, and read them aloud to my father, who suggested further inquiries and advised me what medicines to give, which I made up myself. At one time I had at least a dozen patients, and I felt a keen interest in the work. My father, who was by far the best judge of character whom I ever knew, declared that I should make a successful physician,—meaning by this one who would get many patients. He maintained that the chief element of success was exciting confidence; but what he saw in me which convinced him that I should create confidence I know not. I also attended on two occasions the operating theater in the hospital at Edinburgh, and saw two very bad operations, one on a child, but I rushed away before they were completed. Nor did I ever attend again, for hardly any inducement would have been strong enough to make me do so; this being long before the blessed days of chloroform. The two cases fairly haunted me for many a long year.

My brother stayed only one year at the University, so that during the second year I was left to my own resources; and this was an advantage, for I became well acquainted with several young men fond of natural science. One of these was Ainsworth, who afterwards published his travels in Assyria; he was a Wernerian geologist, and knew a little about many subjects. Dr. Coldstream was a very different young man, prim, formal, highly religious, and most kind-hearted; he afterwards published some good zoölogical articles. A third young man was Hardie, who would, I think, have made a good botanist, but died early in India. Lastly, Dr. Grant, my senior by several years, but how I became acquainted with him I cannot remember; he published some first-rate zoölogical papers, but after coming to London as Professor in University College, he did nothing more in science, a fact which has always been inexplicable to me. I knew him well; he was dry and formal in manner, with much enthusiasm beneath this outer crust. He one day, when we were walking together, burst forth in high admiration of Lamarck and his views on evolution. I listened in silent astonishment, and as far as I can judge without any effect on my mind.

I had previously read the "Zoonomia" of my grandfather, in which similar views are maintained, but without producing any effect on me. Nevertheless it is probable that the hearing rather early in life such views maintained and praised may have favored my upholding them under a different form in my "Origin of Species." At this time I admired greatly the "Zoonomia;" but on reading it a second time after an interval of ten or fifteen years, I was much disappointed; the proportion of speculation being so large to the facts given.

Drs. Grant and Coldstream attended much to marine Zoology, and I often accompanied the former to collect animals in the tidal pools, which I dissected as well as I could. I also became friends with some of the Newhaven fishermen, and sometimes accompanied them when they trawled for oysters, and thus got many specimens. But from not having had any regular practice in dissection, and from possessing only a wretched microscope, my attempts were very poor. Nevertheless I made one interesting little discovery, and read, about the beginning of the year 1826, a short paper on the subject before the Plinian Society. This was that the so-called ova of Flustra had the power of independent movement by means of cilia, and were in fact larvæ. In another short paper I showed that the little globular bodies which had been supposed to be the young state of *Fucus loreus* were the egg-cases of the wormlike *Pontobdella muricata*.

The Plinian Society was encouraged and, I believe, founded by Professor Jameson: it consisted of students and met in an underground room in the University for the sake of reading papers on natural science and discussing them. I used regularly to attend, and the meetings had a good effect on me in stimulating my zeal and giving me new congenial acquaintances. One evening a poor young man got up, and after stammering for a prodigious length of time, blushing crimson, he at last slowly got out the words, "Mr. President, I have forgotten what I was going to say." The poor fellow looked quite overwhelmed, and all the members were so surprised that no one could think of a word to say to cover his confusion. The papers which were read to our little society were not printed, so that I had not the satisfaction of seeing my paper in print; but I believe Dr. Grant noticed my small discovery in his excellent memoir on Flustra.

I was also a member of the Royal Medical Society, and attended pretty regularly; but as the subjects were exclusively medical, I did not much care about them. Much rubbish was talked there, but there were some good speakers, of whom the best was the present Sir J. Kay-Shuttleworth. Dr. Grant took me occasionally to the meetings of the Wernerian Society, where various papers on natural history were read, discussed, and afterwards published in the "Transactions." I heard Audubon deliver there some interesting discourses on the habits of N. American birds, sneering somewhat unjustly at Waterton. By the way, a negro lived in Edinburgh, who had traveled with Waterton, and gained his livelihood by stuffing birds, which he did excellently: he gave me lessons for payment, and I used often to sit with him, for he was a very pleasant and intelligent man.

Mr. Leonard Horner also took me once to a meeting of the Royal Society of Edinburgh, where I saw Sir Walter Scott in the chair as President, and he apologized to the meeting as not feeling fitted for such a position. I looked at him and at the whole scene with some awe and reverence, and I think it was owing to this visit during my youth, and to my having attended the Royal Medical Society, that I felt the honor of being elected a few years ago an honorary member of both these Societies, more than any other similar honor. If I had been told at that time that I should one day have been thus honored, I declare that I should have thought it as ridiculous and improbable, as if I had been told that I should be elected King of England.

During my second year at Edinburgh I attended ——'s lectures on Geology and Zoölogy, but they were incredibly dull. The sole effect they produced on me was the determination never as long as I lived to read a book on Geology, or in any way to study the science. Yet I feel sure that I was prepared for a philosophical treatment of the subject; for an old Mr. Cotton in Shropshire, who knew a good deal about rocks, had pointed out to me two or three years previously a well-known large erratic bowlder in the town of Shrewsbury, called the "bell-stone"; he told me that there was no rock of the same kind nearer than Cumberland or Scotland, and he solemnly assured me that the world would come to an end before any one would be able to explain how this stone came where it now lay. This produced a deep impression on me, and I meditated over this wonderful stone. So that I felt the keenest delight when I first read of the action of icebergs in transporting bowlders, and I gloried in the progress of Geology. Equally striking is the fact that I, though now only sixty-seven years old, heard the Professor, in a field lecture at Salisbury Craigs, discoursing on a trapdyke, with amygdaloidal margins and the strata indurated on each side, with volcanic rocks all around us, say that it was a fissure filled with sediment from above, adding with a sneer that there were men who maintained that it had been injected from beneath in a molten condition. When I think of this lecture, I do not wonder at all that I determined never to attend to Geology.

From attending ——'s lectures, I became acquainted with the curator of the museum, Mr. Macgillivray, who afterwards published a large and excellent book on the birds of Scotland. I had much interesting natural-history talk with him, and he was very kind to me. He gave me some rare shells, for I at that time collected marine mollusca, but with no great zeal.

My summer vacations during these two years were wholly given up to amusements, though I always had some book in hand, which I read with interest. During the summer of 1826 I took a long walking tour with two friends with knapsacks on our backs through North Wales. We walked thirty miles most days, including one day the ascent of Snowdon. I also went with my sister a riding tour in North Wales, a servant with saddle-bags carrying our clothes. The autumns were devoted to shooting chiefly at Mr. Owen's, at Woodhouse, and at my Uncle Jos's, at Maer. My zeal was so great that I used to place my shooting-boots open by my bed-side when I went to bed, so as not to lose half a minute in putting them on in the morning; and on one occasion I reached a distant part of the Maer estate, on the 20th of August for black-game shooting, before I could see: I then toiled on with the gamekeeper the whole day through thick heath and young Scotch firs.

I kept an exact record of every bird which I shot throughout the whole season. One day when shooting at Woodhouse with Captain Owen, the eldest son, and Major Hill, his cousin, afterwards Lord Berwick, both of whom I liked very much, I thought myself shamefully used, for every time after I had fired and thought that I had killed a bird, one of the two acted as if loading his gun, and cried out, "You must not count that bird, for I fired at the same time," and the gamekeeper, perceiving the joke, backed them up. After some hours they told me the joke, but it was no joke to me, for I had shot a large number of birds, but did not know how many, and could not add them to my list, which I used to do by making a knot in a piece of string tied to a button-hole. This my wicked friends had perceived.

How I did enjoy shooting! but I think that I must have been half-consciously ashamed of my zeal, for I tried to persuade myself that shooting was almost an intellectual employment; it required so much skill to judge where to find most game and to hunt the dogs well.

One of my autumnal visits to Maer in 1827 was memorable from meeting there Sir J. Mackintosh, who was the best converser I ever listened to. I heard afterwards with a glow of pride that he had said, "There is something in that young man that interests me." This must have been chiefly due to his perceiving that I listened with much interest to everything which he said, for I was as ignorant as a pig about his subjects of history, politics, and moral philosophy. To hear of praise from an eminent person, though no doubt apt or certain to excite vanity, is, I think, good for a young man, as it helps to keep him in the right course.

My visits to Maer during these two or three succeeding years were quite delightful, independently of the autumnal shooting. Life there was perfectly free; the country was very pleasant for walking or riding; and in the evening there was much very agreeable conversation, not so personal as it generally is in large family parties, together with music. In the summer the whole family used often to sit on the steps of the old portico, with the flower-garden in front, and with the steep wooded bank opposite the house reflected in the lake, with here and there a fish rising or a water-bird paddling about. Nothing has left a more vivid picture on my mind than these evenings at Maer. I was also attached to and greatly revered my Uncle Jos; he was silent and reserved, so as to be a rather awful man; but he sometimes talked openly with me. He was the very type of an upright man, with the clearest judgment. I do not believe that any power on earth could have made him swerve an inch from what he considered the right course. I used to apply to him in my mind the

well-known ode of Horace, now forgotten by me, in which
the words "nec vultus tyranni, &c.," come in.

Cambridge 1828-1831.—After having spent two sessions in
Edinburgh, my father perceived, or he heard from my sisters,
that I did not like the thought of being a physician, so he
proposed that I should become a clergyman. He was very
properly vehement against my turning into an idle sporting
man, which then seemed my probable destination. I asked
for some time to consider, as from what little I had heard or
thought on the subject I had scruples about declaring my
belief in all the dogmas of the Church of England; though
otherwise I liked the thought of being a country clergyman.
Accordingly I read with care "Pearson on the Creed," and a
few other books on divinity; and as I did not then in the
least doubt the strict and literal truth of every word in the
Bible, I soon persuaded myself that our Creed must be fully
accepted.

Considering how fiercely I have been attacked by the
orthodox, it seems ludicrous that I once intended to be a
clergyman. Nor was this intention and my father's wish ever
formally given up, but died a natural death when, on leaving
Cambridge, I joined the *Beagle* as naturalist. If the phre-
nologists are to be trusted, I was well fitted in one respect to
be a clergyman. A few years ago the secretaries of a German psychological society asked me earnestly by letter for
a photograph of myself; and some time afterwards I received
the proceedings of one of the meetings, in which it seemed
that the shape of my head had been the subject of a public
discussion, and one of the speakers declared, with much posi-
tiveness, that I had the bump of reverence developed enough
for ten priests.

As it was decided that I should be a clergyman, it was
necessary that I should go to one of the English universities
and take a degree; but as I had never opened a classical
book since leaving school, I found to my dismay, that in the
two intervening years I had actually forgotten, incredible as it
may appear, almost everything which I had learnt, even to
some few of the Greek letters. I did not therefore proceed
to Cambridge at the usual time in October, but worked with a
private tutor in Shrewsbury, and went to Cambridge after

the Christmas vacation, early in 1828. I soon recovered my school standard of knowledge, and could translate easy Greek books, such as Homer and the Greek Testament, with moderate facility.

During the three years which I spent at Cambridge my time was wasted, as far as the academical studies were concerned, as completely as at Edinburgh and at school. I attempted mathematics, and even went during the summer of 1828 with a private tutor (a very dull man) to Barmouth, but I got on very slowly. The work was repugnant to me, chiefly from my not being able to see any meaning in the early steps in algebra. This impatience was very foolish, and in after years I have deeply regretted that I did not proceed far enough at least to understand something of the great leading principles of mathematics, for men thus endowed seem to have an extra sense. But I do not believe that I should ever have succeeded beyond a very low grade. With respect to Classics I did nothing except attend a few compulsory college lectures, and the attendance was almost nominal. In my second year I had to work for a month or two to pass the Little-Go, which I did easily. Again, in my last year I worked with some earnestness for my final degree of B.A., and brushed up my Classics, together with a little Algebra and Euclid, which latter gave me much pleasure, as it did at school. In order to pass the B.A. examination, it was also necessary to get up Paley's "Evidences of Christianity," and his "Moral Philosophy." This was done in a thorough manner, and I am convinced that I could have written out the whole of the "Evidences" with perfect correctness, but not of course in the clear language of Paley. The logic of this book and, as I may add, of his "Natural Theology," gave me as much delight as did Euclid. The careful study of these works, without attempting to learn any part by rote, was the only part of the academical course which, as I then felt and as I still believe, was of the least use to me in the education of my mind. I did not at that time trouble myself about Paley's premises; and taking these on trust, I was charmed and convinced by the long line of argumentation. By answering well the examination questions in Paley, by doing Euclid well, and by not failing miserably in Classics, I gained a good place among the οἱ πολλοί or crowd of men who do not go in for honors. Oddly enough, I cannot remember how high I stood, and my memory fluctuates between the fifth, tenth, or twelfth, name on the list.

Public lectures on several branches were given in the University, attendance being quite voluntary; but I was so sickened with lectures at Edinburgh that I did not even attend Sedgwick's eloquent and interesting lectures. Had I done so I should probably have become a geologist earlier than I did. I attended, however, Henslow's lectures on Botany, and liked them much for their extreme clearness, and the admirable illustrations; but I did not study botany. Henslow used to take his pupils, including several of the older members of the University, field excursions, on foot or in coaches, to distant places, or in a barge down the river, and lectured on the rarer plants and animals which were observed. These excursions were delightful.

Although, as we shall presently see, there were some redeeming features in my life at Cambridge, my time was sadly wasted there, and worse than wasted. From my passion for shooting and for hunting, and, when this failed, for riding across country, I got into a sporting set, including some dissipated low-minded young men. We used often to dine together in the evening, though these dinners often included men of a higher stamp, and we sometimes drank too much, with jolly singing and playing at cards afterwards. I know that I ought to feel ashamed of days and evenings thus spent, but as some of my friends were very pleasant, and we were all in the highest spirits, I cannot help looking back to these times with much pleasure.

But I am glad to think that I had many other friends of a widely different nature. I was very intimate with Whitley, who was afterwards Senior Wrangler, and we used continually to take long walks together. He inoculated me with a taste for pictures and good engravings, of which I bought some. I frequently went to the Fitzwilliam Gallery, and my taste must have been fairly good, for I certainly admired the best pictures, which I discussed with the old curator. I read also with much interest Sir Joshua Reynolds' book. This taste, though not natural to me, lasted for several years, and many of the pictures in the National Gallery in London gave me much pleasure; that of Sebastian del Piombo exciting in me a sense of sublimity.

I also got into a musical set, I believe by means of my warm-hearted friend, Herbert, who took a high wrangler's degree. From associating with these men, and hearing them play, I acquired a strong taste for music, and used very often to time my walks so as to hear on week days the anthem in King's College Chapel. This gave me intense pleasure, so that my backbone would sometimes shiver. I am sure that there was no affectation or mere imitation in this taste, for I used generally to go by myself to King's College, and I sometimes hired the chorister boys to sing in my rooms. Nevertheless I am so utterly destitute of an ear, that I cannot perceive a discord, or keep time and hum a tune correctly; and it is a mystery how I could possibly have derived pleasure from music.

My musical friends soon perceived my state, and sometimes amused themselves by making me pass an examination, which consisted in ascertaining how many tunes I could recognize when they were played rather more quickly or slowly than usual. "God save the King," when thus played, was a sore puzzle. There was another man with almost as bad an ear as I had, and strange to say he played à little on the flute. Once I had the triumph of beating him in one of our musical examinations.

But no pursuit at Cambridge was followed with nearly so much eagerness or gave me so much pleasure as collecting beetles. It was the mere passion for collecting, for I did not dissect them, and rarely compared their external characters with published descriptions, but got them named anyhow. I will give a proof of my zeal: one day, on tearing off some old bark, I saw two rare beetles, and seized one in each hand; then I saw a third and new kind, which I could not bear to lose, so that I popped the one which I held in my right hand into my mouth. Alas! it ejected some intensely acrid fluid, which burnt my tongue so that I was forced to spit the beetle out, which was lost, as was the third one.

I was very successful in collecting, and invented two new methods; I employed a laborer to scrape during the winter, moss off old trees and place it in a large bag, and likewise to collect the rubbish at the bottom of the barges in which reeds are brought from the fens, and thus I got some very rare species. No poet ever felt more delighted at seeing his first poem published than I did at seeing, in Stephens' "Illustrations of British Insects," the magic words, "captured by C. Darwin, Esq." I was introduced to entomology by my second cousin, W. Darwin Fox, a clever and most pleasant man, who was then at Christ's College, and with whom I became extremely intimate. Afterwards I became well acquainted, and went out collecting, with Albert Way of Trinity, who in after years became a well-known archæologist; also with H. Thompson of the same College, afterwards a leading agriculturist, chairman of a great railway, and Member of Parliament. It seems therefore that a taste for collecting beetles is some indication of future success in life!

I am surprised what an indelible impression many of the beetles which I caught at Cambridge have left on my mind. I can remember the exact appearance of certain posts, old trees and banks where I made a good capture. The pretty *Panagæus crux-major* was a treasure in those days, and here at Down I saw a beetle running across a walk, and on picking it up instantly perceived that it differed slightly from *P. crux-major,* and it turned out to be *P. quadripunctatus,* which is only a variety or closely allied species, differing from it very slightly in outline. I had never seen in those old days Licinus alive, which to an uneducated eye hardly differs from many of the black Carabidous beetles; but my sons found here a specimen, and I instantly recognized that it was new to me; yet I had not looked at a British beetle for the last twenty years.

I have not as yet mentioned a circumstance which influenced my whole career more than any other. This was my friendship with Professor Henslow. Before coming up to Cambridge, I had heard of him from my brother as a man who knew every branch of science, and I was accordingly prepared to reverence him. He kept open house once every week when all undergraduates, and some older members of the University, who were attached to science, used to meet in the evening. I soon got, through Fox, an invitation, and went there regularly. Before long I became well acquainted with Henslow, and during the latter half of my time at Cambridge took long walks with him on most days; so that I was called by some of the dons "the man who walks with Henslow;" and in the evening I was very often asked to join his family dinner. His knowledge was great in botany, entomology, chemistry, mineralogy, and geology. His strongest taste was to draw conclusions from long-continued minute observations. His judgment was excellent, and his whole mind well balanced; but I do not suppose that any one would say that he possessed much original genius. He was deeply religious, and so orthodox that he told me one day he should be grieved if a single word of the Thirty-nine Articles were altered. His moral qualities were in every way admirable. He was free from every tinge of vanity or other petty feelings; and I never saw a man who thought so little about himself or his own concerns. His temper was imperturbably good, with the most winning and courteous manners; yet, as I have seen, he could be roused by any bad action to the warmest indignation and prompt action.

I once saw in his company in the streets of Cambridge almost as horrid a scene as could have been witnessed during the French Revolution. Two body-snatchers had been arrested, and whilst being taken to prison had been torn from the constable by a crowd of the roughest men, who dragged them by their legs along the muddy and stony road. They were covered from head to foot with mud, and their faces were bleeding either from having been kicked or from the stones; they looked like corpses, but the crowd was so dense that I got only a few momentary glimpses of the wretched creatures. Never in my life have I seen such wrath painted on a man's face as was shown by Henslow at this horrid scene. He tried repeatedly to penetrate the mob; but it was simply impossible. He then rushed away to the mayor, telling me not to follow him, but to get more policemen. I forget the issue, except that the two men were got into the prison without being killed.

Henslow's benevolence was unbounded, as he proved by his many excellent schemes for his poor parishioners, when in after years he held the living of Hitcham. My intimacy with such a man ought to have been, and I hope was, an inestimable benefit. I cannot resist mentioning a trifling incident, which showed his kind consideration. Whilst examining some pollen-grains on a damp surface, I saw the tubes exserted, and instantly rushed off to communicate my surprising discovery to him. Now I do not suppose any other professor of botany could have helped laughing at my coming in such a hurry to make such a communication. But he agreed how interesting the phenomenon was, and explained its meaning, but made me clearly understand how well it was known; so I left him not in the least mortified, but well pleased at having discovered for myself so remarkable a fact, but determined not to be in such a hurry again to communicate my discoveries.

Dr. Whewell was one of the older and distinguished men who sometimes visited Henslow, and on several occasions I walked home with him at night. Next to Sir J. Mackintosh he was the best converser on grave subjects to whom I ever listened. Leonard Jenyns, who afterwards published some good essays in Natural History, often stayed with Henslow, who was his brother-in-law. I visited him at his parsonage on the borders of the Fens [Swaffham Bulbeck], and had many a good walk and talk with him about Natural History. I became also acquainted with several other men older than I, who did not care much about science, but were friends of Henslow. One was a Scotchman, brother of Sir Alexander Ramsay, and tutor of Jesus College: he was a delightful man, but did not live for many years. Another was Mr. Dawes, afterwards Dean of Hereford, and famous for his success in the education of the poor. These men and others of the same standing, together with Henslow, used sometimes to take distant excursions into the country, which I was allowed to join, and they were most agreeable.

Looking back, I infer that there must have been something in me a little superior to the common run of youths, otherwise the above-mentioned men, so much older than I and higher in academical position, would never have allowed me to associate with them. Certainly I was not aware of any such superiority, and I remember one of my sporting friends, Turner, who saw me at work with my beetles, saying that I should some day be a Fellow of the Royal Society, and the notion seemed to me preposterous.

During my last year at Cambridge, I read with care and profound interest Humboldt's "Personal Narrative." This work, and Sir J. Herschel's "Introduction to the Study of Natural Philosophy," stirred up in me a burning zeal to add even the most humble contribution to the noble structure of Natural Science. No one or a dozen other books influenced me nearly so much as these two. I copied out from Humboldt long passages about Teneriffe, and read them aloud on one of the above-mentioned excursions, to (I think) Henslow, Ramsay, and Dawes, for on a previous occasion I had talked about the glories of Teneriffe, and some of the party declared they would endeavor to go there; but I think that they were only half in earnest. I was, however, quite in earnest, and got an introduction to a merchant in London to enquire about ships; but the scheme was, of course, knocked on the head by the voyage of the *Beagle*.

My summer vacations were given up to collecting beetles, to some reading, and short tours. In the autumn my whole time was devoted to shooting, chiefly at Woodhouse and Maer, and sometimes with young Eyton of Eyton. Upon the whole the three years which I spent at Cambridge were the most joyful in my happy life; for I was then in excellent health, and almost always in high spirits.

As I had at first come up to Cambridge at Christmas, I was forced to keep two terms after passing my final examination, at the commencement of 1831; and Henslow then persuaded me to begin the study of geology. Therefore on my return to Shropshire I examined sections, and colored a map of parts round Shrewsbury. Professor Sedgwick intended to visit North Wales in the beginning of August to pursue his famous geological investigations amongst the older rocks, and Henslow asked him to allow me to accompany him. Accordingly he came and slept at my father's house.

A short conversation with him during this evening produced a strong impression on my mind. Whilst examining an old gravel-pit near Shrewsbury, a laborer told me that he had found in it a large worn tropical Volute shell, such as may be seen on the chimney-pieces of cottages; and as he

would not sell the shell, I was convinced that he had really
found it in the pit. I told Sedgwick of the fact, and he at
once said (no doubt truly) that it must have been thrown
away by some one into the pit; but then added, if really em-
bedded there it would be the greatest misfortune to geology,
as it would overthrow all that we know about the superficial
deposits of the Midland Counties. These gravel-beds belong
in fact to the glacial period, and in after years I found in them
broken arctic shells. But I was then utterly astonished at
Sedgwick not being delighted at so wonderful a fact as a
tropical shell being found near the surface in the middle of
England. Nothing before had ever made me thoroughly realize, though I had read various scientific books, that science
consists in grouping facts so that general laws or conclusions
may be drawn from them.

Next morning we started for Llangollen, Conway, Bangor,
and Capel Curig. This tour was of decided use in teaching
me a little how to make out the geology of a country. Sedgwick often sent me on a line parallel to his, telling me to
bring back specimens of the rocks and to mark the stratification on a map. I have little doubt that he did this for my
good, as I was too ignorant to have aided him. On this tour
I had a striking instance of how easy it is to overlook phenomena, however conspicuous, before they have been observed
by any one. We spent many hours in Cwm Idwal, examining all the rocks with extreme care, as Sedgwick was anxious
to find fossils in them; but neither of us saw a trace of the
wonderful glacial phenomena all around us; we did not notice
the plainly scored rocks, the perched bowlders, the lateral
and terminal moraines. Yet these phenomena are so conspicuous that, as I declared in a paper published many years afterwards in the "Philosophical Magazine," a house burnt down
by fire did not tell its story more plainly than did this valley.
If it had still been filled by a glacier, the phenomena would
have been less distinct than they now are.

At Capel Curig I left Sedgwick and went in a straight line
by compass and map across the mountains to Barmouth, never
following any track unless it coincided with my course. I
thus came on some strange wild places, and enjoyed much
this manner of traveling. I visited Barmouth to see some

Cambridge friends who were reading there, and thence returned to Shrewsbury and to Maer for shooting; for at that time I should have thought myself mad to give up the first days of partridge-shooting for geology or any other science.

VOYAGE OF THE "BEAGLE" FROM DECEMBER 27, 1831, TO OCTOBER 2, 1836

On returning home from my short geological tour in North Wales, I found a letter from Henslow, informing me that Captain Fitz-Roy was willing to give up part of his own cabin to any young man who would volunteer to go with him without pay as naturalist to the Voyage of the *Beagle.* I have given, as I believe, in my MS. Journal an account of all the circumstances which then occurred; I will here only say that I was instantly eager to accept the offer, but my father strongly objected, adding the words, fortunate for me, "If you can find any man of common sense who advises you to go I will give my consent." So I wrote that evening and refused the offer. On the next morning I went to Maer to be ready for September 1st, and, whilst out shooting, my uncle sent for me, offering to drive me over to Shrewsbury and talk with my father, as my uncle thought it would be wise in me to accept the offer. My father always maintained that he was one of the most sensible men in the world, and he at once consented in the kindest manner. I had been rather extravagant at Cambridge, and to console my father, said, "that I should be deuced clever to spend more than my allowance whilst on board the *Beagle;*" but he answered with a smile, "But they tell me you are very clever."

Next day I started for Cambridge to see Henslow, and thence to London to see Fitz-Roy, and all was soon arranged. Afterwards, on becoming very intimate with Fitz-Roy, I heard that I had run a very narrow risk of being rejected, on account of the shape of my nose! He was an ardent disciple of Lavater, and was convinced that he could judge of a man's character by the outline of his features; and he doubted whether any one with my nose could possess sufficient energy and determination for the voyage. But I think he was afterwards well satisfied that my nose had spoken falsely.

Fitz-Roy's character was a singular one, with very many

noble features: he was devoted to his duty, generous to a fault, bold, determined, and indomitably energetic, and an ardent friend to all under his sway. He would undertake any sort of trouble to assist those whom he thought deserved assistance. He was a handsome man, strikingly like a gentleman, with highly courteous manners, which resembled those of his maternal uncle, the famous Lord Castlereagh, as I was told by the Minister at Rio. Nevertheless he must have inherited much in his appearance from Charles II., for Dr. Wallich gave me a collection of photographs which he had made, and I was struck with the resemblance of one to Fitz-Roy; and on looking at the name, I found it Ch. E. Sobieski Stuart, Count d'Albanie, a descendant of the same monarch.

Fitz-Roy's temper was a most unfortunate one. It was usually worst in the early morning, and with his eagle eye he could generally detect something amiss about the ship, and was then unsparing in his blame. He was very kind to me, but was a man very difficult to live with on the intimate terms which necessarily followed from our messing by ourselves in the same cabin. We had several quarrels; for instance, early in the voyage at Bahia, in Brazil, he defended and praised slavery, which I abominated, and told me that he had just visited a great slave-owner, who had called up many of his slaves and asked them whether they were happy, and whether they wished to be free, and all answered "No." I then asked him, perhaps with a sneer, whether he thought that the answer of slaves in the presence of their master was worth anything? This made him excessively angry, and he said that as I doubted his word we could not live any longer together. I thought that I should have been compelled to leave the ship; but as soon as the news spread, which it did quickly, as the captain sent for the first lieutenant to assuage his anger by abusing me, I was deeply gratified by receiving an invitation from all the gun-room officers to mess with them. But after a few hours Fitz-Roy showed his usual magnanimity by sending an officer to me with an apology and a request that I would continue to live with him.

His character was in several respects one of the most noble which I have ever known.

The voyage of the *Beagle* has been by far the most important event in my life, and has determined my whole career; yet it depended on so small a circumstance as my uncle offering to drive me thirty miles to Shrewsbury, which few uncles would have done, and on such a trifle as the shape of my nose. I have always felt that I owe to the voyage the first real training or education of my mind; I was led to attend closely to several branches of natural history, and thus my powers of observation were improved, though they were always fairly developed.

The investigation of the geology of all the places visited was far more important, as reasoning here comes into play. On first examining a new district nothing can appear more hopeless than the chaos of rocks; but by recording the stratification and nature of the rocks and fossils at many points, always reasoning and predicting what will be found elsewhere, light soon begins to dawn on the district, and the structure of the whole becomes more or less intelligible. I had brought with me the first volume of Lyell's "Principles of Geology," which I studied attentively; and the book was of the highest service to me in many ways. The very first place which I examined, namely St. Jago in the Cape de Verde islands, showed me clearly the wonderful superiority of Lyell's manner of treating geology, compared with that of any other author, whose works I had with me or ever afterwards read.

Another of my occupations was collecting animals of all classes, briefly describing and roughly dissecting many of the marine ones; but from not being able to draw, and from not having sufficient anatomical knowledge, a great pile of MS. which I made during the voyage has proved almost useless. I thus lost much time, with the exception of that spent in acquiring some knowledge of the Crustaceans, as this was of service when in after years I undertook a monograph of the Cirripedia.

During some part of the day I wrote my Journal, and took much pains in describing carefully and vividly all that I had seen; and this was good practice. My Journal served also, in part, as letters to my home, and portions were sent to England whenever there was an opportunity.

The above various special studies were, however, of no

importance compared with the habit of energetic industry and of concentrated attention to whatever I was engaged in, which I then acquired. Everything about which I thought or read was made to bear directly on what I had seen or was likely to see; and this habit of mind was continued during the five years of the voyage. I feel sure that it was this training which has enabled me to do whatever I have done in science.

Looking backwards, I can now perceive how my love for science gradually preponderated over every other taste. During the first two years my old passion for shooting survived in nearly full force, and I shot myself all the birds and animals for my collection; but gradually I gave up my gun more and more, and finally altogether, to my servant, as shooting interfered with my work, more especially with making out the geological structure of a country. I discovered, though unconsciously and insensibly, that the pleasure of observing and reasoning was a much higher one than that of skill and sport. That my mind became developed through my pursuits during the voyage is rendered probable by a remark made by my father, who was the most acute observer whom I ever saw, of a skeptical disposition, and far from being a believer in phrenology; for on first seeing me after the voyage, he turned round to my sisters, and exclaimed, "Why, the shape of his head is quite altered."

To return to the voyage. On September 11th (1831), I paid a flying visit with Fitz-Roy to the *Beagle* at Plymouth. Thence to Shrewsbury to wish my father and sisters a long farewell. On October 24th I took up my residence at Plymouth, and remained there until December 27th, when the *Beagle* finally left the shores of England for her circumnavigation of the world. We made two earlier attempts to sail, but were driven back each time by heavy gales. These two months at Plymouth were the most miserable which I ever spent, though I exerted myself in various ways. I was out of spirits at the thought of leaving all my family and friends for so long a time, and the weather seemed to me inexpressibly gloomy. I was also troubled with palpitation and pain about the heart, and like many a young ignorant man, especially one with a smattering of medical knowledge, was convinced that I had heart disease. I did not consult any doctor, as I fully expected to hear the verdict that I was not fit for the voyage, and I was resolved to go at all hazards.

I need not here refer to the events of the voyage—where we went and what we did—as I have given a sufficiently full account in my published Journal. The glories of the vegetation of the Tropics rise before my mind at the present time more vividly than anything else; though the sense of sublimity, which the great deserts of Patagonia and the forest-clad mountains of Tierra del Fuego excited in me, has left an indelible impression on my mind. The sight of a naked savage in his native land is an event which can never be forgotten. Many of my excursions on horseback through wild countries, or in the boats, some of which lasted several weeks, were deeply interesting: their discomfort and some degree of danger were at that time hardly a drawback, and none at all afterwards. I also reflect with high satisfaction on some of my scientific work, such as solving the problem of coral islands, and making out the geological structure of certain islands, for instance, St. Helena. Nor must I pass over the discovery of the singular relations of the animals and plants inhabiting the several islands of the Galapagos archipelago, and of all of them to the inhabitants of South America.

As far as I can judge of myself, I worked to the utmost during the voyage from the mere pleasure of investigation, and from my strong desire to add a few facts to the great mass of facts in Natural Science. But I was also ambitious to take a fair place among scientific men,—whether more ambitious or less so than most of my fellow-workers, I can form no opinion.

The geology of St. Jago is very striking, yet simple: a stream of lava formerly flowed over the bed of the sea, formed of triturated recent shells and corals, which it has baked into a hard white rock. Since then the whole island has been upheaved. But the line of white rock revealed to me a new and important fact, namely, that there had been afterwards subsidence round the craters, which had since been in action, and had poured forth lava. It then first dawned on me that I might perhaps write a book on the geology of the various countries visited, and this made me thrill with delight. That was a memorable hour to me, and how distinctly I can call to mind the low cliff of lava beneath which I rested, with the sun glaring hot, a few strange desert plants growing near, and with living corals in the tidal pools at my feet. Later in the voyage, Fitz-Roy asked me to read some of my Journal, and declared it would be worth publishing; so here was a second book in prospect!

Towards the close of our voyage I received a letter whilst at Ascension, in which my sisters told me that Sedgwick had called on my father, and said that I should take a place among the leading scientific men. I could not at the time understand how he could have learnt anything of my proceedings, but I heard (I believe afterwards) that Henslow had read some of the letters which I wrote to him before the Philosophical Society of Cambridge, and had printed them for private distribution. My collection of fossil bones, which had been sent to Henslow, also excited considerable attention amongst palæontologists. After reading this letter, I clambered over the mountains of Ascension with a bounding step, and made the volcanic rocks resound under my geological hammer. All this shows how ambitious I was; but I think that I can say with truth that in after years, though I cared in the highest degree for the approbation of such men as Lyell and Hooker, who were my friends, I did not care much about the general public. I do not mean to say that a favorable review or a large sale of my books did not please me greatly, but the pleasure was a fleeting one, and I am sure that I have never turned one inch out of my course to gain fame.

FROM MY RETURN TO ENGLAND (OCTOBER 2, 1836) TO MY MARRIAGE (JANUARY 29, 1839)

These two years and three months were the most active ones which I ever spent, though I was occasionally unwell, and so lost some time. After going backwards and forwards several times between Shrewsbury, Maer, Cambridge, and London, I settled in lodgings at Cambridge on December 13th, where all my collections were under the care of Henslow. I stayed here three months, and got my minerals and rocks examined by the aid of Professor Miller.

I began preparing my "Journal of Travels," which was not hard work, as my MS. Journal had been written with care, and my chief labor was making an abstract of my more interesting scientific results. I sent also, at the request of Lyell, a short account of my observations on the elevation of the coast of Chile to the Geological Society.

On March 7th, 1837, I took lodgings in Great Marlborough Street in London, and remained there for nearly two years, until I was married. During these two years I finished my Journal, read several papers before the Geological Society, began preparing the MS. for my "Geological Observations," and arranged for the publication of the "Zoölogy of the Voyage of the *Beagle*." In July I opened my first note-book for facts in relation to the Origin of Species, about which I had long reflected, and never ceased working for the next twenty years.

During these two years I also went a little into society, and acted as one of the honorary secretaries of the Geological Society. I saw a great deal of Lyell. One of his chief characteristics was his sympathy with the work of others, and I was as much astonished as delighted at the interest which he showed when, on my return to England, I explained to him my views on coral reefs. This encouraged me greatly, and his advice and example had much influence on me. During this time I saw also a good deal of Robert Brown; I used often to call and sit with him during his breakfast on Sunday mornings, and he poured forth a rich treasure of curious observations and acute remarks, but they almost always related to minute points, and he never with me discussed large or general questions in science.

During these two years I took several short excursions as a relaxation, and one longer one to the Parallel Roads of Glen Roy, an account of which was published in the "Philosophical Transactions." This paper was a great failure, and I am ashamed of it. Having been deeply impressed with what I had seen of the elevation of the land of South America, I attributed the parallel lines to the action of the sea; but I had to give up this view when Agassiz propounded his glacier-lake theory. Because no other explanation was possible under our then state of knowledge, I argued in favor of sea-action;

and my error has been a good lesson to me never to trust in science to the principle of exclusion.

As I was not able to work all day at science, I read a good deal during these two years on various subjects, including some metaphysical books; but I was not well fitted for such studies. About this time I took much delight in Wordsworth's and Coleridge's poetry; and can boast that I read the "Excursion" twice through. Formerly Milton's "Paradise Lost" had been my chief favorite, and in my excursions during the voyage of the *Beagle*, when I could take only a single volume, I always chose Milton.

FROM MY MARRIAGE, JANUARY 29, 1839, AND RESIDENCE IN
UPPER GOWER STREET, TO OUR LEAVING LONDON
AND SETTLING AT DOWN, SEPTEMBER 14, 1842

After speaking of his happy married life, and of his children, he continues:—

During the three years and eight months whilst we resided in London, I did less scientific work, though I worked as hard as I possibly could, than during any other equal length of time in my life. This was owing to frequently recurring unwellness, and to one long and serious illness. The greater part of my time, when I could do anything, was devoted to my work on "Coral Reefs," which I had begun before my marriage, and of which the last proof-sheet was corrected on May 6th, 1842. This book, though a small one, cost me twenty months of hard work, as I had to read every work on the islands of the Pacific and to consult many charts. It was thought highly of by scientific men, and the theory therein given is, I think, now well established.

No other work of mine was begun in so deductive a spirit as this, for the whole theory was thought out on the west coast of South America, before I had seen a true coral reef. I had therefore only to verify and extend my views by a careful examination of living reefs. But it should be observed that I had during the two previous years been incessantly attending to the effects on the shores of South America of the intermittent elevation of the land, together with denudation and the deposition of sediment. This necessarily led me to reflect much on the effects of subsidence, and it was easy to replace in imagination the continued deposition of sediment by the upward growth of corals. To do this was to form my theory of the formation of barrier-reefs and atolls.

Besides my work on coral-reefs, during my residence in London, I read before the Geological Society papers on the Erratic Bowlders of South America, on Earthquakes, and on the Formation by the Agency of Earth-worms of Mold. I also continued to superintend the publication of the "Zoology of the Voyage of the *Beagle*." Nor did I ever intermit collecting facts bearing on the origin of species; and I could sometimes do this when I could do nothing else from illness.

In the summer of 1842 I was stronger than I had been for some time, and took a little tour by myself in North Wales, for the sake of observing the effects of the old glaciers which formerly filled all the larger valleys. I published a short account of what I saw in the "Philosophical Magazine." This excursion interested me greatly, and it was the last time I was ever strong enough to climb mountains or to take long walks such as are necessary for geological work.

During the early part of our life in London, I was strong enough to go into general society, and saw a good deal of several scientific men, and other more or less distinguished men. I will give my impressions with respect to some of them, though I have little to say worth saying.

I saw more of Lyell than of any other man, both before and after my marriage. His mind was characterized, as it appeared to me, by clearness, caution, sound judgment, and a good deal of originality. When I made any remark to him on Geology, he never rested until he saw the whole case clearly, and often made me see it more clearly than I had done before. He would advance all possible objections to my suggestion, and even after these were exhausted would long remain dubious. A second characteristic was his hearty sympathy with the work of other scientific men.

On my return from the voyage of the *Beagle*, I explained to him my views on coral-reefs, which differed from his, and I was greatly surprised and encouraged by the vivid interest which he showed. His delight in science was ardent, and he felt the keenest interest in the future progress of mankind.

He was very kind-hearted, and thoroughly liberal in his religious beliefs, or rather disbeliefs; but he was a strong theist. His candor was highly remarkable. He exhibited this by becoming a convert to the Descent theory, though he had gained much fame by opposing Lamarck's views, and this after he had grown old. He reminded me that I had many years before said to him, when discussing the opposition of the old school of geologists to his new views, "What a good thing it would be if every scientific man was to die when sixty years old, as afterwards he would be sure to oppose all new doctrines." But he hoped that now he might be allowed to live.

The science of Geology is enormously indebted to Lyell—more so, as I believe, than to any other man who ever lived. When [I was] starting on the voyage of the *Beagle*, the sagacious Henslow, who, like all other geologists, believed at that time in successive cataclysms, advised me to get and study the first volume of the "Principles," which had then just been published, but on no account to accept the views therein advocated. How differently would any one now speak of the "Principles"! I am proud to remember that the first place, namely, St. Jago, in the Cape de Verde archipelago, in which I geologized, convinced me of the infinite superiority of Lyell's views over those advocated in any other work known to me.

I saw a good deal of Robert Brown, "facile Princeps Botanicorum," as he was called by Humboldt. He seemed to me to be chiefly remarkable for the minuteness of his observations, and their perfect accuracy. His knowledge was extraordinarily great, and much died with him, owing to his excessive fear of ever making a mistake. He poured out his knowledge to me in the most unreserved manner, yet was strangely jealous on some points. I called on him two or three times before the voyage of the *Beagle,* and on one occasion he asked me to look through a microscope and describe what I saw. This I did, and believe now that it was the marvelous currents of protoplasm in some vegetable cell. I then asked him what I had seen; but he answered me, "That is my little secret."

He was capable of the most generous actions. When old,

much out of health, and quite unfit for any exertion, he daily visited (as Hooker told me) an old man-servant, who lived at a distance (and whom he supported), and read aloud to him. This is enough to make up for any degree of scientific penuriousness or jealousy.

I may here mention a few other eminent men, whom I have occasionally seen, but I have little to say about them worth saying. I felt a high reverence for Sir J. Herschel, and was delighted to dine with him at his charming house at the Cape of Good Hope, and afterwards at his London house. I saw him, also, on a few other occasions. He never talked much, but every word which he uttered was worth listening to.

I once met at breakfast at Sir R. Murchison's house the illustrious Humboldt, who honored me by expressing a wish to see me. I was a little disappointed with the great man, but my anticipations probably were too high. I can remember nothing distinctly about our interview, except that Humboldt was very cheerful and talked much.

—— reminds me of Buckle whom I once met at Hensleigh Wedgwood's. I was very glad to learn from him his system of collecting facts. He told me that he bought all the books which he read, and made a full index, to each, of the facts which he thought might prove serviceable to him, and that he could always remember in what book he had read anything, for his memory was wonderful. I asked him how at first he could judge what facts would be serviceable, and he answered that he did not know, but that a sort of instinct guided him. From his habit of making indices, he was enabled to give the astonishing number of references on all sorts of subjects, which may be found in his "History of Civilization." This book I thought most interesting, and read it twice, but I doubt whether his generalizations are worth anything. Buckle was a great talker, and I listened to him saying hardly a word, nor indeed could I have done so for he left no gaps. When Mrs. Farrer began to sing, I jumped up and said that I must listen to her; after I had moved away he turned around to a friend and said (as was overheard by my brother), "Well, Mr. Darwin's books are much better than his conversation."

Of other great literary men, I once met Sydney Smith at Dean Milman's house. There was something inexplicably amusing in every word which he uttered. Perhaps this was partly due to the expectation of being amused. He was talking about Lady Cork, who was then extremely old. This was the lady who, as he said, was once so much affected by one of his charity sermons, that she *borrowed* a guinea from a friend to put in the plate. He now said, "It is generally believed that my dear old friend Lady Cork has been overlooked," and he said this in such a manner that no one could for a moment doubt that he meant that his dear old friend had been overlooked by the devil. How he managed to express this I know not.

I likewise once met Macaulay at Lord Stanhope's (the historian's) house, and as there was only one other man at dinner, I had a grand opportunity of hearing him converse, and he was very agreeable. He did not talk at all too much; nor indeed could such a man talk too much, as long as he allowed others to turn the stream of his conversation, and this he did allow.

Lord Stanhope once gave me a curious little proof of the accuracy and fullness of Macaulay's memory: many historians used often to meet at Lord Stanhope's house, and in discussing various subjects they would sometimes differ from Macaulay, and formerly they often referred to some book to see who was right; but latterly, as Lord Stanhope noticed, no historian ever took this trouble, and whatever Macaulay said was final.

On another occasion I met at Lord Stanhope's house, one of his parties of historians and other literary men, and amongst them were Motley and Grote. After luncheon I walked about Chevening Park for nearly an hour with Grote, and was much interested by his conversation and pleased by the simplicity and absence of all pretension in his manners.

Long ago I dined occasionally with the old Earl, the father of the historian; he was a strange man, but what little I knew of him I liked much. He was frank, genial, and pleasant. He had strongly marked features, with a brown complexion, and his clothes, when I saw him, were all brown. He seemed to believe in everything which was to others utterly incredible. He said one day to me, "Why don't you give up your fiddle-faddle of geology and zoölogy, and turn to the occult sciences?" The historian, then Lord Mahon, seemed shocked at such a speech to me, and his charming wife much amused.

The last man whom I will mention is Carlyle, seen by me several times at my brother's house, and two or three times at my own house. His talk was very racy and interesting, just like his writings, but he sometimes went on too long on the same subject. I remember a funny dinner at my brother's, where, amongst a few others, were Babbage and Lyell, both of whom liked to talk. Carlyle, however, silenced every one by haranguing during the whole dinner on the advantages of silence. After dinner Babbage, in his grimmest manner, thanked Carlyle for his very interesting lecture on silence.

Carlyle sneered at almost every one: one day in my house he called Grote's "History" "a fetid quagmire, with nothing spiritual about it." I always thought, until his "Reminiscences" appeared, that his sneers were partly jokes, but this now seems rather doubtful. His expression was that of a depressed, almost despondent yet benevolent, man; and it is notorious how heartily he laughed. I believe that his benevolence was real, though stained by not a little jealousy. No one can doubt about his extraordinary power of drawing pictures of things and men—far more vivid, as it appears to me, than any drawn by Macaulay. Whether his pictures of men were true ones is another question.

He has been all-powerful in impressing some grand moral truths on the minds of men. On the other hand, his views about slavery were revolting. In his eyes might was right. His mind seemed to me a very narrow one; even if all branches of science, which he despised, are excluded. It is astonishing to me that Kingsley should have spoken of him as a man well fitted to advance science. He laughed to scorn the idea that a mathematician, such as Whewell, could judge, as I maintained he could, of Goethe's views on light, He thought it a most ridiculous thing that any one should care whether a glacier moved a little quicker or a little slower, or moved at all. As far as I could judge, I never met a man with a mind so ill adapted for scientific research.

Whilst living in London, I attended as regularly as I could the meetings of several scientific societies, and acted as secretary to the Geological Society. But such attendance, and ordinary society, suited my health so badly that we resolved to live in the country, which we both preferred and have never repented of.

RESIDENCE AT DOWN FROM SEPTEMBER 14, 1842, TO THE PRESENT TIME, 1876.

After several fruitless searches in Surrey and elsewhere, we found this house and purchased it. I was pleased with the diversified appearance of vegetation proper to a chalk district, and so unlike what I had been accustomed to in the Midland counties; and still more pleased with the extreme quietness and rusticity of the place. It is not, however, quite so retired a place as a writer in a German periodical makes it, who says that my house can be approached only by a mule-track! Our fixing ourselves here has answered admirably in one way, which we did not anticipate, namely, by being very convenient for frequent visits from our children.

Few persons can have lived a more retired life than we have done. Besides short visits to the houses of relations, and occasionally to the seaside or elsewhere, we have gone nowhere. During the first part of our residence we went a little into society, and received a few friends here; but my health almost always suffered from the excitement, violent shivering and vomiting attacks being thus brought on. I have therefore been compelled for many years to give up all dinner-parties; and this has been somewhat of a deprivation to me, as such parties always put me into high spirits. From the same cause I have been able to invite here very few scientific acquaintances.

My chief enjoyment and sole employment throughout life has been scientific work; and the excitement from such work makes me for the time forget, or drives quite away, my daily discomfort. I have therefore nothing to record during the rest of my life, except the publication of my several books. Perhaps a few details how they arose may be worth giving.

My several Publications.—In the early part of 1844, my

observations on the volcanic islands visited during the voyage of the *Beagle* were published. In 1845, I took much pains in correcting a new edition of my "Journal of Researches," which was originally published in 1839 as part of Fitz-Roy's work. The success of this, my first literary child, always tickles my vanity more than that of any of my other books. Even to this day it sells steadily in England and the United States, and has been translated for the second time into German and into French and other languages. This success of a book of travels, especially of a scientific one, so many years after its first publication, is surprising. Ten thousand copies have been sold in England of the second edition. In 1846 my "Geological Observations on South America" were published. I record in a little diary, which I have always kept, that my three geological books ("Coral Reefs" included) consumed four and a half years' steady work; "and now it is ten years since my return to England. How much time have I lost by illness?" I have nothing to say about these three books except that to my surprise new editions have lately been called for.

In October, 1846, I began to work on "Cirripedia." When on the coast of Chile, I found a most curious form, which burrowed into the shells of Concholepas, and which differed so much from all other Cirripedes that I had to form a new sub-order for its sole reception. Lately an allied burrowing genus has been found on the shores of Portugal. To understand the structure of my new Cirripede I had to examine and dissect many of the common forms; and this gradually led me on to take up the whole group. I worked steadily on this subject for the next eight years, and ultimately published two thick volumes, describing all the known living species, and two thin quartos of the extinct species. I do not doubt that Sir E. Lytton Bulwer had me in his mind when he introduced in one of his novels a Professor Long, who had written two huge volumes on limpets.

Although I was employed during eight years on this work, yet I record in my diary that about two years out of this time was lost by illness. On this account I went in 1848 for some months to Malvern for hydropathic treatment, which did me much good, so that on my return home I was able to

resume work. So much was I out of health that when my
dear father died on November 13th, 1848, I was unable to
attend his funeral or to act as one of his executors.

My work on the Cirripedia possesses, I think, considerable value, as besides describing several new and remarkable
forms, I made out the homologies of the various parts—I discovered the cementing apparatus, though I blundered dreadfully about the cement glands—and lastly I proved the existence in certain genera of minute males complemental to and
parasitic on the hermaphrodites. This latter discovery has
at last been fully confirmed; though at one time a German
writer was pleased to attribute the whole account to my fertile imagination. The Cirripedes form a highly varying and
difficult group of species to class; and my work was of considerable use to me, when I had to discuss in the "Origin of
Species" the principles of a natural classification. Nevertheless, I doubt whether the work was worth the consumption of
so much time.

From September 1854 I devoted my whole time to arranging my huge pile of notes, to observing, and to experiment-
ing in relation to the transmutation of species. During the
voyage of the *Beagle* I had been deeply impressed by discovering in the Pampean formation great fossil animals covered
with armor like that on the existing armadillos; secondly,
by the manner in which closely allied animals replace one
another in proceeding southwards over the Continent; and
thirdly, by the South American character of most of the productions of the Galapagos archipelago, and more especially
by the manner in which they differ slightly on each island of
the group; none of the islands appearing to be very ancient
in a geological sense.

It was evident that such facts as these, as well as many
others, could only be explained on the supposition that
species gradually become modified; and the subject haunted
me. But it was equally evident that neither the action of the
surrounding conditions, nor the will of the organisms (especially in the case of plants) could account for the innumerable cases in which organisms of every kind are beautifully
adapted to their habits of life—for instance, a woodpecker or
a tree-frog to climb trees, or a seed for dispersal by hooks or

plumes. I had always been much struck by such adaptations, and until these could be explained it seemed to me almost useless to endeavor to prove by indirect evidence that species have been modified.

After my return to England it appeared to me that by following the example of Lyell in Geology, and by collecting all facts which bore in any way on the variation of animals and plants under domestication and nature, some light might perhaps be thrown on the whole subject. My first note-book was opened in July 1837. I worked on true Baconian principles, and without any theory collected facts on a wholesale scale, more especially with respect to domesticated productions, by printed enquiries, by conversation with skillful breeders and gardeners, and by extensive reading. When I see the list of books of all kinds which I have read and abstracted, including whole series of Journals and Transactions, I am surprised at my industry. I soon perceived that selection was the keystone of man's success in making useful races of animals and plants. But how selection could be applied to organisms living in a state of nature remained for some time a mystery to me.

In October 1838, that is, fifteen months after I had begun my systematic enquiry, I happened to read for amusement "Malthus on Population," and being well prepared to appreciate the struggle for existence which everywhere goes on from long-continued observation of the habits of animals and plants, it at once struck me that under these circumstances favorable variations would tend to be preserved, and unfavorable ones to be destroyed. The result of this would be the formation of new species. Here then I had at last got a theory by which to work; but I was so anxious to avoid prejudice, that I determined not for some time to write even the briefest sketch of it. In June 1842 I first allowed myself the satisfaction of writing a very brief abstract of my theory in pencil in 35 pages; and this was enlarged during the summer of 1844 into one of 230 pages, which I had fairly copied out and still possess.

But at that time I overlooked one problem of great importance; and it is astonishing to me, except on the principle of Columbus and his egg, how I could have overlooked it and its solution. This problem is the tendency in organic beings descended from the same stock to diverge in character as they become modified. That they have diverged greatly is obvious from the manner in which species of all kinds can be classed under genera, genera under families, families under sub-orders and so forth; and I can remember the very spot in the road, whilst in my carriage, when to my joy the solution occurred to me; and this was long after I had come to Down. The solution, as I believe, is that the modified off-spring of all dominant and increasing forms tend to become adapted to many and highly diversified places in the economy of nature.

Early in 1856 Lyell advised me to write out my views pretty fully, and I began at once to do so on a scale three or four times as extensive as that which was afterwards followed in my "Origin of Species;" yet it was only an abstract of the materials which I had collected, and I got through about half the work on this scale. But my plans were over-thrown, for early in the summer of 1858 Mr. Wallace, who was then in the Malay archipelago, sent me an essay "On the Tendency of Varieties to depart indefinitely from the Original Type;" and this essay contained exactly the same theory as mine. Mr. Wallace expressed the wish that if I thought well of his essay, I should send it to Lyell for perusal.

The circumstances under which I consented at the re-quest of Lyell and Hooker to allow of an abstract from my MS., together with a letter to Asa Gray, dated September 5, 1857, to be published at the same time with Wallace's Essay, are given in the "Journal of the Proceedings of the Linnean Society," 1858, p. 45. I was at first very unwilling to consent, as I thought Mr. Wallace might consider my doing so un-justifiable, for I did not then know how generous and noble was his disposition. The extract from my MS. and the letter to Asa Gray had neither been intended for publication, and were badly written. Mr. Wallace's essay, on the other hand, was admirably expressed and quite clear. Nevertheless, our joint productions excited very little attention, and the only published notice of them which I can remember was by Professor Haughton of Dublin, whose verdict was that all that was new in them was false, and what was true was old. This shows how necessary it is that any new view should be explained at considerable length in order to arouse public attention.

In September 1858 I set to work by the strong advice of Lyell and Hooker to prepare a volume on the transmutation of species, but was often interrupted by ill-health, and short visits to Dr. Lane's delightful hydropathic establishment at Moor Park. I abstracted the MS. begun on a much larger scale in 1856, and completed the volume on the same reduced scale. It cost me thirteen months and ten days' hard labor. It was published under the title of the "Origin of Species," in November 1859. Though considerably added to and corrected in the later editions, it has remained substantially the same book.

It is no doubt the chief work of my life. It was from the first highly successful. The first small edition of 1250 copies was sold on the day of publication, and a second edition of 3000 copies soon afterwards. Sixteen thousand copies have now (1876) been sold in England; and considering how stiff a book it is, this is a large sale. It has been translated into almost every European tongue, even into such languages as Spanish, Bohemian, Polish, and Russian. It has also, according to Miss Bird, been translated into Japanese, and is there much studied. Even an essay in Hebrew has appeared on it, showing that the theory is contained in the Old Testament! The reviews were very numerous; for some time I collected all that appeared on the "Origin" and on my related books, and these amount (excluding newspaper reviews) to 265; but after a time I gave up the attempt in despair. Many separate essays and books on the subject have appeared; and in Germany a catalogue or bibliography on "Darwinismus" has appeared every year or two.

The success of the "Origin" may, I think, be attributed in large part to my having long before written two condensed sketches, and to my having finally abstracted a much larger manuscript, which was itself an abstract. By this means I was enabled to select the more striking facts and conclusions. I had, also, during many years followed a golden rule, namely, that whenever a published fact, a new observation or thought came across me, which was opposed to my general results, to make a memorandum of it without fail and at once; for I had found by experience that such facts and thoughts were far more apt to escape from the memory than favorable ones. Owing to this habit, very few objections were raised against my views which I had not at least noticed and attempted to answer.

It has sometimes been said that the success of the "Origin" proved "that the subject was in the air," or "that men's minds were prepared for it." I do not think that this is strictly true, for I occasionally sounded not a few naturalists, and never happened to come across a single one who seemed to doubt about the permanence of species. Even Lyell and Hooker, though they would listen with interest to me, never seemed to agree. I tried once or twice to explain to able men what I meant by Natural Selection, but signally failed. What I believe was strictly true is that innumerable well-observed facts were stored in the minds of naturalists ready to take their proper places as soon as any theory which would receive them was sufficiently explained. Another element in the success of the book was its moderate size; and this I owe to the appearance of Mr. Wallace's essay; had I published on the scale in which I began to write in 1856, the book would have been four or five times as large as the "Origin," and very few would have had the patience to read it.

I gained much by my delay in publishing from about 1839, when the theory was clearly conceived, to 1859; and I lost nothing by it, for I cared very little whether men attributed most originality to me or Wallace; and his essay no doubt aided in the reception of the theory. I was forestalled in only one important point, which my vanity has always made me regret, namely, the explanation by means of the Glacial period of the presence of the same species of plants and of some few animals on distant mountain summits and in the arctic regions. This view pleased me so much that I wrote it out in extenso, and I believe that it was read by Hooker some years before E. Forbes published his celebrated memoir on the subject. In the very few points in which we differed, I still think that I was in the right. I have never, of course, alluded in print to my having independently worked out this view.

Hardly any point gave me so much satisfaction when I was at work on the "Origin," as the explanation of the wide difference in many classes between the embryo and the adult animal, and of the close resemblance of the embryos within the same class. No notice of this point was taken, as far as I remember, in the early reviews of the "Origin," and I recollect expressing my surprise on this head in a letter to Asa Gray. Within late years several reviewers have given the whole credit to Fritz Müller and Häckel, who undoubtedly have worked it out much more fully, and in some respects more correctly than I did. I had materials for a whole chapter on the subject, and I ought to have made the discussion longer; for it is clear that I failed to impress my readers; and he who succeeds in doing so deserves, in my opinion, all the credit.

This leads me to remark that I have almost always been treated honestly by my reviewers, passing over those without scientific knowledge as not worthy of notice. My views have often been grossly misrepresented, bitterly opposed and ridiculed, but this has been generally done, as I believe, in good faith. On the whole I do not doubt that my works have been over and over again greatly overpraised. I rejoice that I have avoided controversies, and this I owe to Lyell, who many years ago, in reference to my geological works, strongly advised me never to get entangled in a controversy, as it rarely did any good whatsoever and caused a miserable loss of time and temper.

Whenever I have found out that I have blundered, or that my work has been imperfect, and when I have been contemptuously criticized, and even when I have been overpraised, so that I have felt mortified, it has been my greatest comfort to say hundreds of times to myself that "I have worked as hard and as well as I could, and no man can do more than this." I remember when in Good Success Bay, in Tierra del Fuego, thinking (and, I believe, that I wrote home to the effect) that I could not employ my life better than in adding a little to Natural Science. This I have done to the best of my abilities, and critics may say what they like, but they cannot destroy this conviction.

During the two last months of 1859, I was fully occupied

in preparing a second edition of the "Origin," and by an enormous correspondence. On January 1st, 1860, I began arranging my notes for my work on the "Variation of Animals and Plants under Domestication;" but it was not published until the beginning of 1868; the delay having been caused partly by frequent illnesses, one of which lasted seven months, and partly by being tempted to publish on other subjects which at the time interested me more.

On May 15th, 1862, my little book on the "Fertilization of Orchids," which cost me ten months' work, was published: most of the facts had been slowly accumulated during several previous years. During the summer of 1839, and, I believe, during the previous summer, I was led to attend to the cross-fertilization of flowers by the aid of insects, from having come to the conclusion in my speculations on the origin of species, that crossing played an important part in keeping specific forms constant. I attended to the subject more or less during every subsequent summer; and my interest in it was greatly enhanced by having procured and read in November 1841, through the advice of Robert Brown, a copy of C. K. Sprengel's wonderful book, "Das entdeckte Geheimniss der Natur." For some years before 1862 I had specially attended to the fertilization of our British orchids; and it seemed to me the best plan to prepare as complete a treatise on this group of plants as well as I could, rather than to utilize the great mass of matter which I had slowly collected with respect to other plants.

My resolve proved a wise one; for since the appearance of my book, a surprising number of papers and separate works on the fertilization of all kinds of flowers have appeared: and these are far better done than I could possibly have effected. The merits of poor old Sprengel, so long overlooked, are now fully recognized many years after his death.

During the same year I published in the "Journal of the Linnean Society" a paper "On the Two Forms, or Dimorphic Condition of Primula," and during the next five years, five other papers on dimorphic and trimorphic plants. I do not think anything in my scientific life has given me so much satisfaction as making out the meaning of the structure of these plants. I had noticed in 1838 or 1839 the dimorphism of *Linum flavum,* and had at first thought that it was merely a case of unmeaning variability. But on examining the common species of Primula I found that the two forms were much too regular and constant to be thus viewed. I therefore became almost convinced that the common cowslip and primrose were on the high road to become diœcious;—that the short pistil in the one form, and the short stamens in the other form were tending towards abortion. The plants were therefore subjected under this point of view to trial; but as soon as the flowers with short pistil fertilized with pollen from the short stamens, were found to yield more seeds than any other of the four possible unions, the abortion-theory was knocked on the head. After some additional experiment, it became evident that the two forms, though both were perfect hermaphrodites, bore almost the same relation to one another as do the two sexes of an ordinary animal. With Lythrum we have the still more wonderful case of three forms standing in a similar relation to one another. I afterwards found that the offspring from the union of two plants belonging to the same forms presented a close and curious analogy with hybrids from the union of two distinct species.

In the autumn of 1864 I finished a long paper on "Climbing Plants," and sent it to the Linnean Society. The writing of this paper cost me four months; but I was so unwell when I received the proof-sheets that I was forced to leave them very badly and often obscurely expressed. The paper was little noticed, but when in 1875 it was corrected and published as a separate book it sold well. I was led to take up this subject by reading a short paper by Asa Gray, published in 1858. He sent me seeds, and on raising some plants I was so much fascinated and perplexed by the revolving movements of the tendrils and stems, which movements are really very simple, though appearing at first sight very complex, that I procured various other kinds of climbing plants, and studied the whole subject. I was all the more attracted to it, from not being at all satisfied with the explanation which Henslow gave us in his lectures, about twining plants, namely, that they had a natural tendency to grow up in a spire. This explanation proved quite erroneous. Some of the adaptations displayed by Climbing Plants are as beautiful as those of Orchids for ensuring cross-fertilization.

My "Variation of Animals and Plants under Domestication" was begun, as already stated, in the beginning of 1860, but was not published until the beginning of 1868. It was a big book, and cost me four years and two months' hard labor. It gives all my observations and an immense number of facts collected from various sources, about our domestic productions. In the second volume the causes and laws of variation, inheritance, &c., are discussed as far as our present state of knowledge permits. Towards the end of the work I give my well-abused hypothesis of Pangenesis. An unverified hypothesis is of little or no value; but if any one should hereafter be led to make observations by which some such hypothesis could be established, I shall have done good service, as an astonishing number of isolated facts can be thus connected together and rendered intelligible. In 1875 a second and largely corrected edition, which cost me a good deal of labor, was brought out.

My "Descent of Man" was published in February, 1871. As soon as I had become, in the year 1837 or 1838, convinced that species were mutable productions, I could not avoid the belief that man must come under the same law. Accordingly I collected notes on the subject for my own satisfaction, and not for a long time with any intention of publishing. Although in the "Origin of Species" the derivation of any particular species is never discussed, yet I thought it best, in order that no honorable man should accuse me of concealing my views, to add that by the work "light would be thrown on the origin of man and his history." It would have been useless and injurious to the success of the book to have paraded, without giving any evidence, my conviction with respect to his origin.

But when I found that many naturalists fully accepted the doctrine of the evolution of species, it seemed to me advisable to work up such notes as I possessed, and to publish a special treatise on the origin of man. I was the more glad to do so, as it gave me an opportunity of fully discussing sexual selection—a subject which had always greatly interested me. This subject, and that of the variation of our domestic productions, together with the causes and laws of variation, inheritance, and the intercrossing of plants, are the sole subjects which I have been able to write about in full, so as to use all the materials which I have collected. The "Descent of Man" took me three years to write, but then as usual some of this time was lost by ill health, and some was consumed by preparing new editions and other minor works. A second and largely corrected edition of the "Descent" appeared in 1874.

My book on the "Expression of the Emotions in Men and Animals" was published in the autumn of 1872. I had intended to give only a chapter on the subject in the "Descent of Man," but as soon as I began to put my notes together, I saw that it would require a separate treatise.

My first child was born on December 27th, 1839, and I at once commenced to make notes on the first dawn of the various expressions which he exhibited, for I felt convinced, even at this early period, that the most complex and fine shades of expression must all have had a gradual and natural origin. During the summer of the following year, 1840, I read Sir C. Bell's admirable work on expression, and this greatly increased the interest which I felt in the subject, though I could not at all agree with his belief that various muscles had been specially created for the sake of expression. From this time forward I occasionally attended to the subject, both with respect to man and our domesticated animals. My book sold largely; 5267 copies having been disposed of on the day of publication.

In the summer of 1860 I was idling and resting near Hartfield, where two species of Drosera abound; and I noticed that numerous insects had been entrapped by the leaves. I carried home some plants, and on giving them insects saw the movements of the tentacles, and this made me think it probable that the insects were caught for some special purpose. Fortunately a crucial test occurred to me, that of placing a large number of leaves in various nitrogenous and non-nitrogenous fluids of equal density; and as soon as I found that the former alone excited energetic movements, it was obvious that here was a fine new field for investigation.

During subsequent years, whenever I had leisure, I pursued my experiments, and my book on "Insectivorous Plants" was published in July 1875—that is, sixteen years after my first observations. The delay in this case, as with all my other books, has been a great advantage to me; for a man after a long interval can criticize his own work, almost as well as if it were that of another person. The fact that a plant should secrete, when properly excited, a fluid containing an acid and ferment, closely analogous to the digestive fluid of an animal, was certainly a remarkable discovery.

During this autumn of 1876 I shall publish on the "Effects of Cross and Self-Fertilization in the Vegetable Kingdom." This book will form a complement to that on the "Fertilization of Orchids," in which I showed how perfect were the means for cross-fertilization, and here I shall show how important are the results. I was led to make, during eleven years, the numerous experiments recorded in this volume, by a mere accidental observation; and indeed it required the accident to be repeated before my attention was thoroughly aroused to the remarkable fact that seedlings of self-fertilized parentage are inferior, even in the first generation, in height and vigor to seedlings of cross-fertilized parentage. I hope also to republish a revised edition of my book on Orchids, and hereafter my papers on dimorphic and trimorphic plants, together with some additional observations on allied points which I never have had time to arrange. My strength will then probably be exhausted, and I shall be ready to exclaim "Nunc dimittis."

Written May 1st, 1881.—"The Effects of Cross and Self-Fertilization" was published in the autumn of 1876; and the results there arrived at explain, as I believe, the endless and wonderful contrivances for the transportal of pollen from one plant to another of the same species. I now believe, however, chiefly from the observations of Hermann Müller, that I ought to have insisted more strongly than I did on the many adaptations for self-fertilization; though I was well aware of many such adaptations. A much enlarged edition of my "Fertilization of Orchids" was published in 1877.

In this same year "The Different Forms of Flowers, &c.," appeared, and in 1880 a second edition. This book consists chiefly of the several papers on Heterostyled flowers originally published by the Linnean Society, corrected, with much new matter added, together with observations on some other cases in which the same plant bears two kinds of flowers. As before remarked, no little discovery of mine ever gave me so much pleasure as the making out the meaning of heterostyled flowers. The results of crossing such flowers in an illegitimate manner, I believe to be very important, as bearing on the sterility of hybrids; although these results have been noticed by only a few persons.

In 1879, I had a translation of Dr. Ernst Krause's "Life of Erasmus Darwin" published, and I added a sketch of his character and habits from material in my possession. Many persons have been much interested by this little life, and I am surprised that only 800 or 900 copies were sold.

In 1880 I published, with [my son] Frank's assistance, our "Power of Movement in Plants." This was a tough piece of work. The book bears somewhat the same relation to my little book on "Climbing Plants," which "Cross-Fertilization," did to the "Fertilization of Orchids"; for in accordance with the principle of evolution it was impossible to account for climbing plants having been developed in so many widely different groups unless all kinds of plants possess some slight power of movement of an analogous kind. This I proved to be the case; and I was further led to a rather wide generalization, viz. that the great and important classes of movements, excited by light, the attraction of gravity, &c., are all modified forms of the fundamental movement of circumnutation. It has always pleased me to exalt plants in the scale of organized beings; and I therefore felt an especial pleasure in showing how many and what admirably well adapted movements the tip of a root possesses.

I have now (May 1, 1881) sent to the printers the MS. of a little book on "The Formation of Vegetable Mold, through the Action of Worms." This is a subject of but small importance; and I know not whether it will interest any readers, but it has interested me. It is the completion of a short paper read before the Geological Society more than forty years ago, and has revived old geological thoughts.

I have now mentioned all the books which I have published, and these have been the milestones in my life, so that little remains to be said. I am not conscious of any change in my mind during the last thirty years, excepting in one point presently to be mentioned; nor, indeed, could any change have been expected unless one of general deterioration. But my father lived to his eighty-third year with his mind as lively as ever it was, and all his faculties undimmed; and I hope that I may die before my mind fails to a sensible extent. I think that I have become a little more skillful in guessing right explanations and in devising experimental tests; but this may probably be the result of mere practice, and of a larger store of knowledge. I have as much difficulty as ever in expressing myself clearly and concisely; and this difficulty has caused me a very great loss of time; but it has had the compensating advantage of forcing me to think long and intently about every sentence, and thus I have been led to see errors in reasoning and in my own observations or those of others.

There seems to be a sort of fatality in my mind leading me to put at first my statement or proposition in a wrong or awkward form. Formerly I used to think about my sentences before writing them down; but for several years I have found that it saves time to scribble in a vile hand whole pages as quickly as I possibly can, contracting half the words; and then correct deliberately. Sentences thus scribbled down are often better ones than I could have written deliberately.

Having said thus much about my manner of writing, I will add that with my large books I spend a good deal of time over the general arrangement of the matter. I first make the rudest outline in two or three pages, and then a larger one in several pages, a few words or one word standing for a whole discussion or series of facts. Each one of these headings is again enlarged and often transferred before I began to write *in extenso*. As in several of my books facts observed by others have been very extensively used, and as I have always had several quite distinct subjects in hand at the same time, I may mention that I keep from thirty to forty large portfolios, in cabinets with labeled shelves, into which I can at once put a detached reference or memorandum. I have bought many books, and at their ends I make an index of all the facts that concern my work; or, if the book is not my own, write out a separate abstract and of such abstracts I have a large drawer full. Before

beginning on any subject I look to all the short indexes and
make a general and classified index, and by taking the one
or more proper portfolios I have all the information collected
during my life ready for use.

I have said that in one respect my mind has changed
during the last twenty or thirty years. Up to the age of
thirty, or beyond it, poetry of many kinds, such as the works
of Milton, Gray, Byron, Wordsworth, Coleridge, and Shelley,
gave me great pleasure, and even as a schoolboy I took intense delight in Shakespeare, especially in the historical
plays. I have also said that formerly pictures gave me considerable, and music very great delight. But now for many
years I cannot endure to read a line of poetry: I have tried
lately to read Shakespeare, and found it so intolerably dull
that it nauseated me. I have also almost lost my taste for
pictures or music. Music generally sets me thinking too en-
ergetically on what I have been at work on, instead of giving
me pleasure. I retain some taste for fine scenery, but it does
not cause me the exquisite delight which it formerly did.
On the other hand, novels which are works of the imagination, though not of a very high order, have been for years
a wonderful relief and pleasure to me, and I often bless all
novelists. A surprising number have been read aloud to me,
and I like all if moderately good, and if they do not end unhappily—against which a law ought to be passed. A novel,
according to my taste, does not come into the first class
unless it contains some person whom one can thoroughly love,
and if a pretty woman all the better.

This curious and lamentable loss of the higher æsthetic
tastes is all the odder, as books on history, biographies, and
travels (independently of any scientific facts which they may
contain), and essays on all sorts of subjects interest me as
much as ever they did. My mind seems to have become a
kind of machine for grinding general laws out of large collections of facts, but why this should have caused the atrophy
of that part of the brain alone, on which the higher tastes
depend, I cannot conceive. A man with a mind more highly
organized or better constituted than mine, would not, I suppose, have thus suffered; and if I had to live my life again,
I would have made a rule to read some poetry and listen to

some music at least once every week; for perhaps the parts of my brain now atrophied would thus have been kept active through use. The loss of these tastes is a loss of happiness, and may possibly be injurious to the intellect, and more probably to the moral character, by enfeebling the emotional part of our nature.

My books have sold largely in England, have been translated into many languages, and passed through several editions in foreign countries. I have heard it said that the success of a work abroad is the best test of its enduring value. I doubt whether this is at all trustworthy; but judged by this standard my name ought to last for a few years. Therefore it may be worth while to try to analyze the mental qualities and the conditions on which my success has depended; though I am aware that no man can do this correctly.

I have no great quickness of apprehension or wit which is so remarkable in some clever men, for instance, Huxley. I am therefore a poor critic: a paper or book, when first read, generally excites my admiration, and it is only after considerable reflection that I perceive the weak points. My power to follow a long and purely abstract train of thought is very limited; and therefore I could never have succeeded with metaphysics or mathematics. My memory is extensive, yet hazy: it suffices to make me cautious by vaguely telling me that I have observed or read something opposed to the conclusion which I am drawing, or on the other hand in favor of it; and after a time I can generally recollect where to search for my authority. So poor in one sense is my memory, that I have never been able to remember for more than a few days a single date or a line of poetry.

Some of my critics have said, "Oh, he is a good observer, but he has no power of reasoning!" I do not think that this can be true, for the "Origin of Species" is one long argument from the beginning to the end, and it has convinced not a few able men. No one could have written it without having some power of reasoning. I have a fair share of invention, and of common sense or judgment, such as every fairly successful lawyer or doctor must have, but not, I believe, in any higher degree.

On the favorable side of the balance, I think that I am superior to the common run of men in noticing things which easily escape attention, and in observing them carefully. My industry has been nearly as great as it could have been in the observation and collection of facts. What is far more important, my love of natural science has been steady and ardent.

This pure love has, however, been much aided by the ambition to be esteemed by my fellow naturalists. From my early youth I have had the strongest desire to understand or explain whatever I observed,—that is, to group all facts under some general laws. These causes combined have given me the patience to reflect or ponder for any number of years over any unexplained problem. As far as I can judge, I am not apt to follow blindly the lead of other men. I have steadily endeavored to keep my mind free so as to give up any hypothesis, however much beloved (and I cannot resist forming one on every subject), as soon as facts are shown to be opposed to it. Indeed, I have had no choice but to act in this manner, for with the exception of the Coral Reefs, I cannot remember a single first-formed hypothesis which had not after a time to be given up or greatly modified. This has naturally led me to distrust greatly deductive reasoning in the mixed sciences. On the other hand, I am not very skeptical,—a frame of mind which I believe to be injurious to the progress of science. A good deal of skepticism in a scientific man is advisable to avoid much loss of time, but I have met with not a few men, who, I feel sure, have often thus been deterred from experiment or observations, which would have proved directly or indirectly serviceable.

In illustration, I will give the oddest case which I have known. A gentleman (who, as I afterwards heard, is a good local botanist) wrote to me from the Eastern counties that the seed or beans of the common field-bean had this year everywhere grown on the wrong side of the pod. I wrote back, asking for further information, as I did not understand what was meant; but I did not receive any answer for a very long time. I then saw in two newspapers, one published in Kent and the other in Yorkshire, paragraphs stating that it was a most remarkable fact that "the beans this year had all grown on the wrong side." So I thought there must be some foundation for so general a statement. Accordingly, I went to my gardener, an old Kentish man, and asked him whether he had heard anything about it, and he answered, "Oh, no, sir, it must be a mistake, for the beans grow on the wrong side only on leap-year, and this is not leap-year." I then asked him how they grew in common years and how on leap-years, but soon found that he knew absolutely nothing of how they grew at any time, but he stuck to his belief.

After a time I heard from my first informant, who, with many apologies, said that he should not have written to me had he not heard the statement from several intelligent farmers; but that he had since spoken again to every one of them, and not one knew in the least what he had himself meant. So that here a belief—if indeed a statement with no definite idea attached to it can be called a belief—had spread over almost the whole of England without any vestige of evidence.

I have known in the course of my life only three intentionally falsified statements, and one of these may have been a hoax (and there have been several scientific hoaxes) which, however, took in an American Agricultural Journal. It related to the formation in Holland of a new breed of oxen by the crossing of distinct species of Bos (some of which I happen to know are sterile together), and the author had the impudence to state that he had corresponded with me, and that I had been deeply impressed with the importance of his result. The article was sent to me by the editor of an English Agricultural Journal, asking for my opinion before republishing it.

A second case was an account of several varieties, raised by the author from several species of Primula, which had spontaneously yielded a full complement of seed, although the parent plants had been carefully protected from the access of insects. This account was published before I had discovered the meaning of heterostylism, and the whole statement must have been fraudulent, or there was neglect in excluding insects so gross as to be scarcely credible.

The third case was more curious: Mr. Huth published in his book on "Consanguineous Marriage" some long extracts from a Belgian author, who stated that he had interbred rabbits in the closest manner for very many generations, without the least injurious effects. The account was published in a most respectable Journal, that of the Royal Society of Belgium; but I could not avoid feeling doubts—I hardly know why, except that there were no accidents of any kind, and my experience in breeding animals made me think this very improbable.

So with much hesitation I wrote to Prefessor Van Beneden, asking him whether the author was a trustworthy man. I soon heard in answer that the Society had been greatly shocked by discovering that the whole account was a fraud. The writer had been publicly challenged in the Journal to say where he had resided and kept his large stock of rabbits while carrying on his experiments, which must have consumed several years, and no answer could be extracted from him.

My habits are methodical, and this has been of not a little use for my particular line of work. Lastly, I have had ample leisure from not having to earn my own bread. Even ill-health, though it has annihilated several years of my life, has saved me from the distractions of society and amusement.

Therefore my success as a man of science, whatever this may have amounted to, has been determined, as far as I can judge, by complex and diversified mental qualities and conditions. Of these, the most important have been—the love of science—unbounded patience in long reflecting over any subject—industry in observing and collecting facts—and a fair share of invention as well as of common sense. With such moderate abilities as I possess, it is truly surprising that I should have influenced to a considerable extent the belief of scientific men on some important points.

CHARLES DICKENS

CHARLES DICKENS

1812-1870

INTRODUCTORY NOTE

In one way the writings of Charles Dickens are all autobiographical; for in his novels he drew constantly upon his own experience, especially those of his impoverished childhood. He had, however, suffered so severely in that childhood that he could never bear to refer to it, even among his closest friends, except in the veiled fashion of fiction. Hence it is himself he describes in "David Copperfield," in "Little Dorrit," and so on; yet only once in his life did he turn openly to autobiography. This was in response to the appeal of his friend John Forster, who wrote the standard "Life of Dickens," which is still in use. In this work of Forster's is inserted the brief autobiographical fragment which Dickens sent him, the fragment given here.

To understand this brief sketch of Dickens' childhood, the reader must know something further of the boy's surroundings. His father was a clerk in government employ, but lost his place through the rearrangement of the department and sank into dire poverty and was ultimately arrested for debt and spent two years in prison. Charles was ten years old at the time of the arrest and was set to work in a blacking factory. James Lamert, manager of the factory, had once boarded with the family, and now offered to help by giving the boy a place. Perhaps if the story of what followed could be told from the viewpoint of the despairing father and sorely harassed mother it might wear a very different aspect; for Dickens is so wrought up over his own childish shame and suffering that he tells his tale wholly in resentment at his grievances.

AN AUTOBIOGRAPHICAL FRAGMENT

In an evil hour for me, as I often bitterly thought, its chief manager, James Lamert, who had lived with us in Bayham Street, seeing how I was employed from day to day, and knowing what our domestic circumstances then were, proposed that I should go into the blacking warehouse, to be as useful as I could, at a salary, I think, of six shillings a week. I am not clear whether it was six or seven. I am inclined to believe, from my uncertainty on this head, that it was six at first, and seven afterward. At any rate the offer was accepted very willingly by my father and mother, and on a Monday morning I went down to the blacking warehouse to begin my business life.

It is wonderful to me how I could have been so easily cast away at such an age. It is wonderful to me, that, even after my descent into the poor little drudge I have been since we came to London, no one had compassion enough on me—a child of singular abilities, quick, eager, delicate, and soon hurt, bodily or mentally—to suggest that something might have been spared, as certainly it might have been, to place me at any common school. Our friends, I take it, were tired out. No one made any sign. My father and mother were quite satisfied. They could hardly have been more so, if I had been twenty years of age, distinguished at a grammar school, and going to Cambridge.

Our relative had kindly arranged to teach me something in the dinner-hour, from twelve to one, I think it was, every day. But an arrangement so incompatible with counting-house business soon died away, from no fault of his or mine; and for the same reason, my small work-table, and my grosses of pots, my papers, string, scissors, paste-pot, and labels, by little and little, vanished out of the recess in the counting-house, and kept company with the other small work-tables, grosses of pots, papers, string, scissors, and paste-pots, down-stairs. It was not long before Bob Fagin and I, and another boy whose name was Paul Green, but who was currently believed to have been christened Poll (a belief which I transferred, long afterward again, to Mr. Sweedlepipe, in "Martin Chuzzlewit"), worked generally side by side. Bob Fagin was an orphan, and lived with his brother-in-law, a waterman. Poll Green's father had the additional distinction of being a fireman, and was employed at Drury Lane theater; where another relation of Poll's, I think his little sister, did imps in the pantomimes.

No words can express the secret agony of my soul as I

sunk into this companionship; compared these every day associates with those of my happier childhood; and felt my early
hopes of growing up to be a learned and distinguished man,
crushed in my breast. The deep remembrance of the sense I
had of being utterly neglected and hopeless; of the shame I
felt in my position; of the misery it was to my young heart
to believe that, day by day, what I had learned, and thought,
and delighted in, and raised my fancy and my emulation up
by, was passing away from me, never to be brought back any
more, cannot be written. My whole nature was so penetrated
with the grief and humiliation of such considerations that even
now, famous and caressed and happy, I often forget in my
dreams that I have a dear wife and children; even that I am
a man; and wander desolately back to that time of my life.

I know I do not exaggerate, unconsciously and unintention-
ally, the scantiness of my resources and the difficulties of my
life. I know that if a shilling or so were given me by any
one, I spent it in a dinner or a tea. I know that I worked,
from morning to night, with common men and boys, a shabby
child. I know that I tried, but ineffectually, not to anticipate
my money, and to make it last the week through; by putting
it away in a drawer I had in the counting-house, wrapped into
six little parcels, each parcel containing the same amount, and
labeled with a different day. I know that I have lounged
about the streets, insufficiently and unsatisfactorily fed. I
know that, but for the mercy of God, I might easily have been,
for any care that was taken of me, a little robber or a little
vagabond.

But I held some station at the blacking warehouse too.
Besides that my relative at the counting-house did what a man
so occupied, and dealing with a thing so anomalous, could, to
treat me as one upon a different footing from the rest, I never
said, to man or boy, how it was that I came to be there, or gave
the least indication of being sorry that I was there. That I
suffered in secret, and that I suffered exquisitely, no one ever
knew but I. How much I suffered, it is, as I have said already,
utterly beyond my power to tell. No man's imagination can
overstep the reality. But I kept my own counsel, and I did
my work. I knew from the first, that if I could not do my
work as well as any of the rest, I could not hold myself above

slight and contempt. I soon became at least as expeditious and as skillful with my hands, as either of the other boys. Though perfectly familiar with them, my conduct and manners were different enough from theirs to place a space between us. They and the men always spoke of me as "the young gentleman." A certain man (a soldier once) named Thomas, who was the foreman, and another man Harry, who was the carman, and wore a red jacket, used to call me "Charles" sometimes in speaking to me; but I think it was mostly when we were very confidential, and when I had made some efforts to entertain them over our work with the results of some of the old readings, which were fast perishing out of my mind. Poll Green uprose once, and rebelled against the "young gentleman" usage; but Bob Fagin settled him speedily.

My rescue from this kind of existence I considered quite hopeless, and abandoned as such, altogether; though I am solemnly convinced that I never, for one hour, was reconciled to it, or was otherwise than miserably unhappy. I felt keenly, however, the being so cut off from my parents, my brothers, and sisters; and, when my day's work was done, going home to such a miserable blank. And *that*, I thought, might be corrected. One Sunday night I remonstrated with my father on this head, so pathetically and with so many tears, that his kind nature gave way. He began to think that it was not quite right. I do believe he had never thought so before, or thought about it. It was the first remonstrance I had ever made about my lot, and perhaps it opened up a little more than I intended. A back-attic was found for me at the house of an insolvent court agent, who lived in Lant Street in the Borough, where Bob Sawyer lodged many years afterward. A bed and bedding were sent over for me, and made up on the floor. The little window had a pleasant prospect of a timber-yard; and when I took possession of my new abode, I thought it was a paradise. . . .

Bob Fagin was very good to me on the occasion of a bad attack of my old disorder, cramps. I suffered such excruciating pain that time, that they made a temporary bed of straw in my old recess in the counting-house, and I rolled about on the floor, and Bob filled empty blacking-bottles with hot

water, and applied relays of them to my side, half the day. I
got better, and quite easy toward evening; but Bob (who was
much bigger and older than I) did not like the idea of my
going home alone, and took me under his protection. I was
too proud to let him know about the prison; and after making several efforts to get rid of him, to all of which Bob Fagin,
in his goodness, was deaf, shook hands with him on the steps
of a house near Southwark Bridge on the Surrey side, making
believe that I lived there. As a finishing piece of reality in
case of his looking back, I knocked at the door, I recollect, and
asked, when the woman opened it, if that was Mr. Robert
Fagin's house.

My usual way home was over Blackfriars Bridge, and down
that turning in the Blackfriars Road which has Rowland
Hill's chapel on one side, and the likeness of a golden dog
licking a golden pot over a shop door on the other. There
are a good many little low-browed old shops in that street,
of a wretched kind; and some are unchanged now. I looked
into one a few weeks ago, where I used to buy bootlaces on
Saturday nights and saw the corner where I once sat down
on a stool to have a pair of ready-made half-boots fitted on.
I have been seduced more than once, in that street on a Saturday night, by a show-van at a corner; and have gone in, with
a very motley assemblage, to see the Fat Pig, the Wild Indian,
and the Little Lady. There were two or three hat manufac-
tories there, then (I think they are there still); and among
the things which, encountered anywhere, or under any circumstances, will instantly recall that time, is the smell of hat-
making.

I was such a little fellow, with my poor white hat, little
jacket, and corduroy trousers, that frequently, when I went
into the bar of a strange public-house for a glass of ale or
porter to wash down the saveloy and the loaf I had eaten in
the street, they didn't like to give it me. I remember, one
evening (I had been somewhere for my father, and was going
back to the Borough over Westminster Bridge), that I went
into a public-house in Parliament Street, which is still there
though altered, at the corner of the short street leading into
Cannon Row, and said to the landlord behind the bar, "What
is your very best—the VERY *best*—ale, a glass?" For, the

occasion was a festive one, for some reason: I forget why. It may have been my birthday, or somebody else's. "Two-pence," says he. "Then," says I, "just draw me a glass of that, if you please, with a good head to it." The landlord looked at me, in return, over the bar, from head to foot, with a strange smile on his face; and instead of drawing the beer, looked round the screen and said something to his wife, who came out from behind it, with her work in her hand, and joined him in surveying me. Here we stand, all three, before me now, in my study in Devonshire Terrace. The landlord in his shirt-sleeves, leaning against the bar window-frame; his wife looking over the little half-door; and I, in some confusion, looking up at them from outside the partition. They asked me a good many questions, as what my name was, how old I was, where I lived, how I was employed, etc., etc. To all of which, that I might commit nobody, I invented appropriate answers. They served me with the ale, though I suspect it was not the strongest on the premises; and the landlord's wife, opening the little half-door and bending down, gave me a kiss that was half-admiring and half-compassionate, but all womanly and good, I am sure.

At last, one day, my father, and the relative so often mentioned, quarreled; quarreled by letter, for I took the letter from my father to him which caused the explosion, but quarreled very fiercely. It was about me. It may have had some backward reference, in part, for anything I know, to my employment at the window. All I am certain of is, that, soon after I had given him the letter, my cousin (he was a sort of cousin by marriage) told me he was very much insulted about me; and that it was impossible to keep me, after that. I cried very much, partly because it was so sudden, and partly because in his anger he was violent about my father, though gentle to me. Thomas, the old soldier, comforted me, and said he was sure it was for the best. With a relief so strange that it was like oppression, I went home.

My mother set herself to accommodate the quarrel, and did so next day. She brought home a request for me to return next morning, and a high character of me, which I am very sure I deserved. My father said I should go back no more, and should go to school. I do not write resentfully or angrily:

for I know how all these things have worked together to make me what I am; but I never afterward forgot, I never shall forget, I never can forget, that my mother was warm for my being sent back.

From that hour until this at which I write no word of that part of my childhood ,which I have now gladly brought to a close, has passed my lips to any human being. I have no idea how long it lasted; whether for a year, or much more, or less. From that hour, until this, my father and my mother have been stricken dumb upon it. I have never heard the least allusion to it, however far off and remote, from either of them. I have never, until I now impart it to this paper, in any burst of confidence with any one, my own wife not excepted, raised the curtain I then dropped, thank God.

RICHARD WAGNER

RICHARD WAGNER

1813-1883

INTRODUCTORY NOTE

Richard Wagner wrote no complete autobiography; he did, however, in his many literary pamphlets, and especially in his letters to that other musical genius, Liszt, write so frequently about himself that the world possesses a good many autobiographical fragments, which might almost be strung together, as those of Luther have been, to form a life-narrative in Wagner's own words.

As a youth, Wagner received an excellent German education at Dresden. He early turned his whole thought to composing music, and after some hardship won success in 1842 with the production of his opera "Rienzi." He was then made the court director of music in Dresden, and there produced the earlier of his great operas, "The Flying Dutchman" and "Tannhäuser." In 1848 he was deprived of office and driven into exile for his support of the people's uprisings of that memorable year. Then followed many weary days of struggle, hardship and even of public ridicule. Not until 1865 did Wagner ultimately find rest and security under the patronage of the music-loving king of Bavaria. In that South-German land, at Munich and afterward at his own specially created theater at Baireuth, he composed his last and greatest music dramas.

WAGNER'S ACCOUNT OF HIMSELF

I was born at Leipzig on May the 22d, 1813. My father was a police actuary, and died six months after I was born. My stepfather, Ludwig Geyer, was a comedian and painter; he was also the author of a few stage plays, of which one, "Der Bethlehemitische Kindermord" (The Slaughter of the Innocents), had a certain success. My whole family migrated with him to Dresden. He wished me to become a painter, but I showed a very poor talent for drawing.

461

My stepfather also died ere long,—I was only seven years old. Shortly before his death I had learned to play "Ub' immer Treu und Redlichkeit" (Ever true and honest) and the then newly published "Jungfernkranz" ("Bridal Wreath") upon the pianoforte; the day before his death, I was bid to play him both these pieces in the adjoining room; I heard him then, with feeble voice, say to my mother: "Has he perchance a talent for music?" On the early morrow, as he lay dead, my mother came into the children's sleeping-room, and said to each of us some loving word. To me she said: "He hoped to make something of thee." I remember too, that for a long time I imagined that something indeed would come of me.

In my ninth year I went to the Dresden Kreuzschule. I wished to study, and music was not thought of. Two of my sisters learnt to play the piano passably; I listened to them but had no piano lessons myself. Nothing pleased me so much as "Der Freischütz"; I often saw Weber pass before our house, as he came from rehearsals; I always watched him with a reverent awe. A tutor who explained to me "Cornelius Nepos," was at last engaged to give me pianoforte instructions; hardly had I got past the earliest finger exercises, when I furtively practiced, at first by ear, the overture to "Der Freischütz"; my teacher heard this once, and said nothing would come of me. He was right; in my whole life I have never learnt to play the piano properly. Thenceforward I only played for my own amusement, nothing but overtures, and with the most fearful fingering. It was impossible for me to play a passage clearly, and I therefore conceived a just dread of all scales and runs. Of Mozart, I only cared for the "Magic Flute"; "Don Juan" was distasteful to me, on account of the Italian text beneath it: it seemed to me such rubbish.

For a while I learnt English also, merely so as to gain an accurate knowledge of Shakespeare; and I made a metrical translation of Romeo's monologue. Though I soon left English on one side, yet Shakespeare remained my exemplar, and I projected a great tragedy which was almost nothing but a medley of "Hamlet" and "King Lear." The plan was gigantic in the extreme; two-and-forty human beings died in the course of this piece, and I saw myself compelled, in its working-out, to call the greater number back as ghosts, since otherwise I should have been short of characters for my last acts. This play occupied practically all my leisure for two whole years.

From Dresden and its Kreuzschule, I went to Leipzig. In the Nikolaischule of that city I was relegated to the third form, after having already attained to the second in Dresden. This circumstance embittered me so much, that thenceforward I lost all liking for philological study. I became lazy and slovenly, and my grand tragedy was the only thing left me to care about. Whilst I was finishing this I made my first acquaintance with Beethoven's music, in the Leipzig Gewandhaus concerts; its impression upon me was overpowering. I also became intimate with Mozart's works, chiefly through his "Requiem." Beethoven's music to "Egmont" so much inspired me, that I determined—for all the world—not to allow my now completed tragedy to leave the stocks until provided with such like music. Without the slightest diffidence, I believed that I could myself write this needful music, but thought it better to first clear up a few of the general principles of thorough-bass. To get through this as swiftly as possible, I borrowed for a week Logier's "Method of Thorough-bass," and studied it in hot haste. But this study did not bear such rapid fruit as I had expected; its difficulties both provoked and fascinated me; I resolved to become a musician.

During this time my great tragedy was unearthed by my family: they were much disturbed thereat, for it was clear as day that I had woefully neglected my school lessons in favor of it, and I was forthwith admonished to continue them more diligently. Under such circumstances, I breathed no more of my secret discovery of a calling for music; but, notwithstanding, I composed in silence a sonata, a quartet, and an aria. When I felt myself sufficiently matured in my private musical studies, I ventured forth at last with their announcement. Naturally, I now had many a hard battle to wage, for my relations could only consider my penchant for music as a fleeting passion—all the more as it was unsupported by any proofs of preliminary study, and especially by any already won dexterity in handling a musical instrument.

I may pass over the endless variety of impressions which exercised a lively effect upon me in my earliest youth; they were as diverse in their operation as in their source. Whether, under their influence, I ever appeared to any one an "infant prodigy," I very much doubt: mechanical dexterities were never drubbed into me, nor did I ever show the slightest bent toward them. To play-acting I felt an inclination, and indulged it in the quiet of my chamber; this was naturally aroused in me by the close connection of my family with the stage. The only remarkable thing about it all was my repugnance against going to the theater itself; childish impressions which I had imbibed from the earnestness of classical antiquity, so far as I had made its acquaintance in the Gymnasium, may have inspired me with a certain contempt, nay, an abhorrence of the rouged and powdered ways of the comedian. But my passion for imitation threw itself with greatest zest into the making of poetry and music—perhaps because my stepfather, a portrait-painter, died betimes, and thus the pictorial element vanished early from among my nearer models; otherwise I should probably have begun to paint too, although I cannot but remember that the learning of the technique of the pencil soon went against my grain. First I wrote plays; but the acquaintance with Beethoven's Symphonies, which I only made in my fifteenth year, eventually inflamed me with a passion for music also, albeit it had long before this exercised a powerful effect upon me, chiefly through Weber's "Freischütz." Amidst my study of music, the poetic "imitative-impulse" never quite forsook me; it subordinated itself, however, to the musical, for whose contentment I only called it in as aid. Thus I recollect that, incited by the Pastoral Symphony, I set to work on a shepherd-play, its dramatic material being prompted by Goethe's "Lovers' Fancies" ("Laune der Verliebten"). I here made no attempt at a preliminary poetic sketch, but wrote verses and music together, thus leaving the situations to take their rise from the music and the verses as I made them.

In the summer of 1834, I took the post of Music Director at the Magdeburg theater. The practical application of my musical knowledge to the functions of a conductor bore early fruit; for the vicissitudes of intercourse with singers and singeresses, behind the scenes and in front of the footlights, completely matched my bent toward many-hued distraction. The composition of my "Liebesverbot" (Forbidden Love) was now begun. I produced the overture to "Die Feen" (The Fairies) at a concert; it had a marked success. This notwithstanding, I lost all liking for this opera, and, since I was no longer able to personally attend to my affairs at Leipzig, I soon resolved to trouble myself no more about this work, which is as much as to say that I gave it up.

In the midst of all this the "earnestness of life" had knocked at my door; my outward independence, so rashly grasped at, had led me into follies of every kind, and on all sides I was plagued by penury and debts. It occurred to me to venture upon something out of the ordinary, in order not to slide into the common rut of need. Without any sort of prospect, I went to Berlin and offered the Director to produce my "Liebesverbot" at the theater of that capital. I was received at first with the fairest promises; but, after long suspense, I had to learn that not one of them was sincerely meant. In the sorriest plight I left Berlin, and applied for the post of Musical Director at the Königsberg theater, in Prussia— a post which I subsequently obtained. In that city I got married in the autumn of 1836, amid the most dubious outward circumstances. The year which I spent in Königsberg was completely lost to my art, by reason of the pressure of petty cares. I wrote one solitary overture: "Rule Britannia."

In the summer of 1837 I visited Dresden for a short time. There I was led back by the reading of Bulwer's "Rienzi" to an already cherished idea, viz., of turning the last of Rome's tribunes into the hero of a grand tragic opera. Hindered by outward discomforts, however, I busied myself no further with dramatic sketches. In the autumn of this year I went to Riga, to take up the position of first Musical Director at the theater recently opened there by Holtei. I found there an assemblage of excellent material for opera, and went to its employment with the greatest liking. Many interpolated passages for individual singers in various operas, were composed by me during this period. I also wrote the libretto for a comic opera in two acts: "Die Glückliche Barenfamilie," the matter for which I took from one of the stories in the "Thousand and One Nights." I had only composed two "numbers" for this, when I was disgusted to find that I was again on the high road to music-making *à la Adam*. My spirit, my deeper feelings, were wounded by this discovery, and I laid aside the work in horror. The daily studying and conducting of Auber's, Adam's, and Bellini's music contributed its share to a speedy undoing of my frivolous delight in such an enterprise.

When, in the autumn, I began the composition of my "Rienzi," I allowed naught to influence me except the single purpose to answer to my subject. I set myself no model, but gave myself entirely to the feeling which now consumed me, the feeling that I had already so far progressed that I might claim something significant from the development of my artistic powers, and expect some not insignificant result. The very notion of being consciously weak or trivial—even in a single bar—was appalling to me.

My voyage to London, in a sailing vessel in the summer of 1839, I never shall forget as long as I live; it lasted three and a half weeks, and was rich in mishaps. Thrice did we endure the most violent of storms, and once the captain found himself compelled to put into a Norwegian haven. The passage among the crags of Norway made a wonderful impression on my fancy; the legends of the Flying Dutchman, as I heard them from the seamen's mouths, were clothed for me in a distinct and individual color, borrowed from the adventures of the ocean through which I then was passing.

Before I set about the actual working-out of the "Flying Dutchman," I drafted first the Ballad of Senta in the second act, and completed both its verse and melody. In this piece, I unconsciously laid the thematic germ of the whole music of the opera: it was the miniature of the whole drama, such as it stood before my soul; and when I was about to betitle the finished work, I felt strongly tempted to call it a dramatic ballad. In the eventual composition of the music, the thematic picture, thus evoked, spread itself quite instinctively over the whole drama, as one continuous tissue; I had only, without further initiative, to take the various thematic germs included in the ballad and develop them to their legitimate conclusions, and I had all the chief moods of this poem, quite of themselves, in definite thematic shapes before me. I should have had stubbornly to follow the example of the self-willed opera composer, had I chosen to invent a fresh motive for each recurrence of one and the same mood in different scenes; a course whereto I naturally did not feel the smallest inclination, since I had only in my mind the most intelligible portrayal of the subject-matter, and not a mere conglomerate of operatic numbers.

"Tannhäuser" I treated in a similar fashion, and finally "Lohengrin," only that I here had not a finished musical piece before me in advance, such as that ballad, but from the aspect of the scenes and their organic growth out of one another I first created the picture itself on which the thematic rays should all converge, and then let them fall in changeful play wherever necessary for the understanding of the main situations. Moreover, my treatment gained a more definite artistic form, especially in "Lohengrin," through a continual remodeling of the thematic material to fit the character of the passing situation; and thus the music won a greater variety of appearance than was the case, for instance, in the "Flying Dutchman," where the reappearance of a theme had often the mere character of an absolute reminiscence—a device that had already been employed, before myself, by other composers.

QUEEN VICTORIA

QUEEN VICTORIA

1819-1901

INTRODUCTORY NOTE

Perhaps no sovereign has ever been more beloved by a nation than was Queen Victoria. Her long life was given earnestly and solemnly to the British people and they returned her devotion by an intense and unwavering affection. She became queen in 1837, just after her eighteenth birthday, and found a Liberal government then in power under Lord Melbourne. His kindly manner and constant thoughtfulness made the young queen attach herself to him very devotedly; but in after years when his cabinet was superseded by a Conservative one, she learned to trust quite as confidently in them.

Queen Victoria had always a methodical inclination toward the keeping of a diary. Her first effort was begun at fourteen and continued until after her marriage. In later years she kept occasional journals while traveling.

This diary brings forth beautifully the tender nature of the young girl, and in the present version of it many of the long records of talks with Lord Melbourne have been omitted, the heart of the diary is all preserved. It includes her first meeting with Prince Albert, their wooing—with all its perplexing intricacies of state precedent—and finally their marriage. Albert was the second son of the ruler of the German state of Saxe-Coburg. They were married February 10, 1840, and continued very happy until Albert's death in 1861. Sorrow for her dearly beloved husband clouded all the queen's long forty years of widowhood.

VICTORIA'S DIARY

I

Friday, 24th May [1833].—To-day is my birthday. I am to-day fourteen years old! How *very old!!* I awoke at ½

past 5 and got up at ½ past 7. I received from Mamma a
lovely hyacinth brooch and a china pen tray. From Uncle
Leopold a very kind letter, also one from Aunt Louisa and
sister Feodora. I gave Mamma a little ring. From Lehzen
I got a pretty little china figure, and a lovely little china
basket. I gave her a golden chain and Mamma gave her a
pair of earrings to match. From my maids, Frances and
Caroline, I also got little trifles of their own work. From
Sir Robert Gardiner,[1] a china plate with fruit. From Victoria and Emily Gardiner, two screens and a drawing done
by them. From the Dean, some books. My brother Charles's
present was not ready. At about ½ past 10 came Sir John
and his three sons. From Sir John [2] I received a very pretty
picture of Dash, very like, the size of life. From Jane, Victoire, Edward, Stephen, and Henry, a very pretty enamel
watch-chain. From Lady Conroy a sandalwood pincushion
and needlecase. From Victoire alone, a pair of enamel earrings. The Duchess of Gordon sent me a lovely little crown
of precious stones, which plays ''God save the King,'' and
a china basket. At 12 came the Duchess of Northumberland
(who gave me an ivory basket filled with the work of her
nieces), Lady Charlotte St. Maur a beautiful album with a
painting on it; Lady Catherine Jenkinson a pretty night-
lamp. Lady Cust, a tray of Staffordshire china. Sir Frederick Wetherall, two china vases from Paris. Doctor Maton,[3]
a small cedar basket. Lady Conroy, Jane, Victoire, Sir
George Anson, Sir John, and the Dean came also. Lady
Conroy brought Bijou (her little dog) with her, and she
gave me a little sweet smelling box. They stayed till ½ past
12. Victoire remained with us. I gave her a portrait of
Isabel, her horse. At 1 we lunched. Victoire stayed till ½
past 2. At ½ past 2 came the Royal Family. The Queen
gave me a pair of diamond earrings from the King. She
gave me herself a brooch of turquoises and gold in the form
of a bow. Aunt Augusta [4] gave me a box of sandalwood.

[1] General Sir Robert Gardiner was Principal Equerry to Prince Leopold of Saxe-Coburg at his marriage with Princess Charlotte.
[2] Sir John Conroy, Comptroller to the Duchess of Kent.
[3] W. G. Maton, M.D., Physician to the Duchess of Kent and Princess
Victoria.
[4] 1768-1840. Daughter of George III.

From Aunt Gloucester,[5] Aunt Sophia, and Uncle Sussex, a féronière of pearls. From Aunt Sophia[6] alone, a bag worked by herself. From the Duke of Gloucester, a gold ink-stand. From the Duke and Duchess of Cumberland, a brace-let of turquoise; and the Duchess brought me a turquoise pin from my cousin George Cumberland. From Princess Sophia Mathilda, a blue topaz watch-hook. From George Cam-bridge,[7] a brooch in the shape of a lily of the valley. Lady Mayo,[8] who was in waiting on the Queen, gave me a glass bottle. They stayed till ½ past 3 and then went away. I had seen in the course of the day, Sarah, my former maid, and Mrs. Brock. Ladies Emma and Georgiana Herbert[9] sent me a sachet for handkerchiefs worked by themselves. Ladies Sarah and Clementina Villiers[10] sent me some flowers as combs and a brooch. Mr. Collen sent me a little painting for my album. At a ¼ to 6 we dined.

Monday, 1st July.—I awoke at ½ past 4 and got up at a ¼ past 5. At a ¼ past 6 we all breakfasted. At 7 o'clock we left Kensington Palace, Sir John going in a post-chaise before us, then our post-chaise, then Lehzen's landau, then my Cousins' carriage, then Charles's,[11] then Lady Conroy's, and then our maids'. It is a lovely morning. 5 minutes past 8—we have just changed horses at Esher. At 4 we arrived at Portsmouth. The streets were lined with soldiers, and Sir Colin Campbell[12] rode by the carriage. Sir Thomas Wil-

[5] Mary, fourth daughter of George III, and wife of William Frederick, Duke of Gloucester, her cousin.

[6] 1777-1848. Daughter of George III.

[7] George (1819-1904), afterwards Duke of Cambridge and Commander-in-Chief. He was two months older than the Princess.

[8] Arabella, wife of the fourth Earl, a Lady-in-waiting to Queen Adelaide.

[9] Daughters of the eleventh Earl of Pembroke. Lady Emma afterwards married the third Viscount de Vesci, and Lady Georgiana the fourth Marquess of Lansdowne.

[10] Daughters of the fifth Earl of Jersey. Lady Sarah afterwards married Prince Nicholas Esterhazy. Lady Clementina died unmarried in 1858.

[11] Charles, Prince of Leiningen, son of the Duchess of Kent by her first marriage.

[12] Major-General Sir Colin Campbell (1776-1847), at this time Lieut.-Governor of Portsmouth and afterwards Governor of Ceylon. He had served with distinction in the Peninsular War and had received the Gold Cross and 6 clasps.

liams,[13] the Admiral, took us in his barge, on board the *dear Emerald*. The Admiral presented some of the officers to us. We stayed about ½ an hour waiting for the baggage to be put on board the steamer, which was to tow us. We then set off and arrived at Cowes at about 7. We were most civilly received. Cowes Castle, the yacht-club, yachts, &c., &c., saluting us. We saw Lord Durham [14] who is staying at Cowes. We drove up in a fly to Norris Castle, where we lodged two years ago, and where we are again living. My cousins and my brother were *delighted* with it.

Monday, 8th July.—At about 10 we went on board the *Emerald* with Alexander, Ernst,[15] Lady Charlotte, Lady Conroy, Jane, Victoire, Sir John and Henry. We were towed up to Southampton by the *Medina* steam-packet. It rained several times very hard, and we were obliged to go down into the cabin very often. When we arrived at Southampton, Mamma received an address on board from the Corporation. We then got into the barge and rowed up to the new pier. The crowd was tremendous. We went into a tent erected on the pier, and I was very much frightened for fear my cousins and the rest of our party should get knocked about; however they at last got in. We then got into our barge and went on board the *Emerald* where we took our luncheon. We stayed a little while to see the regatta, which was going on, and then sailed home. It was a very wet afternoon.

II

Wednesday, 18th May [1836].—At a ¼ to 2 we went down into the Hall, to receive my Uncle Ernest, Duke of Saxe-Coburg-Gotha, and my Cousins, Ernest and Albert, his sons. My Uncle was here, now 5 years ago, and is looking extremely well. Ernest is as tall as Ferdinand and Augustus; he has dark hair, and fine dark eyes and eyebrows, but the nose and mouth are not good; he has a most kind, honest

---

[13] Admiral Williams had rendered valuable services in conjunction with the army in the Low Counties, 1794-5; he became G.C.B. in 1831.

[14] John George Lambton (1792-1840), the first Baron (and afterwards first Earl of) Durham, son-in-law of Lord Grey, had been Ambassador to St. Petersburg, and was now Lord Privy Seal.

[15] Sons of Alexander, Duke of Würtemburg.

and intelligent expression in his countenance, and has a very
good figure. Albert, who is just as tall as Ernest but stouter,
is extremely handsome; his hair is about the same color as
mine; his eyes are large and blue, and he has a beautiful
nose and a very sweet mouth with fine teeth; but the charm
of his countenance is his expression, which is most delightful;
c'est à la jois full of goodness and sweetness, and very clever
and intelligent. We went upstairs with them, and after staying a few minutes with them, I went up to my room. Played
and sang. Drew. At a little after 4 Uncle Ernest and my
Cousins came up to us and stayed in my room till 10
minutes past 5. Both my Cousins are so kind and good; they
are much more *formés* and men of the world than Augustus;
they speak English very well, and I speak it with them.
Ernest will be 18 years old on the 21st of June and Albert
17 on the 26th of August. Dear Uncle Ernest made me the
present of a most delightful *Lory,* which is so tame that it
remains on your hand, and you may put your finger into its
beak, or do anything with it, without its ever attempting to
bite.

Saturday, 21st May.—At ½ past 7 we dined with Uncle
Ernest, Ernest, Albert, Charles, Lady Flora, Count Kolowrat,
Baron Alvensleben, &c. I sat between my dear Cousins.
After dinner came Princess Sophia. Baron de Hoggier, who
had arrived from Lisbon the day before, came after dinner,
and took leave, on his way home. I sat between my dear
Cousins on the sofa and we looked at drawings. They both
draw very well, particularly Albert, and are both exceedingly
fond of music; and they play very nicely on the piano. The
more I see them the more I am delighted with them, and the
more I love them. They are so natural, so kind, so *very*
good and so well instructed and informed; they are so well
bred, so truly merry and quite like children and yet very
grown up in their manners and conversation. It is delightful
to be with them; they are so fond of being occupied too;
they are quite an example for any young person.

Friday, 10th June.—At 9 we all breakfasted for the *last*
time together! It was our last HAPPY HAPPY breakfast, with
this dear Uncle and those *dearest,* beloved Cousins, whom I *do*
love so VERY VERY dearly; *much more dearly* than any other

Cousins in the *world*. Dearly as I love Ferdinand, and also good Augustus, I love Ernest and Albert *more* than them, oh yes, MUCH *more*. Augustus was like a good, affectionate child, quite unacquainted with the world, phlegmatic, and talking but very little; but dearest Ernest and dearest Albert are so grown-up in their manners, so gentle, so kind, so amiable, so agreeable, so very sensible and reasonable, and so *really* and truly good and kind-hearted. They have both learnt a good deal, and are very clever, naturally clever, particularly Albert, who is the most reflecting of the two, and they like very much talking about serious and instructive things and yet are so *very very* merry and gay and happy, like young people ought to be; Albert used always to have some fun and some clever witty answer at breakfast and everywhere; he used to play and fondle Dash so funnily too. Both he and Ernest are extremely attentive to *whatever* they hear and see, and take interest in everything they see. They were much interested with the sight of St. Paul's yesterday. At 11 dear Uncle, my *dearest beloved* Cousins, and Charles left us, accompanied by Count Kolowrat. I embraced both my dearest Cousins most warmly, as also my dear Uncle. I cried bitterly, very bitterly.

III

Wednesday, 24th May [1837].—Today is my 18th Birthday! How old! and yet how far am I from being what I should be. I shall from this day take the *firm* resolution to study with renewed assiduity, to keep my attention always well fixed on whatever I am about, and to strive to become every day less trifling and more fit for what, if Heaven wills it, I'm some day to be! At ½ p. 10 we went to the ball at St. James's with the Duchess of Northumberland, dear Lehzen, Lady Flora and Lady Conroy, &c. The King though much better was unable of course to be there, and the Queen neither, so that, strange to say, Princess Augusta made the *honneurs!* I danced first with Lord Fitzalan,[1] 2ndly with Prince Nicholas Esterhazy,[2] who is a very amiable, agreeable,

---

[1] Grandson of the twelfth Duke of Norfolk who died in 1842. He succeeded as fourteenth Duke and died in 1860.
[2] Son of Prince Paul Esterhazy, Austrian Ambassador.

gentlemanly young man; 3rdly with the Marquis of Granby; [3] 4thly with the Marquis of Douro [4] who is very odd and amusing; and 5thly and lastly with the Earl of Sandwich [5] who is an agreeable young man. I wished to dance with Count Waldstein who is such an amiable man, but he replied that he could not dance quadrilles, and as in my station I unfortunately cannot valse and gallop, I could not dance with him. The beauties there were (in my opinion) the Duchess of Sutherland, Lady Frances (or Fanny) Cowper, who is very pleasing, natural and clever-looking. . . . The Courtyard and streets were crammed when we went to the Ball, and the anxiety of the people to see poor stupid me was very great, and I must say I am quite touched by it, and feel proud which I always have done of my country and of the English Nation. I forgot to say that before we went to dinner we saw the dear children. I gave my beloved Lehzen a small brooch of my hair.

Thursday, 15th June.—The news of the King are so very bad that all my lessons save the Dean's are put off, including Lablache's, Mrs. Anderson's, Guazzaroni's, &c., &c., and we see *nobody.* I regret rather my singing-lesson, though it is only for a short period, but duty and *proper feeling* go before *all pleasures.*—10 minutes to 1,—I just hear that the Doctors think my poor Uncle the King cannot last more than 48 hours. Poor man! he was always kind to me, and he *meant* it well I know; I am grateful for it, and shall ever remember his kindness with gratitude. He was odd, very odd and singular but his intentions were often ill interpreted!—Wrote my journal. At about a ¼ p. 2 came Lord Liverpool and I had a highly important conversation with him—*alone.*

Tuesday, 20th June.—I was awoke at 6 o'clock by Mamma, who told me that the Archbishop of Canterbury and Lord Conyngham were here, and wished to see me. I got out of bed and went into my sitting-room (only in my dressing-gown), and *alone,* and saw them. Lord Conyngham (the

---

[3] Charles (1815-88), afterwards sixth Duke of Rutland, K.G.; he died unmarried. A man of grim manners but not unkindly heart.

[4] Arthur Richard (1807-84), afterwards second Duke of Wellington, K.G. Almost better known by his courtesy title of Lord Douro.

[5] John William (1811-84), seventh Earl of Sandwich, afterwards Master of the Buckhounds.

Lord Chamberlain) then acquainted me that my poor Uncle, the King, was no more, and had expired at 12 minutes p. 2 this morning, and consequently that I am *Queen*. Lord Conyngham knelt down and kissed my hand, at the same time delivering to me the official announcement of the poor King's demise. The Archbishop then told me that the Queen was desirous that he should come and tell me the details of the last moments of my poor, good Uncle; he said that he had directed his mind to religion, and had died in a perfectly happy, quiet state of mind, and was quite prepared for his death. He added that the King's sufferings at the last were not very great but that there was a good deal of uneasiness. Lord Conyngham, whom I charged to express my feelings of condolence and sorrow to the poor Queen, returned directly to Windsor. I then went to my room and dressed.

Since it has pleased Providence to place me in this station, I shall do my utmost to fulfill my duty towards my country; I am very young and perhaps in many, though not in all things, inexperienced, but I am sure, that very few have more real good will and more real desire to do what is fit and right than I have.

Breakfasted, during which time good faithful Stockmar came and talked to me. Wrote a letter to dear Uncle Leopold and a few words to dear good Feodore. Received a letter from Lord Melbourne [6] in which he said he would wait upon me at a little before 9. At 9 came Lord Melbourne, whom I saw in my room, and of COURSE *quite* ALONE as I shall *always* do all my Ministers. He kissed my hand and I then acquainted him that it had long been my intention to retain him and the rest of the present Ministry at the head of affairs, and that it could not be in better hands than his. He then again kissed my hand. He then read to me the Declaration which I was to read to the Council, which he wrote himself and which is a very fine one. I then talked with him some little longer time, after which he left me. He was in full dress. I like him very much and feel confidence in him. He is a very straightforward, honest, clever and good man. I then wrote a letter to the Queen. At about 11 Lord Melbourne came

---

[6] William Lamb, Viscount Melbourne (1779-1848), was at this time Prime Minister and fifty-eight years old.

again to me and spoke to me on various subjects. At about
½ past 11 I went downstairs and held a Council in the red
saloon. I went in of course quite alone, and remained seated
the whole time. My two Uncles, the Dukes of Cumberland [7]
and Sussex,[8] and Lord Melbourne conducted me. The declaration, the various forms, the swearing in of the Privy Coun-
cilors, of which there were a great number present, and the
reception of some of the Lords of Council, previous to the
Council in an adjacent room (likewise alone) I subjoin here.
I was not at all nervous and had the satisfaction of hearing
that people were satisfied with what I had done and how I
had done it. Receiving after this, Audiences of Lord Melbourne, Lord John Russell, Lord Albemarle (Master of the
Horse), and the Archbishop of Canterbury, all in my room
and alone. Saw Stockmar. Saw Clark, whom I named my
Physician. Saw Mary. Wrote to Uncle Ernest. Saw Ernest
Hohenlohe who brought me a kind and very feeling letter
from the poor Queen. I feel very much for her, and really
feel that the poor good King was always so kind personally
to me, that I should be ungrateful were I not to recollect it
and feel grieved at his death. The poor Queen is wonderfully composed now, I hear. Wrote my journal. Took my
dinner upstairs alone. Went downstairs. Saw Stockmar.
At about 20 minutes to 9 came Lord Melbourne and remained
till near 10. I had a very important and a very *comfortable*
conversation with him. Each time I see him I feel more confidence in him; I find him very kind in his manner too. Saw
Stockmar. Went down and said good-night to Mamma &c.
My *dear* Lehzen will ALWAYS remain with me as my friend
but will take no situation about me, and I think she is right.

Wednesday, 21st June.—At ½ p. 9 I went to St. James's

---

[7] Ernest Augustus (1771-1851), fifth son of George III. He was
considered unscrupulous, and was certainly most unpopular in this country. He now succeeded William IV. as King of Hanover. Although of
autocratic temperament, he granted his subjects a democratic constitution, much to their surprise.

[8] Augustus Frederick (1773-1843), sixth son of George III. His marriage to Lady Augusta Murray was declared void under the Royal
Marriages Act. He had by her two children, Sir Augustus d'Este
and Mlle. d'Este (afterwards wife of Lord Chancellor Truro). He
married, secondly, Lady Cecilia Buggin (*née* Gore, daughter of the Earl
of Arran), and to her was granted the title of Duchess of Inverness.

in state. Mamma and Lady Mary Stopford were in my carriage, and Lord Albemarle, Col. Cavendish, Lady Flora Hastings, and Col. Harcourt in the others. . . . After the Proclamation Mamma and the ladies repaired to an adjoining room and left me in the Closet. I gave audiences to Lord Melbourne (a long one), the Earl Marshal (Duke of Norfolk), and Garter King at Arms (Sir William Woods), relative to the funeral of my poor Uncle the late King; to Lord Albemarle, Lord Hill, Lord Melbourne (again for some time), and the Lord President (Lord Lansdowne). I then held a Privy Council in the Throne Room. It was not fully attended and was not the third part so full as it had been on the preceding day. The Marquis of Anglesey, the Chancellor of the Exchequer (Mr. Spring Rice), Lords Wharncliffe, Ashburton, and Wynford, Sir Hussey Vivian, and some Judges were sworn in as Privy Councillors and kissed hands. After the Council I gave audiences to Lord Melbourne, the Archbishop of Canterbury, and all the Bishops except one or two, the Lord Chancellor and all the Judges; Sir Hussey Vivian (Master General of the Ordnance), Lord John Russell, Lord Glenelg, Mr. Poulett Thomson, Lord Howick, Lord Palmerston, and Lord Minto. I then returned home at 1. I must say it was quite like a dream and a sad one, when I was seated in the Closet where but barely 5 weeks ago I beheld for the last time my poor Uncle.

Thursday, 22nd June.—At 12 came the Judge Advocate General (Mr. Cutlar Ferguson) to submit various sentences of Court Martial to me. He is a very clever intelligent man and explained all the cases very clearly to me. I, of *course* saw him alone.

Friday, 23rd June.—I do not mention the VERY *frequent* communications I have with Lord Melbourne, Lord John Russell, &c., &c., &c., as also the other official letters I have to write and receive, for want of time and space. Saw good Stockmar, who remained in my room for some time. Saw the Marquis of Conyngham, then Lord Hill, who explained to me finally about the Court Martials, then Sir Henry Wheatley and Col. Wood, who as Executors of the late King, brought me his will.

Saturday, 24th June.—At 11 came Lord Melbourne and

stayed till 12. He is a very honest, good and kind-hearted, as well as very clever man. He told me that Lady Tavistock had accepted the situation. And he read to me the answer which I was to give to the address from the House of Lords. He told me that the Duke of Argyll would bring the Address but would not read it; and consequently I was not to read mine.

Monday, 26th June.—At ½ p. 9 went with Mamma to Windsor. I was attended by Lady Tavistock and Colonel Cavendish, and Mamma by Lady Flora Hastings. We arrived at the Castle, which looked very mournful and melancholy with the flag half mast high, at about a ¼ p. 11. We went instantly to the poor Queen's apartments. She received me *most kindly* but was at first much affected. She however soon regained her self-possession and was wonderfully calm and composed. She gave us many painfully interesting details of the illness and last moments of my poor Uncle the late King. He bore his dreadful sufferings with the most exemplary patience and always thanked Heaven when these sufferings were but slightly and momentarily alleviated. He was in the happiest state of mind possible and his death was worthy his high station. He felt so composed and seemed to find so much consolation in Religion. The Queen is really a most estimable and excellent person and she bears the prospect of the great change she must soon go through in leaving Windsor and changing her position in a most admirable, strong and high-minded manner. I do not think her looking ill and the widow's cap and weeds rather become her.

I forgot to say that Lord Melbourne told me that the Duchess of Sutherland has accepted the office of Mistress of the Robes, and the Countess of Charlemont of one of my ladies of the Bedchamber. At ½ p. 2 came the Duchess of Sutherland, whom I am delighted to have as my Mistress of the Robes; she was looking so handsome and nice. At about 10 minutes to 4 came Lord Melbourne and stayed till ½ p. 4. I talked with him as usual on Political affairs, about my Household, and various other *Confidential* affairs.

Tuesday, 27th June.—At a little after ½ p. 12 came Lord Palmerston and stayed till a little p. 1. He is a clever and agreeable man. Saw Lord John Russell and Lord Melbourne for a minute. At a few minutes p. 2 I went down into the saloon with Lady Lansdowne; Col. Cavendish, the Vice-Chamberlain (Lord Charles Fitzoy), and the Comptroller (Mr. Byng) were in waiting. Lord Melbourne then came in and announced that the Addresses from the House of Commons were ready to come in. They were read by Lord John Russell, and I read an answer to both. Lord Melbourne stood on my left hand and Lady Lansdowne behind me. Most of the Privy Councillors of the House of Commons were present. After this Lord Palmerston brought in the Earl of Durham, who is just returned from St. Petersburg. I conferred on him the Grand Cross of the Bath. I knighted him with the Sword of State which is so enormously heavy that Lord Melbourne was obliged to hold it for me, and I only inclined it. I then put the ribbon over his shoulder. After this the foreign Ambassadors and Ministers were severally introduced to me by Lord Palmerston. I then went upstairs and gave audiences to the Earl of Mulgrave and to the Earl of Durham. The latter gave a long account of Russia. Did various things.

Saturday, 1st July.—I repeat what I said before that I have *so many.* communications from the Ministers, and from me to them, and I get so many papers to sign *every* day, that I have always a *very great* deal to do; but for want of time and space I do not write these things down. I *delight* in this work. Saw Lord Melbourne. At about ½ p. 11 or a ¼ to 12 came Mr. Spring Rice. Saw Lord John Russell. Wrote &c. At 2 came Sir Henry Wheatley to kiss hands upon being appointed my Privy Purse.

Sunday, 2nd July.—At 10 minutes to 2 came Lord Melbourne till a few minutes p. 3. Talked with him about many important things. He is indeed a most truly honest, straightforward and noble-minded man and I esteem myself *most* fortunate to have such a man at the head of the Government; a man in whom I can safely place confidence. There are not *many* like him in this world of deceit!

Saturday, 8th July.—At a ¼ p. 7 I, Mamma, Mary and Lehzen dined, Charles having gone at 5 o'clock to Windsor to attend the funeral of my poor Uncle, the late King. It was very very sad to hear from ½ p. 8 till nearly 10 o'clock those dreadful minute guns! Alas! my poor Uncle, he now reposes in quiet and peace! As Lord Melbourne said to me, the first morning when I became Queen, that the poor King "had his faults as we all have, but that he possessed many valuable qualities." I have heard from all sides that he was really very fond of me, and I shall *ever* retain a grateful sense of his kindness to me and shall never forget him. Life is short and uncertain, and I am determined to employ my time well, so that when I am called away from this world my end may be a peaceful and a happy one!

Wednesday, 12th July.—At a little before 2 I went with Mamma and the Duchess of Sutherland (in my carriage), Charles and Mary and Lady Tavistock and Lord Albemarle (in the next carriage), and Lady Mary Stopford and Colonel Cavendish in another. I was in full dress and wore the Order of the Bath. I went in state with a large escort. I was received at the door by the Lord Chamberlain, the Lord Steward, &c., &c., and was by them conducted into the Closet, where some people kissed hands. I then went into the Throne Room, Lord Conyngham handing me in, and a Page of Honor (Master Ellice) bearing my train. I sat on the Throne. Mamma and Mary stood on the steps of the Throne on one side, and the Duchess of Sutherland and Lady Tavistock stood near me (behind). I then received the two Addresses (of which, as also of all the other things, I subjoin an account), and read Answers to both. I then returned to the Closet; and went into another room to put on the Mantle of the Bath (of crimson satin lined with white silk); I then saw Lord Melbourne in the Closet for a few minutes. After this I went again into the Throne-room, and seated myself on the Throne. I then conferred the Order of the Bath (*not sitting* of course) upon Prince Esterhazy. After this I held a Privy Council. After the Council I gave audiences to the Earl of Yarborough (who thanked me very much for having appointed his amiable daughter, Lady Charlotte Copley, one of my Bedchamber Women); to Lord Melbourne, Lord John Russell, Lord Mulgrave, and Lord Hill. I then left the Palace, the Duchess of Sutherland (who looked lovely, as she always does), and Lady Tavistock, going with me in my carriage, in the same way as I came, and got home at a ¼ to 5.

Thursday, 13th July.—Got up at 8. At ½ p. 9 we break-fasted. It was the *last time* that I slept in this poor old Palace, as I go into Buckingham Palace to-day. Though I rejoice to *go* into B.P. for many reasons, it is not without feelings of regret that I shall bid adieu *forever* (that is to say *forever* as a DWELLING), to this my birth-place, where I have been born and bred, and to which I am really attached! I have seen my dear sister married here, I have seen many of my dear relations here, I have had pleasant balls and *delicious* concerts here, my present rooms upstairs are really very pleasant, comfortable and pretty, and *enfin* I like this poor Palace. I have held my first Council here too! I have gone through painful and disagreeable scenes here, 'tis true, but still I am fond of the poor old Palace. At a little after 2 I went with Mamma and Lady Lansdowne (in my carriage), Lehzen, and Col. Cavendish (in the next) to Buckingham Palace. I am much pleased with my rooms. They are high, pleasant and cheerful. Arranged things.

Friday, 14th July.—At a few minutes to 2 I went with Mamma and the Duchess of Sutherland (in my carriage), Lady Charlemont and Lord Albemarle (in the next carriage), and Charles, Mary, and Lady Flora (in the other) to St. James's. I was in full dress and wore the blue ribbon and star of the Garter, and the Garter round my arm. I was received in the same way as before. I went into the Throne Room, sat on the Throne, and received three Addresses in the same way as on Friday. Two of the Addresses were very fully attended and the room became intensely hot. I then put on the Mantle and Collar of the Garter (of dark blue velvet lined with white silk). Gave a few minutes' audience to Lord Melbourne. I then went into the Throne Room (did not sit on the Throne), held a Chapter of the Garter and conferred that Order on Charles. Mamma, Charles and Mary went away immediately after this, but I remained and gave a long audience to Lord Melbourne, who read to me the Speech which I am to deliver when I prorogue Parliament. He reads so well and with *so* much good feeling. I am sorry to see him still looking ill. I then saw the Duke of Devonshire. Came home with my two Ladies at ½ p. 4.

Saturday, 15th July.—At a few minutes p. 2 I went into

one of the large drawing-rooms and held a Cabinet Council, at which were present all the Ministers. The Council lasted but a very short while. I then went into my Closet and received Lord Melbourne there. He stayed with me till 20 minutes to 4. He seemed and said he was better. He has such an honest, frank, and yet gentle manner. He talks so quietly. I always feel peculiarly satisfied when I have talked with him. I have *great* confidence in him. After dinner, at 10 o'clock came *Thalberg*,[9] the most famous pianist in the world! He played four things, all by heart. They were all Fantasias by him; (1) on *The Preghiera of Mosé*, (2) on "God save the King" and "Rule Britannia," (3) on *Norma*, (4) on *Les Huguenots*. *Never, never* did I hear anything at all like him! He combines the most *exquisite, delicate* and touching feeling with the most wonderful and powerful execution! He is unique and I am quite in ecstasies and raptures with him. I sat quite near the piano and it is quite extraordinary to watch his hands, which are large, but fine and graceful. He draws tones and sounds from the piano which no one else can do. He is *unique*. He is quite young, about 25, small, delicate-looking, a very pleasing countenance, and extremely gentlemanlike. He is modest to a degree and very agreeable to talk to. J'étais en extase!

Monday, 17th July.—At ½ p. 1 I went in state to the House of Lords, with the Duchess of Sutherland and the Master of the Horse in my carriage, and Lady Lansdowne and Lady Mulgrave in another. Had I time I would give a very minute account of the whole, but as I have *very* little, I will only say what I feel I wish particularly to name. I went first to the Robing-room, but as there was so many people there I went to a Dressing-room where I put on the Robe which is enormously heavy. After this I entered the House of Lords preceded by all the Officers of State and Lord Melbourne bearing the Sword of State walking just before me. He stood quite close to me on the left-hand of

---

[9] Sigismund Thalberg (1812-71) was now in the full flood of success. He wrote many fantasias on operatic themes, *e.g.* on *Robert le Diable*, *Zampa*, etc. In 1845 he married a widow, the daughter of Lablache. As a composer he never succeeded in emulating his success as a pianist. Later in life he abandoned music, and became a professional vine-grower.

the Throne, and I feel always a satisfaction to have him near me on such occasions, as he is such an honest, good, kind-hearted man and is my *friend,* I know it. The Lord Chancellor stood on my left. The house was very full and I felt somewhat (but very little) nervous before I read my speech, but it did very well, and I was happy to hear people were satisfied. I then unrobed in the Library and came home as I went, at 20 minutes p. 3.

Wednesday, 19*th July.*—I gave audiences to various foreign Ambassadors, amongst which were Count Orloff, sent by the Emperor of Russia to compliment me. He presented me with a letter from the Empress of Russia accompanied by the Order of St. Catherine all set in diamonds. (I, of course, as I generally do every evening, wore the Garter.) The Levee began immediately after this and lasted till ½ p. 4 without one minute's interruption. I had my hand kissed nearly *3000* times! I then held a Council, at which were present almost all the Ministers.

IV

Friday, 23*rd February* [1838].—I lamented my being *so* short, which Lord M. smiled at and thought no misfortune. Spoke to him of the Levee, the place where I stood which some people objected to, which led him to speak of the old Court in the time of George III., when a Levee and also a Drawing-room was like an Assembly; the King and Queen used to come into the room where the people were already assembled, and to walk round and speak to the people; they did not speak to everybody, and it was considered no offense, he said, if they did not. I asked him when he first went to Court; he said in the year 1803, he thought; it was at the time when everybody volunteered their services and when he was in a Volunteer Corps. Spoke of Lord Howe, his remaining about the Queen; [1] and when he was made to resign.

Tuesday, 27*th February.*—I said to Lord Melbourne that Uncle Leopold was amazingly frightened when the Prince of Orange came over with his sons, as he always imagined that

---

[1] Lord Howe's attitude was one of hostility to the Government. He had been Lord Chamberlain to Queen Adelaide and was believed to have encouraged her in inciting the King against the ministry of Lord Grey.

the late King had *some intentions* about that; (meaning a marriage between me and one of the young Princes). "And so he had," said Lord Melbourne decidedly. "He sounded me about it," and Lord Melbourne wrote to him (the late King) to say that in a political point of view, he did not think it a desirable thing; that the country would not like a connection with Holland; the King was much disappointed at this, Lord Melbourne said; he (the King) had always a fear about a marriage; he was afraid Mamma had intentions, which I observed she certainly had; and that the King therefore thought "he must *dévancer* her"; that Lord Melbourne told him, if he wished such a thing he had better be sure first if the *Parties* themselves liked it; for that he never could force such a thing; of which Lord Melbourne said the King never seemed sensible; at which I laughed. He said that the Prince of Orange also came to him (Ld. M.) from the King, and asked him if he or the Government had any objection to such a connection. "Personally," Lord Melbourne said to him, "there could be no objection; no more than to any other Prince in Europe"; but at the same time he must tell him that his (the Prince's) country was so situated that it would be constantly involved in war if any war was to break out; "I told him as much as that," Lord Melbourne said, "and that I could not say anything until we saw it in some sort of shape or other." This was all very curious and interesting for me to hear.

BUCKINGHAM PALACE, *Wednesday, 7th March.*—Dressed for riding. At a few m. p. 12 I *rode* out with Lord Conyngham, Lord Uxbridge, dear Lehzen, Miss Cavendish, Col. Cavendish, and Sir G. Quentin and Mr. Fozard. I mounted in the garden just under the terrace in order that nobody should know I was going to ride out. I rode my dear favorite Tartar who went perfectly and *most delightfully,* never shying, never starting through all the *very* noisy streets, rattling omnibuses—carts—carriages, &c., &c. I quite *love* him. We rode out through the garden, through the gate on Constitution Hill; round the park by the water, out at the new gate, by Lord Hill's former villa, a good way on the Harrow Road, I should say within 4 or 5 miles of Harrow—then down a pretty narrow lane where one could fancy oneself 2 or 300

miles from London, out by Willesden Field (where I had
never been), and Kilburn, down the Edgware Road—Connaught Place, through omnibuses, carts, &c., &c., in at Cumberland Gate, galloped up to Hyde Park Corner—and in at
the same garden gate at Constitution Hill, and safely to
the Palace at 10 m. to 3. It was a lovely day, a beautiful and
delicious ride, and I have come home quite charmed and delighted.

Wednesday, 15th August.—I asked Lord Melbourne if it
ever had been usual for the Sovereign to *read* the Speech *after*
the Prime Minister had done so at the Council, as Lord Lansdowne had twice asked that question. Lord Melbourne said,
never; but that the late King had done it once, when he was
in a great state of irritation, and had said, "I will read it
myself, paragraph by paragraph." This was the last time
the late King ever prorogued Parliament in person. I asked
if Brougham was in the House; he said no, he was gone. I
told him I heard Brougham had asked Lady Cowper down
to Brougham Hall; but that she wouldn't go; I asked if she
knew him (Brougham) well; Lord Melbourne said very well,
and "I've known him all my life; he can't bear me now;
he won't speak to me; I've tried to speak to him on ordinary
subjects in the House of Lords, but he won't answer, and
looks very stern"; Lord Melbourne said, laughing, "Why,
we've had several severe set-to's, and I've hit him very
hard." I asked if he (B.) didn't still sit on the
same bench with Lord Melbourne. "Quite on the gangway;
only one between," replied Lord Melbourne. Lord Melbourne and I both agreed that it was *since* the King's death
that Brougham was so enraged with Lord Melbourne; for,
till then, he would have it that it was the *King's* dislike to
him (and the King made no objection whatever to him, Lord
Melbourne told me) and *not Lord Melbourne;* "he wouldn't
believe me," Lord M. said: "And *now* he's undeceived."
Brougham always, he said, used to make a great many
speeches. I observed that I thought if his daughter was to die,
he would go mad; but Lord Melbourne doesn't think so; and
said, "A man who is always very odd never goes really mad."

Thursday, 16th August.—"You were rather nervous," [2] said

[2] This refers to the reading by the Queen of her "Speech."

Lord Melbourne; to which I replied, dreadfully so; "More so than any time," he continued. I asked if it was observed; he said, "I don't think any one else would have observed it, but I could see you were." Spoke of my fear of reading it too low, or too loud, or too quick; "I thought you read it very well," he said kindly. I spoke of my great nervousness, which I said I feared I never would get over. "I won't flatter Your Majesty that you ever will; for I think people scarcely ever get over it; it belongs to a peculiar temperament, sensitive and susceptible; that shyness generally accompanies high and right feelings," said Lord Melbourne most kindly; he was so kind and paternal to me. He spoke of my riding, which he thought a very good thing. "It gives a feeling of ease the day one has done with Parliament," said Lord Melbourne. He spoke of the people in the Park when I went to the House; and I said how very civil the people were—*always*—to me; which touched him; he said it was a very good thing; it didn't do to rely too much on those things, but that it was well it was there. I observed to Lord Melbourne how ill and out of spirits the Duke of Sussex was; "I have ended the Session in great charity," said Lord Melbourne, "with the Duke of Wellington, but I don't end it in charity with those who didn't vote with the Duke when he voted with us"; we spoke of all that; "The Duke is a very great and able man," said Lord Melbourne, "but he is more often wrong than right." Lord Holland wouldn't allow this; "Well, let's throw the balance the other way," continued Lord Melbourne, "but when he is wrong he is *very* wrong."

Friday, 17th August.—I then told Lord Melbourne that I had so much to do, I didn't think I possibly could go to Windsor on Monday; he said if I put off going once for that reason, I should have to put it off again, which I wouldn't allow; I said there were so many things to go, and to pack,— and so many useless things; "I wouldn't take those useless things," said Lord Melbourne laughing. I then added that he couldn't have an idea of the number of things women had to pack and take; he said many men had quite as much,— which I said couldn't be, and he continued that Lord Anglesey had *36* trunks; and that many men had 30 or 40 different waistcoats, and neck-cloths, to choose from; which made me laugh; I said a man *couldn't* really want more than 3 or 4 coats for some months. He said in fact 6 were enough for a year,—but that people had often fancies for more. I said our dresses required such smooth packing; "Coats ought to be packed smooth," replied Lord Melbourne.

Saturday, 8th September.—We rode round Virginia Water. As I was galloping homewards, before we came to the Long Walk, on the grass and not very fast, Uncle left my side and I went on alone with Lord Melbourne, when something frightened Uxbridge, who was alarmed at being left without his second companion, and he swerved against Lord M.'s horse so much, that I came *off;* I fell on one side sitting, not a bit hurt or put out or frightened, but astonished and amused,— and was up, and laughing, before Col. Cavendish and one of the gentlemen, all greatly alarmed, could come near me, and said, "I'm not hurt." Lord M.'s horse shied away at the same moment mine did; *he* was much frightened and turned quite pale, kind, good man; he said, "Are you sure you're not hurt?" I instantly remounted and cantered home; Lord M. was rather alarmed again and thought Uxbridge was inclined to shy. I sat between Uncle and Lord Melbourne. Uncle talked much, and praised me for my behavior during my *feat* of falling! Lord Melbourne said most kindly and anxiously, "Are you *really* not the worse?" He repeated this twice. We spoke of how it happened; he said he didn't *see* me fall, but *heard* me fall; he said it was fortunate his horse jumped away, else I might have been hurt.

V

Sunday, 24th February [1839].—Talked of Lord Douro's marriage to Lady Elizabeth Hay,[1] one of Lord Tweeddale's daughters, being settled; both Lady Normanby and I said we should not believe it till we saw Lord Douro really married, for that he was so very changeable; they said Lord Duoro had been out shopping with the young lady; and Lord M. said, "Shopping is very demonstrative," which made us laugh; and "There is a day when even the most *volage* is

---

[1] Daughter of eighth Marquess of Tweeddale. She became Lady Douro, and afterwards Duchess of Wellington. She outlived the Duke many years.

fixed, and has his wings clipped." Talked of the picture of Van Amburgh and the Lions Landseer is making. "Why, he" (V. Amburgh) "quite brings Daniel down," said Lord M.; and he talked of the Power the ancients had with Music over beasts, and passions; we said that would have no effect on him (Ld. M.); he said Orpheus would; which made us laugh; he said the formation of the organ of the ear was different, and also that the dislike came from want of attention. "I have music in me," he said, "if it was awoke; only I never attended to it." If he really had *liked* it, I said, he must have attended to it. "I never could dance in time," he said; "I never knew when it began. Sir Isaac Newton said," he continued, " 'The only difference between me and a carter, is attention.' " "I despised music when I was young, beyond everything," said Lord M., "and everybody who liked it; I was very foolish." It was the fashion, he said, then, to dislike music and dancing, and to lounge upon the sofas.

Tuesday, 5th March.—Lord M. said that he had received a letter from the Duke of Wellington the day before yesterday, in which the Duke says that there is a gentleman in Hampshire whose son was Aide-de-Camp to the Emperor of Russia, and that he had written over (I suppose to his Father) that he had seen a large plan on the Emperor's table of an intention to attack the East Indies with his fleet, that the Emperor had referred it to his Ministers, and that he had afterwards seen it on the Emperor's table marked "approved"; the Duke says he does not think it at all probable that such a large and difficult undertaking should really be in contemplation, but he thinks it possible that the Emperor would get his Fleet into the Mediterranean, and wishes that something should be done to prevent their coming out; the Duke thought this intelligence ought not to be totally disregarded and therefore brought it before the Government. "I don't think it very probable," said Lord M., "but it mustn't be totally disregarded." [2] Lord M. then said he was afraid they were in a scrape about the Registrar's Certificate for a marriage, of

[2] This ridiculous story was proved afterwards to be a pure fabrication. It is interesting as an illustration of the type of sensational gossip that finds credence in all countries and under all forms of government.

which he already told me the other night; it sounds exceedingly absurd, a man has married his grandmother; Lord M. told me the case; an old man of 70 named John Payne married a girl of 17; he had a grown-up son who had an illegitimate son; and on the death of the old man, this same natural son married his grandfather's widow,—which is, of course, quite wrong; and the mistake arose, Lord M. said, from the Registrar saying that an illegitimate child was no relation, "nullius filius," Lord M. said, and that therefore he might marry his grandmother; now, Lord M. said, this is quite wrong, and only applies to inheritance of property and not to a thing of this sort; "else," he said, "a man might marry his Mother or his Sister."

Monday, 11th March.—Talked of the late King's serious and real intention to marry me to the second son of the Prince of Orange; "He was very eager about it," said Lord M., "he was very angry with me about that, for I made a great many objections to it." Lord M. said the King meant to have managed it any how, and he was always afraid of being "forestalled" about it, which I said he very likely would have been. "The Prince of Orange was very anxious about it," Lord M. continued; "he came to me about it, and said the King wished it very much, but that he knew that wasn't the only thing in this country; and he wished to know if I had any decided objection to it." I talked of my Uncle being greatly alarmed about it. Pozzo, Lord M. said, and all the Russians, were anxious and always wishing for the Dutch alliance. I asked Lord M. did he think Pozzo was still for it; Lord M. said, of course they always wished for such an alliance; I asked was there in general much said about my marrying. "I haven't heard anything," he said, "but there will be some day a great deal; but I'll ask." "The best way to prevent that," I said, "was by never marrying at all," and that I used to frighten my relations by saying so. I asked him did he think the Country was anxious I should marry, for that I wished to remain as I was for some time to come; he said he didn't believe they showed any wish for it as yet.

Wednesday, 13th March.—I said to Lord M. I knew I had been very disagreeable and cross in the morning, which he didn't allow. I said I had been exceedingly angry with John Russell for not letting me go to Drury Lane; Lord M. laughed and said, "But it can't be." I couldn't get my gloves on, and Lord M. said, "It's those consumed rings; I never could bear them." I said I was fond of them, and that it improved an ugly hand. "Makes it worse," he replied; I said I didn't wear them of a morning. *"Much* better," he said, "and if you didn't wear them, nobody else would." Ear-rings he thinks barbarous. I said I thought I was not getting stronger. "Why, you have every appearance of getting stronger," he said, and "You should take the greatest care of your health; there's nothing like health; particularly in your situation; it makes you so independent; bad health puts you into the power of people."

Friday, 15th March.—I said I hoped he would always tell me whatever he heard; he said, "I always do." "Not lately," I said; "I haven't heard anything lately." "For," I added, "I was sure I made a great many mistakes"; "No, I don't know that at all. People said," he continued, "that I was 'lofty, high, stern, and decided,' but that's much better than that you should be thought familiar. I said to Stanley,"[3] he continued, "it's far better that the Queen should be thought high and decided, than that she should be thought weak. 'By God!' he said, 'they don't think that of her; you needn't be afraid of that.'" Lord M. seemed to say this with pleasure. "The natural thing," he continued, "would be to suppose that a girl would be weak and undecided; but they don't think that." I said that I was often very childish, he must perceive; "No, not at all, I don't see that in any respect," he said.

Sunday, 17th March.—Talked of the Archbishop of York and his being so wonderful for his age; I made Lord M. laugh by saying he told me that Lord M. had said to him, "You Bishops are sad dogs." "He's a good-natured lively man," said Lord M. "He was always very kind to me when I asked his advice about people." Lord M. went to the Speaker's Levee[4] after his dinner. Lord M. said Prime Ministers

[3] Afterwards Earl of Derby, and Prime Minister.
[4] The Speaker's Levee still remains an institution. The Commander-in-Chief's Levee died with the office in 1904.

always used to have them, and they were given up by Mr.
Pitt out of laziness; they used to be in the morning and Lord
M. said there was a curious account of the Duke of Newcastle's
levees in one of Smollett's novels; "He used to run in to it
half shaved, with the lather on one side of his face," said
Lord M., "but that was the right thing; it's meant to be while
you are getting up; I hold a levee; I see people while I'm
dressing." I asked him if that didn't tire him. "No, not
at all, and it don't keep them waiting," he replied.

Friday, 22nd March.—Got up at ½ p. 9. Very anxious
and nervous. Saw by the papers we were beat by 5; and
they had sat till 4! I am in a sad state of suspense; it is
now ¾ p. 12, and I have not yet heard from Lord Melbourne;
I hear he was still asleep when my box arrived, and I desired
they shouldn't wake him. Arranged things; wrote. Heard
from Lord Melbourne: "It is now twelve o'clock and Lord
Melbourne was so tired with the debate of last night that he
has slept until now. The majority, as your Majesty sees, was
very small. We must have a Cabinet this morning in order
to consider what steps are to be taken. It must be at Lord
Lansdowne's, as he is confined with the gout and cannot go
out. Lord Melbourne will be with Your Majesty by one—if
possible."

At about 5 m. to 2 he came and stayed with me till at
¼ p. 2. I asked how he was and if he wasn't very tired. "Not
very," he replied, "I was very tired last night." It was so
late. "I don't know what's to be done, really," he said. "We
are going to have a Meeting at Lansdowne's to consider the
question; it's a direct censure upon the Government." I
asked Lord M. who had been appointed on this Committee of
Inquiry into the state of Ireland. "Oh! they have appointed
it fairly enough; we can't complain of unfairness in the appointing of it; but it is *having* the Committee that is the
difficulty to get over," said Lord M. Lord Melbourne told
me he was sure we would be beat last night, and expected "by
a much larger majority." He also said to me, "I'm afraid
you were very uneasy at not hearing, but I thought 5 o'clock
was too late to send." Received at a ¼ to 5 the following
communication from Lord Melbourne: "that the Cabinet have
decided—1st, that it is impossible to acquiesce in the Vote of

last night in the House of Lords; 2ndly, that it would not be justifiable to resign in the face of the declaration which I made in the year 1836, in the House of Lords, that I would maintain my post as long as I possessed the confidence of the Crown and of the House of Commons, particularly as there is no reason to suppose that we have lost the confidence of that House. 3rdly, that the course to be pursued is to give notice in the House of Commons to-night, that the sense of that House will be taken immediately after the Easter Holidays upon a Vote of approbation of the principles of Lord Normanby's Government of Ireland. If we lose that question or carry it by a small majority, we must resign. If we carry it, we may go on.—This is a plain statement of the case, and this course will at least give Your Majesty time to consider what is to be done.''—I forbear making any observations upon this until I have talked fully to Lord Melbourne upon it, with the exception of one, which is—that as for ''the confidence of the Crown,'' God knows! *no Minister, no friend* EVER possessed it so entirely as this truly excellent Lord Melbourne possesses mine! [5]

Lord M. didn't hear Lord Carew, as he went out of the House for a moment when he was speaking; I said I heard he didn't speak well; ''He speaks with that Wexford shriek,'' said Lord M. He said to Lady Normanby, ''Normanby is too thin-skinned, too susceptible; and that's his fault; he shouldn't mind being abused; nobody should mind that. Brougham said to Duncannon, 'Tell that foolish friend of yours, Normanby, not to mind being abused, for he is paid to bear it.' '' Talked of Brougham being a bad man with no heart; Lord M. said, ''No, he *has* a heart; he has feeling, I should say he was too susceptible and acted from sudden impulses.'' Talked of contradicting abuse in the papers, and

[5] NOTE BY QUEEN VICTORIA, *1st October*, 1842.—Reading this again, I cannot forbear remarking what an artificial sort of happiness *mine* was *then*, and what a blessing it is I have now in my beloved Husband *real* and solid happiness, which no Politics, no worldly reverses *can* change; it could not have lasted long, as it was then, for after all, kind and excellent as Lord M. is, and kind as he was to [me], it was but in Society that I had amusement, and I was only living on that superficial resource, which I *then fancied* was happiness! Thank God! for *me* and others, this is changed, and I *know what* REAL happiness is.—V. R.

Lord M. said, there might one day come something one couldn't well contradict, and therefore it was better not to contradict at all. We were seated much as usual, my truly valuable and excellent Lord Melbourne being seated near me. I said to Lord M. that I was sure I never could bear up against difficulties; Lord M. turned round close to me, and said very earnestly and affectionately, "Oh! you will; you must; it's in the lot of your Station, you must prepare yourself for it." I said I never could, and he continued, "Oh! you will; you always behaved very well." I said to Lord M. I was sure he hadn't a doubt we should carry it.[6] I said I felt so helpless; "I don't see what any Sovereign can do, old or young, male or female," he said, "but to put themselves into the hands of the person that they have chosen as Minister;" talking of the whole thing, Lord M. said, "We'll do everything we can to avert it; I never thought we should have carried you on as far as we have done."

Friday, 12th July.—Talked of my fearing that too many of my relations had come over this year, which Lord M. didn't think, and said there had been no remarks made about it. Talked of my Cousins Ernest and Albert coming over,—my having no great wish to see Albert, as the whole subject was an odious one, and one which I hated to decide about; there was no engagement between us, I said, but that the young man was aware that there was the possibility of such a union; I said it wasn't right to keep him on, and not right to decide before they came; and Lord M. said I should make them distinctly understand anyhow that I couldn't do anything for a year; I said it was disagreeable for me to see him though, and a disagreeable thing. "It's very disagreeable," Lord M. said. I begged him to say nothing about it to anybody, or to answer questions about it, as it would be very disagreeable to me if other people knew it. Lord M. I didn't mind, as I told him everything. Talked of Albert's being younger. "I don't know that that signifies," said Lord M. "I don't know what the impression would be," he continued, "there's no anxiety for it; I expected there would be." I said better wait till impatience was shown. "Certainly better wait for a year or two," he said; "it's a very serious question." I said I wished

[6] The vote of confidence to be moved in the House of Commons.

if possible never to marry. "I don't know about *that*," he replied.

Sunday, 14th July.—Talked of the foliage being in beauty, and I said neither the lime blossoms or the flowers smelt hardly at all in this garden; Lord M. wouldn't believe it, and said, "Everything does better in London; London beats the country hollow in flowers." Talked of the garden being, as I said, very dull; "All gardens are dull," said Lord M., "a garden is a dull thing." Talked of the garden in St. James's Park, and Lord M. said there was a great piece of work about the old Swan being killed, in consequence of their having brought in too many other swans; this swan was called Old Jack, and had been hatched in the year '70!! "They are very angry with me," said Lord M. I asked why; "Because I didn't see that it was taken care of."

Wednesday, 17th July.—Talked of the fate of Edward II. and Richard II. being so alike, and so uncertain; the one by his wife's connivance. Talked of Edward III.'s *seven* sons; of Henry V.'s widow marrying Owen Tudor, who was illegitimately descended from John of Gaunt. "They didn't mind what a Queen Dowager did then," Lord M. said; "they seldom returned." Anne of Cleves for instance lived and died here. Talked of Henry VIII. behaving very ill to her; he called her "a Flanders mare"; of his using his other wives so ill; Jane Seymour, I said, narrowly escaped being beheaded. "Oh! no, he was very fond of her," said Lord M., which I denied. "She died in child-bed when Edward VI. was born." And poor Catherine of Aragon he ill-used, I said; "He got tired of her," said Lord M., "she was a sad, groaning, moaning woman," which made me laugh. "She had always an idea that her marriage was formed in blood," he said, on account of the poor Earl of Warwick's death, which always hung upon her mind. Talked of Catherine Parr's narrowly escaping death. Lord M. said, "He got to be dreadfully tyrannical; when he began he had every sort of good feeling." Talked of Mary. "She was dreadfully bigoted, she would have sacrificed everything to her religion," he said. Talked of her cruelty—her having poor Jane Grey, her own cousin, executed. Talked of her (J. Grey's) sister, who died in prison, and whom Queen Elizabeth ill-treated because she married somebody without her leave. "Oh! she was dreadfully tyrannical," said Lord M., "just like her father; very stern; she was a Roman Catholic in fact, except the supremacy of the Pope; that she would never submit to." Talked of poor Mary of Scots' execution, which M. said Elizabeth delayed too long, for that her Ministers had been urging it. "When she signed it," said Lord M., "she said, 'I know Lord Walsingham will die of grief when he hears it'; it wasn't right of her to joke at such a moment." Talked of poor Mary. "She was a bad woman," said Lord M., "she was a silly, idle, coquettish French girl." I pitied her; talked of Darnley's brutality about Rizzio; Lord M. fears there's no doubt about her being aware of the intention of murdering Darnley, talked of her unhappiness, and the roughness of the Scotch towards her; of her brother Moray, whom Lord M. admires.

"Macaulay says," said Lord M., "no Christian Prince ever mourned for a Mahommedan; and Mahommedans never wear mourning; they take off their turbans and put ashes on their heads, but never change their garb." "I was speaking to Palmerston about Peel the other day, and he said," continued Lord M., " 'The Queen would have liked Peel better when she knew him'; he says that he is much the best of them, that he is a very fair man; that he is not a very *high-minded* man, and has shown himself less so than he thought he had been."

Saturday, 27th July.—"Party went off well?" he asked. I replied Yes, but that a Concert always dragged, as people couldn't and mustn't talk. "You say the Queen Dowager was rather affected," he said, (I wrote to him last night,) "the same plate, the same servants," he observed (quite touched). I said I had great difficulty in persuading her to go before me, for that she said that really was *too* wrong, that she couldn't think of doing it, but I forced her to do it; she said to me, "I must obey." "I was sure she wouldn't like that," said Lord M. with tears in his eyes, and he was also much affected when I told him that she said she *felt* kind intentions. Talked of my fearing to go to Windsor this year; of my getting tired of the place; of George III. living almost always at Windsor, hunting 6 times a week, which Lord M. thinks he did till 1800; certainly after his 1st illness in 1788.

Wednesday, 31st July.—At 5 I went downstairs with Lehzen and Matilda to the Equerries' room, where Lord Melbourne was sitting to Grant [7] (since a ¼ p. 4) on that wooden horse without head or tail, looking so funny, his white hat on, an umbrella in lieu of a stick in one hand, and holding the reins which were fastened to the steps in the other; he sat there so patiently and kindly, doing just what he was told[8]; but, as Grant said, he is not easy to paint, for he either looks grave and absorbed, or laughs and goes into the other extreme; he is always changing his countenance; I was *so* amused. Grant kept telling him, "Now Lord Melbourne, hold your head in the right position,"—for he kept looking at Islay and trying to touch him with his umbrella; and then, "Now sit up, Lord Melbourne." Grant has got him so like; it is such a happiness for me to have that dear kind friend's face, which I do like and admire so, so like; his face, his expression, his air, his white hat, and his cravat, waistcoat and coat, all just as he wears it.

Talked of Lord M.'s having had his umbrella in the room, and I said he always took it about with him. He replied laughing, "You should never quit your umbrella when it rains." What use was it in a close carriage? I said. "Might be upset," he said, "I might want to get out; suppose I might be stopped and put out of the carriage, which may happen one of these days,—at least leave me the umbrella to go on with," he said laughing very much and making us all laugh too.

Thursday, 10th October.—Got up at ½ p. 10 and saw to my astonishment that a stone, or rather 2 stones, had been thrown at my dressing-room window and 2 glasses broken; the stone was found under the window; in the little blue room next the audience room another window broken and the stone found in the room; in the new strong room another window broken, and in one of the lodging rooms next to this, another broken and the stone found in the middle of the room. This is a very strange thing, and Lehzen told Lord Surrey of it. At ½ p. 7 I went to the top of the staircase and received my 2 dear cousins Ernest and Albert,—whom I found grown and changed, and embellished. It was with some emotion that I beheld

[7] Sir Francis Grant, elected P.R.A. in 1866.

[8] The sitting was for a picture which now hangs in the corridor at Windsor. The Queen is shown riding out from the Castle accompanied by her Court.

Albert—who is *beautiful*. I embraced them both and took them to Mamma; having no clothes they couldn't appear at dinner. At 8 we dined. Besides our own party, Lady Clanricarde, Lord and Lady Granville, Baron Brunow, Lord Normanby, the Hon. William Temple, and Mr. Murray (who returned), dined here. I sat between Baron Brunow and Lord Melbourne. Talked to Lord Melbourne of my cousins having no baggage; I said I found my cousins so changed. Talked of my cousins' bad passage; their not appearing on account of their *négligé*, which Lord M. thought they ought to have done, *at* dinner and certainly after. "I don't know what's the dress *I* wouldn't appear in, if I was allowed," said Lord M., which made us laugh. After dinner my Cousins came in, in spite of their *négligé*, and I presented them to Lord Melbourne. I sat on the sofa with Lady Clanricarde, Lord Melbourne sitting near me, and Ernest near us and Albert opposite—(*he* is so handsome and pleasing), and several of the ladies and gentlemen round the sofa. I asked Lord M. if he thought Albert like me, which he is thought (and which is an immense compliment to me). "Oh! yes, he is," said Lord M., "it struck me at once."

Friday, 11th October.—Got up at ½ p. 9 and breakfasted at 10. Wrote to Lord Melbourne. Signed. My dear Cousins came to my room and remained some little time; Albert really is quite charming, and so excessively handsome, such beautiful blue eyes, an exquisite nose, and such a pretty mouth with delicate moustachios and slight but very slight whiskers; a beautiful figure, broad in the shoulders and a fine waist.—At about ½ p. 10 dancing began. I danced 5 quadrilles; (1) with Ernest; (2) with dearest Albert, who dances so beautifully; (3) with Lord Alfred; (4) with Ernest; and (5) with dearest Albert again. After the 1st quadrille there was a Valse; after the 2nd and 3rd Gallops; and after the 4th another Valse; it is quite a pleasure to look at Albert when he gallops and valses, he does it so beautifully, holds himself so well with that beautiful figure of his.

Saturday, 12th October.—At 20 m. p. 3 I rode out with my cousins, Mamma, Lord Melbourne, Daisy, and the same party as the day before with the exception of Lord Granville, Lord Normanby, Lord Surrey and Mr. Byng; and came home at

½ p. 5. I rode Friar, who went beautifully. I rode the whole time between Albert (with whom I talked a good deal) and Lord Melbourne, who, out of anxiety lest I should suffer from his horse shying against me, rode his white-faced horse, which he has not ridden since he came down with him, and which isn't half as easy as the other, nor so safe; it was so kind and I felt it so much, but it grieved me; luckily the horse went safe and quiet.

Sunday, 13th October.—At 11 I went to church with Mamma and my beloved cousins (in my carriage) and all the other ladies (except Daisy) and gentlemen, to St. George's. Besides Mamma and my 2 cousins, Lady Sandwich, Lord Melbourne, Lord Palmerston, Lord Falkland and Alvensleben were in the Closet with me. Dearest Albert sat near me, who enjoyed the music excessively and thought it quite beautiful.

Lord M. said he had a gossiping letter from Lady Holland, which he read to me; as he thought I couldn't read it. Talked of Spain; Alava's pleasure at being asked, and his saying in a letter he did not wish to change his name for any other. Talked of my cousins having gone to Frogmore; the length of their stay being left to me; and I said seeing them had a good deal changed my opinion (as to marrying), and that I must decide soon, which was a difficult thing. "You would take another week," said Lord M.; "certainly a very fine young man, very good-looking," in which I most readily agreed, and said he was so amiable and good tempered, and that I had such a bad temper; of my being the 1st now to own the advantage of beauty, which Lord M. said smiling he had told me was not to be despised, in spite of what I had said to him about it. Talked of my cousin being religious. "That strong Protestant feeling is a good thing in this country," he said, "if it isn't intolerant,"—which I assured him it was not. I had great fun with my dear cousins after dinner. I sat on the sofa with dearest Albert; Lord Melbourne sitting near me, Ernest playing at chess, and many being seated round the table. I looked at some drawings by Stephano della Bella and Domenichino, with Albert, and then we gave them to Lord Melbourne.

Monday, 14th October.—Talked of my Cousins' having gone out shooting. After a little pause I said to Lord M., that I

had made up my mind (about marrying dearest Albert).—
"You have?" he said; "well then, about the time?" Not for
a year, I thought; which he said was too long; that Parliament must be assembled in order to make a provision for him,
and that if it was settled "it shouldn't be talked about," said
Lord M.; "it prevents any objection, though I don't think
there'll be much; on the contrary," he continued with tears
in his eyes, "I think it'll be very well received; for I hear
there is an anxiety now that it should be; and I'm very glad
of it; I think it is a very good thing, and you'll be much
more comfortable; for a woman cannot stand alone for long,
in whatever situation she is." Lord M. said then that he won-
dered if I didn't wish to have it directly (which I said I
didn't), as in that case Parliament would have to be assembled
before; but if I didn't, that it had better be in January or
February, after Parliament met; not later; upon which I observed, "So soon." "You are rather alarmed when it comes
to be put in that way," he said laughing; which I assured
him I was not. Then I asked, if I hadn't better tell Albert
of my decision soon, in which Lord M. agreed. How? I asked,
for that in general such things were done the other way,—
which made Lord M. laugh. That Uncle Leopold and Uncle
Ernest should know it; of settling my own time; and then for
some time of what should be done for him; George of Denmark would be the person to look back to; he was Lord High
Admiral, Lord M. said; of making him a Peer—my being
against it. A Field Marshal he ought to be made, just like
Uncle; and anyhow a Royal Highness; of how I should say it
to Albert; Lord M. thought there was no harm in people's
guessing the thing; he said that he would mention it to John
Russell and Palmerston, and perhaps the Chancellor. When
we got up, I took Lord M.'s hand, and said he was always *so*
kind to me,—which he has always been; he was *so* kind, *so*
fatherly about all this. I felt *very* happy. Read dispatches.
Wrote to Ernest and Albert sending them things. Wrote my
journal.

At 8 o'clock we all dined. Prince Esterhazy, Lord Uxbridge
and the Ladies E. and C. Paget dined here. Prince Esterhazy led me in, and I sat between him and my dearest Albert,
with whom I talked a great deal. Lord Melbourne sat oppo-

site between Lady C. Dundas and Ellen. Talked to Lord Melbourne after dinner of my hearing Albert couldn't sleep these last few days; nor I either, I added; that he asked a good deal about England, about which I tried to give him the most agreeable idea. "I mentioned it to J. Russell," said Lord M., but that J. Russell was very anxious it should be told to very few, as it was so difficult to *deny* such a thing when it was really settled; and that if I could talk to Albert about it and settle it with him but no one else, which I said I would. "I'll talk to you about it more fully to-morrow," Lord M. said.

Tuesday, 15th October.—Saw my dear Cousins come home quite safe from the Hunt, and charge up the hill at an immense pace. Saw Esterhazy. At about ½ p. 12 I sent for Albert; he came to the Closet where I was alone, and after a few minutes I said to him, that I thought he must be aware *why* I wished them to come here,—and that it would make me *too happy* if he would consent to what I wished (to marry me). We embraced each other, and he was *so* kind, *so* affectionate. I told him I was quite unworthy of him,—he said he would be very happy "das Leben mit dir zu zubringen," and was so kind, and seemed so happy, that I really felt it was the happiest brightest moment in my life. I told him it was a great sacrifice,—which he wouldn't allow; I then told him of the necessity of keeping it a secret, except to his father and Uncle Leopold and Stockmar, to whom he said he would send a Courier next day,—and also that it was to be as early as the beginning of February. I then told him to fetch Ernest, which he did and he congratulated us both and seemed very happy. I feel the happiest of human beings.

At 25 m. p. 1 came Lord Melbourne and stayed with me till 20 m. p. 2. He was well and had slept well. Talked of the weather; he read me a letter about this Lord Huntingdon, who seems to be very proud and tenacious of his rights and rank, as Lord M. already knew, and as his Uncle-in-law Lord Carew writes. Talked of that, of William Cowper's coming down, and George Anson; I then began and said I had got well through this with Albert. "Oh! you have," said Lord M.; and I continued that he had said he would let no one perceive that anything of the kind had taken place;

that he seemed very happy, and his brother as happy as him, only that *he* (E.) said he was the only loser by it, as his brother had been everything to him. Lord M. then said—if I had wished to have it immediately—that Parliament must be assembled. He said there was a great deal of talking going on about it; Lady Holland had written about it. Before this Lord M. said, "You can then (when married) do much more what you like." "Normanby wishes it," said Lord M. "He wishes the thing should be done and thinks it the best." "John Russell said," continued Lord M. with tears in his eyes, "his only wish is that you should be happy," which I said I hadn't a doubt of.

Wednesday, 16th October.—Talked of Albert's behaving so wonderfully, so that no one could imagine that anything had taken place; Ernest's saying *he* couldn't bear it, if he was in such a situation. "I find you must declare it in Council," said Lord M., when it is to be announced; "it is quite done by you; you assemble the Privy Councillors and announce it to them; that is what George III. did." Talked of making him a Peer, which Lord M. said he should like to take other people's opinion upon; but I talked of the necessity of his having precedence of every one else. "There'll be no difficulty about that," said Lord M., "as everybody will see the propriety of that."

Saturday, 19th October.—My dearest Albert came to me at 10 m. to 12 and stayed with me till 20 m. p. 1. Such a pleasant happy time. He looked over my shoulder and watched me writing to the Duchess of Northumberland, and to the Duchess of Sutherland; and he scraped out some mistakes I had made. I told him I felt so grateful to him and would do everything to make him happy. I gave him a ring with the date of the ever dear to me *15th* engraved in it. I also gave him a little seal I used to wear. I asked if he would let me have a little of his dear hair.

Thursday, 28th November.—Talked of having good news from my Cousins, and their thinking Uncle so well; Albert's having talked to Uncle Leopold about his being a Peer, Uncle's giving many reasons for having it, but Albert's saying it was best to wait and see. Lord M. said he had seen Sir William Woods, who told him the Garter could easily be seen at any time; he had shown Lord M. some very curious precedents of former Royal Marriages, of Queen Mary's and Philip's [9]; and that George III.'s [10] was the scene of the greatest confusion that ever took place; he has notes which show that *none* of that procession took place, and that we must make this different; and there was one curious thing, Lord M. said; I had observed that George III. didn't lead the Queen out; well, it was settled they should go separate, but by these Notes it says the King insisted on leading her out and did so. Talked of the Chapel Royal; Uncle Leopold's being married at Carlton House in private.

Friday, 29th November.—"I've got all these papers," he said, and he read me a letter from Sir William Woods to Anson, and then a very curious account of Queen Mary's marriage to Philip, who was only *Prince* of Spain then; and it was announced in the Cathedral at Winchester, where they were married, that his father gave him the Kingdom of Naples; Queen Mary was given away by 3 of her gentlemen in the name of the *realm*. Lord M. then showed me the Act of naturalization of George Prince of Denmark; and read me an account of the marriage of the Princess Royal to the Hereditary Prince of Würtemburg.[11] Lord M. said he would get these papers copied for me.

Friday, 6th December.—Talked of the attacks against the omission of the word "Protestant" in the Declaration. "You mustn't think it belongs to the Party," [12] said Lord M., "now you'll see not one word will be said about it in Parliament"; that he heard Lyndhurst deplored it very much; I thought it was Croker's doing, as he had asked Lord M. about the word Protestant being left out. Lord M. said he *on purpose* left out what was put in George III.'s Declaration, which was, that the Princess was a lineal descendant of a House which had always been warmly attached to the Protestant Religion, as that didn't say anything about *her* religion; and Lord M.

[9] Philip and Mary were married with great pomp in Winchester Cathedral, 25th July, 1554.
[10] George III. was married in the Chapel Royal, St. James's, at 10 o'clock in the evening of 8th September, 1761.
[11] The marriage of George III.'s eldest daughter to Frederick Charles, Duke and afterwards King of Würtemburg, took place in 1797.
[12] The Tory Party.

said he left that out on purpose *not* to attract attention, as else they would have said that wasn't true, and that many of the family had collapsed into Catholicism.

Saturday, 7th December.—Talked of Philip, Queen Mary's husband, having been Titular King of England, which however Lord M. said he disliked so much, and that he disliked her. Talked of Princess Charlotte having always said she would make Uncle King if she came to the Throne. Talked of William III. having insisted on being King *de facto,* which Bishop Burnet settled with Queen Mary for him, and William said he (Bp. B.) had settled in an hour what he had been contemplating for years. I said she (Mary) was a cruel woman, which Lord M. wouldn't allow, and said, "She had been the handsomest woman in Europe." He said William always left her to settle his affairs while he was abroad; she died in '93 or '94, he thinks. Talked of Queen Anne, who he said had also been handsome, which I said couldn't be the case, and that the Bust of her in the Gallery here was very ugly. "That was done when she was old," said Lord M., "when she had had 15 or 16 children."

Sunday, 8th December.—Uncle is also full of the necessity of a Marriage Treaty. "I think the best, Ma'am, would be," said Lord M., "if you approve, for Stockmar to be instructed with all they wish to be done, and to be sent over here directly, so as to settle it here before the Meeting of Parliament," which I quite agreed in. Lord M. observed Uncle thought a Treaty safer, and perhaps it might be, though he thought an Act of Parliament equally so. Talked of my letter from Albert being from Coburg. Talked of sending a drawing of these Arms to Albert, and how we should settle about the Seal. "The Arms [13] are rather a ticklish thing to meddle with," said Lord M., "as they are not *your* Arms but the Arms of the Country,"—which is very true.

Wednesday, 11th December.—"Here's the Chancellor's answer about this bill of naturalization," said Lord M. "I wrote to him to consider it," and Lord M. then read it; he thinks the same course as that pursued in Uncle Leopold's case should be followed; and agreed that Albert should cer-

[13] The Queen had sent a little drawing of the Arms made by herself to the Prince at Coburg.

tainly have precedence [14] over the Royal Dukes. "And now he mentions what I never thought of when I talked of it to Your Majesty, 'and even I think before the *Queen's Children*,' " Lord M. read. Lord M. then said he thought he never could go before the Prince of Wales, before the Heir-Apparent; but *I* said *they* never could go before their father. The Chancellor concludes by saying, it would be very disagreeable if the Parties concerned were not to concur; I said I felt certain both the Duke of Sussex and the Duke of Cambridge would *not* object to this, and that otherwise Albert's position would *not* be bearable. He talked of Mrs. Hamilton (Margaret Dillon), and Lord M. asked, "How many children? Why, the measure of married happiness is to have a great number of children," said Lord M.

Wednesday, 18th December.—Then he talked of a mistake there was in those "points" they had written from Coburg, viz. that I had the right to appoint my Husband Regent, which I have not. Lord M. says he must consult the Chancellor about many other things. George IV. bought a good deal of property, he said. There was a bill brought in, in George III.'s reign, Lord M. continued, enabling him to make a will, which till then no King could.

Sunday, 22nd December.—I continued Albert's position would be too difficult if he must go after *all*, that he *ought* to have the title of King, that power wasn't worth having if I couldn't even give him the *rank* he ought to have. "You can't give it him but by Act of Parliament," [15] said Lord M. "Here's the Chancellor's answer to that letter" (those questions and propositions from Coburg), which Lord M. then read to me, and which are very clear and good. Respecting the Succession to Coburg, he says *they* may settle *there* what they like, to which we shall not dissent but agree; but that *we* cannot *legislate here* about a Foreign Succession. He states likewise that I cannot appoint Albert Guardian to my children—for that if my son was of age when I died, he, as *King*, would be Guardian of his brothers and sisters, and if he were

[14] Lord Melbourne ultimately advised the Queen that it was unnecessary to say anything about the Prince's precedence in the Bill, as she could, by her own Sovereign Act, grant him any precedence she pleased.

[15] This refers to the Title of King. Any other rank the Queen could bestow by her own act.

not of age, then there would be a Regency. "These are our laws," he said, and he added laughing, "I don't know if they are right." He wished me to send a copy of these answers to Albert, and he would send one to Uncle Leopold.

Monday, 23rd December.—Lord M. said how singular it was, that since William the Conqueror, that there had only been 3 Queens, and that those were only Queens by extraordinary circumstances; the title of Prince of Wales only belongs to a man, he said, there can be no Princess of Wales (in her own right). Talked of Queen Mary having been a good deal persecuted and ill-used by Edward VI., and Lord M. said, as a proof, Edward said he hoped he should not be obliged to proceed to violent measures against her. Talked of Hallam's not having a good opinion of Cranmer; saying what he had done when he became Archbishop, but that as he was burnt, everybody thought him a Saint. Lord M. said he was "very shuffling," and that he heard that somebody was going to publish a life of Cranmer, tending to lower him very much in the eyes of the world,—upon which the Archbishop of Canterbury wrote to say he had better not do it, "not rake all that up," for that "after all he is our first Protestant Archbishop."

Sunday, 29th December.—Talked of the Provost of Eton,[16] his having looked so ill at church. Lord M. always liked him, and said he taught so well. "Very clever man," said Lord M., "he wrote Latin verses as quick as he could speak; I think he made his house gentlemanlike, which was rather wanted when I was there; he was what is the worst thing for a schoolmaster, a timid man; he was a very good-natured man. School-boys certainly are the greatest set of blackguards," he continued; "sure sign of a shuffling blackguard at school, is to have no hat, and a great-coat without another coat under it, and no book."

Tuesday, 31st December.—I said funnily I thought Lord M. didn't like Albert so much as he would if he wasn't so strict. "Oh! no, I highly respect it," said Lord M. I then talked of A.'s saying I ought to be severe about people. "Then you'll be liable to make every sort of mistake. In this country all should go by law and precedent," said Lord M., "and not by what you hear."[17]

[16] Dr. Goodall.
[17] It must be remembered that the Prince was little over nineteen

VI

Wednesday, 1st January, [1840].—I feel *most grateful* for all the blessings I have received in the past year, the acquaintance and love of dearest Albert! I only implore Providence to protect me and those who are most dear to me in *this* and many succeeding years, and to grant that the *true* and *good* cause may prosper for *this year* and *many* years to come, under the guidance of my kind Lord Melbourne!

Thursday, 2nd January.—Talked of Hallam, and his account of Jane Grey's having 2 sisters. "He tells it very clearly," Lord M. said; "that was a sad scene" and not poor Jane's fault. Talked of Elizabeth's imprisoning that unfortunate sister of Jane's, Catherine, for marrying; Lord M. said, "When the Princess Elizabeth" (our Queen) "was sent to the Tower, she inquired very particularly if Jane Grey's scaffold was still up."

Monday, 13th January.—I asked if on the Wedding day, as I should *not drive* in full state, and Albemarle said he did not make a point of going with me, I should take Mamma with me. "Yes, I think so," said Lord M. "I think it would be a very right thing to do on that day." Talked of the Treaty being settled easily; of the Cabinet dinner at the Chancellor's in the evening. "We shall settle the Speech to-night," he said, "and let you have it to-morrow morning." I said I felt very nervous about reading it and beginning with my Marriage. "If you say it to 20, or 20,000, it's the same thing," he said, which is true enough.

Tuesday, 14th January.—Talked of other things; of absurd reports in the papers of Lord M.'s resigning after my marriage; he said he *never* dropped a word which could give rise to such a report. "I'm afraid it's our own people who spread these reports," he said, "Bannerman and Ellice" (who always go together). "When people say a report prevails it generally makes me suspect that they spread it," Lord M. said. Talked of Stockmar, and how he was, and Lord M. said, "I should like to see him when he has seen people and made his

years old, and that his standards of right and wrong, always high and noble, were tinged at this time with the uncompromising severity of youth. In after-years he adopted to the full Lord Melbourne's formula, and never acted upon hearsay.

estimate of the state of things; I think he is about the cleverest man I ever knew in my life,'' he added, ''a little misanthropic''; and a good man, I said. ''An excellent man,'' Lord M. replied, ''he has rather a contempt of human affairs and means; a bad digestion.''

Thursday, 16th January.—At ½ p. 1 I set off in the State Coach, with Lord Albemarle and the Duchess of Sutherland, and the whole procession just as usual, to the House of Lords. The House was very full; my good Lord Melbourne just as usual standing close next to me. Wonderful to say, I was less nervous than I had ever been. The Duke of Cambridge was there. There was an immense crowd of people outside, and both coming and going I was loudly cheered, more so than I have been for some time. Uxbridge told me the Duke of Wellington had made a sad mistake by moving that the word *Protestant* be put into the address, and saying [1] it was left out to please O'Connell!! and that Lord Melbourne had replied beautifully to it. Then that Sir John Yarde-Buller had given notice in the House of C. of a Motion on the 28th of want of confidence in Ministers!! I was so angry. Immediately after dinner I wrote to Lord M. begging he would come. Meanwhile I received a letter from him giving an account of the Debate; and very soon after a note saying he was undressed, but would dress and come directly. At ½ p. 10 my good Lord Melbourne came and stayed with me till 5 m. to 11. I saw him upstairs as of a morning. I said I was shocked to have made him come out, but that I hadn't then received his box, and Uxbridge had alarmed me. He was quite dressed, —really so *very, very* kind of him to come. The Duke of W. had been very foolish, he said; Lord M., however, consented to the word being inserted. ''J. Russell sent to say he wished it should be put in,'' Lord M. said, ''as he thought there might be an awkward division about it in the House of Commons.'' Lord M. asked if I had heard from the H. of C.; I replied I had about this Notice of Sir J. Yarde-Buller's, but that I thought there could be no alarm about it. ''No, I hope not,'' Lord M. replied, and we agreed this was the best shape they

[1] The Queen wrote to the Prince that ''The Tories made a great disturbance, saying that you are a Papist, because the words *a Protestant Prince* have not been put into the Declaration—a thing which would be quite unnecessary, seeing that I *cannot* marry a *Papist.*''

could put it into for us, as our people will be sure to go with us upon this. "They say they wish to see which is the strongest," Lord M. said. Talked of a General Election. "We have always lost (by that) hitherto since the Reform Bill," he said.

Friday, 17th January.—After dinner Lord Melbourne and I looked at the picture of Albert. "The head is like," he said, "very good—fine expression—melancholy" (as it is), "which is good for a picture." Lord M. don't like a *fine hand* or a *fat* hand for a man. He made me laugh by saying, "The arms are one of the principal points in a woman." He looked at the picture of Queen Mary (which with one of William III. and 2 other portraits have replaced those 4 landscapes), and he said, "She was the handsomest woman in Europe; I consider her as the first of the Stuarts; she managed everything so well, and the perfect confidence he had in her." We looked at William III., whom he again praised very much and said wasn't cruel. "It was only that accident at Glencoe," he said.

Sunday, 19th January.—Talked of Albert's indifference about Ladies, and Lord M. said, "A little dangerous, all that is,—it's very well if that holds, but it doesn't always," Lord M. said. I said this was very wrong of him, and scolded him for it. "It's what I said at Windsor; I think I know human nature pretty well." I said not the *best* of human nature. "I've known the best of my time," he said, "and I've read of the best."

Monday, 20th January.—Talked of Mr. Wakley attacking the Tories for disloyalty. Talked of Hallam and my liking it so much; his giving an account of the persecutions in Elizabeth's reign; of Queen Mary of Scots and her innocence. "All the ladies take Queen Mary's part," Lord M. said, "all those who reason like Hallam do quite admit her to be guilty, and all those who consult their feelings, do not." Talked of Darnley's murder, which I maintained her not to have knowledge of, but which Lord M. says she *did* know of. "I think she was quite right to have him knocked on the head," Lord M. said funnily, which made me laugh. Talked of Rizzio's murder, and poor Mary's cruel fate. Lord M. said Elizabeth was very reluctant to have her executed, and that the whole country demanded it. I said Hallam says that Walsingham and

Leicester urged Elizabeth to persecute the Roman Catholics; Lord M. said, as I know and Hallam says, that Leicester was a bad man. "Whenever he (Lord Burleigh) put anything before her," Lord M. continued, "he always put the reasons on both sides in 2 columns, which may have been a very good way, but I think a way to puzzle," in which I quite agree; I couldn't bear it, I'm sure. Talked of Essex—his being a fine character—his conduct in Ireland—his sudden return—his unfortunate death, and the possibility of his having been saved if it had not been for the Countess of Nottingham. "It killed her" (Elizabeth), Lord M. said. Talked of Hallam containing so much knowledge which one hadn't before known, and Lord M. said he couldn't recommend a better book. I observed to Lord M. he didn't seem at all low. "No, I'm much better," he replied, "but still I'm not well." I entreated him to take some good advice about his health. "That won't do any good," he said, "it's age and that constant care"; which alas! alas! is but too true. "I'm nearly 61," he continued, "many men die at 63, and if they get over that, live till 70." I told him he mustn't talk in that way. "People like me grow old at once, who have been rather young for their age." I said he still was that. "Still, I feel a great change since last year," he said.[2] I feel certain his valuable health and life will be spared yet many a year. His father lived to be 83, but was very feeble, he said, for many years, and that it was not worth living then; his mother died at 66. "She had been a very strong woman till then," Lord M. said, "but she declined and sank rapidly." I begged Lord M. to take great care of himself, as he belonged to all of us; and he promised he would.

Tuesday, 21st January.—I showed him Uncle Leopold's letter. I also showed Lord M. Stockmar's letter, in which he talks of a Clause in the 2nd Article of the Marriage Treaty, which Stockmar had taken upon himself to agree to; it's about Albert's having no other Claims besides the £50,000 [3]

[2] He died aged sixty-nine, but, like his father, much enfeebled.
[3] This was the amount proposed by the Government. Mr. Hume proposed to cut it down to £21,000, but this was negatived by a large majority. The whole Conservative party, however, supported an amendment of Colonel Sibthorp to make the Prince's income £30,000 only, and this was carried by 262 to 158.

settled on him. "It's the same which was put in to Queen
Mary's with Philip," Lord M. said. "It is impossible to say
what claims a man may have who marries a Queen,
over the property of the Crown; I'm afraid there'll be a good
deal of observation about the Prince's Provision; they'll say
it's too much"; which I said would be wrong. The Prince's
position was disagreeable enough as it was, I said, but this
would make it too bad; that I wouldn't do it for the world.
"You wouldn't do it," Lord M. said laughing; "still, if he
is a man of discretion he may make it" (his position) "a very
considerable one," he added.

Wednesday, 22nd January.—I then said I was so vexed and
distressed by poor dear Albert's letter yesterday; that I feared
they made him believe abroad that we wanted to degrade him
here.⁴ His letter to Lord M., and also to me, were misappre-
hensions about his Household, and about Lord M.'s letter.
"We can't proceed to form his Household now," Lord M.
said. I said, Oh! yes, for that I would be answerable for it;
that I thought Albert didn't quite understand the difference
between "standing by" and "acting." "I don't quite *understand* his letter," Lord M. said; therefore, I replied, Stockmar
and I would let Lord M. have the letter back again. "At the
same time, 2 Households are very awkward," Lord M. said,
and that there had been great trouble about the Queen Dowager's. We think the number of Albert's ought to be reduced.
Talked of my being vexed about the whole; of all that; of its
being unfair that the *Queen's husband* should have so much
less than the *King's wife* in which Lord M. agreed. Talked
of various things, and German being so difficult. "So everybody says," Lord M. said. "Is it possible to be so difficult?"
"Oughtn't to know more than one language," he continued.
"You can't *speak* one purely if you know a great many,—
you mix them. They say you needn't know more than Latin
and French"; Greek, Lady Lyttelton mentioned. "There's
no necessity for it," he said; its being difficult; "a very
copious language," he replied. I observed learning much as

⁴ The Prince was naturally much annoyed by the attacks and criti-
cisms in Parliament and in certain organs of the Press. They were of
a purely party character, and although plainly understood in England, were
misapprehended abroad, where the match was believed to be unpopular
among the English people. This was not the case.

I did at once, prevented one from learning anything very well, and bewildered one. "That's very true what you say," Lord M. said, "that's the fault now, they teach too much at once." Talked of teaching being a dreadful thing, the poor children being more eager to learn than the higher classes, and Lady Lyttelton saying the Irish children were so very much quicker in learning than the English. "It's that quickness that leads to that disregard of truth," Lord M. said, "for when you ask them anything, they don't think of what you *say*, but of what they think will *please* you." He told me at dinner that he was having a new *full-dress* coat made, for the *great* occasion, which was "like building a 74-gun ship" in point of trouble and work, and that he had had the man with him in the morning, trying it on and pinning here and stitching there.

After this some new *Assam* Tea, which Sir J. Hobhouse had sent me, was brought in, and I gave Lord M. a printed paper which had been sent me with it, which he read out loud and so funnily; there was the opinion of a *Dr. Lum Qua* quoted, which name put him into paroxysms of laughter, from which he couldn't recover for some time, and which did one good to hear. After this I said to him he had been so very kind about all that matter which vexed me so yesterday. "The advantage of Monarchy is unity," Lord M. said, "which is a *little* spoiled by 2 people,—but that must be contended against." "I've no doubt," he continued, "that is what kept Queen Elizabeth from marrying; but you mustn't think that I advocate that; I think that's not right, it's unnatural, and nothing's right that's unnatural." I said I was certain that Albert wouldn't interfere. "Oh! I haven't the slightest doubt that he won't interfere," he replied warmly; and I added that that was the very reason why he might run into the other extreme. "My letter may have appeared dictating," he said, which I said was not the case; "that's my way of writing, I write so to you, and did to the King." I said I was sure it would all do very well in a little time. "*You* understand it all," he said, "you have always lived here"; and I had had three years' experience, I said. "But you had just the same capability for affairs," Lord M. said, "when you came to the Throne, as you have now,—you were just as able; I'm for making people of age much sooner." He again went into an amazing fit of laughter about *Dr. Lum Qua.*

Thursday, 23rd January.—Talked of a novel by Miss Martineau called *Deerbrook*, which Lady Lyttelton was praising very much, and which she said was about the Middle Classes. "I don't like the Middle Classes," Lord M. said, "they say that the Upper and Lower Classes are very much like each other in this country; the Middle Classes are bad; the higher and lower classes there's some good in, but the Middle Classes are all affectation and pretense and concealment." I said to Lord M. he so often kept one in hot water by saying *such* things before, and to, people; "It's a good thing to surprise," he said. I said he said such things of people's families to them. "That's a very good thing," he replied funnily, "I do that on purpose, I think it right to warn people of the faults in their families"; and he turned to Lilford [5] and said, "Your family has always been reckoned very prosing, so I warn you of that," which made us laugh so. I said to Lord M. I had told Stockmar what Lord M. had said to me here and at Windsor, about those very high principles like A.'s not *holding* often, upon which Stockmar said, generally speaking that was true, but that he didn't think that would be A.'s case.

Thursday, 30th January.—Talked of Miss Eden and her jumping into the river at Hampton Court and saving a child who fell in. "It was a courageous thing to do," he said. Of Lady Mayo,[6] and her being such a quiz. "Lady Mayo said to Lady Glengall," [7] Lord M. continued, " 'I understand you said I was the ugliest woman in the world'; so Lady Glengall, quite driven to the wall, said, 'Well, I must say, Lady Mayo, I think you are the most frightful woman I ever saw in my life.' " Talked of the Herald's Office, and Sir Wm. Woods, and Lord M. said, "They were very foolish about those Arms" (A.'s) "when they had the precedent under their very nose," which is quite true. "Old Lord Pembroke, who was then Lord Chamberlain," Lord M. continued, "said at the Coronation

---

[5] Thomas Atherton, third Lord Lilford (1801-61).

[6] Arabella, wife of John, fourth Earl of Mayo, a Lady-in-Waiting to Queen Adelaide. She was daughter of William Mackworth-Praed.

[7] Margaret Lauretta, wife of Richard, second Earl of Glengall, and daughter and co-heiress of William Melhuish of Woodford, Essex.

of George II., to Anstis,[8] who was Garter, 'Thou silly knave, that dost not even know thy silly work!' "

Lord M. sent me a letter from the Duke of Sussex before dinner, so delighted at giving me away, and I received one after dinner from him, which I gave Lord M., and he said in returning it, "He is very much pleased; I'm very glad."

We were seated as usual, Lord Melbourne sitting near me. He said he was quite well, but never *felt* quite well, which I said was the constant care and wear; and that he never felt quite free from some little ailing, nor did anybody; when he was young, he said, he never felt unwell, and used "only to live for my amusement," he said, and that if he were to begin life again he would do only that and not enter Politics at all. I said I thought people who only lived for their amusement bad, and that I was sure we should all be punished hereafter for living as we did without thinking at all of our future life. "That's not my case," Lord M. said; and we talked of living our life and beginning it again, and if it were possible, we agreed, we should try and correct ourselves. Talked of his having told me at Windsor that the young men in his day and he himself had been so very impudent; he said I must have misunderstood him, "for I was very shy; there never was a shyer man."

Friday, 31st January.—Then he showed me a note from Lady Burghersh saying she had seen the Duke, who would be anxious not to do anything to embarrass the Government, but that the Precedence lay rather on awkward ground; and that they wouldn't oppose the 2nd reading, but make alterations in the Committee. The remainder of the time that Lord M. was with me, we talked almost entirely about this ill-fated Precedence, and I fear I was violent and eager about it. I said to Lord M. he must fight it out. The House of Lords *might* sit next day, he said, in order to get on with it; and in answer to my saying it was so dreadful not to have the Power even to give my Husband rank, Lord M. said I couldn't, that that was "the law of the Country," and he thinks convenient at times.

Friday, 7th February.—Just before I went out I received

───────

[8] John Anstis, the elder, Garter 1718-44. Part of the time he was joint holder of the office with his son, who held it till 1754.

a delightful letter from dearest Albert from Dover, written in the morning; he suffered most dreadfully coming over; he is much pleased with the very kind reception he met with at Dover. Talked to Lord M. of Albert's letter, and one from Torrington saying dearest Albert's reception had pleased him so, as A. feared he wouldn't be well received; but Lord M. agreed with me that a Vote of the H. of Commons had nothing whatever to do with that. At this moment I received a letter, and a dear one, from dearest Albert from Canterbury, where he had just arrived, and where he had also been very well received, as I told Lord M., who said, "I've no doubt; his reception has been such that he must take care not to be intoxicated by that," which I said I was quite sure he needn't fear. Talked of Soult and his reception here having made him so friendly to England; of Sebastiani's removal; of Guizot. "You can always tell him you have read his book," Lord M. said laughing. As usual Lord Melbourne sitting near me, talked of my being a little agitated and nervous; "Most natural," Lord M. replied warmly; "how could it be otherwise?" Lord M. was so warm, so kind, and so affectionate, the whole evening, and so much touched in speaking of me and my affairs. Talked of my former resolution of never marrying. "Depend upon it, it's right to marry," he said earnestly; "if ever there was a situation that formed an exception, it was yours; it's in human nature, it's natural to marry; the other is a very unnatural state of things; it's a great *change*—it has its inconveniences; everybody does their best, and depend upon it you've done well; difficulties may arise from it," as they do of course from everything. Talked of popular assemblies, of my having grown so thin. "You look very well," he said; "after all," he continued, much affected, "how anybody in your situation can have a moment's tranquillity!—a young person cast in this situation is very unnatural. There was a beautiful account in a Scotch paper," he said, "of your first going to prorogue Parliament; 'I stood close to her,' it says, 'to see a young person surrounded by Ministers and Judges and rendered prematurely grave was almost melancholy'; 'a large searching eye, an open anxious nostril, and a firm mouth.'" Lord M. repeated this several times, looking so kindly and affectionately at me; "A very true representation," he said, "can't be a finer physiognomy"—which made me smile, as he said it so earnestly. Talked of Albert's being a little like me; of the Addresses and dinners A. would be plagued with; of my taking him to the Play soon. "There'll be an immense flow of popularity now," Lord M. said. Talked of the difficulty of keeping quite free from all Politics. I begged Lord M. much to manage about Thursday, which he promised he would, as I said it always made me so happy to have him. "I am sure none of your friends are so fond of you as I am," I said. "I believe not," he replied, quite touched, and I added also he had been always so very kind to me I couldn't say *how* I felt it.

Saturday, 8th February.—At ½ p. 4 the Carriage and Escort appeared, drove through the center gate, and up to the door; I stood at the very door; 1st stepped out Ernest, then Uncle Ernest, and then Albert, looking beautiful and so well; I embraced him and took him by the hand and led him up to my room; Mamma, Uncle Ernest, and Ernest following. After dinner Albert and Ernest shook hands with Lord Melbourne. "I think they look very well," Lord M. said when he came up to me; "I think he (A.) looks very well." Talked of their passage; Lord M. said it was such a very good thing that Albert attended service in the Cathedral at Canterbury. I sat on the sofa with my beloved Albert, Lord Melbourne sitting near me. Talked of the gentlemen that Uncle had with him. Lord M. admired the diamond Garter which Albert had on, and said "Very handsome." I told him it was my gift; I also gave him (all before dinner) a diamond star I had worn, and badge. Lord M. made us laugh excessively about his new Coat, which he said, "I expect it to be the thing most observed."

Sunday, 9th February.—Received a beautiful Prayer-book from Mamma; breakfasted at 10. Wrote to Lord M. Dearest Albert and Ernest came in, Albert looking so well, with a little of his blue ribbon showing.[9] He brought me 4 beautiful old Fans. At 12 I went down to Prayers with my beloved Albert, Mamma, Ernest, and my ladies and gentlemen. Mr.

[9] The ribbon of the Garter was at this time worn by day. The Duke of Wellington constantly wore it, with a white waistcoat. The star was sometimes worn *without* the ribbon.

Vane read and the Bishop of London preached a very fine sermon. The Service was over at 5 m. p. 1. Talked of dearest Albert's being agitated. "That's very natural," Lord M. said, "I don't wonder at it." Lord M. promised to stay Thursday. I took his hand and pressed it, and thanked him for all his kindness, which I hoped he would continue. I couldn't believe what was to happen next day, I said. At a ¼ to 6 my beloved Albert came to me and stayed with me till 20 m. to 7. We read over the Marriage Service together and tried how to manage the *ring*. Wrote my journal. At 8 we dined. The dinner was just the same as the day before with the exception of Lord Albemarle, Lord Erroll, Lord Byron, Col. Grey and Stockmar; and with the addition of Lord Surrey and Col. Cavendish. Albert led me in and I sat between him and Uncle E. It was my last unmarried evening, which made me feel so odd. I sat on the sofa with dearest Albert, Lord Melbourne sitting near me. Talked of A.'s having talked to him (L. M.); of guessing words; the Lord's Prayer being almost entirely composed of Saxon words, all but 4; of the Cathedral at Canterbury and Bishop Chicheley [10] being buried there.

Monday, 10th February.—Got up at a ¼ to 9—well, and having slept well; and breakfasted at ½ p. 9. Mamma came before and brought me a Nosegay of orange flowers. My dearest kindest Lehzen gave me a dear little ring. Wrote my journal, and to Lord M. Had my hair dressed and the wreath of orange flowers put on. Saw Albert for the *last* time *alone*, as my *Bridegroom*. Dressed.

Saw Uncle, and Ernest whom dearest Albert brought up. At ½ p. 12 I set off, dearest Albert having gone before. I wore a white satin gown with a very deep flounce of Honiton lace, imitation of old. I wore my Turkish diamond necklace and earrings, and Albert's beautiful sapphire brooch. Mamma and the Duchess of Sutherland went in the carriage with me. I never saw such crowds of people as there were in the Park, and they cheered most enthusiastically. When I arrived at St. James's, I went into the dressing-room where my 12 young Train-bearers were, dressed all in white with

---

[10] Henry Chichele, or Chicheley, prelate and statesman. Archbishop of Canterbury and Founder of All Souls' College, Oxford. Died 1443.

white roses, which had a beautiful effect. Here I waited a
little till dearest Albert's Procession had moved into the
Chapel. I then went with my Train-bearers and ladies into
the Throne-room, where the Procession formed; Lord Melbourne in his fine new dress-coat, bearing the Sword of State,
and Lord Uxbridge and Lord Belfast on either side of him
walked immediately before me. Queen Anne's room was full
of people, ranged on seats one higher than the other, as also
in the Guard room, and by the Staircase,—all very friendly;
the Procession looked beautiful going downstairs. Part of
the Color Court was also covered in and full of people who
were very civil. The Flourish of Trumpets ceased as I entered the Chapel, and the organ began to play, which had a
beautiful effect. At the Altar, to my right, stood Albert;
Mamma was on my left as also the Dukes of Sussex and Cambridge, and Aunt Augusta; and on Albert's right was the
Queen Dowager, then Uncle Ernest, Ernest, the Duchess of
Cambridge and little Mary, George, Augusta, and Princess
Sophia Matilda. Lord Melbourne stood close to me with the
Sword of State. The Ceremony was very imposing, and fine
and simple, and I think OUGHT to make an everlasting impression on every one who promises at the Altar to *keep* what he
or she promises. Dearest Albert repeated everything very
distinctly. I felt so happy when the ring was put on, and by
Albert. As soon as the Service was over, the Procession returned as it came, with the exception that my beloved Albert
led me out. The applause was very great, in the Color Court
as we came through; Lord Melbourne, good man, was very
much affected during the Ceremony and at the applause. We
all returned to the Throne-room, where the Signing of the
Register took place; it was first signed by the Archbishop,
then by Albert and me, and all the Royal Family, and by:
the Lord Chancellor, the Lord President, the Lord Privy
Seal, the Duke of Norfolk (as Earl Marshal), the Archbishop
of York, and Lord Melbourne. We then went into the Closet,
and the Royal Family waited with me there till the ladies had
got into their carriages. I gave all the Train-bearers as a
brooch a small *eagle* of turquoise. I then returned to Buckingham Palace alone with Albert; they cheered us really most
warmly and heartily; the crowd was immense; and the Hall

at Buckingham Palace was full of people; they cheered us again and again. The great Drawing-room and Throne-room were full of people of rank, and numbers of children were there. Lord Melbourne and Lord Clarendon, who had arrived, stood at the door of the Throne-room when we came in. I went and sat on the sofa in my dressing-room with Albert; and we talked together there from 10 m. to 2 till 20 m. p. 2. Then we went downstairs where all the Company was assembled and went into the dining-room—dearest Albert leading me in, and my Train being borne by 3 Pages, Cowell, little Wemyss, and dear little Byng. I sat between dearest Albert and the Duke of Sussex. My health and dearest Albert's were drunk. The Duke was very kind and civil. Albert and I drank a glass of wine with Lord Melbourne, who seemed much affected by the whole. I talked to all after the breakfast, and to Lord Melbourne, whose fine coat I praised. Little Mary [11] behaved so well both at the Marriage and the breakfast. I went upstairs and undressed and put on a white silk gown trimmed with swansdown, and a bonnet with orange flowers. Albert went downstairs and undressed. At 20 m. to 4 Lord Melbourne came to me and stayed with me till 10 m. to 4. I shook hands with him and he kissed my hand. Talked of how well everything went off. "Nothing could have gone off better," he said, and of the people being in such good humor and having also received him well; of my receiving the Addresses from the House of Lords and Commons; of his coming down to Windsor in time for dinner. I begged him not to go to the party; he was a little tired; I would let him know when we arrived; I pressed his hand once more, and he said, "God bless you, Ma'am," most kindly, and with such a kind look. Dearest Albert came up and fetched me downstairs, where we took leave of Mamma and drove off at near 4; I and Albert alone.

[11] Princess Mary of Cambridge, Duchess of Teck, mother of Queen Mary.

OSCAR WILDE

OSCAR WILDE

1856-1900

INTRODUCTORY NOTE

It was about the year 1880 that the name of Oscar Wilde first became a frequent one in common conversation; and from that time until Wilde's death in 1900 he was continually furnishing the English speaking world with new shocks, new interests, new excitements. Wilde was born in Dublin, the son of a noted Irish physician, and first became known as the leader of the aesthetic craze of the '80's. As a student at Oxford he talked scornfully of collegiate athletics, praised idle leisure and dreamy ecstasy, and adorned his room with peacock-feathers, sunflowers and lilies. A great many people enjoyed laughing at Wilde and his cult, but it had a distinct artistic influence. He wrote a novel, "The Picture of Dorian Grey," and then in 1892 achieved a much more distinct and virile fame as a playwright with his drama of "Lady Windermere's Fan." One witty, paradoxical play after another increased his reputation until the sudden disastrous climax in 1896. He was accused and convicted of gross immoralities of life and was sentenced to two years in prison. Some rumor or flavor of immorality had clung about Wilde ever since his Oxford days, but had been disbelieved by the better class of friends and critics who admired his real abilities; now his guilt was manifest and beyond society's condoning. After serving his sentence Wilde lived abroad for the brief remnant of his life under the name of Sebastian Melmoth, a pseudonym borrowed from an old romance of a homeless, sinful wanderer. During his prison life he produced two works which perhaps mark the highest reach of his genius, one, a poem, "The Ballad of Reading Gaol"; the other, an explanation or defense of his career, including a picture of his jail life and mental suffering.

This remarkable work, "De Profundis," has been widely read and accepted as a classic. It was issued by Messrs. Putnam's Sons in 1905, and its sales formed the chief fund for the provision of Wilde's unhappy family. Only the more directly autobiographical portion of the work can be given here, but the reader will find equal value in the remainder of the book.

525

DE PROFUNDIS

SUFFERING is one very long moment. We cannot divide it by seasons. We can only record its moods, and chronicle their return. With us time itself does not progress. It revolves. It seems to circle round one center of pain. The paralyzing immobility of a life every circumstance of which is regulated after an unchangeable pattern, so that we eat and drink and lie down and pray, or kneel at least for prayer, according to the inflexible laws of an iron formula: this immobile quality, that makes each dreadful day in the very minutest detail like its brother, seems to communicate itself to those external forces the very essence of whose existence is ceaseless change. Of seed time or harvest, of the reapers bending over the corn, or the grape gatherers threading through the vines, of the grass in the orchard made white with broken blossoms or strewn with fallen fruit: of these we know nothing, and can know nothing.

For us there is only one season, the season of sorrow. The very sun and moon seem taken from us. Outside, the day may be blue and gold, but the light that creeps down through the thickly muffled glass of the small, iron-barred window beneath which one sits is gray and niggard. It is always twilight in one's cell, as it is always twilight in one's heart. And in the sphere of thought, no less than in the sphere of time, motion is no more. The thing that you personally have long ago forgotten, or can easily forget, is happening to me now, and will happen to me again to-morrow. Remember this, and you will be able to understand a little of why I am writing, and in this manner writing.

A week later, I am transferred here. Three more months go over and my mother dies. No one knew how deeply I loved and honored her. Her death was terrible to me; but I, once a lord of language, have no words in which to express my anguish and my shame. She and my father had bequeathed me a name they had made noble and honored, not merely in literature, art, archæology, and science, but in the public history of my own country, in its evolution as a nation. I had disgraced that name eternally. I had made it a low byword among low people. I had dragged it through the very mire. I had given it to brutes that they might make it brutal, and to foes that they might turn it into a synonym for folly. What I suffered then, and still suffer, is not for pen to write or paper to record. My wife, always kind and gentle to me, rather than that I should hear the news from indifferent lips, traveled, ill as she was, all the way from Genoa to England to break to me herself the tidings of so irreparable, so irredeemable, a loss. Messages of sympathy reached me from all who had still affection for me. Even people who had not known me personally, hearing that a new sorrow had broken into my life, wrote to ask that some expression of their condolence should be conveyed to me.

Three months go over. The calendar of my daily conduct and labor that hangs on the outside of my cell door, with my name and sentence written upon it, tells me that it is May.

Prosperity, pleasure, and success, may be rough of grain and common in fiber, but sorrow is the most sensitive of all created things. There is nothing that stirs in the whole world of thought to which sorrow does not vibrate in terrible and exquisite pulsation. The thin beaten-out leaf of tremulous gold that chronicles the direction of forces the eye cannot see is in comparison coarse. It is a wound that bleeds when any hand but that of love touches it, and even then must bleed again, though not in pain.

Where there is sorrow there is holy ground. Some day people will realize what that means. They will know nothing of life till they do. —— and natures like his can realize it. When I was brought down from my prison to the Court of Bankruptcy, between two policemen, —— waited in the long dreary corridor that, before the whole crowd, whom an action so sweet and simple hushed into silence, he might gravely raise his hat to me, as, handcuffed and with bowed head, I passed him by. Men have gone to heaven for smaller things than that. It was in this spirit, and with this mode of love, that the saints knelt down to wash the feet of the poor, or stooped to kiss the leper on the cheek. I have never said one single word to him about what he did. I do not know to the present moment whether he is aware that I was even conscious of his action. It is not a thing for which one can render formal thanks in formal words. I store it in the treasure-house of my heart. I keep it there as a secret debt that I am glad to think I can never possibly repay. It is embalmed and kept sweet by the myrrh and cassia of many tears. When wisdom has been profitless to me, philosophy barren, and the proverbs and phrases of those who have sought to give me consolation as dust and ashes in my mouth, the memory of that little, lovely, silent act of love has unsealed for me all the wells of pity: made the desert blossom like a rose, and brought me out of the bitterness of lonely exile into harmony with the wounded, broken, and great heart of the world. When people are able to understand, not merely how beautiful ——'s action was, but why it meant so much to me, and always will mean so much, then, perhaps, they will realize how and in what spirit they should approach me.

The poor are wise, more charitable, more kind, more sensitive than we are. In their eyes, prison is a tragedy in a man's life, a misfortune, a casualty, something that calls for sympathy in others. They speak of one who is in prison as of one who is "in trouble" simply. It is the phrase they always use, and the expression has the perfect wisdom of love in it. With people of our own rank it is different. With us, prison makes a man a pariah. I, and such as I am, have hardly any right to air and sun. Our presence taints the pleasures of others. We are unwelcome when we reappear. To revisit the glimpses of the moon is not for us. Our very children are taken away. Those lovely links with humanity are broken. We are doomed to be solitary, while our sons still live. We are denied the one thing that might heal us and keep us, that might bring balm to the bruised heart, and peace to the soul in pain.

I must say to myself that I ruined myself, and that nobody great or small can be ruined except by his own hand. I am quite ready to say so. I am trying to say so, though they may not think it at the present moment. This pitiless indictment I bring without pity against myself. Terrible as was what the world did to me, what I did to myself was far more terrible still.

I was a man who stood in symbolic relations to the art and culture of my age. I had realized this for myself at the very dawn of my manhood, and had forced my age to realize it afterwards. Few men hold such a position in their own life-time, and have it so acknowledged. It is usually discerned, if discerned at all, by the historian, or the critic, long after both the man and his age have passed away. With me it was different. I felt it myself, and made others feel it. Byron was a symbolic figure, but his relations were to the passion of his age and its weariness of passion. Mine were to something more noble, more permanent, of more vital issue, of larger scope.

The gods had given me almost everything. But I let myself be lured into long spells of senseless and sensual ease. I amused myself with being a *flâneur*, a dandy, a man of fashion. I surrounded myself with the smaller natures and the meaner minds. I became the spendthrift of my own genius, and to waste an eternal youth gave me a curious joy. Tired of being on the heights, I deliberately went to the depths in the search for new sensation. What the paradox was to me in the sphere of thought, perversity became to me in the sphere of passion. Desire, at the end, was a malady, or a madness, or both. I grew careless of the lives of others. I took pleasure where it pleased me, and passed on. I forgot that every little action of the common day makes or unmakes character, and that therefore what one has done in the secret chamber one has some day to cry aloud on the housetop. I ceased to be lord over myself. I was no longer the captain of my soul, and did not know it. I allowed pleasure to dominate me. I ended in horrible disgrace. There is only one thing for me now, absolute humility.

I have lain in prison for nearly two years. Out of my nature has come wild despair; an abandonment to grief that was piteous even to look at; terrible and impotent rage; bitterness and scorn; anguish that wept aloud; misery that could find no voice; sorrow that was dumb. I have passed through every possible mood of suffering. Better than Wordsworth himself I know what Wordsworth meant when he said:

> "Suffering is permanent, obscure, and dark,
>   And has the nature of infinity."

But while there were times when I rejoiced in the idea that my sufferings were to be endless, I could not bear them to be without meaning. Now I find hidden somewhere away in my nature something that tells me that nothing in the whole world is meaningless, and suffering least of all. That something hidden away in my nature, like a treasure in a field, is Humility.

It is the last thing left in me, and the best: the ultimate discovery at which I have arrived, the starting-point for a fresh development. It has come to me right out of myself, so I know that it has come at the proper time. It could not have come before, nor later. Had any one told me of it, I would have rejected it. Had it been brought to me, I would have refused it. As I found it, I want to keep it. I must do so. It is the one thing that has in it the elements of life, of a new life, a *Vita Nuova* for me. Of all things it is the strangest. One cannot acquire it, except by surrendering everything that one has. It is only when one has lost all things, that one knows that one possesses it.

Now I have realized that it is in me, I see quite clearly what I ought to do; in fact, must do. And when I use such a phrase as that, I need not say that I am not alluding to any external sanction or command. I admit none. I am far more of an individualist than I ever was. Nothing seems to me of the smallest value except what one gets out of oneself. My nature is seeking a fresh mode of self-realization. That is all I am concerned with. And the first thing that I have got to do is to free myself from any possible bitterness of feeling against the world.

I am completely penniless, and absolutely homeless. Yet there are worse things in the world than that. I am quite candid when I say that rather than go out from this prison with bitterness in my heart against the world, I would gladly and readily beg my bread from door to door. If I got nothing from the house of the rich I would get something at the house of the poor. Those who have much are often greedy; those who have little always share. I would not a bit mind sleeping in the cool grass in summer, and when winter came on sheltering myself by the warm close-thatched rick, or under the pent-house of a great barn, provided I had love in my heart. The external things of life seem to me now of no importance at all. You can see to what intensity of individualism I have arrived—or am arriving rather, for the journey is long, and "where I walk there are thorns."

Of course I know that to ask alms on the highway is not to be my lot, and that if ever I lie in the cool grass at night-time it will be to write sonnets to the moon. When I go out of prison, R—— will be waiting for me on the other side of the big iron-studded gate, and he is the symbol, not merely of his own affection, but of the affection of many others besides. I believe I am to have enough to live on for about eighteen months at any rate, so that if I may not write beautiful books, I may at least read beautiful books; and what joy can be greater? After that, I hope to be able to recreate my creative faculty.

But were things different; had I not a friend left in the world; were there not a single house open to me in pity; had I to accept the wallet and ragged cloak of sheer penury: as long as I am free from all resentment, hardness, and scorn, I would be able to face the life with much more calm and confidence than I would were my body in purple and fine linen, and the soul within me sick with hate.

And I really shall have no difficulty. When you really want love you will find it waiting for you.

I need not say that my task does not end there. It would be comparatively easy if it did. There is much more before me. I have hills far steeper to climb, valleys much darker to pass through. And I have to get it all out of myself. Neither religion, morality, nor reason can help me at all. . . .

I want to get to the point when I shall be able to say quite simply, and without affectation, that the two great turning points in my life were when my father sent me to Oxford, and when society sent me to prison. I will not say that prison is the best thing that could have happened to me; for that phrase would savor of too great bitterness towards myself. I would sooner say, or hear it said of me, that I was so typical a child of my age, that in my perversity, and for that perversity's sake, I turned the good things of my life to evil, and the evil things of my life to good. . . .

While I was in Wandsworth prison I longed to die. It was my one desire. When after two months in the infirmary I was transferred here, and found myself growing gradually better in physical health, I was filled with rage. I determined to commit suicide on the very day on which I left prison. After a time that evil mood passed away, and I made up my mind to live, but to wear gloom as a king wears purple: never to smile again: to turn whatever house I entered into a house of mourning: to make my friends walk slowly in sadness with me: to teach them that melancholy is the true secret of life: to maim them with an alien sorrow: to mar them with my own pain. Now I feel quite differently. I see it would be both ungrateful and unkind of me to pull so long a face that when my friends came to see me they would have to make their faces still longer in order to show their sympathy; or, if I desired to entertain them, to invite them to sit down silently to bitter herbs and funeral baked meats. I must learn how to be cheerful and happy.

The last two occasions on which I was allowed to see my friends here, I tried to be as cheerful as possible, and to show my cheerfulness, in order to make them some slight return for their trouble in coming all the way from town to see me. It is only a slight return, I know, but it is the one, I feel certain, that pleases them most. I saw R—— for an hour on Saturday week, and I tried to give the fullest possible expression of the delight I really felt at our meeting. And that, in the views and ideas I am here shaping for myself, I am quite right is shown to me by the fact that now for the first time since my imprisonment I have a real desire for life.

There is before me so much to do that I would regard it as a terrible tragedy if I died before I was allowed to complete at any rate a little of it. I see new developments in art and life, each one of which is a fresh mode of perfection. I long to live so that I can explore what is no less than a new world to me. Do you want to know what this new world is? I think you can guess what it is. It is the world in which I have been living. Sorrow, then, and all that it teaches one, is my new world.

I used to live entirely for pleasure. I shunned suffering and sorrow of every kind. I hated both. I resolved to ignore them as far as possible: to treat them, that is to say, as modes of imperfection. They were not part of my scheme of life. They had no place in my philosophy. My mother, who knew

life as a whole, used often to quote to me Goethe's lines—
written by Carlyle in a book he had given her years ago, and
translated by him, I fancy, also:—

> "Who never ate his bread in sorrow,
>   Who never spent the midnight hours
> Weeping and waiting for the morrow,—
>   He knows you not, ye heavenly powers."

They were the lines which that noble Queen of Prussia,
whom Napoleon treated with such coarse brutality, used to
quote in her humiliation and exile; they were the lines my
mother often quoted in the troubles of her later life. I absolutely declined to accept or admit the enormous truth hidden
in them. I could not understand it. I remember quite well
how I used to tell her that I did not want to eat my bread
in sorrow, or to pass any night weeping and watching for a
more bitter dawn.

I had no idea that it was one of the special things that the
Fates had in store for me: that for a whole year of my life,
indeed, I was to do little else. But so has my portion been
meted out to me; and during the last few months I have,
after terrible difficulties and struggles, been able to comprehend some of the lessons hidden in the heart of pain. Clergy-
men and people who use phrases without wisdom sometimes
talk of suffering as a mystery. It is really a revelation. One
discerns things one never discerned before. One approaches
the whole of history from a different standpoint. What one
had felt dimly, through instinct, about art, is intellectually
and emotionally realized with perfect clearness of vision and
absolute intensity of apprehension.

I now see that sorrow, being the supreme emotion of which
man is capable, is at once the type and test of all great art.
What the artist is always looking for is the mode of existence
in which soul and body are one and indivisible: in which the
outward is expressive of the inward: in which form reveals.
Of such modes of existence there are not a few: youth and
the arts preoccupied with youth may serve as a model for us
at one moment: at another we may like to think that, in its
subtlety and sensitiveness of impression, its suggestion of a
spirit dwelling in external things and making its raiment of

earth and air, of mist and city alike, and in its morbid sympathy of its moods, and tones, and colors, modern landscape art is realizing for us pictorially what was realized in such plastic perfection by the Greeks. Music, in which all subject is absorbed in expression and cannot be separated from it, is a complex example, and a flower or a child a simple example, of what I mean; but sorrow is the ultimate type both in life and art.

Behind joy and laughter there may be a temperament, coarse, hard, and callous. But behind sorrow there is always sorrow. Pain, unlike pleasure, wears no mask. Truth in art is not any correspondence between the essential idea and the accidental existence; it is not the resemblance of shape to shadow, or of the form mirrored in the crystal to the form itself; it is no echo coming from a hollow hill, any more than it is a silver well of water in the valley that shows the moon to the moon and Narcissus to Narcissus. Truth in art is the unity of a thing with itself: the outward rendered expressive of the inward: the soul made incarnate: the body instinct with spirit. For this reason there is no truth comparable to sorrow. There are times when sorrow seems to me to be the only truth. Other things may be illusions of the eye or the appetite, made to blind the one and cloy the other, but out of sorrow have the worlds been built, and at the birth of a child or a star there is pain.

More than this, there is about sorrow an intense, an extraordinary reality. I have said of myself that I was one who stood in symbolic relations to the art and culture of my age. There is not a single wretched man in this wretched place along with me who does not stand in symbolic relation to the very secret of life. For the secret of life is suffering. It is what is hidden behind everything. When we begin to live, what is sweet is so sweet to us, and what is bitter so bitter, that we inevitably direct all our desires towards pleasures, and seek not merely for a "month or twain to feed on honeycomb," but for all our years to taste no other food, ignorant all the while that we may really be starving the soul. . . .

I hope to live long enough and to produce work of such a character that I shall be able at the end of my days to say, "Yes! this is just where the artistic life leads a man!" Two